BANKING IN THE AMERICAN WEST
From the Gold Rush to Deregulation

The bank at Bodie, a California ghost town, has long ago disappeared. Left behind is the bank's brick vault, above, which contains the sturdy black safe, below. (*Photos by Lynne Pierson Doti*)

BANKING IN THE AMERICAN WEST

From the Gold Rush
to Deregulation

LYNNE PIERSON DOTI
and
LARRY SCHWEIKART

UNIVERSITY OF OKLAHOMA PRESS
NORMAN AND LONDON

To our families

Doti, Lynne Pierson.
    Banking in the American West : from the Gold Rush to deregulation
    / Lynne Pierson Doti and Larry Schweikart.
        p.   cm.
    Includes bibliographical references and index.
    ISBN 0-8061-2373-7
    1. Banks and banking—West (U.S.)—History—20th century.
    I. Schweikart, Larry. II. Title.
    HG2609.D68   1991
    332.1'0978—dc20   91-50302
                                                               CIP

The paper in this book meets the guidelines for permanence and durability of the Committee
on Production Guidelines for Book Longevity for the Council on Library Resources, Inc. ⊗

CONTENTS

TABLES

PREFACE

As this goes to press, American banking has entered another phase of its reassessment of regulatory policies. Secretary of the Treasury Nicholas Brady recently sent to Congress a plan for reducing deposit insurance, consolidating the federal regulatory agencies from four to two, and strengthening the capital base of existing banks. The American Bankers Association followed suit with its own reforms, while House Banking and Finance Committee chairman Henry Gonzalez issued his own suggestions for revision of bank regulations. All of those plans, in general, represent continued deregulation of banking, with the limitations placed on banks, especially prohibitions against branch banking, lifted. The trends bode well for American banking.

For banking in the American West, some of the developments seem to vindicate those strategies of the region's lawmakers and entrepreneurs. Not all western states followed similar patterns of development, of course, and not all established similar regulatory structures. Indeed, many midwestern states led the way in establishing deposit insurance systems, and, as of 1991, states such as Colorado remain committed to unit banking. Nevertheless, the banking systems in many western states have survived in the face of the most dire predictions of looming disaster related to the energy bust and the savings and loan collapse. Following publication of a sharply critical book on the Bank of America that all but predicted the demise of that institution, the Bank of America abruptly reversed course and has revived, if not thrived. Elsewhere, the real-estate recession in many western cities may yet result in large numbers of failed banks. For the most part, however, western banks seem to have weathered the storm, and now ride toward recovery. The next 150 years of western banking promise to be at least as interesting as the first.

Throughout our journey into western banking's past we have incurred the usual debts, and we take pleasure in acknowledging those who supported and encouraged this work. Both Chapman College and the University of Dayton, especially the University of Dayton Research Institute and George Noland, provided financial and other support. Larry Schweikart would like to thank the Charles Redd Center for Western Studies and the Earhart Foundation for research support grants. Librarians who made special efforts on our behalf include Lisa Backman of the Denver Public Library; Walter Jones of the Marriott Library at the University of Utah, who personally oversaw copying and mailing of many dissertations on Utah banking to us; John C. Borst at the South Dakota Historical Society; Margaret N. Haines of the Oregon Historical Society; John E. Bye of the North Dakota Institute for Regional Studies; Eric Moody at the Nevada Historical Society; Ellie Arguimbau of the Montana Historical Society Library, who made outstanding efforts to find obscure documents; Robert P. Hendrickson, who furnished us with materials from the First Bank of Bismarck; Debby Barlett at Bank IV, Wichita, who supplied us with a copy of the bank's history; and Thomas G. Alexander at the Charles Redd Center. We would also like to thank librarians at the following institutions that assisted our research: Arizona State University; Brigham Young University; Chase Bank of Arizona, Scottsdale; Colorado Historical Society; City Bank of Leadville; Kansas Historical Society; Museum of New Mexico; National Archives; Nebraska State Historical Society; Northern Arizona University; Oklahoma Bankers Association; Oklahoma Historical Society; South Dakota State Archives; Stanford University; University of Arizona; University of California, Berkeley; University of New Mexico; University of Oregon; Utah State Historical Society; and Valley National Bank.

We take special pleasure in acknowledging the assistance of several individuals who made our work much easier and more complete, through either their advice or their contributions to research, including Thomas Noel, Jay Fell, Tiarr Martin, Nen Kheng Hay, Thomas Jaehn, and Esther Ng. Linda McKinley and Jennifer Davis provided excellent typing and layout support. Among our colleagues who read either all or parts of the manuscript, Charles Calomiris, Leonard Arrington, Elliott Brownlee, Edwin Perkins, Marc Weiss, James Smallwood, Michael Konig, and Dwight Lee all made excellent suggestions or criticisms, as did participants in panels at the Durrell Conference on Money and Banking, the Western Economic Association, and the Social Science History Association. Robert Chandler, of Wells Fargo Bank, provided us with particularly useful comments. Eric Monkkonen at *Urban Studies* encouraged the publication of an essay on financing urban growth in the West. Thanks are also due to editors and referees at the *Pacific Historical Review*, the *Journal of Arizona History*, the *Journal of the Southwest*, the *Journal of the West*, the *New*

Mexico Historical Review, and *Essays and Monographs in Colorado History* for their comments on essays that were published in those journals.

At the University of Oklahoma Press, we are indebted to John Drayton, who broke the trail for us to undertake this project, as well as to other University Press staff who helped shape and improve the manuscript.

Because any book ultimately is a collective effort funnelled through the word processor of, in this case, two people, we cheerfully recognize the contributions of our families. They gave of their time and, to the degree that it was a sacrifice, of us. For their part in this book, we dedicate *Banking in the American West* to them.

LYNNE PIERSON DOTI
LARRY SCHWEIKART

Anaheim, California
Dayton, Ohio

BANKING IN THE AMERICAN WEST
From the Gold Rush to Deregulation

1

NO MONEY IN KANSAS

Few Americans have any sympathy for bankers. Inheriting a literary portrait of Shylock from their forebears, throughout our past one group or another has seen banks as the source of economic instability on the one hand and of tightfistedness on the other. The Jacksonians won countless elections by attacking banks as the tools of elites. Sixty years later, many Americans nodded in agreement with the Populists as they railed against the "moneybags of the east" made up of "money changers waxing richer and richer." The moneylender, intoned the *Farmer's Alliance*, "must be dethroned."[1] The national banking system they dominated was called by one polemicist the "Financial Devil Fish of America."[2] He only reinforced the view of many that "Wall Street owns the country."[3] As late as 1985, Iowa farmers circulated a pamphlet entitled "Billions for Bankers, Debt for the People."[4] Still others raced to the doors of closing and insolvent institutions in the 1930s, and, then, in the 1970s and early 1980s, shrugged in ambivalence to the desperate straits of many modern banks' Third World loans. More regulation, less profit, state bank monopolies, a federal presence on boards of directors, and barriers to entry—whatever it took to make banks completely safe, solvent, and yet freer with credit for the common man—was, to many Americans at different times, completely justified.[5] Certainly one would conclude as much reading William Greider's diatribe against the "wealth holders," "stable money," and "free rein of the *rentier*."[6]

Yet the public's concerns about banks, distrust of bankers, and alarms about the conspiracy of bankers have perhaps been overplayed by historians. After all, it made a good story—the rich and powerful against the common man. But if the story was true for sections of the country at certain times, it was hardly applicable to the frontier West. As the nation expanded westward, pioneers took a somewhat different view of the local banker, if for no other reason than he was one of them, a merchant, farmer, or miner made good. Westerners learned important lessons from the poor regulations that had afflicted the Old Northwest and the cotton-rich Southeast, and had less interest in prohibiting banks than had Arkansas, Wisconsin, and several other states at one time or another.[7] Indeed, the mines, lumber camps, farms, transportation and shipping businesses, and basic manufacturing that sprang up in California, Colorado, Arizona, Washington, Montana, and elsewhere in the region needed capital. The railroads acquired their own financing, but the settlers who followed wanted banks.

Western values demanded openness and fairness in competition, which translated into unit-bank laws from Texas to North Dakota. Only a few states—sometimes by accident—managed to resist the bias against branch banking, until the Great Depression forced a reassessment. Westerners valued safety and solvency even more than competition, but this goal too had to be reached in a typically western fashion. Sons of well-to-do easterners were not automatically respected in the West, and few western banking houses were founded with predominantly outside capital. Instead, western bankers followed a different pattern. They established their personal reputations, then constructed imposing, solidly built, permanent facilities to prove that their bank was indeed safe. Most western banks were homegrown, and the image, at least, was that little of the banking community represented outside interests. In most western towns the banker could still call individual customers by their names as recently as the Great Depression.

Perhaps for these reasons, western bankers, unlike bankers in previous times of crisis, did not experience public anger or resentment or represent a "moneyed conspiracy" to their depositors, as had bankers in other parts of the nation. Even the western Populists, who expressed considerable disdain over financial institutions, tended to point their venom east, away from their own bankers. In money-starved Kansas in 1859, despite the temptation to blame others for the absence of credit and currency, the *Elmwood Free Press* recognized that "when we become producers the cry 'no money' will cease," and Kansan John J. Ingalls matter-of-factly noted that the "actual exports of the country . . . has [sic] not yet been enough to pay for the whiskey that is drank [sic] every month."[8] Even when the local residents decried shinplasters and wildcat bank notes—"fog money"—they tended to blame immigrants who brought the money with them, not the banks.[9]

SCOPE OF THE STUDY

Not only does the West provide a regional study by virtue of its post–Civil War growth, but it also has been viewed by historians as a region with special and separate characteristics from the South, the East, the Old Northwest or even the border Midwest of Minnesota, Iowa, and Missouri.[10] We have chosen, therefore, to include in the West all states to the west of the Minnesota-Iowa-Missouri-Arkansas border. This definition fits almost exactly with that of Gerald Nash (who broke down the West into even further categories with a "wet West and a dry West").[11] Texas is an important exception. Insofar as historians have sometimes grouped Texas with the southern states, it poses a dilemma. This problem is magnified when we include Oklahoma. Still, our inclination is to omit Texas and include Oklahoma, whose similarities to Kansas and Nebraska make it part of the plains. Where more recent developments, such as the creation of the Dallas Federal Reserve District, might have put it in the West, we have incorporated relevant material. Since our study begins well before the creation of the Federal Reserve System districts, we did not feel obliged to organize it along the lines of those districts, but instead used the comptroller of the currency's old divisions: originally, western and Pacific states, and later, southwest, Mountain, and Pacific (excluding Alaska and Hawaii).[12]

Western historians recently have made significant contributions toward a broader picture of the economy in the region, but they have almost universally ignored banking and its effects. Although a recent historiographical essay on the economic development of the American West includes a brief discussion of banking on the frontier, its sources are dated and do not address any region of the West beyond the Mississippi.[13] However, a few important exceptions stand out: Leonard Arrington long ago began to integrate finance into his accounts of Utah's history; W. Turrentine Jackson has undertaken an extensive study of Wells Fargo and Company; Kirkpatrick Sale noted the crucial role western banks played in shifting political and economic power from the Rustbelt to the Sunbelt; and Gerald Nash has consistently incorporated economic history into his many works.[14] A number of other authors have assumed the tedious but important task of detailing the financial and banking history of individual states.[15] All of that work has provided necessary snapshots of banking growth, but has by its very nature been uneven, highly specialized, and narrowly focused.

Another layer of individual institutional histories has appeared.[16] Such studies received considerable monetary support from their hosts, and often yielded expectedly biased—but nevertheless useful—accounts, however limited, often providing to the public access to internal documents that would otherwise be unavailable to historians.[17] Over this patchwork of fragmented histories, a number of economists have engaged in statistical studies of specific periods or policies, resulting in an overlay of highly technical macroeconomic analysis relatively insensitive to local historical factors. Economists Charles Calomiris, Lance Davis, Milton Friedman,

Richard Sylla, and Eugene White, for example, have produced sophisticated studies that in one way or another cover the period from 1865 to 1913.[18] Generally those studies have ignored unique aspects of the West. Ross Robertson, in *The Comptroller and State Supervision,* discussed issues of free banking, noting that the rush of charter requests after the second BUS (Bank of the United States) closed made it expeditious for states to adopt free-banking laws. He commented that "the idea of readily available charters and bond-secured note issues was quickly becoming accepted throughout the country," yet in 1850, as the free-bank movement bloomed, California's state constitution prohibited all incorporated banks, free or otherwise.[19] Where historians have rendered broad works dealing with banking—Bray Hammond, James Livingston, and Robert Craig West come to mind—they have focused more on national politics and culture than on the interaction between banks and the regions in which they exist.[20]

Our goal, then, is to set banking and finance in the West in its historical and economic perspective. Was western banking distinctly different than banking in other sections of the country? If so, how? Did western banks draw money from the East without becoming a colony to eastern financial centers? Despite the influence of the Bank of America, were other western banks able to establish themselves as regional powers? What characteristics were peculiar to the economies of western states that changed banking and finance there? Many western states had extensive influence in shaping federal banking policy proportionate to their population. What factors contributed to that influence? As the political and economic power of the nation began to shift in the 1960s from the Rust Belt to the Sun Belt, what role did banks and bankers play in initiating and then stimulating and encouraging this realignment? Finally, how did they respond to: first, the energy bust; then, the related real-estate collapse; and, ultimately, the challenge of foreign competitors in an international market?

While we rely on statistical analysis for some of our discussion, we have avoided forays into detailed econometrics in order to remain focused on the larger picture. In general, then, we have concentrated on an overview of banking trends heavily laced with the particulars of individual banks and bankers, rather than studying the microeconomics of state banking or specific regions. However, as a point of departure for future statistical studies, researchers should consult the Appendix, tables 1 and 2, which provides yearly totals for all banks in the West by state, along with their yearly total resources.

Attempting such a broad synthesis on a topic that is broader still has its share of hazards. The sheer economic might of California—by 1988 the *world's* seventh largest economy—without the counterbalance of Texas, tends to slant any regional study of the West to at least some degree. But then, the same argument could be made about Louisiana's role in the antebellum economy or New York's in the late 1800s.[21] Another pitfall is that some among this diverse group of states entered the Union as late as 1912, giving the states an uneven history of regulation. Nevertheless, patterns of development are detectable, and the western states have more in common with each other than not. When L. Milton Woods described Cheyenne, Wyoming, as having had "a cemetery before it had truly become a town," he could easily have described countless western settlements, but not too many in South Carolina or Connecticut.[22] Of course, the continuity of the West's development extends far beyond burial plots, which, along with saloons, general stores, and blacksmith shops, dotted every frontier town. So did banks.

Early Banks and Currency

One of the most common threads in the expansion of the western economy has been the rapidity with which banking services appeared. Lord and Williams, a mercantile and freighting partnership, essentially provided banking in Tucson (Arizona Territory) with a "service area" that reached New Mexico at least fifty years before Arizona claimed statehood.[23] But compared to other western territories, even that looked a little slow. In California many banks existed less than three years after the arrival of the first gold miners, highlighted by the creation of the Miners Bank in 1848. •When Dexter Horton formalized his banking business in Seattle, there were only four hundred residents, whose contact with the outside world was limited to the weekly steamer.[24]

Another common thread, and a more important one, is the reason banks appeared. Here, the West is in sharp contrast to the South and parts of the Old Northwest. Unlike many southern banks, which had been specifically created by state legislatures to expand the credit generating capacity, western banks sprang up almost exclusively as a response to an insufficient money supply. The problem was currency not credit.[25]

Fur traders and trappers had established an extensive frontier "currency" system based on pelts as early as 1784. In Missouri after 1805, "it was legal to pay taxes in shaven deer skin at three pounds to one dollar," and consequently merchants who stored the fur bales issued warehouse receipts for leather and pelts that soon circulated as money.[26] Before long, warehousers in St. Louis, operating on the "goldsmith principle" (in which ancient goldsmiths had discovered that their depositors wanted redemption only in gold coins of the same weight, not identical coins) soon entered into a form of merchant banking. Equally important, they began to anticipate demand of future fur deliveries, which allowed them to issue warehouse receipts redeemable in furs at a future date. Although eastern merchants demanded payment from the Missouri customers in specie or recognized notes, the St. Louis banks—the Bank of Missouri and the Bank of St. Louis, both of which were chartered in 1816—found it as easy to verify the value and authenticity of pelts as to check bank notes from unfamiliar institutions hundreds of miles away.

Pelts and furs also constituted much of the early currency in the Pacific Northwest and Oklahoma, and visitors to California observed hides, tallow, and sea otter skins passing for money.[27] Similar observations could be made at any number of western locations. Oklahoma traders, who also handled furs, were epitomized by former Cincinnati banker Hugh Glenn, who lost his fortune and in 1820 started anew with a post near present-day Chase, Oklahoma.[28] There, Glenn accepted fur deposits and advances of credit. As with many early trading posts, licenses granted by the War Department gave the illusion of regulation, although the posts mostly policed themselves.[29] Merchants, however, traded in furs and whatever notes circulated among the soldiers, and extended considerable credit to Native Americans. Local tribes cast out from the East had often attained as much financial sophistication as whites, and they quickly found that they needed trading-post bankers nearby. Consequently, many merchants established permanent banking posts in Native American settlements, such as the depots in Doaksville, Skullyville, and Boggy Depot. These served the Choctaw Nation, and by the Civil War the Creek and Cherokee also had full-time banking offices that often consisted of only a cash box standing in a store's corner enclosed with chicken wire.[30]

The shortage of money in the 1820s, however, necessitated constant trips for merchants in the territory to Fort Smith or New Orleans. Transporting furs, gold, and silver coin overland to their trading posts, these merchants offered easy marks for bandits who waited until the traders entered Indian Territory and attacked there.[31] The cost of transporting gold, silver, and notes thus reflected both the distances that separated major banking centers and the risks associated with transport.

Use of furs and hides as money pushed further west and south not long after the Missouri banks opened, giving way to a more formalized banking system, but the early traders had already contributed to a developing financial network of considerable sophistication. When larger numbers of permanent settlers arrived, they brought with them eastern and southern paper currency, which then circulated on a regular basis. Because of the severe banking troubles in Wisconsin, Michigan, Minnesota, and Illinois in the 1850s, the Old Northwest played a relatively minor role in supplementing the frontier money supply. Minnesota, Illinois, Wisconsin, and Iowa had at one time or another prohibited banks, and even though Minnesota, Michigan, Ohio, Indiana, Illinois, and Wisconsin eventually did permit free banking laws, most of the free banks collapsed because of difficulties related to depressed bond prices.[32]

Nor did the western frontier receive an increasing flow of money from southern banks: despite the presence of growing or reviving financial systems in Tennessee, Louisiana, Alabama, Georgia, the Carolinas, and Virginia, parts of the South nearest the frontier and most likely to transmit a circulating medium had not yet recovered from the panic of 1837.[33] Arkansas, for example, prohibited banks altogether and was bankless by 1845 except for a dozen private bankers who by law were prohibited from issuing notes.[34] Mississippi had only two small chartered banks in operation on the eve of the Civil War,[35] and Texas had passed a somewhat porous law banning banks.[36] A few banks appeared there, but provided little money. Despite the antibank sentiment in Texas—much of which arose from the Republic's generous issue "of treasury notes, audited drafts and other types of paper money"—Texas traders quickly recognized their need for currency.[37] William M. Gouge, the famous Philadelphia monetary theorist, visited Texas as a bank examiner in 1852, and wrote a treatise called *The Fiscal History of Texas*, in which he noted the scarcity of money.[38]

Other gateways to the frontier also lacked banks. Prior to 1858, Missouri allowed only the State Bank of Missouri to issue notes, and its money "was doing duty in California, Oregon, and New Mexico whither it had been carried by emigrants and traders."[39] When the Nebraska legislature passed its first criminal code in 1855, bankers were defined among the criminals and banking was made illegal.[40] After 1857, a change in the law permitted a number of wildcat banks to appear. Thus, states that bordered the new frontier offered little to expand circulation of currency in Oklahoma, Kansas, Nebraska, or the Dakota Territory, although immigrants obviously brought some notes and specie with them. The editor of the *Kansas City Journal of Western Commerce* estimated that as much as $800,000 a year came into his town, then left for points west, and some settlers, such as Thomas C. Wells, who put down roots in Manhattan, arrived with more than $2,000.[41] Other money entered the western territory through gifts from friends, families, and relief organizations. John and Sarah Everett of Osawatomie, for example, received frequent cash gifts following their arrival in 1855.[42] Still other funds come from groups such as the National Kansas Committee and the Boston Relief Committee, which together poured almost $300,000 into Kansas in the late 1850s.[43] Other sources of funds existed, including (in the mid-1850s) pro- and antislavery groups, payments to Native American tribes, and federal government expenditures, not to mention cash that slid into the territory through gunrunning and other illegal activities.[44] Nevertheless, these sources could not have sufficiently supplied the rapidly developing economies of the plains states, and the Jacksonian hostility toward banks still carried some weight in Kansas and Nebraska. Kansas's three territorial governors all held antibank views: Robert J. Walker commented that he "would not sanction the establishment of any bank of issue in the territory," while James Deaver thought Congress did not give the states the power to charter banks, and Samuel Medary described banks as "demoralizing and seductive."[45] With those sentiments widely held, the 1855 Kansas territorial legislature prohibited nonbanking corporations from carrying on any banking operations, and two years later all existing unchartered banks were declared illegal. Thus, limited to tiny amounts of cash brought in from outside, settlers certainly had a complaint: there was no circulating medium to speak of. And the cry "There is no money in Kansas" might well have described the situation in neighboring plains territories as well.[46]

Circumstances differed in Colorado, California, and Montana, where abundant gold, gold dust, and silver constituted a temporary, if inconvenient, local circulating medium. Colorado's earliest banks began as bullion-purchasing offices and their founders were involved in gold brokerage before they formed the Exchange Bank in Denver in 1861 and the First National Bank of Denver in 1865.[47] As one observer of Denver's early saloons remarked, "whether buying a beer or a town lot, Coloradans typically pulled out pouches filled with yellow dust and nuggets."[48] Montana's first recorded exchange of gold dust, which, according to Lt. James H. Bradley, occurred in the mid-1850s, brought $1,525 in cash. Bradley sold the dust, for which he had exchanged $1,000 worth of "horses, arms, blankets, tobacco, etc."[49] Montana banks soon learned, as had those in Colorado, that they needed a regular gold business to remain profitable.

Indeed, for those inclined toward dishonesty, gold dust, unlike the pelts, offered a number of opportunities to engage in shenanigans such as dilution by mixing gold with brass fillings. Pure gold dust, which sold for twenty dollars an ounce, could be detected by rubbing it against ironstone. Gold dust also suffered from problems of divisibility, portability, and exactness of value. Small scales adorned saloon counters, with neither merchant nor customer fully trusting the other. A drink generally went for "a pinch," with the saloonkeeper permitted the honor. Barkeeps soon sported longer fingernails, and their libations accordingly reflected the increased prices.[50] The abundant gold supply soon forced all prices in the region up: eggs sold for two dollars a dozen and interest rates at Brown Brothers, the first unchartered bank in Denver, topped 25 percent.[51] Banks routinely sought the services of assayers, and bankers themselves quickly developed a proficiency for determining gold-dust value. Naturally, banks and other gold-dust buyers complained that miners received too much for their dust. Barrows, Millard and Company, an Omaha firm, praised the efforts of future Denver banker David Moffat for "moving the price of Dust . . . to what it's really worth[.] We have been bored to death here just by the foolish way you men have traded at Denver, allowing $16 for Dust that is not worth $14."[52]

The problems of divisibility and exactness of value of gold dust were solved when Austin W. Clark, Milton E. Clark, and Emmanuel Gruber, three Leavenworth, Kansas, gold dealers who had entered operations in 1858, decided to open an office in the gold-producing region of Colorado. They had often payed for shipping on $300,000 worth of gold dust at a given time, and hoped to reduce the overhead on transportation. Clark, Gruber and Company did more than simply relocate, for the firm quickly entered the coining and minting business. Its Denver office opened in July 1860, hauled in mint dies and a steam press, purchased gold dust at twelve to sixteen dollars an ounce, and minted coins in two and one-half–dollar, five-dollar, ten-dollar, and twenty-dollar gold pieces. In addition, as permitted by Colorado law, the company issued one-dollar and five-dollar notes, redeemable in gold, which were soon in greater demand than greenbacks. Like "George Smith's money" in Wisconsin, these notes constituted a currency more trusted and more soundly secured than even that of the U.S. government.[53] However, the firm also put scrip of questionable value into circulation. Just before the Denver office opened, Clark, Gruber and Company purchased scrip issued by the federal court in payment of trial expenses with the anticipation of circulating it.[54]

Another Denverite, Henry J. Rogers, issued $300 worth of a fractional currency that violated territorial laws (although he was not prosecuted), notes which, according to the Denver Rocky Mountain News, resembled "a piece of tissue paper dyed in indigo."[55] The success at note issue enjoyed by Rogers and Clark, Gruber and Company lasted only a few days until the National Bank Act drove privately issued notes out of existence. Meanwhile, Denverites, led by the Clarks and Gruber, lobbied for an official U.S. mint in Denver, with no illusions about who would receive the printing patronage. In 1863, Denver had its mint. Clark, Gruber and Company sold its press and two-story building to the federal government for $25,000, although the firm continued to handle all the actual minting work. Numerous other local businesses had made the transition from gold buyers to bankers, and a few had issued their own short-lived currency.[56]

Even the proximity to local mines did not ensure increasing prosperity or abundant currency. The Denver Rocky Mountain News in July 1860 noted that "money, just now, is pretty tight, collections are critical, and Denver drummers have generally to promise to 'call again.' . . ." It also repeated the claim that some lenders could receive "25% per month for as many thousands as they might lend" (although one Montana banker, John Owen, lent money on occasion to trappers at no interest).[57] Nevertheless, the city continued to attract entrepreneurs. In November 1862, the handsome young Luther Kountze, who had volunteered among his family members to expand their Omaha banking office founded in 1857, arrived in Colorado Territory. Two years later, his shy younger brother Charles joined him. The chief attractions of the Kountze Brothers banking house were buying and selling gold dust, and dealing in currency shipped in from their Omaha bank.[58] By 1868, R. G. Dun and Company, the eastern credit and business rating firm, concluded that "Kountze Bros. . . . are consider[ed] the best bankers west of the Mo[.] River."[59] But even then, Luther's conservative brother in Omaha, Augustus, warned that "operating in Gold has got to be nothing more or less than Gambling. . . . Gold would drop down 10 or 15% a day. . . ."[60] On the other hand, Allen and Millard in the mid-1860s made substantial profits from their Virginia City operation. One of Millard's friends wrote that Millard "has $80,000 on the road. . . . Profit on this . . . is $16,000. . . . Millard only has capital of $10,000. He says he made $10 per ounce on all the dust he handled last year and that he always expects 10 percent profit on all his home transactions."[61]

Idaho, Montana, and the Dakotas also witnessed gold strikes: Idaho in 1861–62, Montana in 1862 (plus silver and quartz discoveries), and the Black Hills in 1876. Each strike brought successive flocks of miners and settlers. At Fort Benton, on the upper Missouri, steamers discharged ten thousand people in 1876 alone.[62] Others trudged in on trails or followed in wagon trains from Minnesota. Montana historian Clark Spence assessed this population as "fluid, mobile . . . ready to move at slightest rumor of precious metal. . . ."[63] A need developed in these areas to assess the value of the gold and to supply the miners with basic necessities. It is hardly surprising, then, that the first bankers were either gold brokers or merchants. Major John Owen, who ran a trading post at Bitterroot Valley, conducted banking operations, including issuing drafts and making loans, as early as 1850.[64] Andrew Jackson Davis, a pioneer banker in Butte, Montana, began as a freighter who delivered merchandise all over the state.[65] Thousands flocked to the Black Hills after hearing the rumors of gold. Naturally, the first bank in the area, Miller and McPherson Bankers, originated as a brokerage house for gold dust.[66] One observer noted that in these gold towns "the first two signs to appear [were] 'saloon' and 'bank,' " the latter filling a need exemplified by fur trader Pierre Narcelle, who, for lack of a bank, kept up to $60,000 buried in the ground.[67] The profits to be made from gold and exchange on gold encouraged such influential banks as J. and W. Seligman to locate associates in Helena and other remote spots.

But ores brought a problem well known on the plains: with dozens of miners wishing to exchange their gold and silver on a regular basis, the early bankers desperately needed currency. So, in an ironic sense, Montana and Kansas shared the problem of "no money." Consider the letters of Hussey, Dahler, and Company, a pre-1860 Helena bank that was related to Warren Hussey's Salt Lake City firm. Charles Dahler, in charge of the Montana operations, expressed his frustration as early as 1867 when he wrote Hussey: "What are we to do for currency[?] the country is most effectively drained . . . and here we are less than [$]500 in sight to buy dust. . . . But there is one thing, we are in as good [a] fix as our neighbors."[68] Later, the currency shortage at Hussey, Dahler, and Company grew so intense that Dahler wrote to a commission merchant in Fort Benton asking that he try to get currency from passengers on a steamboat bound for St. Louis.[69] One night the bank closed with only sixty-five dollars in cash in its vault, and on another occasion Dahler noted dourly to the Virginia City office: "Am dead broke today and all banks are short."[70]

California had already experienced similar growing pains, in addition to others that the rest of the West had not yet known. As late as 1847, San Franciscans were still exchanging skins and cattle hides as money.[71] If any "banking" services existed, they came from the Hudson's Bay Company, which supplied most of the skins and what little gold coin circulated among the fifty or so citizens of Yerba Buena (as it was then called). Hudson's Bay abandoned the location in 1846, but Richard Dana nonetheless predicted that "if California ever becomes a prosperous country, this bay will be the center of its prosperity."[72] With the outset of the Mexican War, a new group of settlers moved into the Sacramento Valley. Still, an 1847 newspaper account listing the occupations of 169 people recorded no bankers.[73] American coins brought in by soldiers soon circulated with the Spanish and Mexican real.

The small flood of settlers turned into a tidal wave of speculators and prospectors with the publicity attending the discovery at Sutter's Mill in January 1848. By June 1849, gold dust had eclipsed pelts and coin as the preferred circulating medium, trading at U.S. $16 an ounce.[74] As in Denver, the abundant gold forced prices up. Between April and August 1848, for example, flour prices increased 300 percent.[75] The price of gold dust made it profitable to ship gold to New York or to the Philadelphia Mint, and several companies stepped in to develop this business.[76] Ads in local papers expressed a willingness to buy or sell gold or U.S. and Spanish coin, or offered interest-bearing notes. Local merchants who accumulated gold receipts, which they had to take to eastern urban centers for new wares, reasoned that they could circumvent these expensive trips and the burdensome journeys with gold dust if they could locate buyers in the East. Many of the merchants began a conversion to banking, with its convenient correspondent relationships with other banks. Consequently, over a fifteen-year period, hundreds of new banks had appeared, the foremost being the Bank of California, which was opened in June 1864 by William Chapman Ralston and Darius Ogden (D.O.) Mills with great fanfare and $2 million in capital.[77]

The appearance of any banks at all in California was noteworthy, due to the state's constitutional provision which outlawed chartering them. To say that this provision was ignored understates the case: by 1852 the San Francisco tax assessor listed fourteen banks among the occupants of downtown buildings. Despite the lack of concern about enforcing the antibanking law, the legislature did police the regulations against private note issue, strengthening those laws when the prominent firm of Page, Bacon & Co. failed in 1855 and precipitated a general panic.[78]

Meanwhile, the discovery of gold in the Gold Canyon area of Nevada lured in miners, many of whom had migrated first to California and its mining boom. From 1850 to 1859 this area supported between 100 and 180 miners who extracted $642,000 worth, even while they cast away the black sand—silver ore—they found with the gold. As early as 1853 Ethan and Hosea Grosh began to keep the silver ore and mine it with the gold. They landed on the Silver City branch of the Comstock Lode, but both died in tragic accidents before they found the actual Comstock.[79] Their loss was others' gain. By 1859, discovery of new ore deposits in the Comstock drew thousands more "new Californians" back across the Sierra Nevada, and "from 1859 to 1880 the history of the Comstock [was] the history of Nevada."[80] Virginia City and other Nevada towns soon experienced the same problems with a circulating medium as had Colorado and California: there was plenty of the valuable stuff, but it was inconvenient to use, hard to carry, difficult to measure for exact quality, and its very abundance encouraged rising prices.[81] Attempting to solve this problem, more than two hundred private banks supplied money in Nevada.

From the outset, Nevada's history had been interwoven with Utah's (due to the initial groups of Mormon settlers in Nevada) and with California's (because of the miners). California quickly expanded its influence beyond supplying a labor force, miners, and some early entrepreneurs, to establishing a branch of the Bank of California. Ralston, having had contact with the Comstock Lode in 1860, turned a defeat into a victory when he established a branch of the newly formed Bank of California in Virginia City.[82] Historians of California and Nevada differ over the details of the affair, but apparently the events unfolded as follows: one of the Bank of California's major Virginia City correspondents, Stateler and Arrington, a bank formed in 1861, attempted to defraud the Bank of California after Stateler got deeply into debt by trying to cash a huge overdraft on the California bank. When that overdraft was not approved, the Nevada bank went under. Ralston sent a representative, William Sharon (later a U.S.

senator from Nevada), to press claims and during Sharon's stay he decided that a branch would be profitable. A local banking firm, Arnold and Blauvelt joined the Bank of California agency to create an early interstate banking system. Sharon, a frail Ohio native and Quaker who had trekked west with the forty-niners to mine in California, had already made—and lost—a fortune in mining-stock speculation. Under Sharon's leadership, the Bank of California brought permanent circulation of bank notes.[83]

Other Nevada banks existed before the Bank of California although none had "bank" in its corporate title.[84] Wells Fargo, B. F. Hastings and Company, and Thornburgh, Ruhling and Company all made loans at 3 to 5 percent interest per month, but none of them issued notes, and miners needed a circulating medium. Thus, although the Bank of California offered far lower lending rates than the prevailing 3 to 5 percent, it gained its dominant position in Nevada as a source of notes, which it could generate easily in San Francisco.[85]

Noticeably different in its experiences with money from other parts of the Rockies, Utah filled its need for cash and early banking services principally through a scrip system under the watchful eye of the Church of Jesus Christ of Latter-day Saints.[86] From 1847 to 1863, local merchants, like their San Francisco, Virginia City, and Denver counterparts, bought and sold gold dust and issued their own notes.[87] More important than merchants, however, was the church tithing office and storehouse. This office used a system of debits and credits to control deposits and withdrawals from a community storehouse. Often the church-issued receipts for such withdrawals served as drafts or bank notes. Despite the sophistication of this system, it took the fortuitous return of members of the Mormon Battalion from Sutter's Mill with California gold to alleviate the money shortage in Salt Lake City and other communities.[88] The soldiers "deposited the gold dust with the [church] presidency," which minted it and in December of 1848 issued forty-six ten-dollar gold coins.[89] These and other coins served as a basis for several note issues from 1849 to 1858, and initially the notes circulated on a par with gold.

Temporary disruptions caused by the 1858 Utah War resulted when non-Mormon traders and merchants hastily left, "taking with them a major portion of the money supply."[90] Brigham Young, the charismatic and occasionally ruthless Mormon leader, had grasped the lessons of the ill-conceived banking institution at Kirtland, Ohio, where Joseph Smith's Safety Society Anti-Banking Co. collapsed in the panic of 1837.[91] Young wanted no part in a repeat performance of that crisis, but Utah needed money. He therefore authorized the establishment the Deseret Currency Association. This company issued notes, which Young called on church members to accept as gold. In a display of the advantages of a theocracy, church members complied, and when they did not, Young's response was swift. A group of church-licensed butchers refused to accept the first issues of the notes in 1849, and Young threatened to revoke their licenses. They immediately accepted the notes.[92] Still, non-Mormons increasingly regarded the church paper as of dubious value—notes ran at 60 percent discount—further emphasizing differences between the Mormons and Gentiles in Utah.[93] The U.S. territorial marshall confiscated the plates and forced retirement of the Mormon scrip in late 1858, but Young had already sermonized about "the propriety of having a Bank."[94] He had organizers support the concept and report "names in favor of the bank in my ward."[95]

Mormon colonies extended into Wyoming (then mostly in Dakota Territory), which too had subsisted on fur money and foreign coins. In 1857, the government prohibited foreign coins, further constricting the already scarce money supply, forcing early Wyoming settlers to rely on postage stamps for small change. These passed through several hands until they became so mutilated that "the post office refused to exchange them for new stamps, and the Treasury refused to accept them because they were not issued by that particular branch of government."[96]

Whereas the slavery issue had drawn both southern and freesoil settlers to Kansas in a political competition to dominate the state's constitution, and gold had been the magnet that attracted the first major population waves to Sutter's Mill, Virginia City, and Denver, the desolate town named Cheyenne represented just another supply depot for the Union Pacific Railroad. General Grenville M. Dodge and General Christopher C. Auger laid plans for an army post and settlement in 1867, and both sites had occupants even before they were completed.[97] Soldiers and railroad workers contributed to the currency supply with regular infusions of outside cash. Still, the paint on the town had scarcely dried by the time a local merchant, N. H. Heath and Company, advertised its safe and its willingness to accept deposits.[98] Several days later, on October 1, 1867, H. J. Rogers of Denver announced he was opening a banking business in Cheyenne.[99] Another settlement based on mining developed at South Pass, and a banking house opened there in 1868 or earlier, again created by the need for currency in that remote location. As in Denver and Virginia City, the miners needed a convenient way to exchange and transport gold dust.[100]

Gold had attracted business to the Pacific Northwest, not as much because of the relatively minor gold discoveries there, but because Oregon City (a village of less than a thousand in 1851) and Seattle had become important supply points for the California forty-niners.[101] Earlier developments had been limited to the fur trade and a Methodist mission consisting of thirty people in the Willamette Valley. All were dependent for supplies on the Hudson's Bay Company until 1840, the year in which fifty-one new missionaries arrived. One of them, George Abernathy, a former accountant, set up a store on an island in the Willamette River.[102] By the mid-forties both the Hudson's Bay Company and Abernathy were supplementing their merchant income with interest in the credit they had extended settlers.[103] When the missionaries decided to close their secular pursuits in 1846, debts to the mission totalled $30,000. George Abernathy bought these debts for $20,000 cash plus an interest-free note for $10,000, thus beginning a very long and prosperous career in Oregon business.[104]

Other merchant and express companies specialized in the safekeeping of money in the early 1850s. Ladd and Tilton Bank in Portland, Baker and Boyer Bank in Walla Walla, Dexter Horton's bank in Seattle, G. A. Barnes and Company of Olympia, and A. M. Cannon of Spokane Falls all grew out of mercantile businesses.[105] Dexter Horton, in fact, had stored his customers' deposits in a coffee barrel until he decided to get a safe and a set of books in 1870.[106] Several private banks that circulated their own notes appeared before 1860.[107] Henry Failing and Henry W. Corbett, two of the most important bankers—early competitors really—turned their merchant businesses into banks and ultimately joined forces to control First National Bank in Portland.[108]

With the mines nearby (and earlier, the fur business), westerners did not lack the ability to make purchases, nor the value with which to make them. They lacked a convenient means of exchange. It is noteworthy that the cry was not "There is no *credit* in Kansas" (as might have been applicable in Arkansas or Alabama at times), but that there was *no money*.

The federal government by the 1860s had preempted the chief cause of the credit demand elsewhere—land—by selling it cheaply, giving it away or subsidizing the railroads, which sold it on favorable terms.[109] And where large-scale plantations had required huge capital investments on a yearly basis for cotton, sugar, rice, or tobacco, the single-family western farms survived on far less, although, they, too, obviously needed seed, plows, horses, and so on. Still, the origins of the State Bank of Alabama, Real Estate Bank of Arkansas, Union Bank of Florida, and Planters Bank of Mississippi (to name but very few) demonstrate clearly that credit generation topped the list in the motivations of the founders. In stark contrast, virtually no western bank in the early period saw lending as its central business.

Another early motivation for bank creation, especially in Virginia, Georgia, Kentucky, Ohio, and Pennsylvania, had been to fund internal improvements, especially railroads and canals.[110] The later development of the West, however, diverted some of those demands as well for banks to act as agents of the state. The record on that, westerners knew, was not good. By the 1860s, the major railroads had already entered the New York money markets for financing through national bond issues.[111] Improvement banks in Ohio and Louisiana and elsewhere had disappointed their investors. One massive railroad and banking company, which planned to extend from Cincinnati to Charleston, found negotiating the state legislatures much more difficult than negotiating the mountain passes.[112]

Finally, the Civil War stimulated a tremendous burst of credit by the federal government, although, again, little currency actually arrived in the West.[113] With the onus of having to generate loans for specific pressure groups lifted, western banks found themselves, through circumstances, timing, and luck, largely unbeholden to politicians for their existence. To a greater degree than bankers elsewhere, western bankers had to establish their individual trustworthiness, for no state government or canal or railroad stood behind them ready to put up its assets to bail the bankers out in an emergency. Often, early western bankers ignored or outright violated territorial and state laws with impunity. More important, the authorities did not seem to mind. As a result, it fell to western bankers to regulate themselves, at least during the frontier stages of their history. Self-regulation rested on a personal relationship of trust with depositors and borrowers, and on outwardly visible symbols that reassured the community of a banker's permanent commitment and of his bank's safety. In the frontier period of the West, no balance sheet was as important to the bankers as are these symbols of safety.

2

SYMBOLS OF SAFETY: BANKING IN THE FRONTIER PERIOD, 1849–1893

The frontier period in the West, as applied to banks, effectively began when the first official (self-proclaimed or chartered) banks appeared. During this era, bankers virtually regulated themselves and made a transition from a freewheeling, entrepreneurial economy to a more structured economy of banking codes, corporations, and managerial hierarchies. Indeed, one can argue that it is the appearance of comprehensive codes that marks the end of the frontier period insofar as banking is concerned. Although banking was one of the earliest industries, in almost every western state many years passed before state officials borrowed from the more developed eastern states the concept of state-imposed regulation of bank operations.

During this unregulated period, bankers developed their own system for winning the confidence of potential depositors. In all cases, the system of self-regulation that resulted contained certain components. Two of the most critical were the personal reputation of the bank owner and certain architectural features of the bank building. As might be predicted, then, these factors became less important as the regulatory environment shifted the burden of proving safety away from the individual to the government, and from his frequently personal reassurances that the customers' dollars were safe to the written reports of examiners, agents, and state bureaucrats. By the late 1800s, the long arms of state and federal agencies reached out to touch all incorporated bankers and many private bankers in the West on a regular basis.

In the early 1850s, however, such developments could not have been further from the imagination (or nightmares) of the earliest gold-exchange agents, mercantile store owners, and pioneer merchants who would found the western banking empires. These entrepreneurs often moved from makeshift barter techniques to standard banking practices in the space of just a few years. For example, Lewis Atherton's detailed studies of Missouri and Kansas merchants in the 1830s reveal a system that accepted beeswax in return for whiskey, tallow and sugar for linen, and hard labor for basic staples. He found that the merchants themselves frequently remitted in goods.[1] In Missouri, for a short time, the merchants' produce trade had set them against proposed banking legislation, which in turn induced the farmers to form a cooperative exchange.[2] Quickly, however, these early pioneer merchants developed commission and forwarding businesses, then exchange and banking functions, and ultimately intricate correspondent relationships. Erling Erickson's assessment of the appearance of banks in frontier Iowa—that they "can be traced to an established business, such as a commission house, land agency, law practice, or general store"—applies equally to Arizona, Kansas, Colorado, and other points west of Iowa.[3]

Even before the merchants arrived, frontier areas frequently developed another potential source of bankers—the land agents. Land sales in territories depended entirely on an ever-changing kaleidoscope of federal laws and Native American treaties.[4] President James Buchanan angered the entire population of eastern Kansas when he abruptly reversed a policy of permitting settlers to "squat" on land for a period until they had accumulated enough capital to purchase it.[5] But when the preemption policies had been in effect, farmers had every incentive to speculate rather than farm: they had no clear title until the government surveyed, consequently their land could not serve as collateral for loans. Cyrus K. Holliday summed up the situation to his wife when he wrote: "investing in property in Kansas is like buying tickets in a lottery."[6] One constant remained in that the government accepted only specie in payment for lands. Land agents who had gold purchased the government land for cash, then sold it to settlers for credit. Even with land as collateral, lending rates hit 4 to 5 percent per month, and without land, rates could be higher.[7] To modern borrowers, and many outraged historians, these rates seemed steep at best, ruinous at worst.[8] But in fact, as Allan and Margaret Bogue discovered, speculators in Nebraska would have made some profits, but hardly of the windfall variety that contemporaries had charged.[9] More recent research suggests that speculators "could not have significantly retarded or distorted the settlement of the public lands."[10] And, despite their careful calculations, the Bogues never sufficiently weighed the risk factor, which may have more than justified rates of 40 to 50 percent per year.[11] Certainly debtors thought the interest rates high. The *Elmwood Free Press*, always ready to comment on monetary matters, clamored that "the people of Kansas have been cursed with exorbitant rates of interest," namely three percent per month."[12] Across the continent, in California, Wells, Fargo, and Company's banking agent reported that, as of 1853, "money commands from 3 to 10 prct. a month. . . ."[13] Hence, one has to treat cries of usury with care.

Whether or not the frontier speculators made the spectacular profits that newspapers such as the *Free Press* claimed, they nevertheless served important intermediary exchange functions and performed some routine lending in Kansas and Nebraska. For example, Cook and Sargent, a land agent in Davenport, Iowa, operated a branch office in Florence, Nebraska.[14] Plenty of competition existed, including Henn, Williams and Company of Fairfield, which had a connection with the Western Exchange, Fire and Marine Insurance Company of Omaha.[15] Nevertheless, Cook and Sargent remained the most important and the largest land agency (valued at $1 million) and, with their land-office brethren, the company sought to escape the provisions against banking that emanated from their own legislature in 1846 by simply moving their operations across state borders—in most cases, Nebraska's.

Desperate for circulation, Iowans, led by the firm of Greene and Weare of Cedar Rapids, and prompted by Thomas Hart Benton (nephew of "Bullion" Benton and an officer in Greene and Weare), incorporated the Western Exchange in collaboration with Henn and Williams.[16] Ironically, Bernhard Henn and Jesse Williams were loyal "hard money" Democrats, as were Morgan Reno, William F. Coolbaugh, George Greene, and J. L. Langworthy, and they all remained in theory committed to the radical wing of the antibank Jacksonians.[17] Conveniently, they forgot they had earlier demanded the extinction of all banks of issue and instead either directly or indirectly associated themselves with out-of-state note-issuing banks![18] While the incorporation act passed by the Nebraska legislature in fact prohibited the Western Exchange Company from note emission, it permitted it to receive deposits and issue certificate "receipts" for the deposits, a practice that curiously resembled issuing notes. Thus, Nebraska's first wildcats began surreptitiously.[19]

Western Exchange's notes soon covered not only parts of Nebraska Territory, but Iowa as well. When the bank folded in the panic of 1857, its note holders were badly burned. Before the panic, however, Nebraskans and Iowans faced a critical shortage of money, and "at the request of Iowa bankers" (i.e., the former land agents), the Nebraska legislature chartered five new banks in 1855.[20] Iowans soon purchased or controlled three of the five Nebraska banks: Fontanelle Bank of Bellevue, the Bank of Florence, and the Bank of Nebraska.[21] Ebenezer Cook of Davenport and Hugh D. Downey of Iowa City served as incorporators of the Bank of Florence, giving Cook an interlocking directorship on two Nebraska banks and their Iowa "land office," with its branch offices in Iowa City, Des Moines, Rock Island (Illinois), and Boston.[22] No wonder Cook, Sargent, and Downey acquired the label the "Pierpont Morgans of their day."[23]

The Bank of Florence circulated its notes in Iowa through the Cook and Sargent branches, significantly described as "fine and commodious" bank buildings.[24] In passing, it is important to note that in the years before the Civil War even "nonbank" land-agent banks and wildcat banks found it necessary to provide at least some symbols of safety to customers. It went well beyond facade: in Iowa, Cook and Sargent circulated statements promising full responsibility for the Nebraska notes.[25] During the panic of 1857, the Nebraska wildcat notes plunged, and, after an angry and violent crowd gathered in Davenport to protest, Cook and Sargent redeemed all of the Bank of Florence money.[26]

A third Iowa-owned Nebraska wildcat, the Bank of Nebraska at Omaha, featured Des Moines bankers Benjamin F. Allen and Hoyt Sherman as incorporators.[27] It, too, failed, but Allen redeemed all outstanding notes. The Fontanelle Bank of Bellevue, although founded by a local general, L. L. Bowen, soon passed into the hands of Iowans Greene and Weare of Cedar Rapids, another land agency with seven Iowa branches. Like other Nebraska wildcats, this bank failed in 1857. Unlike the others, however, it never redeemed its $150,000 worth of outstanding notes.[28]

With records such as those established by the early Nebraska banks, it is hardly surprising that in this region the term "wildcat bank" was usually uttered with contempt. Yet several points should be made about these institutions. First, as best can be determined, the Nebraska lawmakers had not based their legislation on any of the existing free-banking laws, especially in states where free banks had met with success, such as New York, Ohio, Illinois, and Tennessee.[29] Second, that the majority of the Nebraska banks created in 1855 and 1856 operated under control from outside the state offered both a curse and a blessing: the Iowa land agent–bankers had no stake in Nebraska's banks, making them less responsive and stable, but the branch structure of the Iowans' banks diversified their portfolios, spread the risk, and ultimately (in Nebraska's case) made the insolvent solvent. Essentially worthless shinplasters were redeemed at par, thanks to assets the land agents had amassed in Davenport, Des Moines, Rock Island (Illinois), and Boston. Thus vindicated, branch- and chain-banking structure should have been welcomed—or at the very least received a serious look—by Cornhusker and Jayhawk legislators (or even by Iowans when they legalized banks of issue in 1857).[30]

Free-banking principles had penetrated as far west as Santa Fe, where in 1863 a group of prominent citizens, spurred by the absence of money, obtained a provisional charter from the territorial legislature for a bank.[31] Sigmund Seligman, Cerain St. Vrain, Levi Speigelberg, and others proposed an institution called the Bank of New Mexico, a combination property bank and free bank. According to the charter, when the president and directors turned over title for real estate and property to, *or* when they had deposited the bank's own stock or United States 6 percent bonds with, the governor's office, they could incorporate the bank.[32] Although Congress never acted on this charter, this unique approach to banking law, derailed by national legislation, adds further evidence to the arguments advanced by many historians and economists that variants of free banking were increasingly favored prior to Civil War centralization.[33]

Certainly Nebraska's unfortunate experience did not discredit the idea of free banking. The foolish bank ban had made the population money-starved, and one who is thirsty enough will drink even salt water. Nor is it entirely clear that Nebraskans failed to appreciate the dubious value of the wildcat money, despite the vociferous crowd in Davenport. Arthur Rolnick and Warren Weber have shown that Minnesotans, in similar circumstances, saw the free-bank notes as speculative currency from the outset and treated them as such.[34] It is essential to note, however, that free banking in many ways constituted a much more regulated type of banking than that found under state chartering regulations: no branches were permitted and the portfolio mix was of a predictable, fixed, inflexible nature.

NATIONAL BANKING

The National Bank and Currency Acts rendered free-banking laws and note-issue by banks moot subjects. Many of the newer western states thus avoided the policy debacles of the antibank Jacksonian-influenced states, but they also lost the opportunity to fashion laws that met their own area's peculiar demands. Under the new federal legislation, individuals wishing to start a bank could obtain a charter from the U.S. government, regardless of state policies.[35] The acts further placed a 2 percent, then 10 percent tax on notes issued by private banks or state-chartered banks (i.e., any but a national bank), driving all independent note-issuing banks out of the business of printing money.[36] These acts established minimum capitalizations, depending on the size of the urban area: $50,000 for towns of six thousand or fewer; $100,000 for more than six thousand but less than fifty thousand people; and $200,000 for cities of over fifty thousand.[37] The high capitalization requirements discriminated against developing areas such as the West and the rebuilding South. Few towns of under six thousand could easily accumulate the $50,000 capitalization, let alone an individual merchant. In California as late as 1899 only 31 percent of the private bankers and only 55.7 percent of all banks had over $50,000 in capital.[38] Hence, in addition to eliminating banks of issue, the federal acts at least slowed down the process by which merchants became bankers. Moreover, only banks that had branches when they joined the system were permitted branches at all. Small towns and the plains West, which had developed their banking theory under the fuzzy-thinking Jacksonians and had con-cluded that only unit banks ensured adherence to Jacksonian egalitarian-ism, were thus denied the benefits of branching.[39]

The new laws also included prohibitions against lending on real estate under most conditions, especially making direct first mortgage loans. According to Section 28 of the National Bank Act, the only conditions under which banks could hold or convey real estate were: if it proved necessary for the immediate accommodation or transaction of its business; for the security of debts previously contracted; or as it was acquired through judgments, decrees, etc. The act prohibited the possession of real estate under mortgage or to secure any debt for more than five years. Some historians and economists have seen this provision itself as discriminatory against the West because it reduced the ability of national banks to promote urban development and settlement, and supposedly placed them at a disadvantage compared to state banks.[40] Whether it indeed reduced over-all mortgage lending by national banks is itself debatable. Richard Keehn and Gene Smiley, for example, have found that "lending by national banks was substantially greater than the magnitudes suggested by [other studies]," especially because of indirect lending.[41] National banks, for example, could make personal or commercial loans and renew them as mortgage loans, or accept additional property as collateral for existing loans. But even if national banks faced a disadvantage in mortgage lending, they were more than adequately compensated by their powers of note issue, returns on government bonds, potential profits through being desig-nated a federal depository, and the free advertising on their bills, to name just a few advantages that they had over state banks.[42] Irrespective of these considerations, the most significant effect of the mortgage-lending prohibitions and the new web of federal homestead laws and railroad-subsidy acts was to exclude many of the land-agent bankers who had so carefully cultivated their businesses in this respect. Thanks to these laws, the merchant emerged victorious over the land agent (or, if you will, "speculator"), as the natural precursor to the banker and financier of the West.

Passage of these acts not only gave the government much-needed credit, but it established complete control over the process of currency creation and, temporarily, bank chartering in many areas. This was especially true in the western territories, wherein the Congress had the final right of approval over all bank charters, as well as the South, whose state-chartered banks had collapsed attempting to prop up the Confederacy.[43] Moreover, awarding charters provided a neat method of rewarding political friends and punishing enemies, and occasionally the victorious Union could ac-complish both at once, especially when it came to authorizing carpetbagger banks in the South. Lincoln's administration had thus presided over a massive shift of financial power from the West and growing South to Washington, D.C., although for several decades the government remained financially dependent on New York's banks.

Since most of the West consisted of isolated towns too small to sustain a national bank, and the territorial and state governments were unable or unwilling to charter banks, merchants more than ever became the natural financial intermediaries. The mercantile store owners had access to credit in urban centers to the east and in San Francisco, and they also had a regular flow of money. Nearly all settlers, sooner or later, had to come to the merchant, and, because frequent trips were expensive and time consuming, the imperative to obtain all of one's supplies at one time usually dictated "running a tab." Since simple necessities did not come cheap on the frontier—flour in Tucson sold for twenty-five dollars worth of silver per barrel—further demands for credit were placed on the store owner.[44] Such prices hardly represented "gouging," either, as a typical freighting trip by water from San Francisco to Yuma, then overland to Tucson, took an average of sixty days.[45] During the entire overland journey, wary wagoners kept a watchful eye for Apaches and run-of-the-mill bandits. From the demand side, merchants had a ready credit market; and from the supply side, although they no longer enjoyed the privileges of printing notes, they still frequently represented the only major depot for hundreds of miles. They therefore controlled, to some degree, the flow of money in the territories (and hence, its velocity). Not surprisingly, then, many of the bankers in the West, especially after the Civil War, came from the ranks of merchants.

MERCHANT BANKERS

Simply having access to credit and a demand for it did not suffice to create a bank. Without local regulations, and without an obvious federal presence in local banking activities, customers relied on a variety of indicators to determine a bank's stability and safety. The most obvious indicator to any customer or depositor was the background, business experience, and reputation of the founder or founders of the bank. And, on a day-to-day basis, the business most visible to the community was a mercantile operation.

The Mark I. Jacobs Company in Tucson exemplified the general store that made a transition to banking.[46] San Francisco merchant Mark Jacobs saw the wild Arizona Territory as a business opportunity, and in 1867 he dispatched his two sons, Lionel and Barron, to establish a mercantile operation in Tucson.[47] Dealing in everything "from hairpins to harmonicas," the brothers secured capital from California to exchange gold and silver for army drafts.[48] Admonished by their father not to forget "the great power of money," Lionel and Barron entered into the lending arena once their business had stabilized.[49] Their father's exhortation to "deal less in calico and more in money" led them to contemplate founding a bank.[50] By 1871, thanks to the Jacobs Company, Tucson had a primitive banking system six years before the first chartered bank, the Bank of Arizona in Prescott, opened.[51]

Oklahoma witnessed a similar evolution of merchants-turned-bankers. Doaksville, the major settlement in the Choctaw Nation, featured competition between the Doak and Times Mercantile Company and Berthelet, Heald, and Company, both of which performed basic banking functions.[52] Other merchants engaged in banking in Micco, Three Forks, Tahlequah, and North Fork Town.[53] The most influential of these early Oklahoma merchant-bankers, J. J. McAlester, met with such success that residents named a town for him.[54] McAlester, a Confederate veteran who gained mercantile experience in Stonewall (where else?) from 1865 to 1870, opened a store with a partner at the "Crossroads," a major point on the Texas Road. Soon his partner quit, but McAlester expanded his mercantile business to include banking. He also engaged in basic mineral exploration, which resulted in his discovery of a huge coal deposit. The Oklahoma Mining Company, founded by McAlester, generated one of the earliest energy booms in the state.[55]

In addition to providing credit, several other western mercantile businesses engaged in freighting, which included another bank-related function, that of accepting goods on deposit and issuing a receipt. Among the frontier entrepreneurs who engaged in freighting businesses, William Ralston, the Bank of California's founder, managed a shipping firm before he and his partners started a bank, and Lord and Williams in Tucson often had $1 million in deposit from army payrolls, customers, or simply awaiting shipment to San Diego.[56] Other examples of mercantile freighting firms are Todd and Company, an Oregon firm founded in 1851; and a joint arrangement between the H. W. Corbett Company and Abernathy, Clark and Company, which shipped goods in and out of Portland.[57]

Of course, the most important western overland shipping firm, Wells, Fargo and Company, founded in 1852, remains a bank to the present.[58] Henry Wells and William G. Fargo took their concept from the uneducated but determined New Yorker John Butterfield, who had advanced through the ranks from driving a stagecoach to controlling his employer's firm.[59] He went on to dominate mail and passenger lines in northern and western New York, and he epitomized the concept of express-mail service—fast and safe package shipment. In 1849 he merged his infant express company, Butterfield and Wasson, with those of Wells and Company and Livingston, Fargo and Company, to form the American Express Company, better known in the 1970s and 1980s for its worldwide credit cards than for its mail service.[60] Yet the principle was the same: rapid transfer of goods or services across vast distances. Wells was the first president of American Express until 1867, when Fargo succeeded him.

Henry Wells, like Butterfield a New Yorker, had involved himself in civic and business activities in Aurora, eventually founding Wells College. Kindly but serious, Wells's long white beard concealed his youth. At the age of forty-five he joined Butterfield's venture, having already distinguished himself as a railroad promoter and bank president.[61] In contrast, the more rugged William Fargo, thirteen years younger than Wells, although an active business promoter in Buffalo, had a better feel for politics, having served two mayoral terms in Buffalo.[62]

Wells and Fargo, in spite of their New York loyalties, saw the opportunities offered by California and a general western freight operation. Butterfield and other directors wanted no part of such an ambitious expansion at that time, but agreed to let Wells and Fargo create a separate, cooperating business. On March 18, 1852, Wells, Fargo, and other associates met at New York's Astor House to announce the formation of Wells, Fargo and Company, and within months opened a San Francisco office on Montgomery Street.[63] Significantly, two representatives of the company arrived in California, one in charge of express business and one specifically for banking operations.[64] By 1855, at least fifty-five Wells Fargo agencies operated throughout California and Oregon, gracing towns with names such as Yankee Jim's, Rattlesnake Bar, and Rough-n-Ready. Wells, Fargo and Company not only mastered overland mail and freight with its stagecoaches, but shipped gold by water along the California coast and rivers in the steamer *Antelope*, known as the "gold boat."[65]

Adams and Company, Wells Fargo's chief competitor, in the express business, also offered banking services. This company and other rivals collapsed in the financial debacle of 1855 in California. Wells Fargo, still quite solvent, took advantage of the competitors' difficulties to establish new contracts with their depots.[66] It thus placed itself in an excellent position to control California express services and also expanded its banking opportunities, which prepared it for an even greater role in western development. Wells, Fargo and Company had cooperated with American Express since its founding, and in 1857, with the announcement by Congress that the postmaster general would be authorized to contract for overland mail service between the Mississippi River and the Pacific Coast, John Butterfield proposed a new venture. Although the government selected a route that passed through El Paso, Yuma, and Los Angeles, then turned north to San Francisco (instead of a more direct route), Butterfield believed that the Wells Fargo stagecoaches would handle that segment of the trip. Thus, Butterfield, Wells, Fargo, and representatives from U.S. and Adams express companies (the two major competitors), created the joint-stock Overland Mail Company. Butterfield's adept organization, however, soon found itself in a sea of debt, most of it to Wells, Fargo and Company, which "from the beginning . . . served as the 'banker' for The Overland Mail Company. . . ."[67] Moreover, Wells, Fargo and Company dominated Overland's investors and directors. The Wells Fargo–dominated board ousted Butterfield from the presidency of the Overland Mail Company in 1860.[68] By 1865, following a rerouting of the stage lines north to the California Trail, and after a series of corporate "force-outs" and outright sales, Wells, Fargo and Company had gained virtually complete control of all lines west of the Missouri River.[69]

Wells Fargo, like so many other freighting and depot businesses, entered the field of banking services when it issued certificates of exchange, the first appearing on July 13, 1852.[70] Being well-versed in the difficulties and dangers of transportation, the company took precautions to ensure reliable transfers of funds with such bills, sending three copies between remitters and receivers in the East and West. The first to arrive was recorded as the official transaction and paid, and the others were void if and when they arrived. So prominent had the banking services become that Wells Fargo's advertisement in the *San Francisco Business Directory* in 1852 mentioned the express business in tiny letters three lines down from the huge headline "Bankers and Exchange Dealers."[71] By California's banking crisis in 1855, Wells, Fargo and Company had increased its capital and expanded its services to Sacramento, Stockton, and even Portland. When it opened its banking house in Los Angeles, its capital had reached $1 million.[72]

Clearly, Wells Fargo's transportation network gave it an advantage over other mercantile operations, and yet the mail contract that had given the company its boost now proved an invaluable assistance to competitors, who could use those same mail routes for their own exchange business. Among the dozens of merchants who used mercantile business as a springboard to banking were the Jacobs brothers and Martin Kales, and Solomon Lewis in Arizona; J. A. Patterson and P. S. Hoffman, J. B. Charles, and E. L. Conklin in Oklahoma; the Speigelbergs and Felipe Chavez in New Mexico; Edward Ivenson and D. K. Allen in Wyoming; Henry J. Rogers, John William Hugus, and Luther and Charles Kountze in Nebraska. The Kountzes later expanded into Colorado and Wyoming.

California entrepreneurs who founded the largest and most important banks came from mercantile backgrounds. D. O. Mills came to Sacramento to prospect, opened a mercantile establishment instead, and quickly added banking to his activities.[73] Isaias W. Hellman, president of Farmers and Merchants Bank of Los Angeles and Nevada Bank of San Francisco, started as an employee in his relatives' dry goods store.[74] Charles Crocker (Crocker

Bank), the son of an unsuccessful liquor distributor, was an iron forge operator, then a dry goods store owner; John Downey, later a California governor, was a merchant who opened the first bank in Los Angeles; and the Bank of California's chief competitor, James Flood and William O'Brien, two of the founders of the Bank of Nevada, had been partners in a San Francisco saloon.[75]

The Mormons, too, followed this pattern with the creation of the Bank of Deseret in 1871, although a private mercantile business, Walker Brothers, also evolved into a powerful bank, Walker Bank and Trust Company.[76] Lewis H. Hershfield, an Oneida, New York, merchant, brought his business to Helena in 1865, formalizing his gold-trading brokerage into a bank. In 1882, he and his brother received a national charter for their newly named Merchants National Bank.[77] Even in Nevada, with its Bank of California branch in Virginia City (which had emerged from Joseph Donohoe and William Ralston, a private banking company, itself born of the freight business), and the Wells Fargo agencies there, merchants overwhelmingly dominated the ranks of western bankers.[78]

From these numerous merchants, we can select a few as case studies that represent a fairly common experience. The Speigelberg brothers— Solomon, Levi, Willi, and Lehman—are an outstanding example of a merchant family in New Mexico. Levi remained with his own New York banking house while the others ventured west in the 1850s to open their general store in Santa Fe. They labored at this business for twenty years, building a broad clientele and a local reputation for honesty.[79] In April 1872, the Santa Fe Speigelbergs organized a bank with the intent of obtaining a national charter.[80] Their major competitor, the well-rooted First National Bank of Santa Fe, had deep local loyalties and aggressive directors. Its chief founder, Lucien B. Maxwell, capitalized the bank at $150,000 through sales of his extensive Beubien and Miranda ́Grant properties in New Mexico.[81] In September 1870 Maxwell had joined John Watts, Peter Maxwell, Charles Holly, and Henry Hooper to execute the articles of incorporation for New Mexico's first bank. Within a year, these owners sold control to the bank's attorneys, Thomas Catron and Stephen Elkins, who placed themselves on the board.[82] Elkins was the new president. Despite receiving the designation of U.S. depository from the federal government, First National had difficulty attracting deposits, so it was not surprising that Elkins was alarmed at the prospect of having the Speigelbergs as competitors. Writing his New York brokers, Northrup and Chick, Elkins warily noted "some jews [sic] of this place together with one of the Speigelbergs of New York are attempting . . . to establish a 2d Nat. Bank here. . . . Of course, it is to our interest to defeat their project if possible and to this end I have . . . written a short note to the Comptroller of the Currency suggesting . . . that the First National Bank is amply able to do the business of this place. And the establishment of a 2nd Bank would render the success of both quite doubtful."[83]

On the contrary, both succeeded. Second National Bank opened in the late summer of 1872, capitalized at $150,000, with the obvious objective of gaining broad local support. Not only had the Speigelbergs recruited prominent local miller Felipe Chavez to serve on the board, but of the stockholders listed in 1880, thirteen of the twenty-three were New Mexicans, seven of them from Santa Fe.[84] Chavez also brought two other assets to the young bank. First, his connections to the Hispanic community promised to tap that group, which saw the "Santa Fe gang" of Elkins and Catron as elitist. More important, however, Chavez, like the Speigelbergs, was a merchant-trader and owner of the first steam-driven flour mill in New Mexico. The intentions behind having Chavez on the board were abundantly clear in Willi Speigelberg's notification of his reappointment as a director in 1879, which was, according to Speigelberg, due to "your great financial abilities as well as your *universally known reputation*" (emphasis added).[85] The threat posed by Second National concerned Elkins enough that he wrote existing First National customers to make certain they did not move their accounts, and in this he was successful.[86] First National had made its share of enemies, though. Levi Speigelberg assured a New York banker that "our chances of getting plenty of business are good," because a number of friends and customers "[do] not desire to do business elsewhere if they can possibly help it."[87] By October, the bank reported its business "steadily increasing" with the "promise of being one hundred times [better] than we expected."[88] Willi Speigelberg's optimistic reports to the contrary, the bank's profits were so strained that Lehman Speigelberg, Second National's president, requested that the comptroller of the currency deposit the bank's current installment of currency with a New York bank to the order of Second National's cashier, Willi Speigelberg, to avoid stagecoach freight charges.[89]

Both banks, as it happened, prospered. Santa Fe had enough business for two banks, at least for a while. Second National reported business "steadily increasing" in October, while First National declared 4 percent, then 7 percent dividends over a twelve-month period.[90] By 1874, Felipe Chavez noted that Second National had done better than he expected, and both banks weathered the panic of 1873.[91] The success of these institutions, but of Second National in particular, illustrates the evolution of merchants into bankers. The Speigelbergs voluntarily closed their bank and returned to New York in 1892, before the signs of the coming depression had appeared, because the bank, though entirely solvent, had not grown as they had expected. At the time of its liquidation all stockholders received their investment, although Chavez and some others thought the institution was "rather slow in making settlement."[92]

Perhaps the most famous of the merchant bankers, another brother team—the Kountzes—established Colorado's oldest bank. Luther, who opened Kountze Brothers Bank on December 2, 1862, was the son of Christian Kountze, a German immigrant from Saxony. Christian had come to the United States in 1820 as a twenty-five-year-old peddler, traveling the country until he reached Osnaburg, Ohio.[93] En route, Kountze had sold his wares in Pittsburgh, where he met Charles Brewer, a local business leader. Brewer backed Kountze's business, helped to establish him in Osnaburg. There, Christian met his future wife and saw his mercantile business blossom. Although Christian never entered banking itself, it is clear his sons had that inclination from the outset. One mysteriously died attempting to open a branch of Kountze Brothers Bank in Dakota City, Nebraska, some eighty-five miles from Omaha. Augustus, the oldest son, and Herman had opened their Omaha bank in 1857 in a small shack. They quickly established sterling reputations in Omaha and then in Denver. R. G. Dun and Company noted of Augustus and Herman, after they opened the Omaha bank: "First class men. G[oo]d hab[it]s in every way; men of hon[esty] and consid[erable] responsibility. . . ." Of Luther and Charles in 1863, the Dun Report noted they were "consid[ered] reg[ular] and reliab[le] and good for any and all contracts they make."[94]

The Kountzes' primary Denver competition, Milton E. and Austin W. Clark and Emmanuel Gruber of Clark and Company, ironically also hailed from Ohio. They had left Brown County in 1857 to open a merchandising house in Leavenworth, Kansas. Although they participated in land speculations, the solemn, distinguished-looking trio turned their attention to a mercantile store, then, when they arrived in Denver, to gold-dust exchange. The Clarks and Gruber spent little time in Denver after their mint swung into operation, instead promoting George T. Clark (no relation to Austin and Milton) as manager. Like the other Clarks, George had business experience, having worked in an express company.[95]

Clearly, a background in mercantile operations or gold exchange characterized most successful western bankers. Seldom did an already established banker in the East travel west, although of course exceptions existed. The pioneer Montana bank Allen and Millard, opened in 1864, actually represented an extension of Des Moines financier Benjamin F. Allen's Iowa business. He sent J. H. Millard to Virginia City to establish the first official bank in the territory, even though a few other merchants, including Major John Owen, had engaged in banking for several months.[96] Other bankers came west in an assortment of roles. William J. Murphy, the railroad contractor hired by the Arizona Canal Company to construct the canal project, learned upon accepting the job that his contract included a clause that required him to raise capital through the sale of mortgage bonds.[97] His limited experience in this area led him to local banker Martin Kales, who had opened an agency of the Bank of Arizona in Phoenix. Kales, however, showed no interest in the project, and Murphy found himself searching elsewhere for financial help. He asked an acquaintance, Iowa banker William Christy, to supervise the financial aspects of the project, and as a vehicle to sell bonds, the canal group organized First National Bank of Phoenix in September 1883.[98]

Kales, meanwhile, became the chief obstacle to the Arizona Canal Company and First National Bank. Murphy, writing his wife in March 1884, reported that a friend advised him that "the enemy faction [Kales and his associates] are doing their best to break me and the bank." Murphy realized that in Kales he had "an active enemy."[99] Christy and First National had given Kales some ammunition by lending more than was permitted under its national charter, which Kales gleefully reported to bank examiners. But when the examiners showed up on April 12, 1884, to investigate Kales's reports of excessive lending at the "national" bank, they found instead Valley Bank of Phoenix, reorganized literally overnight by Christy, Murphy, W. J. Bennett, and Moses H. Sherman.[100]

The Arizona Canal opened in June 1885, with much of the credit for its success belonging to Christy, but other transplanted bankers left far different legacies. J. M. Ragsdale and C. R. McLin, two Kansas bankers, organized a chain of banks in Oklahoma and operated them for two years before leaving the territory with the funds. Many depositors suffered at the hands of these "interstate bankers."[101] It was probably just as well that established bankers stayed out of the West: a Montana settler, S. H. Bohm, conned New York banker J. W. Seligman out of more than $175,000 in a few short years for investment in Bohm's Helena Bank.[102] Usually, however, one found reports such as that in the *Denver Tribune* of September 14, 1882, describing the founders of the Bank of Durango as "gentlemen well known and holding high rank in financial circles."[103]

No one fit this description better than Portland banker Henry W. Corbett. A New Yorker who arrived in the Willamette Valley in 1851, Corbett had worked for seven years prior to his trek west with the New York dry goods firm of Williams, Bradford and Company, which sponsored his Northwest venture.[104] Purchasing general merchandise, then shipping it to Portland, he opened his own mercantile establishment. Corbett had all the desirable characteristics of a potential banker: he avoided risk, shunned speculation, and insisted on complete control of his own funds. An individualist quite capable of business innovation, Corbett developed a strong reputation with local customers. By devising his own system of purchasing on remittances, and insisting on high quality and exact standards, Corbett laid the foundation for his own bank. He observed in a letter to an eastern firm, "we experience the benefit of having no Banks in the Pacific [Northwest]," and, presaging his entry into banking, he noted to another firm, "we have no banks on the Pacific," and later said that he relied entirely upon "receipts from my own business."[105] By the 1860s, Corbett had "begun more or less informally to fulfill the function of a banker."[106] His weaknesses—conservatism and a methodical approach to business—were also his strengths. Henry Failing, his competitor and eventual partner, observed that Corbett's company "has never made money as fast as we have yet he has kept his capital all in his business and a great deal outside which he can call in at any moment."[107] Failing, who in 1869 joined Corbett to gain control of the four-year-old First National Bank, not surprisingly, had started his career in merchandising.[108]

In neighboring Washington, at Walla Walla, flour miller and merchant A. H. Reynolds joined J. H. Day, a local physician whose keen eye for gold dust—which he often took in payment for his services—to create a mercantile company that emerged in 1869 as the Reynolds and Day bank.[109] Ironically, their chief competitor, the Boyer-Baker Bank, also had been founded by a physician-merchant duo, Dr. Dorsey F. Baker and John Boyer. Their bank opened only a few months after that of Reynolds and Day. These two banks served entirely different clienteles, with Boyer-Baker financing wheat farmers and fruit growers and Reynolds and Day concentrating on cattle ranchers and miners.

To achieve a solid local reputation, businessmen had to put down local roots, and already-established bankers seldom uprooted to come west. In the few cases in which they did, their relocation represented part of a family branch-bank extension, as occurred with the Speigelbergs and the Kountzes. Much more common were bankers such as John H. Dill, a sewing-machine salesman who lent money at interest until he amassed $750 capital and opened what eventually became Commercial National Bank in Muskogee.[110] Another typical merchant, Edward Ivinson, a West Indian native, arrived in Laramie in 1868 "with three or four carloads of merchandise to open the first mercantile establishment [there]."[111] Then, a remarkable transformation occurred that mirrored the development of banking everywhere in the West. According to Ivinson, "It so happened that I had the only safe in town and the merchants and businessmen deposited their funds with me."[112] John William Hugus, the post trader at Fort Fred Steele, started his own mercantile operations the same year as Ivinson but brought with him from Omaha some banking experience related to his work with J. A. Ware and Company, a partnership between Hugus and Nebraska banker J. A. Ware.[113] Hugus established combination mercantile operations/banks in Rawlins and Saratoga.[114]

At least eight mercantile businesses in early Utah Territory became banks, some of which continue to operate in one form or another.[115] Two of the most important, Walker Brothers and Hooper, Eldredge and Company, began in 1859. Walker Brothers operated as a general store until 1871, and even after beginning banking it continued its merchandising operations until 1885. Prominent merchants William H. Hooper and Horace S. Eldredge formed Hooper, Eldredge and Company in 1858 and carried on a banking business until the Zion Co-operative Mercantile Institution absorbed the merchant side of their business in 1869. The company reorganized as an official banking company the following year.[116] Other firms originated as gold agents or freighting companies in Utah, including a Salt Lake City branch of Wells Fargo. Some Utah bankers, including transplanted Denver gold broker Warren Hussey, branched into operations in Montana. Along with Charles Dahler, the Denver agent of Ben Holladay's Overland Stage Line, Hussey put together banking enterprises in Central City and Denver, as well as in Virginia City and Helena.[117] Hussey personally managed the Utah and Montana banks, the most prominent of which was First National Bank of Utah (successor to Hussey and Dahler's Miner's National). A man of boundless energy and vision, and gifted with exceptional promotional talents, Hussey, who anticipated the completion of the transcontinental railroad, created First National, obtaining the necessary organizational papers well before his partnership acquired the assets of Miner's National.[118] This bank failed during the panic of 1873, largely because Hussey retained his considerable profits himself rather than returning them to the bank's surplus account.[119] Undeterred, and possessing no small amount of money, Hussey continued banking operations as a promoter in Montana (1874–79), then, after a brief stay in New York to generate stock sales for his Colorado mines, he moved to northern Idaho to establish a new bank, headquartered in a tent.[120]

Just as Hussey crossed from Utah to Idaho and Montana, an Idaho merchant moved to Salt Lake City to create Utah's third national bank. B. M. Du Rell, who had followed the mining boom to Idaho from 1862 to 1864 and established a mercantile business geared to supplying prospectors, called B. M. Du Rell and C. W. Moore. They soon received deposits and opened offices in Ruby City, Boise City, and Idaho City. Du Rell noticed that his supplies all passed through the important distribution center at Salt Lake City.[121] In 1871 he left Boise, where he had established the First National Bank of Idaho in 1867 (although he and Moore could not obtain any national bank notes until late 1867, and not until 1871 did the bank have enough notes to actually open for business). Finally seeing the bank successfully launched, Du Rell left for the Wasatch foothills, where he used a capital of $100,000 to found Salt Lake City National Bank of Utah.[122]

On a far smaller scale, but no less adventurous, were the exploits of Kansas banker Silas D. Aulls and Montana banker Andrew Jackson Davis. A small-business owner from Avoca, New York, Aulls established the Bank of Bucklin and the Western Banking Company in Bucklin, Kansas in 1887. In letters to his brother-in-law, Ambrose Hewlett, Aulls not only perceptively noted the money shortage in Kansas, but left an interesting record of the origins of a small country bank. A letter written in August 1888 contains Aulls's observation that he saw "many chances to make money here but . . . a person must have some *capital*. . . . A small amount of capital will answer very well here. . . ." Several days later he advised Hewlett of his attempt to "make arrangements to get in some office here. . . . [I] shall buy very small notes & handle real estate soon. . . ." Aulls recalled that "Hutchinson Bros [Bank, of Pratt, Kansas] commenced business here 3 years ago without any capital except what they borrowed from St. Louis."[123] Davis, a man of many hats, had operated a grist mill in Iowa, and had shipped goods to Bannack, Montana, after the discovery of gold there. He had made a living as an Indian trader, a river merchant, a farmer, and a miller. Arriving in Montana in 1863, before long he had established the state's first flour mill. His freighters brought in the first reaper and threshing machine in the area, and soon supplied other general-merchandise store owners with their wares. In 1886, when Samuel T. Hauser organized S. T. Hauser and Company, soon to convert to First National Bank of Helena, Davis was a prime investor as well as vice president. Davis struck out on his own, establishing a partnership that retained the name S. T. Hauser and Company in Butte on February 6, 1877, for which he provided most of the capital himself. The bank incorporated as Butte National Bank in 1881, and three years later Davis acquired sole ownership.[124]

Hauser, of course, had a background as diverse as that of Davis. A Kentuckian who saw the potential for profits in the gold-dust trade, Hauser arrived in Montana at age twenty-nine, and two years later, in 1864, created a corporation called the American Gold and Silver Mining Company of Montana, with investors who included George Peabody and W. A. Dodge. Although, unlike many other western bankers, he borrowed $15,000 from an eastern source (George Kennedy, a contractor on the Pacific Railroad in Missouri) to start his Virginia City banking operation, when he attempted to convert it into a national bank in 1865 his partners explained to him the importance of a local reputation. New York financier Thomas Akers wrote Hauser admonishing him: "What we need of you is not money so much as names. . . . You would furthermore be expected to name other men who would *nominally* become stockholders. In short . . . do everything necessary to be done in organizing *except* furnish the money" (emphasis added).[125] Clearly, then, even when capital was abundant, the frontier bankers needed something money alone could not buy: a reputation.

Since a quantitative study identifying all merchants who became bankers is virtually impossible, we must rely on qualitative evidence. From Wyoming to California, Idaho to Oklahoma, the pattern remained the same for the appearance of banks: a merchant established a business in which he gained—or improved—his commercial experience, and provided a record that the public could trust. This qualitative evidence is overwhelming in revealing that bankers universally came from the ranks of merchants and dealers in gold dust, not railroaders, lawyers, soldiers, or any other group. It is also clear that most of these merchants were self-made individuals of little inherited wealth and often with little cash at the time they started their banks. Finally, their success depended, to some degree, on establishing a reputation for stability and prosperity.

This pattern correlates with that discovered by Harry Stevens in his study of Cincinnati bankers in the frontier period. Stevens found that the "largest proportion were or had been merchants."[126] Unlike the Cincinnati bankers, however, once the western merchants decided to enter banking, they did so wholeheartedly and usually without returning to their original mercantile businesses, although many expanded their businesses beyond banking into mining, railroads, and industry.

SYMBOLS OF SAFETY

After deciding to become bankers, the merchants acquired some means of storing or otherwise protecting valuables. Gallant D. Dickinson kept a "vault" under his bed, an excavated hole protected by his Colt revolver; and J. W. "Joe" McNeal of Medicine Lodge, Kansas, opened his Guthrie, Oklahoma, bank in a tent, kept his deposits in a money belt, and was "protected day and night by two guards armed with Winchesters." Needless to say, "McNeal never lost a penny."[127] These eccentric and unusual methods of keeping deposits safe should not be interpreted as meaning that bank buildings and safes were not important. Indeed, we contend that these physical manifestations constituted an indispensable component of the public perception of a bank. And, not surprisingly, all successful bankers quickly abandoned the rattlesnakes, woodpiles, and Winchester-armed bodyguards in favor of more practical, visible, and permanent facilities. Certainly some of the more "normal" facilities that characterized banks were no more safe than the twenty-four-hour-a-day guards, but unquestionably the public perceived them as such.

Interim quarters, however, required that the merchant store the money somewhere. First National Bank of Helena operated from a corner in a grocery store.[128] Oklahoma merchants separated their safe area with chicken wire.[129] Wyoming storekeeper/bankers simply put money in marked envelopes, while the I. E. Solomon General Store in Solomonville, Arizona, did not even indulge in that formality, as Isadore Solomon kept the accounts in his head.[130] Still other bankers, at one time or another, conducted business from home, using the safe for a table; from a hotel; or even from a corner of another bank.[131] A chain of Oklahoma banks operated in box-framed buildings as auxiliaries to a network of department stores. Sweetwater County State Bank, lacking a suitable building, leased a butcher shop, "which never lost the aroma of its former life."[132] Exchange National Bank of Perry, Oklahoma, set up shop in what was formerly Jack Leon's Kentucky Liquor Store, and it is doubtful that it ever smelled much better than Sweetwater Bank. Indeed, at first, confused customers slapped their money on the counter and expected a drink in return.[133] A South Dakota bank had "scales, a counter, and a 'safe' . . . made of pine boards, but a can of black paint made it look like cast iron," while another bank in Blunt, South Dakota, took over a local Masonic temple.[134]

None of these temporary facilities was located in, nor did these strange methods of keeping deposits (not to mention the books) take place in, a bank building. The building and its chief component, the vault and/or safe, constituted the second major symbol of safety that complemented the banker's business experience and reputation. Historians have glossed over the cultural and economic significance of the physical manifestations of banking, but the constant references in contemporary newspapers and even the correspondence of bankers to the buildings and safes suggests that they played a critical role, and one that extended beyond the actual protection of deposits.

Historians long ago should have been alerted to the significance of safes, vaults, and bank buildings by the sheer number of references to them in early accounts. A report describing Albuquerque National Bank in 1890, for example, mentions the "handsomely paved" floor, the fixtures, and the vault, noting there was "not a stronger vault in the United States."[135] When Colorado National Bank, formerly Kountze Brothers Bank (which had obtained a national charter in 1866), constructed a new building in 1882, the *Denver Republican* published an extensive account of the $100,000 three-story building. "The Colorado National Bank," noted the paper, "has spared no expense, aiming only to obtain perfect security."[136] The Bank of Arizona in Prescott, as seen by the *Prescott Miner* in 1878, had the "appearance of a bonanza house of the metropolis."[137] Clark, Gruber and Company had an imposing two-story building as early as 1860, replete with brick and fronted by four stone pillars. Inside, broad counters and etched glass greeted customers. The building for the First National Bank of Denver, in 1865, had a large directors' room, etched glass, and by the

1870s, gas lights. The bank constructed the building at a cost of $45,000 and eventually added a third floor.[138]

Or consider the extravagant Citizens Bank of Wichita in 1887. Its beautiful tiled floors, ornately designed ceiling, handsome carved wooden counters and tables, spacious lobby, and richly detailed walls testified to the bank's considerable wealth. And it had both gas and electric fixtures.[139] Helena's First National Bank similarly sported a luxurious interior, replete with ornate brass designs on the tellers' cages.[140]

Many of the early California banks show the desire for concrete symbols of safety. Not only did Ralston's Bank of California showcase the bank, it gave the architect, David Farquharson, a stellar reputation with other bankers, who hired him to design London and San Francisco Bank in 1873 and Nevada Bank in 1875. Indeed, Farquharson became so immersed in banking that he helped to capitalize, then serve as president of, the California Savings and Loan Society (a bank despite its name) in 1873.[141] William Tecumseh Sherman, in his brief career as a San Francisco banker, erected a building which still stands, but during the construction he complained mightily of his experienced cashier's spending on the vault.[142]

When the stern Thatcher brothers, Mahlon and Joseph, established First National Bank at Fourth Street and Santa Fe Avenue in Pueblo, Colorado, the *Pueblo Chieftain* commented on the black-walnut counter ornamented with massive carved brackets. It was, as the paper stated, "really an elegant affair." A detailed report of the bank's interior followed, and the report concluded: "In a word, the room contains all the modern improvements of a model banking house."[143] The tiny Bank of Arizona, perhaps a third the size of the Thatcher brothers' Pueblo institution, displayed similar fine wood and brass, ornate wallpaper and fixtures, and intricate tellers' cages.[144]

Why the fascination with ornate design, rich woods, marble, brass, and other ostentatious flourishes, even in small towns and in banks of relatively low capitalizations? Were these bankers reckless, tossing away investors' money on mere trappings? Except for perhaps saloons, certainly no other buildings in most western towns would have such furnishings, and few buildings were as well constructed as banks. Was this, too, mere extravagance?

Despite the absence of direct discussions on the subject by bankers, their actions, seen through the institutions they constructed, reveal a great deal. It is clear that the bank building itself constituted a symbol of safety, perhaps the most significant of all the symbols not only to the banker but to the public. The bank building fulfilled this purpose on at least two levels, one practical and the other visual. On the practical side, the bank building of course safely contained the wealth of depositors in its safe and vault. Although it is unlikely that any bank building offered much of a deterrent to robbery aside from the heavy vaults and safe it contained, it provided important physical security by its very location. The typical bank stood close to the center of town, far enough away from the saloon to discourage alcohol-induced midnight pilgrimages by the bar patrons, but close enough that the next morning those same bleary-eyed (and broke) revelers could obtain more cash. The bank's interior wall bordered another business, and the vault usually was set into that wall or placed in the basement to prevent break-ins from outside directly into the vault. Thus, any attempt at burglary or robbery involved getting inside the building, which was in the middle of town, then inside the vault, which was in the most protected part of the building. At that point, if the robbers planned an after-hour heist, they still had to deal with the safe and vault. Early ball-safe designs featured a large, extremely heavy ball, in which the money was kept, that was joined by a thin welded strip to a box-like base. Any attempt to blow open the ball simply caused it to break off and roll around the floor. It was far to heavy to carry and its absence of angles left no spot to which a thief could apply explosives, which, in those days, were too primitive to blow open the ball anyway. Plain blasting powder, which was used until dynamite was discovered in 1867, would destroy just about anything around the safe but it is unlikely that it could have penetrated the thick shielding. On the other hand, a daylight raid carried entirely different risks. An escape with stolen money risked every gun in town being brought to bear on a set of rather obvious desperadoes.

Much more eminent than the threat of robbery was fire. San Francisco, for example, burned five times between 1848 and 1851, and in Montana, First National Bank of Butte burned during the disastrous fire of 1889 (it is worth noting that the Butte bank's vault passed the test). A bank had to protect against this danger first and foremost. Banks thus not only routinely used fireproof safes and vaults but often fireproof buildings as well. In the case of James King, originally from William, California, one of San Francisco's first bankers, the protection against fire could be carried too far. Convinced his fireproof building offered complete safety, he stayed in the bank during the San Francisco fire of 1851. While the building indeed protected him from the flames, the heat and smoke nearly killed him before he finally escaped.[145] Most bankers, lacking King's eccentricities, felt no such compulsion to demonstrate the sturdiness of their vaults, although three San Francisco chroniclers reported that some bankers in that city indeed perished attempting to duplicate King's feat.[146]

On one level the bank building represented physical security, but it also secured deposits and capital through investment in the building and its fixtures, thus the ornamentation and rich interiors. In the period from

1879 to 1890, the average bank building cost from $8,500 to $250,000 and some of these structures stood in "metropolises" such as Pueblo, Colorado, and Laramie, Wyoming, scarcely population centers on a par with Cincinnati and St. Louis. For a bank such as Colorado National Bank, capitalized at $100,000, a $45,000 investment in its building represented a major portfolio choice—almost fifty percent of its capital—but one that the investors could see and assess on a daily basis.[147] In a less populated city such as Pueblo, the Thatcher brothers' bank, capitalized at $50,000, purchased its structure at Fourth and Santa Ana for $8,750, or just over 17 percent of its capital.[148] Ralston's Bank of California building, constructed at a cost of $250,000, represented 12.5 percent of the initial capital.[149] Ladd and Tilton, bankers in Portland, showed the total of their real estate entry at the closing of the first day's books (namely, their bank building) to be $23,753.08, against capital of $50,000 (48 percent).[150] William Sherman commenced construction of Lucas Turner & Co. Bank based on an estimated cost of $53,000 out of initial capital of $200,000 (27 percent).[151] Sherman's bank building, owned by one of his St. Louis partners, rented the facilities that the bank did not need, adding to its revenue. Not only did expenditure on a building establish a permanent, visible record of the bank's assets, but it also infused a considerable amount of its capital into the town. Thatcher Brothers' investment amounted to just under 2 percent of the real-estate value *in all of Pueblo* in the year it was built.[152] Russell County, Kansas, with a population of scarcely four hundred, sported a two-story bank, L. Banker Mercantile Company, which one pioneer called "the biggest building west of Salina [Kansas]."[153] In Helena, Montana, a town of three thousand in 1870, Bohm and Aub announced plans to put up a $9,000 banking house. The bank's announced capital was only $25,000, although Bohm had important connections to J. W. Seligman of New York at that time.[154] Bank buildings consistently were big as early as the 1850s, with the Miner's Exchange Bank towering four stories above the San Francisco skyline in the mid-1850s. Christopher Nelson, a student of western bank architecture, dates the "golden age of monumental banks" in the West from David Farquharson's 1886 design for the Bank of California, with its arched facade, and finely cut bluestone Doric and Ionic columns.[155] It is clear that expensive, and big, bank buildings typified western banking houses even earlier.

How much did bankers deliberately construct elaborate buildings to display their wealth and stability? Direct comments on the subject from nineteenth-century bankers are scarce, possibly because they knew that their ability to attract and hold deposits rested in such mercurial intangibles as the appearance of the bank and, on occasion, even the girth of the banker. They had to be careful not to give away this secret. But some commentators broke the silence. An anonymous critic in 1855 observed

that "the architecture of the banking house . . . should be marked exter-
nally, internally, and throughout, by stability as its leading feature."[156]
Another observer noted that "it has seemed necessary to make something
of a show, to express in the building the fact that banks . . . are suffering,
as it were, from the possession of too much cash. . . ."[157] Thus even in
Vermillion, South Dakota, a bank owned the "largest and most costly
building in town."[158] Buildings and fixtures also provided tangible investments, about which twentieth-century bankers have exhibited more can-
dor. One Scottsdale, Arizona, banker, scolded in the local press for building a "Taj Mahal" headquarters in April 1980, lectured the critics by
pointing out that the classical art, tapestries, fixtures, and ornate facilities
represented an investment whose increased value beat the rate of inflation
every year.[159] Floors of marble, chandeliers, Persian carpets, fine wood
furniture, and exquisite paintings were goods that, unlike bonds, could
find a market in almost any rapidly growing city. Bank buildings and their
contents acted as a safe but visible investment: the best advertising that
the institution was "safe and sound" was the view of stately columns in front
of an imposing-looking building, which, on closer inspection, sheltered a
seemingly impregnable vault housing the ultimate of banking symbols, the
safe. Not surprisingly, the bank building itself developed as an important
advertising tool. Long before San Francisco's Transamerica "pyramid"
acquired quick recognition from the public, bankers used pictures of their
banks on letterheads and in advertising, as well as on exchange drafts.[160]

The bankers' belief in the importance of an expensive building was
enhanced in many cases by regulations prohibiting or restraining the
ownership of other real estate. For example, national banks were not,
under most circumstances, permitted to lend on real estate or to own real
estate other than the bank premises. Ownership of the bank building then
remained their only method of participating in a real-estate boom. Since
in the frontier era few states prohibited the ownership of real estate, the
tendency of banks to construct buildings with a great deal of surplus office
space that was rented to other firms occurred when the laws changed after
1900.

According to a 1905 article reviewing the floor plans for existing banks,
two basic alternatives predominated, with most architects accepting only
minor modifications to these plans.[161] One plan grouped the tellers in the
middle of the banking room. This was the design followed in 1867 by
Ralston's architects for the Bank of California.[162] The other plan had the
tellers along the outside walls, such as in the Bank of Arizona, Prescott
(circa 1878), and the San Francisco Wells Fargo banking department in
the Parrott Building (circa 1858).[163] Either design, however, maximized
visibility of the vault area, which had to be available to public inspection.
According to architectural historian Win de Wit, "The vault was another

item whose location in the bank was prescribed virtually from the outset. Situated at the end of the room on a direct axis with the bank's entrance, the vault and its gigantic open door would inspire confidence in the strength and security of the bank to incoming clients."[164]

Few buildings consistently captured these qualities as well as those designed by Louis Sullivan, America's premier architect of the nineteenth century. Sullivan, blackballed by the architectural community in the late 1800's, was forced to turn to bank design and construction, mostly in the Midwest (although some of his projects were in border areas, such as Iowa, that we have excluded from our study). Although coming at the end of the frontier period for the communities in which he built, Sullivan's work, especially when examined in the light of the floor plans, clearly illustrates how the characteristics of safety, and yet open views of the vault, were crucial in every western bank. For example, the bank in Grinnell, Iowa, the largest building in town in its time, displayed extensive ornamentation on the outside. In the interior, the vault area remained in view behind the tellers' cages. Sullivan's bank building in Cedar Rapids, People's Savings Bank, although much smaller, still retained the typical view of the vault.[165]

The best testimony to the bankers' emphasis on vaults, or at least, to their understanding of the public's perceptions about what was important in a bank, comes from their advertising. Banks in the nineteenth century rarely advertised (compared to modern banks with their barrages of ads), but when they did, the ads emphasized the size, strength, and safety of the vault and/or safe, or, occasionally, the banks's capitalization. This is typified by the *Ruby City Owyhee Avalanche* ad in 1866 for King, Webb and Company's "magnificent Fire & Burglar-Proof Vault."[166] William Young, owner of First National Bank of Colorado Springs, boasted that his bank's "safe was larger than those of his infant rivals, the Peoples [Bank] and the El Paso County [Bank]."[167] The same bank, when vice president James Hagerman took over as president, was torn down in order that a new building could be constructed in 1890. Despite the steam heating, the hardwood paneling, and the Italian marble floors, the focal point of the attention was the $15,000 bank vault created by Hall Safe and Lock Company of Cincinnati. (Hall was one of the major safe suppliers; Diebold Safe and Lock was the other.) The Hall vault measured thirteen by eighteen feet, with a two-and-one-half-ton outer door and a fifteen-hundred-pound inner door, and had three-foot-thick walls. According to the safe's manufacturer, it afforded protection "against fire, burglary, dynamite or mobs."[168] The Thatcher brothers, the first bankers in Pueblo, Colorado, advertised in the *Colorado Chieftain* ownership of a safe weighing two tons: "a marvel of beautiful and substantial workmanship and looks defiance [sic] at burglars and fire."[169]

One South Dakota banker thought the safe so vital an investment that he bought it on time from the Diebold Safe and Lock Company, and did not pay off the debt until he liquidated his bank.[170] When boasting about the sturdiness of their vaults and safes to local papers, bankers spared no detail. Cook, Sargent, and Parker, in Nebraska, described their vault as follows: "Sheet steel a quarter of an inch thick, in giant slabs, was ordered from the Pennsylvania Mills. . . . There are more than 2,000 riveted bolts. . . . And at the very thinnest place in the armor this mighty steel jacket is 19 inches thick . . . besides the . . . sheet metal protection, there was from two to four feet of masonry about it, above and at strategic points."[171]

Countless bankers found that, above all, they needed a safe to enter the banking business. The French brothers of The Dalles, Oregon, parlayed their ownership of a very large safe used initially for their own cash to provide a safekeeping depository for their customers' cash, which in turn allowed them to start a bank.[172] First National Bank of Portland reimbursed its president, L. M. Starr, for several items, including a safe, when the bank opened for business. Within a month, the bank recorded ownership of two safes. A new safe, which cost $2,636, was purchased when a new building was erected.[173]

Silas Aulls thought a safe constituted virtually all he needed to enter banking in Kansas. He noted the sale of a "banking outfit" in 1888 for $125—"a bargain"—with a "fire-and burglar-proof chest in the safe with a time lock . . . and a wire railing."[174] Unfortunately, Aulls already had one.[175] Most bankers spared no expense for their safes (with the exception of William Sherman, who criticized a subordinate for what he viewed as an "unnecessarily strong" vault, by which Sherman meant "unnecessarily expensive").[176] Often they competed for the prestige of owning the safest safe. A letter to Cook and Sargent from St. Louis bankers E. W. Clarke and Brothers promised to build Cook and Sargent's vault "like the one in our Bank in Springfield . . . for $550 which is an increase on the former price" due to the cost of iron. Nevertheless, Cook and Sargent were expected to "prefer the $550 [vault]." Clark and Brothers noted "it is one got up for the New York World's Fair where it was on exhibition and is . . . nicer than usual. . . ."[177] Even when the bank fell prey to fire or flood, the safe remained. In the ghost town of Bodie, California, a solidly constructed vault stands amidst the faint traces of a bank building long gone. The safe remains behind the iron grilled door, still an eloquent symbol.[178]

If the safe performed a symbolic as well as a practical function, it had to stand in public view, at least to some degree. Hence designs placed the vault and safe in visible positions inside the bank. However, other symbols served much more utilitarian purposes. The teller's window, which some-times developed into a telephone-booth-like cage, but generally remained a regular counter with bars to separate the teller from the customer, offered some protection to the teller, and, more importantly, kept money physically separated from normally honest customers who might find themselves tempted. However, there was a psychological element to the teller's window in that it promoted a distinction between customer and banker, thus further professionalizing the business. It lent an air of "expertise" and mystique to the fairly dull business of counting and separating money. Even so, many western banks tried through their design to create an atmosphere of openness and democracy, especially in more settled communities where bankers' reputations were well established and elitism had become a concern. In many of Louis Sullivan's banks, the desks of the officers stood in plain view, and a customer did not have to traverse stairs or cross physical boundaries to gain access to the president. The phenomenon developed somewhat later in the West than in the Midwest, as evidenced by the surprised reaction of the San Francisco community when A. P. Giannini established this pattern in his Bank of Italy branches during the years 1909 to 1915.[179]

The vaults, safes, and buildings in western banking thus constituted the second major symbol of safety that buttressed the merchant's reputation and business experience. Together, they allowed the banker to send a message to the community that his bank was safe. In turn, the bank offered a promotional tool to attract wealth into the community. Bank buildings in this respect constituted the most basic form of boosterism. Just as the banker himself had announced his permanence in the community by constructing a magnificent banking house at no small cost to himself, so the community announced to the world that it was indeed "here to stay" by virtue of the fact that it now had a real bank.

Given, then, the tremendous concern for an image of stability, solvency, safety, and respectability, no thought troubled the banker more than the threat of robbery. Even if a successful thief took little money, the damage done to the edifice built by the banker's symbols of safety was almost irreparable. As a result, a great mythology has grown up around western bank robberies—the stylized romantic scenes of a few desperate men riding into town, grabbing the cash, and hightailing it out with a posse hot on their heels—but it is typically a false picture. In fact, one story of a horseback robbery reveals quite a different scenario. Brigands assaulted First National Bank of Newport (now Newport Beach), California, in 1912. Three doses of explosives were needed to penetrate the vault, awakening many of the townspeople. A gun battle ensued between two local bartenders (who kept late hours anyway) and the thieves. Confusion and poor vision in the early morning light left none of the principals damaged, but an innocent bystander—a fisherman—was hit before the bandits commandeered a buggy drawn by a single horse. Although they escaped, the robbers left behind the money in the horse's nosebag.[180]

Other examples of bank robberies are extremely rare. In Arizona, for example, excluding a single 1896 robbery in Nogales (a town on the Mexican border), there is no record of a bank robbery until 1923, and none were recorded in Nevada before the Bank of Winnemucca robbery in 1900.[181] Likewise, in New Mexico, few, if any, confirmed bank robberies occurred until well into the twentieth century, nor, apparently, did any bank robberies occur in Montana. Other state histories reveal similar situations.

The source of the mythology is unclear, perhaps stemming from the Jesse James raids in Minnesota and Missouri, or drawing from episodes in Texas. Certainly the Dalton Gang attempted to "take down" the two banks in their home town of Coffeeville, Kansas, but the townspeople shot all but one of the gang in a wild gun battle before the Daltons ever got close to the bank, further underscoring the "safety of location" thesis.[182] A spectacular robbery did occur in 1889 at First National Bank of Denver, but rather than unfolding like the plot of a Hollywood Western, it more closely resembled a modern bank holdup. The robbery featured the infamous Butch Cassidy and others in a complex plot in which a man entered the office of bank president David Moffat, pulled out a pistol and a bottle that he claimed was nitroglycerine, and in hostage fashion obtained $11,000 in paper money and coin and $10,000 in a marked gold note. Although the felons escaped, they found they could not cash the marked note. The "nitroglycerine" turned out to be salad oil.[183] So even if a few examples can be produced, bank robberies hardly constituted the norm among western criminal elements.

To say that robberies were rare, however, does not mean that bankers themselves did not have a genuine concern about them. Cashier Moses B. Hazeltine of the Bank of Arizona told the A. C. Cook Mining Company that "the country is wild and it is considered unsafe to carry large amounts of coin in our vaults."[184] Of course, Hazeltine may have been an alarmist. His older brother, the previous cashier at the bank, had chosen to keep sacks of gold in the wastebasket, covered with paper, instead of the vault, despite the fact that the bank had never experienced a robbery attempt. Trains and stagecoaches presented far more tempting targets and entailed less risk for the return. Nor would banks tolerate robberies. No bank could survive more than a couple of robberies and expect to remain in business, even if little money was lost. Its image as an unsafe bank would convince consumers to take their money elsewhere or keep it at home. Without doubt these circumstances drastically changed when bandits acquired motorized vehicles. Until that time, however, most western bankers' emphasis on their symbols of safety worked well and deterred robberies, and most losses due to theft came from the inside. For example, the *Helena Weekly Herald* reported in 1869 that "Cashier J. W. Stateler . . . on Sunday night at a late hour took a tearful but not unwilling congé of his mountain metropolis while its inhabitants were profoundly sleeping the happy hours away. . . . The manner in which [M]any of our most worthy citizens were swindled out of their accumulated savings was particularly aggrevating. . . ."[185]

Of course, J. W. Seligman also suffered from the scandal involving Bohm and Aub. S. H. Bohm had convinced Seligman to back his bank, only to divert funds for his own purposes.[186]

Did that mean that, lacking the danger and possible glory associated with shoot-outs and desperate escapes, bankers' lives followed a fairly dull and routine path? In a word, yes, although they found excitement in other pursuits. Normally, though, daily activities consisted of counting coin, weighing dust, stacking bills, checking addition, and writing an endless series of letters acknowledging receipt of this draft or a payment late on that account.[187] Even such routine matters as these, of course, could occasionally generate interesting events, such as when Barrows, Millard and Company, Omaha bankers, noted that they had to pay gold coin for dust and "to offer a return miner anything like [currency] or Draft sets him to swearing, or he goes out the door kiting."[188] The differences between drafts and coin is apparent in the record of a heated exchange between Eugene Kelly and J. A. Donohue in 1864. Kelly held two drafts totalling $50,000 on C. K. Garrison that William Ralston guaranteed. Garrison refused to supply coin to meet the obligation. His son, who had signed the note, claimed he signed only out of friendship to Ralston, who owed the funds to yet another party and had used the draft as a means to delay actual payment. Finally, Ralston claimed he could not be held responsible for the funds since his firm, Donohue and Ralston, had entered into liquidation. Kelly ultimately received his money but lamented: "It [was] an ugly transaction and ought not to see the light of day."[189] Typically, neither the owners nor the president ran the routine business of their bank, although at Kountze Brothers, Valley Bank of Phoenix, Second National Bank of Santa Fe, and the Bank of California, to name but four examples, the owners oversaw all aspects of the institution's activities.[190]

Where the owner or branch manager did have relatively complete control, a different type of excitement awaited. For some, the prospect of opening new areas to business and the opportunities offered by virgin lands lured them away from their musty buildings for more wide-open banking. Silas Aulls, the Bucklin, Kansas, banker, captured in his correspondence the excitement he felt when opening his small bank. He began by "trying to make arrangements to get in some office here. Can go into the banking business with Thompson [and] buy very small notes & handle real estate. . . ." Aulls found an important difference between banking in the West and his banking practice in Avoca, New York: "here it requires no book-keeping and for that reason there is no work in connection with the business." Although it is doubtful that Aulls found banking quite so easy after several months on the job, he certainly never lost his optimism about banking's future in Bucklin. In May 1888 he observed that the "banking business is the safest and best business in the state and will be for some time," and instructed his brother-in-law: "this is no Avoca banking business. . . . [A] man is a fool to loan money in the east when he can come here and get any such rates and security." Aulls concluded an 1888 letter with a prediction that he no doubt regretted a year later, stating that "one person can run a bank here."[191]

Many others thought opportunities existed for great wealth in similar small-town one-person banks. J. Rogers, the assistant cashier of Cloud County Bank in Kansas saw a chance to open a chain-related office in Great Bend, where "the native banker . . . is not very well liked. I am sure that just dealing [there] will bring us a good share of the business." Yet, after doing business in Great Bend for only two months, Rogers's tune changed, and he pleaded for help from H. C. Harrison at the parent bank. "We ought to have more money," he wrote. "I am constantly on the anxious seat for fear [that] some delay in the mail will make our remittances too late to cover our drafts."[192] These boom/bust extension houses characterized all areas of the West. Joseph Leet of the Denver Investment and Banking Corporation, looking to "expand my loan business in Wyoming," promised that within a year "the Colorado boom will get up there. And the Colorado boom is a doozy."[193] At the same time Leet tried to attract investors into Wyoming, which he called an "unsettled repetition of Colorado with the precious minerals left out." Leet boasted "the Denver boom grows apace," and he begged for money from a relative, claiming to have lost $100,000 because investors refused to back his land speculations.[194]

Such freewheeling agents plied their trade in the employ of existing banks or on their own until well after the turn of the century, keeping alive a tradition of loose procedure, individual decisions, and quick riches or losses. By the 1890s, however, most western states had passed through their frontier period and more formal structures within banks were necessary. Even Leet, lamenting the failure of another Wyoming agent-banking operation, observed that the owners were "liberal to the needy. It was noble but it was not banking."[195] On the other hand, Lyle W. Dorsett, examining the reports of R. G. Dun and Company in early Denver, found access to credit remarkably open, even to women, minorities, and a special group of risky borrowers, saloon keepers.[196] It appears from general records that bankers extended credit freely—once. If a borrower earned a reputation for defaulting, he usually did not get another loan or have his notes extended, at least with the same bank. Bankers, especially those who acted as one-man banks, had considerable freedom in this respect. One Butte banker extended a $9,000 loan to a rancher without collateral, while Robert S. Ford gained the reputation as the father of the northern Montana cattle industry because he granted loans on easy terms to "those he felt were trustworthy."[197] A Dillon, Montana, banker "handed out money to the penniless but promising members of the community."[198]

THE FRONTIER BANKER'S DAY

Without the glory of quick wealth or the pulse-pounding din of gunfire that accompanied a robbery, bankers adjusted to a routine and usually dull set of operations that characterized banking on a daily basis. Extremely small banks utilized one person to handle all the business. Issac Moore, who worked for Nowlan and Weary, a firm that operated out of Helena, Virginia City, and possibly Bannack, Montana, (with one account recording a bank in operation as early as 1863), served as cashier, teller, and janitor. He wrote his brother explaining, "I am still running [the bank] alone, being President, Cashier and Clerk all in one. . . . We sometimes carry more gold dust in the safe than 2 or 3 men can carry. . . . We sell one man currency, or greenbacks as you call them, [then sell] the next a foreign draft on London, Dublin or Germany and perhaps the very same day buy back drafts, gold dust and currency."[199] The amount of business forced most banks to hire a cashier who oversaw all aspects of the bank's daily activities and procedures. George Clark managed First National Bank of Denver, and Will Hazeltine at the Bank of Arizona and Rufus J. Palen at First National Bank of Santa Fe performed similar functions. J. A. Graves, an attorney, ran Farmers and Merchants Bank in Los Angeles while the founder and president, Isaias W. Hellman, resided in San Francisco.[200]

Depending on the size of the bank, anywhere from one to several tellers might stand behind the cages at a given time. Nearby they kept the tools of their trade, including a scratch pad for making quick computations, a signature book for comparing the handwriting of endorsers to drafts that bore their names, small scales for weighing gold dust, and daily ledger books, which the cashier totaled and balanced each night. Most of the daily activities still involved receiving deposits, cashing drafts, extending and collecting loans, then spending long hours posting these transactions in a flowing Spencerian script into the bank's leatherbound account books. The employees performed virtually all this work by hand or in their heads, although at Ladd and Tilton Bank in Oregon, the president saw a small adding machine left by a salesman and told a young messenger to play with it all he liked, "then send it back."[201]

In addition to those duties, the cashier maintained the balances of correspondent accounts with banks in other cities, and used numerous onionskin letterbooks for official correspondence with customers, correspondent banks, and absentee managers. He retained a copy of the correspondence for the bank (although these were often barely legible and easily destroyed by water). Typewriters worked their way west in the 1890s, but banks did not witness their common use until after the turn of the century.[202] This made the correspondence duties of the cashier often overwhelming. Most correspondence dealt with deposits or payments from customer accounts. The following abbreviated samples, the first to a customer and the second to an absentee owner, are typical of cashiers' letters.

Santa Fe, N.M. May 28, 1872

Felipe Chavez
Belen, New Mexico
    We can receive your gold and silver and issue a certificate of deposit payable in cash but we do not think it would be received for duties of the custom house, as it is customary to receive only certificates of the United States Treasury.

S. B. Wheelock, A. Cashier
First National Bank of Santa Fe

San Francisco, September 4, 1856

Lucas Turner Bank
St. Louis, Missouri
    One of our notes for $7000 laid over today [became past due]. We take it the house—Lowe, Ebbets & Company—has failed. We held 200 barrels of butter as collateral which I think will cover principal and interest. . . .

William Sherman[203]

Occasionally, the cashier injected a personal note to familiar customers or to business associates, who frequently asked for investment advice, but none of the correspondence suggests that banking carried much excitement. Lionel Jacobs, in a letter to his nephew, reported: "I am well busy with routine matters." Later, he wrote: "I am very busy doing drudgery work as usual." Still again, "Am busy daily from 10 AM to 3 PM doing Yeoman duty as Paying and Receiving Teller for which my reward is—the consciousness of duty done and expectations which the future may fulfill."[204] Jacobs exaggerated—he was, after all, an owner of the Pima County Bank—but he aptly captured the dreary sameness of bank work. Lost money, unreliable mail, writing customers, and dealing with gold dust constituted his daily routine.

    Gold dust, in fact, presented additional opportunities for profit to a perceptive banker. Many of them in mining towns sported long beards to capture flecks of gold that flew about during weighing. At the end of the day, a good combing might yield a few dollars.[205] Likewise, it behooved bankers to fastidiously sweep their floors and thus collect the gold along with the regular dust. But beards could be a liability, too. One Prescott customer, turned down for a loan, reached across the counter, grabbed the teller by his beard, and shook his head vigorously.[206]

Other perils also afflicted daily operations. Mails, notoriously unreliable, and overland shipping of gold and silver, kept much of the bankers' instruments of liquidity in a constant state of flux. In the fall of 1872, a lack of silver plagued First National Bank of Santa Fe, and by December the cashier urged shippers to "hurry up silver fast as possible."[207] Problems such as these often applied to only a single bank. Across town the Speigelbergs' Second National Bank still had large reserves, and in November Willi Speigelberg requested that gold balances be transferred to the currency account because "our gold business [is] not likely to be very large."[208] Technology offered some improvement in placing orders and transfers of exchange, with its own share of special problems. Telegraph codes, necessitated by the openness of the medium, allowed bankers to send orders for coin or exchange in such a way that the telegraphers themselves would not understand their contents. However, telegraph codes required that banks keep handy cipher books, in which different codes, each corresponding to a different day of the week, signified transactions. If the two corresponding bankers were not literally on the same page, telegraph costs would skyrocket and deposits or withdrawals might occur at the wrong time. S. G. Murphy, the cashier of the Pacific Bank in San Francisco, "continually annoyed" and "put to . . . expense" other bankers by not having or using his codes. Such a code might read "Instinct Knoll to Afgan Calico," and could mean "Deposit to the account of Pacific Bank." But even the messages could get mixed up in transmitting or receiving, as when a mystified customer received a message containing the phrase "wet adpole," which was supposed to be "We telegraph exchange on. . . ."[209] These codes were in use from Chicago to San Francisco, but how many bankers adopted them is not clear.

Whether or not telegraph cipher codes constituted an essential part of every western banker's procedures, several practices typified virtually all bank operations. Among other common events, at least once a month, and occasionally more frequently, the cashier met with the directors to discuss the current status and direction of the bank. Usually the subject of the bank's discount line led to the most heated discussions. On the surface, it appears that many factors about a bank's lending policies should have been cut and dried. After all, the loan and discount lines had limits, the bank had criteria for borrowers, and the directors supposedly had no partiality in lending except for profit. Such a scenario might make sense in a world of pure laissez-faire capitalism or theoretical Marxism; in the banker's world it was fantasy.

The directors frequently received their appointments on the basis of the amount of business they brought to a bank. This meant lending as well as deposit business. Not surprisingly, the documents of the board of directors of First National Bank of Santa Fe reveal bitter struggles between the independent cashier Major Rufus J. Palen and the principal borrower (and director) Thomas Catron, later a U.S. senator from New Mexico. Palen had joined the bank as an assistant cashier in 1878 from the employ of Mutual Life Insurance Company on the recommendation of Stephen Elkins, Catron's law partner (later U.S. senator from West Virginia and a sponsor of the 1903 Elkins Act that regulated railroad rates).[210] Although he retained his insurance agency for several years after joining the bank, Palen acquired enough stock from his mother to also become a director. On June 11, 1883, he replaced William Griffen as cashier, and took office with the goal of ending loans to the directors. Catron, the central culprit, had outstanding loans (or was security on loans) of $30,000 and had attempted to shift his debts by borrowing $25,000 from others. By October 1883, Palen warned Elkins that Catron had debts of $150,000. The cashier had "no confidence" in Catron "morally, financially, or otherwise," and he pointed out to one of Catron's potential lenders who asked for a reference Catron's "large amount of indebtedness."[211] In 1894, with the bank staggering under large debts to Catron and other directors, Palen forced a reorganization, and made some changes. Still, Catron remained a large debtor and vice president.[212]

Such internal problem loans plagued every bank. The failure of the Bank of California in great part occurred because William Ralston himself owed the bank as much as $9.5 million.[213] Minutes of the board of City Bank of Leadville, Colorado, mention that C. C. Howell "had on diverse occasions used his official position as President . . . for the purpose of obtaining [funds for] his own private purposes" and "signed drafts for private use."[214] The bank directors removed him from his position and attempted to rescue the bank. Its investigations uncovered a host of irregularities, including the revelation that Howell's personal secretary and assistant cashier "was in the habit of drawing drafts [of] which the cashier was not aware," violating a fundamental banking procedure.[215] Efforts to attach Howell's property in April 1883 failed to restore the bank's asset base, and it closed on January 16, 1884.[216] Denver National Bank experienced rapid turnover of its officers and cashiers between 1882 and 1892, much of it associated with control of stock.[217] Thus, while cashiers had ample opportunity to advance, they also bore much of the responsibility for failures. Palen, Will Hazeltine, Charles Kountze, George

Clark, and A. G. Swain of Wyoming National exemplified cashiers who tasted the rewards of western banking. On the other end of the spectrum was Clarence S. Dunbar, an ill-fated Laramie merchant who had come from Boston and had opened a private bank with Henry Wagner. In 1878, while duck hunting on Hutton Lake, Dunbar stood up in his boat to take an ill-advised shot. The recoil sent him into the icy water, and it took five days for search parties to locate his frozen body.[218]

The expanding influence of the cashiers in many banks symbolized an even greater fundamental change that was slowly taking place in western banking by the late 1870s. Financial structures had evolved along with the frontier in which they operated, a frontier that was disappearing. Territorial governments had given way to state constitutions. State banking departments appeared and often demanded an accounting from bankers.[219] Railroads had crisscrossed many of the regions, adding to the populations. In large cities such as Denver, San Francisco, Omaha, Tucson, Salt Lake City, and others, wide open frontier habits had been tempered by more conservative practices. Several banks had already changed from loose, frontier banking (recalling Silar Aulls's comment about not keeping books), to more structured, formal procedures, epitomized by the cashiers. In nineteenth-century banks, the cashier came closest of all bankers to the role of manager as described by Alfred Chandler.[220] Banks still had a long way to go before they would resemble the corporations taking shape in the East, with their managerial hierarchies. But they clearly had entered a transitional period, one marked by the rise of state banking regulations, and for the first time in their careers, bankers found themselves reacting to events rather than initiating them.

In an age of agrarian unrest, silverite agitation, and bankers' conspiracies, the symbols of safety no longer carried the assurance that they once had. On the other hand, bankers, to protect their own investment in those expensive symbols, began to exert their political strengths to address several problems, including the elasticity of the money supply and unsound banking practices by new entrants. Lawmakers, always anxious to appear active in solving problems, quickly turned their attention to banking, whose relatively unregulated beginnings had laid a solid foundation of growth in the western frontier.

3

CONTROLLING THE "INJUDICIOUS BANKER": FROM FRONTIER TO REGULATION, 1893–1913

Bankers had done a fairly good job of regulating themselves and had by 1873 instituted some examination and regulation procedures, but they were sorely tested by the bank panics of 1873, 1893 and 1907. These panics put some banks into difficulty and gave the more conservative bankers a chance to insist on limiting the activities of their more adventure-some colleagues.

One way the bankers sought to increase the safety of the industry was through bank clearinghouses. When this proved inadequate the states began requiring examination, minimum capitalization, and deposit insur-ance. National laws were also being strengthened at this time. With rules and regulations replacing personal reputation, banking became a profession.

Regulation to constrain competition and the professionalization of bank-ing reinforced the public's fear of a "money power" conspiracy, and banks had indeed professionalized and started to regulate themselves partly in response to the more risky activities of some of their colleagues. Perhaps no fear gripped the common man more in the late nineteenth century than that a large, monopolistic business conspiracy of some sort controlled his or her life. The "money power" conspiracy usually topped the list, and there could be little question that New York banks dominated much of the nation's finances. Some thought that the banks and railroads wielded more power than they did, and even a recent historian of the age, Gabriel Kolko, in his revisionist study of railroad regulation, advanced the thesis that railroad owners, seeing the handwriting on the wall, took the initiative to regulate themselves.[1] They accomplished that by forming pools and cartels to reduce competition, and, when it became apparent that the government would involve itself on behalf of shippers and consumers, railroads "captured" regulatory agencies at the state and national level, packing those bodies with their own pro-railroad policymakers. Thus while they accepted some regulation, it was of their own choosing and slant.

Bankers in the West had already beaten the railroaders to the punch. Not that they "captured" anybody, for bankers seldom agreed on specific policies except for the unit bankers' cohesion in opposition to branching. Nor did the state houses listen seriously to bankers' proposals. Occasionally lawmakers changed a tax here, opened a regulation there, but they did so grudgingly, and often only under the most dire financial conditions. Rather, bankers in the 1870s and 1880s had already embarked on a wide-spread program of self-regulation. They needed no government agency to threaten them or establish guidelines. Instead, in an informal coalescence of practices and procedures, western bankers made some sense out of a regulatory mishmash of federal laws that overlaid a system of the different regulations—concerning unit banking, chain banking, group banking, interstate banking, real estate, and mortgage lending services, and insurance sales—in fifteen states.

EARLY REGULATIONS AND EXAMINATIONS

At the sixteenth annual Kansas Bankers Association meeting in 1903, Morton Albaugh, the state bank commissioner, delivered an address, apparently well received, entitled "The Injudicious Banker and How to Control Him." Albaugh's speech, without so intending, outlined the changes in regulation that bankers had undergone in the previous forty years. His villains—those "injudicious bankers"—displayed precisely the characteristics that had fueled the booms in most western cities. Exactly what were the characteristics of an "injudicious banker?" For one, the banker who failed to "avail himself of the assistance, judgement, the experience, and the advice of his directors . . . is imprudent." While a judicious banker "will exert himself to know thoroughly everyone of his patrons," the injudicious banker would lend recklessly, without checking the background of his borrowers.[2] Overlending to officers and directors and a tendency to speculate also marked poor banking practices. (Of course, most directors originally founded such banks to provide their farms, ranches, mines, or railroads with loans. As banks took in increasing amounts of deposits, they found themselves less dependent on the capital of the directors, and thus, less obliged to grant their loans.)[3] Albaugh found "no banker so utterly or so inexcusably imprudent as the one who fails on every occasion to follow the provisions of the law."[4]

Conditions had indeed changed; Albaugh would scarcely have recognized Kansas banking as it operated in the 1870s. Across the Kansas borders in Nebraska and Colorado, and as far away as California, bankers

violated nineteenth-century laws governing their profession with regularity. Not only did some twenty-four private bankers, plus Wells Fargo
agencies, operate in California, according to an 1855 list of private bankers,
but entrepreneurs there created the huge Miners Bank, capitalized at
$200,000 in open defiance of the state's constitutional provisions against
corporate banking.[5] State officials universally winked at such infractions.
Even when bankers complied with the law, they took full advantage of
every cranny in the code: the cashier of the Cloud County Bank in Kansas,
writing to the owner, H. C. Harrison, noted that if the two of them
planned to organize a new bank "it would be better [to do it] at once, or
at least before the first of March . . . to avoid as much tax as possible
without making any false statements."[6] Certainly no one thought it dangerous that a banker did not keep his books up to date. (To Albaugh that was
inexcusable: "The prudent banker will be prompt in all things. The report
. . . required by law . . . will always be on time. His books will be posted
and in order for inspection any day.")[7] Not surprisingly, this 1903 lecture
on good banking came from a regulator, not a banker or merchant, and
emphasized formal reports, compliance with the law, strict adherence to
legal lending limits, and so on. Banking had changed, from the emphasis on
symbols of safety and the banker's reputation to an emphasis on regulation.
Bankers were admonished under no circumstances to break the law. To a
certain degree, good accounting—or at least, good-looking accounting—
had replaced good character.

The journey from Silas Aulls's statement that banking in Kansas required
no bookkeeping to Albaugh's view, which, judging from his featured
position at the convention, probably reflected the views of his audience,
took a somewhat circuitous route. Changes did not occur overnight.

In the 1850s, New York banker A. B. Johnson penned a tract called *A
Treatise on Banking*, wherein he offered advice to bankers on behavior
appropriate for lending reserve levels, interest, and so on. Johnson warned
that "men who are prone to extravagance in their domestic or personal
expenditures, rarely possess the amount of property they are reputed to
possess . . . [whereas] the rich are usually more inclined toward
parsimony. . . ." The morality of the debtor was paramount in establishing
security: "debts are rarely collectable from the property of the
endorser. . . ." He instructed that "when no safe business offers, no business should be transacted by a banker who entertains a proper respect
for himself. . . ." Johnson offered basic guides on the selection of loans,
showing the sale of exchange must be defined "to business which brings
with it circulation or deposits." Finally, Johnson dedicated a small but
concluding section to the character of the banker.[8]

Thirty years later, those same views still prevailed. In Central City,
Colorado, Joseph A. Thatcher, the president of the First National Bank,

anticipating his forthcoming trip to Europe, prepared detailed instructions for his cashier to operate the bank in his absence. Thatcher had been a merchant at twenty-five, a clerk and bookkeeper with the Central City branch of the Denver private bank Warren Hussey and Company.[9] Promoted to manager of the Warren Hussey Central City bank in 1863, Thatcher joined with Joseph Standley to purchase the bank seven years later, establishing Thatcher, Standley and Company. They converted to a national charter in 1874, renaming their bank First National Bank of Central City, capitalized at $50,000. Six years later, with the bank thriving against strong competition by Henry M. Teller's Rocky Mountain National Bank, Thatcher felt confident leaving it in the hands of his cashier.

Among Thatcher's orders, the bank "shall not loan any one individual or firm more than 10 per cent of our capital—that is, $5000."[10] Even so, he continued, for the most valued customers, whom the bank occasionally had to accommodate to greater amounts, "we must break or evade the law, and take our chances."[11] This statement was a far cry from the norm espoused by Albaugh. But Thatcher hardly represented an irresponsible banker, instructing the cashier: "Do not make loans to any one outside of your own customers," and "Do not carry overdue paper." He made certain that the bank kept enough currency on hand during busy periods of the month. More important, Thatcher's orders show a concern with "doctoring" the reports to the comptroller of the currency, who would call for five statements per year. The inside schedule—the crux of the report—needed to show "a large proportion of 'two-name' paper," as "small a proportion as possible" on real estate or mortgages, few loans to directors, and so on.[12] It is noteworthy that Thatcher did not instruct the cashier to avoid the *practices*, which he, himself, clearly endorsed and followed, but their appearance on the official reports.

Equally important, Thatcher left a record of the bank's customers with comments on their character, credit history, and ability to pay. For example, the Artic Mining Company, an Ohio firm, "must not overdraw one dollar.—Don't know anything about them."[13] Or on the opposite extreme, Silas Bertenshaw of the Black Hawk Foundry—"a fair, honorable man and a good account," was "good up to $2,000 on personal note." J. W. Drips of Hughesville "must not overdraw," as his small silver-mining company was "of no value," while the Gunnel Company was "good for any amount they will ask for, when guaranteed (as it always will be) by Kimber and Fullerton, who practically control the stock."[14]

It is significant that Thatcher was a national banker. Even had he and his fellow chartered bankers all demonstrated great enthusiasm for following the letter of the law (and it is clear they often did just the opposite), many deliberately avoided charters because of the regulation involved, choosing to remain private bankers.[15] And the mounting task that faced authorities attempting to monitor the activities of banks was monumental. Nebraska alone had ten national banks, more than one hundred state banks, and up to forty-six private banks by 1880; by 1890 these numbers may have ballooned up as high as 119 national banks and over five-hundred state and private banks. But even these numbers are extremely unreliable and lack any official source of reporting, as the Department of State Banking was not created until 1890.[16] Until then, the comptroller of the currency published numbers, but even these were not complete reports (see Appendix, table 1). Within Albaugh's tenure as bank commissioner, the number of state banks to examine easily had reached between three hundred and 525.[17]

Everywhere new demands had been placed on state and territorial governments by the growing number of banks. Simply keeping track of the incorporations and officers presented a burden unheard of in 1860. For those states that had attempted to construct a thorough banking law, agencies also had to sift through piles of statements, traipse around the state for examinations, and try to gain some credible information about the officers and directors. Unit bank laws made such examinations ludicrous, especially if the forlorn examiner had to ride to his bleak destinations on horseback. The 1863 and 1864 laws provided for the pay of bank examiners by the examined bank at the rate of five dollars a day for the actual exam and two dollars for every twenty-five miles traveled to perform the duty. In 1875 Congress changed the fee to a scale based on the capital of the bank examined, with fees ranging from twenty to seventy-five dollars. All of Oregon, Nevada, and California, plus banks in reserve cities, had fees set by Congress.[18]

William Brownfield Thorpe (1845–1924), an entrepreneur who had opened a bank in Butler County, Nebraska, in 1877, served as the state bank examiner for Nebraska in the 1890s. His diary and examination books leave a fascinating firsthand account of the procedures of such investigations and the condition of the banks he visited.[19] A typical entry appears in Table 3-1. Note first of all the examiner valued the bank building in this small town at over $8,000. As important as the figures, however, were his comments, which ranged from "Loans: Well distributed. Well served and Well Looked After," to "books not balanced sometimes for a long time." Thorpe realized that almost no one kept records except for a journal or ledger. Records traversed a broad range in their condition and detail, beginning with such poor examples as those of White River Valley Bank, about which Thorpe recorded: "records, none—no articles filed." Likewise, the entry for Farmers and Merchants Bank of Hay Springs carried a single word summation of its records: "bad." Despite the horrifying state of the books, Thorpe noted that White River Valley Bank "can pay deposits in full" and labeled its reserves "ok." Northwestern State

Table 3.1   The Chadron Banking Company, Examined Ausut 12, 1890

Assets		Liabilities	
1. Notes	$47,471.66	1. Capital stock	$25,300.00
2. Demand loans	2,000.00	2. Surplus fund	
3. Overdrafts	1,677.21	3. Other undivided profits, viz:	
4. U.S. Bonds		Discount	
5. Other stocks & bonds	194.00	Exchange	
6. Premiums		Rent	
7. Cash items		Profit & Loss	697.36
8. Due from Natl banks, viz:		4. Due to national banks, viz:	
Merc. Natl. Bank,		5. Due to state banks & bankers, viz:	
Omaha	1,200.00	6. Dividends unpaid	
Mer. Loan & Co.,		7. Individual deposits, viz:	
Chicago	403.60	Subject to check	15,752.58
Hanover Natl, NY	1,230.80	Time certificates	14,766.47
Nebraska Natl, Omaha	53.25	Cashiers checks	30,519.05
Fredonia Natl,		8. Notes & Bills	
Fredonia, NY	1,024.31	rediscounted	3,500.00
9. Due from state banks and		9. Bills payable	5,000.00
bankers, viz:			
Sundry bank (collections)	154.00		
10. Exchanges			
11. Checks			
12. Nat. bank notes			
13. Fractional paper currency			
14. Silver dollars	3,030.50		
15. Fractional coin			
16. Gold coin			
17. Legal tender notes			
18. Banking house	8,341.50		
19. Other real estate	2,308.33		
20. Current expenses	19.24		
Total	$65,016.41		$65,016.41

Source: William B. Thorpe, Examination Book, Box 1, Folder 1, MS 3838, NHR.

Bank's loans were "well distributed, well secured and well looked after." Most entries contained comments of a similar nature. Thorpe knew that he dealt with intangibles, such as character, which could not be confined to the few small categories in his books. One can also sense the futility of trying to make judgments about so many banks and so many accounts on only the briefest of visits. By the early 1900s, the burden had become so great that Walter Fulkerson, the national bank examiner from Missouri, wrote to Charles Sumner Jobes, a Kansas bank examiner and former Mississippi banker, about his experiences. Fulkerson was "pretty tired. I have made thirteen examinations since the 25th of last month. . . ."[20]

Jobes, who had run his own bank in Kosciusko, Mississippi, from 1874 to 1878, came to Kansas and received his examiner's job as a plum from the spoils system. Banks paid a fee for their examinations, a percentage of which went to the examiner. Jobes had on his own list "112 Kansas banks 17 in Ind[ian] Territory and 8 in Kansas City Mo., making 137 in all," and, according to the benefactor who had gotten Jobes appointed, these examinations "are worth $8000 to you annually."[21] California examiners, who complained about low pay, reflected somewhat different circumstances two decades later, although by 1913 North Dakota examiners received twenty-five dollars per examination (if the examiners had Jobes's schedule, they would have received over $1,400 per year).[22] The Kansas district had not been Jobes's first choice, as he had asked for Oklahoma, but Congressman Chester Long, his benefactor, advised Jobes that Charles Dawes, the comptroller, had just removed another western examiner and Jobes should be grateful he was left "unmolested." Jobes not only conducted routine exams, (averaging a bank every three days), but also made special investigations at the comptroller's request.[23] On top of those duties, the comptroller expected examiners to assist in the prosecution of felonious bank officials.[24] In at least one case, a banker thought the timing and method of the bank examinations were politically motivated.[25] Certainly, as regulation grew more all-inclusive it would be increasingly easy for politicians to use the regulatory system for their own ends, as bankers in the 1930s frequently charged.

Mortgage Lending and Community Involvement

That burden would have been difficult enough on regulators in stable times, using a universal set of bank regulations that everyone clearly understood. In the period in which Thorpe and Jobes worked, however, the practice of banking was far more inclusive than it was seventy-five years later, especially among the private banks and the little-regulated state banks. Mortgage lending still comprised an important part of their business, as did insurance-policy sales, especially fire, hail, and tornado

insurance. Those services often provided the sole margin of profit for rural
South Dakota banks.[26] For example, the Bank of Vermillion offered real
estate and insurance services as early as 1877. Its advertisement in the
Vermillion Dakota Republican offered "to buy and sell Real Estate. Pay
taxes and loan money for Eastern Capitalists on real estate security." This
lending of eastern money to new settlers had become "one of the most
important mortgage vehicles in the community" by 1878.[27] Indeed, the
practice of lending eastern funds to develop the West constituted a reverse
colonialism, with local banks building growth from funds that lay hope-
lessly unemployed elsewhere. The bank alone accounted for one-third of
the mortgages negotiated in the county in 1878 and 1888.[28] Many of the
loans came from eastern relatives of the bankers themselves and earned
12 percent interest for five-year mortgages. One of the bank's owners,
Darwin Inman, himself acted as an agent for New York investors. The
bank also engaged in land speculation of its own funds.[29]

One of the most interesting cases of banks' involvement in mortgage
lending involved a Maine mortgage agent, Charles M. Hawkes.[30] After
working in a Chicago bank, then moving to Davenport, Iowa, Hawkes
joined Lynch, Barker and Company in Portland, Maine as a silent partner.
He then began, with $17,000 of his own, to invest in state bonds in the
Missouri area. By the early 1870s, he had acquired an interest in Kansas
mortgages, and asked the Lawrence Savings Bank and the Shawnee
County Bank in Topeka if they knew of potential borrowers. He wanted
the banks to originate the mortgages while he found cash from eastern
lenders. Not only did lenders flock to Hawkes, he reported that he could
not get mortgages "fast enough to supply the demand."[31] Hawkes visited
the West yearly, and had no agents. He negotiated the loans after banks
in Kansas found appropriate borrowers, and tended to collections and
payments to the mortgagees. Westerners benefitted from this process, for
Hawkes's papers make it clear that he and the investors did not want to
acquire any land in Kansas. They sought only safe investments. Interest-
ingly, too, the lenders included as unlikely a source as the Shakers.[32]
Hawkes preferred small loans (as did Arizona banker extraordinaire, Walter Bimson, sixty years later), and he guaranteed his investors 8 to 10
percent interest.

Clearly many banks engaged in mortgage lending in one form or another, or, at the very least, originated mortgage loans.[33] In California,
virtually all of the state banks were lending on real estate. An 1878
report, for example, showed only three banks among the eighty reporting
institutions not engaged in real-estate lending. The real-estate boom in
Wichita peaked in 1887 with transactions totalling more than $9 million,
and although over time savings banks specialized in that activity, the
largest assets of the commercial banks made them perennially important

sources of funds for the real-estate market.[34] Bankers also actively participated in founding western mortgage companies, but, again, those companies sought profitable ways to lend eastern funds, and conversely, safe havens for eastern and European investments. None of them intended either to acquire western land or to become absentee landlords. In fact, several companies encountered difficulties because they cut back western lending after the panic of 1873, concerned about the safety of the loans.[35]

Where they did not originate loans for others, bankers themselves participated in the real-estate market, none more adeptly than William Sargeant Ladd, founder of Ladd and Tilton Bank in Portland, who acquired vast tracts of land, apparently with little intention of turning them into urban or suburban developments. He planned this development, when it eventually did materialize as a residential area, in a radically different form from the grids that crisscrossed the rest of the city. Known as Ladd's Addition, that 126-acre tract, which cost Ladd $10,000 in the 1880s, carried a value of $1 million eleven years later. Ladd's real-estate investments grew so extensive that in 1908 he incorporated the Ladd Estate Company to handle the family's property, and he participated in the mid-1880s with fellow Portland bankers Henry Corbett, Henry Failing, and C. H. Lewis in resurrecting the Portland Hotel, whose foundations had sat exposed for over two years.[36]

Other avenues of profit related to mortgages were open to banks. Banks required mortgagees to insure their properties, and some evidence exists that banks may have either funneled all their business to particular eastern companies or obtained origination fees for the policies.[37] Supplying forts with exchange proved profitable for some banks. The Speigelbergs of Santa Fe at first saw their bank as an aid to their merchandising operations at the local posts, and later decided to shift completely to banking.[38] Still other banks found business with Native Americans profitable. One individual associated with Bismarck National Bank suggested that T. C. Powers, the bank's co-owner from Helena, "arrange to bid on Indian business at a price that will lose us no money. . . ." Although he maintained that the money the bank had lost over the previous two years was "a matter of no mean importance," he in no way suggested that Powers abandon such business, only that he make it profitable again.[39]

Profits also existed at the margins of the national banking laws. Congress, in the original 1863 and 1864 National Banking Acts, allocated $300 million in bank notes to be apportioned among the states according to existing bank capital and population, as well as resources and business of the area. In 1875, after much agitation, a bill reallocating national bank notes was passed. At the same time, obtaining a charter for an existing national bank became easier, and those charters had grown more attractive and desirable. The name "national" in a bank title, according to Comptroller

Thomas Kane in his booklet "The Romance and Tragedy of Banking," was worth $25,000 in the postbellum period, and tremendous benefits accrued from such spoils as the depository system, which identified certain national banks as depositories for U.S. Treasury funds that were designated for payment to government employees or contractors.[40] First National Bank of Santa Fe, which in 1876 was not a depository, sought to acquire this status. On June 29, 1876, the government did away with special depositories and designated certain national banks as depositories. S. B. Wheelock, First National's cashier, learned that over the previous three years, the local depository averaged $300,000 in balances. However, for the privilege of being named a depository, a bank first had to deposit $150,000 in bonds with the U.S. government. If Wheelock relied on an accurate source, the cashier reasoned, the local depository in question would have had an additional $150,000 available for lending after putting up the $150,000 in bonds—quite a tidy sum that competitors would not have. At the time, however, First National did not have a sufficient sum of bonds to deposit as required by law, and to meet the sum the bank would have had to call in outstanding loans. Instead, the directors came up with a plan to lend the bank the necessary money, and by September the institution had achieved its depository status. Within a month the cashier's letter noted that public deposits "considerably exceed what we expected to receive."[41]

Depository status had given Lord and Williams, the early Tucson banking firm, much of its revenue, and First National Bank of Denver found its deposits nearly $200,000 above the levels the bank had expected before status was conferred.[42] There were many other ways a bank could take advantage of dealings with national and local governments. Nearby military installations brought income to dozens of western towns long before the World War II spending boom cited by many historians as the major cause of western growth.[43] Of course, the scale differed greatly between 1866 and 1941; nevertheless, federal involvement in the western economy has deep roots. Every fort and its soldiers needed exchange and banking services. Forts needed a place to deposit payrolls, and soldiers needed to exchange pay drafts if they received anything but gold. The Interior Department passed thousands of dollars of additional money through local banks each year for Indian agencies or other federal offices. State, county, and city governments also kept sizeable accounts with bankers, and handling the deposits and exchange for Denver, Salt Lake City, San Diego, and Portland—not to mention the state of California and the like—provided a bank with obvious advantages over its competitors.

It also entailed certain obligations. The Bank of Vermillion constructed sidewalks and graded streets adjoining its property, and when the city treasurer needed to vacate his office in the 1880s while the new city hall was constructed, the bank provided him with space.[44] Kales and Lewis, bankers for the city of Phoenix—Kales was the city treasurer—lent the city over $1,400 in 1883 to fight a smallpox epidemic.[45] Bankers commonly assisted state, county, and city governments in floating bond issues for the developing infrastructure. William Sherman, for example, reported in 1857 that his bank (Lucas & Turner, Bankers) had loaned $35,000 for construction on Powell Street, and D. O. Mills was a primary mortgage bondholder of the Portland Railway Company.[46] Ladd and Tilton Bank held almost $133,000 of its $1 million assets in bonds, stocks, and warrants as of 1869, while Henry Corbett and Henry Failing actively participated in organizing or directing the City and Suburban Railway Company, the Oregon Railway and Navigation Company, and the Northern Pacific Terminal Company. All told, they, C. H. Lewis, and Ladd backed dozens of paving, cement, gas, electric, and transportation companies in Portland. Indeed, although public philanthropy was not their chief purpose, western bankers gave of themselves and their fortunes. According to even an acerbic critic of the Portland business community, Corbett, Ladd, Failing, and John C. Ainsworth "gave willingly and generously to many worthy cultural and social causes. They were the major supporters of the YMCA, the Humane Society, the Ladies' Relief Society, the Boys and Girls Aid Society and the Children's Home. . . . In proportion to other wealthy families in Portland's early history they contributed more than their fair share."[47]

The wide variety of services offered by banks, when combined with the vast number of banks in operation, certainly diminished the ability of government to regulate banks effectively. Neither factor, however, generated much of the impetus toward regulation that appeared in the late nineteenth century. Instead, two other, connected forces—mergers and panics—accelerated the natural trends toward regulation. Mergers represented a natural, national response of businesses to competition. Bankers, especially, saw consolidation as a route around stifling anti–branch-banking legislation. In addition, most successful banks that had received charters in the 1860s and 1870s entered growth periods a decade later, and started to feel the constraints of branching. Without a more widespread customer and lending base, these banks could grow no further. Mergers offered the only remaining solution, and a rash of them occurred on the Pacific Coast after 1910, capped in 1914 by the merger of First National Bank of Portland and Security Savings and Trust Company. For years, the two institutions had shared the same headquarters building; the latter had been supported by Portland's established banking community since it was founded in 1890.[48]

Such mergers required aggressive leadership. The financial affairs of Absalom V. Hunter provide an interesting study of bank operations. A gold prospector who arrived in Colorado in 1868, Hunter moved to Colorado

Springs after a brief mining career. There, he worked for McFerren Bank and met George Trimble, his future business partner. The two men even married sisters in 1877.[49] Together, they opened Miners Exchange Bank of Leadville in 1878 and later received a national bank charter for their Carbonate National Bank. Hunter was president of the latter institution, and moved to Denver in 1911 to take the presidency and chairmanship of First National Bank of Denver.

Courageous and tough, Hunter lost the use of his feet while fighting a mining fire in 1896, and after taking the helm of First National, he often managed the affairs of the bank from Hot Springs, Arkansas. In letters to Charles Cavender, the attorney for Hunter and Trimble Bankers, the successor firm to Miners Exchange Bank, Hunter left a useful record of a senior officer's view of daily affairs. Hunter received regular reports from Cavender and acknowledged with satisfaction such comments as "everything is going so nicely at both the Bank and the Office." Events of the world had, in Hunter's view, an immediate effect on the bank. In May 1910, with cash "gradually running down," Hunter suggested letting "some of our commercial paper mature" and not replacing it due to uncertainty surrounding the death of Edward VII. When Cavander reported a week later that "cash [is] getting down pretty well," Hunter warned not to let it drop below $300,000, adding: "you and [the assistant cashier] know the conditions better than I at this distance. . . ." Hunter noted that "a line of good commercial paper in cases of stress . . . is certainly one of the most liquid and available assets that any bank can have, as was thoroughly demonstrated in our case during the panic of 1907 and '08."[51]

For a growing bank with aggressive leaders such as Hunter, expanding the bank was a given. Without branching, banks had to rely on takeovers, mergers, and consolidations with troubled banks. Merger activity characterized much of the history of western banking in the late 1800s (with the exception of California, which had few mergers in the 1890s and none in 1899), and many banks in unit-bank states pursued takeover targets. One example that occurred during Hunter's leadership was First National's merger with Capitol National Bank (originally Continental National). Chartered in 1902 by, among others, William F. Hughes and John W. Springer of Denver, the bank voted in 1912 to voluntarily liquidate. However, the directors apparently had a prior understanding with the officers of First National, and the bank's assets merged with those of First National later in the year.[52]

Just before the Capitol merger, Hunter, Henry Porter, Gerald Hughes, and Charles Boettcher formed Denver Securities Company. This company "expected to take over [the Bank of Leadville, in receivership] on the 13th [of June ?, 1911]," but postponed the deal, "having gotten through with the investigation of the affairs of the First National and the Trust Company [by bank examiners]."[53] As the bank's historians concluded, despite the fact that First National and the International Trust Company "were both under the same roof and overseen by [David] Moffat [the bank's second president, who had just died], there was some talk that assets of the two institutions were being intermingled to the advantage of Moffat. . . ." However, the July 1910 report from the comptroller of the currency found "no mingling of assets."[54] With the comptroller's investigation out of the way, bank management then had to deal with a major problem: because of the death in March 1911 of the bank's powerful former president, many of the securities owned by the bank because of his influence suddenly became questionable investments. Hunter, Gerald Hughes, and several others formed a syndicate to purchase the outstanding stock, and, with additional investments from a group of New Yorkers, materially expanded the number of stockholders. Hunter's involvement in an expansionist program had not been the first in the bank's history. In 1882, the directors of Merchants National Bank, then scarcely a year old, voted to liquidate and merge with First National of Denver.[55]

Other banks offered likely takeover targets but somehow maintained their independence, at least for a while. Provo Commercial and Savings Bank (formerly Utah County Savings Bank), organized in 1890, received a delegation from First National Bank of Provo roughly three years after opening for business.[56] Reed Smoot, the president of Provo Commercial and a future U.S. senator from Utah, managed to postpone merger talks for several years. The bank weathered the panic of 1893 apparently without any problems, for the directors' minutebook evidences no concern over the bank's condition during the period. Nevertheless, in 1900 First National again submitted a proposal for a merger with Provo Commercial, and this time it came to a stockholders' vote, where it passed.[57]

PANICS AND BANK RUNS

Provo Commercial may have avoided any ill effects from the panic of 1893, but other banks fared less well. Still, the diversity of western economic interests kept any panic prior to 1907 from affecting the entire region. Panics in 1873, 1877, 1893, and 1907, while serious, were not universally felt. The Panic of 1873 was hardly noticed in the Far West. While some problems appeared, they constituted such rare events as to generate conversation. In San Francisco, which rapidly emerged as a money center for the coastal states, banks weathered this panic without incident, although the East's financial problems made money somewhat scarce, which caused interest rates to rise there and throughout the West.[58] The seventies were marked by the difficult times the economy endured after the completion of the transcontinental railroad brought increased competition and reduced employment. Mining of silver in Nevada and gold in Oregon was also in decline. These factors, rather than eastern bankers' problems, did place stress on western banks.

The closure of the Bank of California in 1875 was one spectacular example of how these forces affected banks. Started in 1864 by William Ralston, with twenty-four of the West's most distinguished business leaders as directors and $200 million in capital, paid in gold, the Bank of California was the first incorporated bank in the state.[59] To start his new bank, Ralston withdrew his share from Donohoe and Ralston and Company, where at least one of his partners disparaged Ralston as too liberal in his lending policies to be a good banker.[60]

Ralston's conception of the proper role of a banker certainly would have appalled his traditional contemporaries. The prevailing doctrine among American bankers stated that banks should lend on the security of short-term, self-liquidating ("commercial") paper. The security implied by that doctrine consisted of inventory, crops, or something the holder could quickly sell in the normal course of business. Proponents of that widely held philosophy objected to investment in bonds, long-term real-estate or speculative loans, or loans the proceeds of which were used for fixed capital.[61]

The Bank of California rapidly assumed the position of the West's largest bank, making loans to develop industry of all kinds in California, Nevada, and Oregon. In November 1864, Ralston accepted stock in a copper mine as payment of a debt, and in 1869 rumors that the Bank of California speculated in mining stock circulated.[62] Indeed, one of the bank's agents complained of this problem. After noting that he had experienced difficulty selling bills bearing the bank's endorsement, he finally heard that the real trouble arose from the bank's having locked several millions of its means in utterly unavailable security such as carriage factories, railroads, land companies and other enterprises, which—however good in themselves when held by capitalists who could wait—were entirely inappropriate as security for bank loans.[63] Even though in 1873 the bank's directors forced Ralston to assume personal responsibility for the loans to George Kimball and Company (carriage builders), New Montgomery Street Real Estate Company (formed for the purpose of removing a hill so as to extend the street), and Pacific Woolen Mills Company totalling $3.5 million, he could not be dissuaded from such investments.[64]

The bank survived these investments and flourished while Ralston's luck in the silver markets held and while San Francisco's growth accelerated. But when both flagged, the bank needed to retrench. Instead, the staid D. O. Mills retired and Ralston proceeded unrestrained. He built a hotel (the Palace) that became a legend, buying a ranch to supply oak for its construction, a foundry for its nails, a furniture factory, and so on, until

William Sharon complained: "when he goes into anything there is no end to it. Never will he beat a retreat until he strikes the ocean."[65]

Ralston struck the ocean on a warm August day. He had been forced to close the bank twenty minutes early the day before, because a dip in the stock market had precipitated a run, and told an Alta reporter: "we do not expect to resume [business]."[66] He then submitted his resignation, which the board accepted, and headed for a swim in San Francisco Bay. Although Ralston was accustomed to swims in the bay's frigid water, the added stress of his resignation may have contributed to his demise. An engineer on a passing steamer noticed him and then saw that the swimmer's movement had ceased. He attempted a rescue, to no avail. Ralston was pronounced dead on the beach.[67] The Bank of California lived, however, and under the leadership of D. O. Mills, whom the board recalled, it revived quickly and moved ahead with conviction, unloading the mining securities and investing heavily in financing trans-Pacific trade.[68] The bank acquired Washington and Oregon banks, and after it received a national charter in 1910 it won a special dispensation to retain these offices as actual interstate branches.[69]

Economies dependent solely on agriculture or mining frequently suffered even in the absence of a general panic. For example, in 1886 the Wichita region experienced a drought, followed by a severe winter, while other regions harvested bumper crops. As a result, by 1892 the city's population had fallen by more than 50 percent and threw Fourth National Bank of Wichita on rocky shoals. The bank survived, only to greet the general depression of 1893, and was forced to sell its real estate holdings at a 90 percent loss in order to survive.[70] A collapse of mining income in the summer of 1892 in Montana decimated banking there. According to the mayor of Bozeman, George Ramsey, "Not counting the faro banks, nor the sand banks, nor the banks of the creek, there is only one banking institution remaining in Bozeman."[71]

Indeed, the local conflagrations may have done more damage than the national panics. Of twenty-eight states and private banks operating in Utah by 1873, according to Roland Stucki's chronology of these institutions, only two could have even remotely attributed their demise to that year's panic.[72] At least two banks entered into operations in Utah in 1873 and three in 1875, indicating that finance there remained relatively untouched. In Wyoming, out of fifteen private, state, and national banks chartered before 1873, seven survived past 1874, but the remainder either merged into one of those seven or disappeared from view immediately after their founding. None of those banks was chartered in 1873, suggesting that the panic had a marginal impact on the state's financial institutions.[73] As Paul Trescott has noted, "bank *failures* were not a major factor in the depressions which followed 1873 and 1884. . . ."[74]

Overall failures may have been few, but to bankers "in the trenches," panic times promised trouble. First National Bank of Wichita, founded by former Indiana minister James C. Fraker, who displayed a "personal lack of preparation in the field of banking," failed as a result of wheat and cattle-trade problems after the panic of 1873.[75] Fraker's first response, to fraudulently report the bank's condition as sound, was ultimately discovered. O. H. Harker, the manager of the Henriett Mine in Leadville, Colorado, wrote of the 1884 panic to David Moffat at First National of Denver: "Matters financially in this village are still in a panicky and chaotic condition. Nothing but rumors &c. An hour ago it was said there was a run on the Carbonate Bank." That rumor proved false: "Tin cans and stockings are now in demand instead of banks."[76] At Denver National Bank, the directors' minutes of August 1, 1893, recorded that the panic had arrived in force. Anxious directors sought ways to reduce overhead expenses, especially employees' salaries, "before determining whether the bank shall resume [paying deposits]." Resolving to cut expenses by 50 percent, the directors decided to resume in two weeks. However, eleven days later the bank found it needed "certain guarantys," especially a $100,000 loan from National Bank of New York.[77] Still, the bank faced desperate times, and opened negotiations with Union National Bank of Denver to buy Denver National in all due haste.[78] By late July the banks had worked out a sale: all assets of Denver National would go to Union National, which would pay $15,000 cash and assume all the troubled bank's debts.[79] The stockholders of Denver National voted down the plan in July, leaving the officers no choice but to put the bank into liquidation. Suddenly, a new player entered the picture—one that most Western bankers had never before encountered in a major business deal and one that symbolized the change in banking—the federal government. The comptroller of the currency refused to allow the bank to liquidate, indeed insisted that Union National purchase it. Faced with the comptroller's edict, the Denver National stockholders agreed to the sale and, by January 1895, the comptroller found that the bank had met all conditions for liquidation.[80] Still, several of Denver National's bad debts almost negated the sale, but by 1900 the final settlement had occurred and by 1902 the board had its last meeting.[81]

Elsewhere, the panic had the same effects as its predecessors in 1873 and 1884. Although Second National Bank of Santa Fe voluntarily closed its operations on July 17, 1892, when most of the Speigelbergs returned to New York, the other major Santa Fe bank, First National Bank, felt the effects of the depression.[82] For the first time in many years, in 1894 it missed a dividend payment.[83] Frank Bond, a prominent sheep rancher from north of Santa Fe, recalled that "banks would not loan a dollar [during the panic]. . . . Most of the merchants had to remit currency for their groceries which they bought in Colorado, as the wholesale grocery dealers were afraid the banks would break before the checks could be paid."[84] Some banks failed simply out of bad timing or corruption. Albuquerque National Bank closed in 1893, paying its depositors in full, after the president, Stephen Folsom, was indicted for making false entries. Likewise, Commercial Bank of Deming, whose chief officer, C. H. Dane, was indicted for his part in First National Bank of Silver City's collapse, also failed.[85] Overall, approximately twenty-five western banks failed during the panic, some due to the activities of officers such as Folsom. Alexander J. Noyes, assessing the panic in *Political Science Quarterly*, thought "defective bank management," and "reckless banking" had caused the majority of the problems with banks.[86] Even so, he agreed with Dun's Mercantile Agency, which reported that the West had 147 of the nation's 213 failed banks in the panic of 1893, although the estimates of both Dun and Noyes probably underestimated the total number of bank failures.

Among the western states, the panic of 1893 was most evident on the Pacific Coast, where eighty-one of the nation's 642 failures occurred.[87] Washington's banking system faced near-total devastation by the financial problems of the early nineties: Spokane lost four of seven banks, Tacoma lost seven of eight, Bellingham lost five out of six. Seattle lost only one bank, albeit one that had been spectacularly successful prior to the panic, Merchants National Bank of Seattle.[88] Many of those failures occurred well after 1893 because the Great Northern Railway reached near enough to Seattle in 1893 to buffer the city's banks from ill effects. But by 1895, when Merchants National Bank closed with an aggregate loss of $231,000, followed by four smaller banks, the panic had reached the city. Even at successful banks, such as People's Savings Bank, the board took drastic action in response to the panic, writing off bad loans, halving the advertising budget and some salaries, borrowing $70,000, and reducing the space that the bank rented in the Occidental Building.[89] The arrival of the steamship *Portland* reassured the population and officially ended the panic in Seattle. In Washington the number of banks dropped from 173 in 1892 to ninety-one in 1896, showing that in that state, at least, failed banks did not reopen and were not replaced by new banks.[90]

Business in Oregon was notably depressed during the summer of 1893, and a general feeling of uneasiness characterized banking relations. The conditions first took their toll on George Markle, an aggressive investor with control of two banks. First one, then the other closed their doors, precipitating a run on other Portland banks. Two other banks failed, and Ainsworth National Bank closed temporarily. First National Bank avoided trouble only when bags of gold from Meier and Frank's well-capitalized merchandise store arrived through the back door. Inland banks then experienced runs. Seven national banks in the state closed, but eventually reopened. Although none of the failures was initiated in any way by the panic in the East (which apparently first manifested itself in Chicago), the general climate of unease contributed to existing problems.[91] Montana suffered a rash of closings, with Samuel Hauser's First National Bank in Helena the best known, and one bank suspended operation because of failures "so near" as Australia. As usual, some failures resulted not from economic conditions but from crime, such as when Livingston National Bank folded after cashier George A. Carey absconded with $100,000.[92] Southern California was the site of the West Coast's first major bank failure, that of the Riverside Banking Company on June 14. During the next month six banks closed in Los Angeles, although all but one eventually reopened.[93] Farmers and Merchants Bank of Los Angeles survived the panic by paying its customers without undue haste while displaying bags of gold, including $250,000 sent by owner Isaias Hellman from San Francisco. Hellman also tried to help the neighboring City Bank, but "threw up his hands in despair when he saw the worthless paper they had taken."[94] City Bank did not survive the panic. San Francisco did not suffer as much as did most cities, probably because of the flexibility those banks were afforded by their international correspondents and their clearinghouse which, unlike the Los Angeles clearinghouse, allowed members to pool their resources to make a show of strength when a run threatened.

Nevertheless, most banks made internal adjustments without excessive external regulation and survived, and most "adjustments" involved trying to get borrowers to repay their loans. Martin Kales, of Kales and Lewis in Phoenix, regretted that he had loaned money to P. J. McCormack, who had written Kales explaining that his own debtors had not yet paid him, and he could not pay the bank. Kales unsympathetically instructed McCormack to "go to Albuquerque and make it a *business to get us some money.*" If he could not get cash from New Mexico, Kales warned, McCormick would have to "come home and sell off something, as we cannot carry you to so large an amount any longer."[95] The panic brought similar threats from the Bank of Arizona, whose cashier told one borrower: "I have told [other debtors] that if their notes are not paid I shall make them trouble and they are rustling to save cash. I tell *you* the same thing. . . . I *want my money*. . . ."[96] To another, the cashier wrote: "This matter has dragged along beyond all decency."[97]

The panic of 1907 proved far more traumatic, and ultimately provided the last straw for even those who had held out against national regulation. Copper prices had already plummeted, causing banks in copper mining areas to close or suspend in droves. Three banks in Globe, Arizona, alone closed, as did one in Bisbee, although its demise was due to the illegal activities of its officers).[98] New Mexico sheepman Frank Bond recalled that "the Roosevelt Panic," as he called it, placed him in tight straits. Cattle feeders who used Bond's many lots and had debts to local banks gave Bond their own checks, which were turned down. When Bond appealed to the source—the banks, especially First National—cashier Rufus Palen told him he would "see [them] through, but to not use the bank any more than [they] had to."[99] Ultimately, however, the New York money panic, not short-term regional conditions, forced most western banks to the point of crisis. William M. Pease, the cashier of Commercial State Bank of Wagner, South Dakota, recalled that he requested additional currency from First National Bank in Sioux City, only to be referred to the president, James F. Toy. Toy informed Pease that the bank couldn't "send out any currency today."[100] As a result, many banks in Pease's region "adopted the 'five dollar' plan," which permitted a customer to withdraw no more than five dollars from an account per day. Local bankers even made a campaign out of persuading individuals who might have money stashed at home to part with it. Only when the Sioux City banks released additional funds in December did panic conditions ease, but by then the banks' reserves had fallen so low that bankers borrowed from individuals who had cash. For a change, the bankers complained of outrageous interest rates.[101] Those effects were not universal, however. Issac P. Baker, the owner of Bismarck National Bank in North Dakota, reported in November that his "cash on hand at present [was] sufficient" and rejected offers of help from the chairman of the Chicago Clearinghouse Association. He observed no hoarding: "Whatever hoarding there is must be carried on in large centers."[102]

Western banks, of course, created their own clearinghouses for relief, among other temporary measures taken to ameliorate the crisis. Banks in Reno and Sparkes, Nevada, established a clearinghouse association in late 1907 to effect "a more perfect . . . settlement of the daily exchanges between them. . . ."[103] Most clearinghouses printed "clearinghouse certificates" backed by the securities of local banks. The banks themselves then subscribed to some of the new paper. Denver's clearinghouse association, formed in 1885, sought to promote sound and conservative banking. The association established regulated banking practices, such as banking hours (10:00 A.M. to 3:00 P.M.), interest rates, and other practices. According to Thomas Noel, a historian of Colorado National Bank, "so powerful were the clearinghouse banks that smaller banks regarded their policies as unofficial law."[104] Indeed, a Minot, North Dakota, banker complained that in 1913 the Minot Clearinghouse Association forced him to lower the interest paid to depositors by 1 percent.[105] San Francisco, Denver, and Globe, Arizona, relied on the use of clearinghouse certificates to relieve the demand for money from suspended banks.[106]

San Francisco and Los Angeles clearinghouses took on the role of regulator before the state banking association existed, and not only regulated

members, but served as a sort of local central bank until the Federal
Reserve System arrived. Bankers established the San Francisco Clearinghouse in 1876 to satisfy the banks' need to reduce the cost of transporting
the gold and silver they used to settle their balances. In the beginning,
the clearinghouse members deposited silver with one member bank and
certificates were issued against the deposits. Later, U.S. Gold Certificates
were used for clearing, and by 1883, the clearinghouse association had
minimum capital requirements of $500,000 for membership.[107]

Panics, of course, tested the effectiveness of the clearinghouse associations, and, where none existed, prompted their creation. On May 1, 1908,
the Los Angeles Clearinghouse appointed an examiner to make periodic
examinations of the local banks. He and his staff examined any bank,
clearinghouse member or not, which could pay for the examination. In
1909 San Francisco appointed an examiner who proceeded to examine all
of the clearinghouse members, and, by 1908, membership in the San
Francisco association was so critical that exclusion from it was "financial
suicide."[108] A copy of the examination of Donohoe and Kelly Banking
Company (an original member of the clearinghouse association), reveals a
very complete examination. Each of the bank's loans was rated with a brief
comment; comparisons were made between the bank and its rivals; and
advice was given on the overall management of the bank's assets.[109] Other
cities began clearinghouses as the number of banks increased. California
had nine such institutions in 1907, and Seattle, Tacoma, and Portland also
operated clearinghouses. Each had made special arrangements to ease
crisis situations at various times, but the financial panic of 1907 brought
them to try a palliative never before used in the paper-shy West. Clearinghouses in San Francisco, Los Angeles, and Sacramento issued specially
printed clearinghouse certificates that circulated among the general population. In San Francisco alone, nearly $2 million worth of this scrip was
issued in denominations as low as one dollar.[110] While most of the emergency clearinghouse certificates issued were quickly retired, those bearing
interest circulated widely and redemption still occurred in the mid-
1920s.[111]

Some bankers found no need for clearinghouses or otherwise anticipated
the panic. Isaias Hellman's assistance to his Los Angeles bank proved
invaluable. In April, 1906, he wrote to his manager in Los Angeles describing the devastation of the earthquake, and while requesting cash for the
Nevada bank, warned him to "keep strong in cash in Los Angeles. Make
no loans for the present except to regular clients and in moderate amounts
only." Hellman directed the manager to call in all loans from New York
and to keep the cash on hand.[112] In general, branching solved many of the
problems of clearinghouses, explaining the slow development of clearinghouse associations in California and other branch-banking states. Rather

than being a sign of market sophistication, clearinghouses were second-best attempts to compensate for many of the advantages offered by branching, though the two existed side by side in several states.[113]

EARLY STATE BANKING REGULATIONS

By 1906, the West had firmly linked itself to the East through mails and rails, an evolution that permitted even greater use of drafts and checks.[114] Thus the transition from currency to credit owed as much to the post office and the railway mail service as it did to banks, especially in the West. Railroads felt constant pressure to give preferred treatment to mail cars even over freight and passenger service. That, in turn, facilitated rapid clearing of checks and aided in the charging and credit process, ostensibly one of the purposes of the clearinghouse associations. But more rapid check-clearing and information transmission—especially if it was news of an eastern panic—exacted a price. The West found itself more vulnerable than ever to eastern shocks, as seen in the panic of 1907.[115] The number of western banks increased by 445 between 1906 and 1908, but resources fell from $2.23 billion to $2.14 billion (see appendix, tables 1 and 2). Those statistics are misleading, however, because the rate of increase had slowed dramatically due to the panic. Moreover, numerous weak banks, although they did not fail outright, followed the course of action of at least six Arizona banks to consolidate, merge, or become a branch of another bank.[116]

As always, some failed banks suffered from owners who operated on the fringes of the law and beyond the limits of good, honest business. Among the early "pyramid-scheme" banks to fail, Denver Savings Bank stood out because of its boldness and sophistication. Leonard Imbolden and J. A. Hill, along with some of their friends, acquired majority control of the bank in September 1904, and within a year they had indebted themselves to the bank by over $600,000. Before Imbolden acquired the bank, he sent soon-to-be president C. B. Wilfley to examine it, with the admission "We need a bank to take care of our interests. . . . We do not want it for an investment or dividends. . . ." Imbolden even instructed Wilfley to make certain the former president was not in the bank at closing of the sale: "He might see some things there. . . ." The new owners already had a plan to link the Denver institution with Mount Vernon National Bank in Boston and a partnership they had in an unincorporated Texas bank, the Bank of Commerce in Fort Worth. They also were associated with trust companies in Fort Worth and Vinita, Oklahoma, in Indian Territory. Needless to say, Imbolden and Hill owed money to each of these. Indeed, in a September 1905 letter, Hill dissuaded Imbolden from unveiling the extent of the network to other partners, reminding Imbolden "we are broke now," and "we must keep our business affairs to ourselves."[117] Colorado authorities caught Imbolden and Hill that year, and they were tried, convicted, and imprisoned. Still, their method was instructive, and predated a similar multistate thrift and bank collapse in the 1970s.[118] Essentially, they operated by using borrowed money from one bank to buy stock in a second, and borrowing from the second to buy stock in the first in order to borrow more, using their new leverage. Before their arrest, Imbolden and Hill owned stock in ten banks and trust companies in four states, plus Indian Territory, and had a large outstanding loan to yet another. Their purchase of Denver Savings Bank, which had failed in 1893, involved an intricate scam of buying the bank with drafts on other Imbolden-Hill banks that were not paid but credited Denver Savings Bank with similar amounts on the books of the Texas banks; then, using the newly created "money," Imbolden borrowed from the Denver bank to pay his original loans.[119]

More than ever, the instability blamed on the financial system prompted citizens, regulators, and bankers alike to press for substantial changes in the banking system. Mergers and financial panics thus constituted the two rising forces that shaped, and were shaped by, banking regulation as formal laws replaced the symbols of safety. Ripples of regulation surged through each state throughout the late 1800s, but not until the panic of 1893 did these forces begin to converge, and they did not crest until the crisis of 1907.

This late development of widespread regulation, first at the state level, then culminating in national legislation with the creation of the Federal Reserve system, has perplexed many historians of the West (as similarly late developments puzzled historians of the antebellum South), even though they acknowledge the burgeoning number of banks and their vast spectrum of services that made regulation a nearly impossible task.[120] In fact, all of the early state and territorial legislatures created banking laws, especially in the 1870s and 1880s. These laws almost universally represented sunshine regulations designed to expose abuses by forcing publication of banks' resources, liabilities, and so on. Occasionally they set basic entry requirements. However, western states and territories refrained for several decades from establishing examiners' offices, bank boards, minimum capitalizations, or other restrictive laws, and not even the sunshine legislation was universally adopted. Washington state, for example, until 1908 required no regular reports to any state office.

No specific events seem to have triggered the shift to greater state regulation on a regional basis, and even on the state level it is difficult to pin down a cause-and-effect relationship between crisis and response. In Wyoming, for example, passage of the "Holliday Bill" in 1888, which set capital requirements for state banks, followed the collapse of several institutions that had financed cattle ranches through the disastrous winter of 1886–87.[121] Specifically, the failure of Maverick Bank in Douglas may have sparked action, but the most recent chronicler of Wyoming's banking past located no real evidence on this point.[122] Wyoming adopted stricter loan limits than the federal statutes allowed, but set lower capital limits. It enacted no legislation either prohibiting or permitting branch banking. But even with the passage of this and another comprehensive law, these acts served as sunshine legislation in requiring reports and publications of statements of condition, and this, too, fit the general pattern of legislation that evolved in western states. Nevertheless, L. Milton Woods concluded correctly that "the 1888 law had very subtly shifted the burden of proof of bank safety from the banker to the territorial government."[123] Indeed, while the symbols of safety remained an important part of banking until the Great Depression, under the new rules virtually anyone who met the paltry $10,000 capitalization minimum for Wyoming banks could cloak himself in the mantle of a respectable banker.

California adopted one of the earliest general banking laws in the West, passing in 1877 legislation that required banks to publish information about their financial condition and also establishing a board of bank commissioners.[124] During its first decade, the board complained that the legislature ignored its reports and suggestions.[125] Commissioners examined each bank twice yearly until 1905, although the frequency and reliability of their published reports left something to be desired.[126] Even so, this practice of examining banks was relatively unique in the nation at this time, with only four northeast states, Indiana, and Iowa requiring regular official inspection of state banks.[127] The promise, or threat, of examination appears to have had some impact: California examiners in 1878 reported one bank on their list closed about the time of the expected visit.[128] Indeed, the examiners closed the first bank they visited (the Masonic Savings and Loan Bank); they found the second acceptable; the third owed over $373,000 and was closed; the fourth—a savings and loan—owed $5.5 million and was closed; and the fifth, Odd Fellows Bank, closed shortly after the examination owing more than $2.1 million. Examiners also closed some inland banks.[129] California's early farsightedness in permitting branching worked better than its early efforts at sunshine legislation. By 1909, new general capitalization laws and other broad bank regulations were in place there. Oregon and Washington quickly copied these laws.

Ironically, the first rash of failures in Oregon came after passage of the new banking law on May 25, 1907, which ostensibly was to make banks safer. The Oregon legislature appointed James Steel, brother-in-law of the Powerful banker William Ladd, as the state's first bank examiner. Less than three months after the new law went into effect, the Oregon Trust and Savings Bank in Portland went into receivership. Steel had not yet had time to make the circuit and examine the state's banks, so he could hardly be blamed. That small bank, organized in 1904 by Lonner O. Ralston and run by W. H. Moore and W. C. Morris, held much of its assets in bonds of telephone companies that had yet to return a nickel.[130] Worse, the officers had skimmed a percentage for selling the bonds to the bank and had retained $20,000 in bank commissions for their own use.[131] Needless to say, the authorities convicted and jailed the officers. But that hardly ended the panic-related problems in Oregon, for no sooner had J. Thornburn Russ, president of the Title Guaranty and Trust Company, boasted that "the banks in Portland have never been in better condition," than his bank collapsed with total liabilities of $2.6 million.[132] Title Guaranty owed much of that amount to Ladd and Tilton, and almost half a million dollars of the $2.6 million was money from the state deposited by the bank examiner's brother and state treasurer, George Steel.[133] Ross received an indictment. For his part, Steel had put state money into the weakest institution imaginable.

Nebraska followed a similar pattern, first enacting sunshine laws in 1876, then setting lending limits and, instead of capitalizations, cash reserve floors in 1889.[134] Only in 1895, as a response to the panic of 1893, in which eighty-five state banks failed as a direct or indirect result of the depression, did the state require all non-national banks to be chartered by a newly created state banking board. Ignoring the exceptional weakness of the rural unit banking system, Nebraska lawmakers instead concentrated on insuring deposits, setting in motion the machinery that produced the Deposit Guaranty Fund.[135]

Kansas, with its first sweeping bank act in 1891, dealt with neither branching nor deposit guarantees.[136] Indeed, no express stipulation against branch banking existed until 1929. Until then, timid Kansas bankers simply refrained from testing the intent of the law. The 1891 legislation sought to rectify a major weakness in the state constitution's article dealing with banks, which dealt only with banks of issue. Once federal legislation ended those banks' activities, the Kansas Bank laws became anachronistic. Little sunshine legislation developed, either, as the legislature in 1891, and revising the laws again in 1897, established capitalization levels, fixed reserves, and a banking department, with the 1897 revisions significantly improving the earlier law.

Utah Territory's 1888 general banking act established the pattern for its banking growth. It set the minimum number of people needed to organize a bank at six; established a minimum capitalization of $20,000; restricted to $10,000 the amount that could be lent to a single officer; gave the territorial secretary bank examiner's powers; and required banks to publish quarterly financial statements.[137] Although a historian of Utah banking has credited the law with reducing bank failures—and the average did drop from 1.5 failed banks per year between 1864 and 1887 to .75 failed banks per year between 1888 and 1895—one could simply conclude that the competition of the market had weeded out the inefficient banks and that the post-1888 period had been affected by a major barrier to entry.[138] Not until 1901 did the legislature establish minimum reserves. In 1903 an office of state bank examiner was created, and subsequent laws toughened enforcement and examinations. Like Nebraska, Kansas, Montana, Oklahoma, and, with certain exceptions, North Dakota, Utah prohibited branching.

Colorado and Montana stood out among the group of states and territories that prohibited branching in that they relied on mining and livestock raising, not farming, as the basis of their economies. The antipathy toward branching had deep rural roots, and consequently its development in Colorado and Montana is more problematic. One explanation for this antipathy, especially in Colorado, might be found in the number of national banks already established at the time: thirteen. At least one bank existed in each of the major population areas, and federal laws allowed branching by national banks only if the states permitted it at the time the banks joined the national system. On the other hand, small towns, which could not meet the minimum capitalization of $30,000 for a state bank, obtained services from private banks that the state laws essentially left outside the administrative powers of the government. In Montana, for example, the minimum capital requirement was $20,000, and although the state auditor had the authority to approve applications, no method of examining the banks appeared until the state created the state examiner's office in 1915. Colorado had required the private banks to adhere to the same rules as state banks by 1910 (A year earlier it had attempted to pass a state guaranty law.) Opposition by the Colorado Bankers' Association led to the substitution of an individual guaranty law.[139] Thus, from both the supply and demand sides, little incentive existed for branch banking, no matter how much sense it would have made for Colorado.[140] Eugene White has found "little discussion of the subject by the public, bankers, academics, or Congress before the 1890s."[141]

Idaho, as of 1895, still stipulated minimum capital requirements in each bank's individual act of incorporation, as did Oregon. By 1909, though, both had adopted uniform minimum requirements. Both, along with Wyoming, also passed new "free banking" laws permitting banks to incorporate under fixed rules rather than apply to the state for charters or use general incorporation laws.[142] Idaho and Oregon, along with Colorado and seven other western states, made private banks comply with the same rules as state banks. Washington's 1908 law gave private banks until 1915 to incorporate and required banks to state their function—savings or commercial—and to report regularly to the newly created office of state bank examiner.

Nevada, in addition to permitting institutions to incorporate to "safely invest [the savings of members] for their common benefit," a provision "open to a wide range of interpretation," also required banks to obtain a license to operate.[141] License fees varied according to the monthly volume of business, and empowered the county sheriffs to collect these fees. They had little incentive or time to perform these duties. Nevada banks had no formal system of reporting or an agency to which to report until 1907. The panic of that year led Nevada lawmakers to attempt to supervise and regulate banks even more, and encouraged passage of several acts limiting nonbanking activities and banning branch banking.[143] Much of the lawmakers' antipathy toward branching came from the domination of the state's early banking system by the Bank of California. Yet, while that institution accumulated massive economic power, there were never suggestions that it failed to provide adequate services at reasonably competitive rates.[144] Arizona followed later than most of its neighbors in passing its general banking laws, with the first appearing in 1893 and broader regulations added in 1897, 1909, and 1912. However, the most significant fact of Arizona's regulation was the almost accidental appearance of branching.

BRANCHING

Within a short time the Bank of Arizona in Prescott, which, as the territory's first chartered bank dated back to 1877, under owners Sol Lewis and Martin Kales, opened an "agency" in Phoenix. For all purposes, they treated the agency as a branch. Other banks followed the Bank of Arizona's lead. By the time lawmakers finally decided to pass bank legislation, branching was a fact of life in Arizona.[145]

Without question, the most significant economic effect of all the western banking regulations was the "California bankers' ability to freely engage in branch banking," although the most spectacular use of branching, by A. P. Giannini's Bank of Italy, had not yet occurred.[144] Branching had a mixed history in other states where it had been tried, mostly because it had been wedded to state monopoly banks.[147] But antebellum Virginia developed a powerful and healthy branch system that proved far more stable than the free-banking systems in other states, and modern studies leave little doubt as to the desirability of branching.[148] Branch banking, though, acquired a bad name for two reasons. First, in those states where state banks had established branches, they also had a monopoly or, at least, a quasimonopoly.[149] Branching, while the brainchild of the antimonopoly Jacksonians, soon joined elites, state banks, and monopolies as singularly evil in the minds of the public. The public's concerns were fueled by a second factor: the failure of several state branch banks during the panic of 1837, especially those in Alabama, Arkansas, and Georgia. The state banks seemed, in the public eye, to fail more spectacularly than other institutions. Some people blamed state banks, others branching. So monopoly branch banks, in their rubble, scarred the memories of the early settlers of the plains. Freeman Clarke, the second comptroller of the currency, further poisoned the well against branching by interpreting section 8 of the National Banking Act as a prohibition against branch banking.[150] By the 1870s, populism fanned those fears even more. Added to all those drawbacks, branching had the inherent disadvantage of seeming to foster absentee capital. When the National Monetary Commission commissioned a study of branching in 1910, the author concluded that the absence of branches was "partly due to the general wish of each American community . . . to have its banks managed by its own citizens. . . ."[151] The wonder of it all was that branching appeared anywhere in the West.

Yet, no system could have better suited diverse and rich California. Mining and farming, later buttressed by trade, manufacturing, and the film industry, each with its own special business cycle, thrived on the abilities of California's banks to shift funds from city to country, northern regions to southern. Initially, however, California's ease of entry for new banks meant branching had little effect. As late as 1905, for example, only five banks had branches. Indeed, one could conclude that this initial weakness itself saved branching from the forces that stirred the nation during this period.[152] In the 1905 and 1907 acts in California, branching was not mentioned, then in 1909 it was specifically allowed. Oregon patterned itself on California's 1907 law, and in 1909 permitted branching, although Washington, which had allowed branching, suddenly prohibited it in that year. Arizona permitted branching from the 1870s. With the exception of Nevada, which had inherited California's branch-banking legislation but specifically prohibited branching in 1909 out of concern for a repeat of the early domination that had occurred by the Bank of California, the entire Pacific Slope accepted a system uniquely conducive to western growth.

A considerable body of economic theory on branching exists, much of it favorable to the effects branching brings in customer responsiveness, availability of branching services, average asset size, and risk diversification.[153] No one has argued more forcefully that branching could have produced a much more stable U.S. banking system in the late nineteenth and early twentieth century than has Eugene N. White. White has shown, especially in comparisons with Canadian banking, that weaknesses in the American system stemmed from the lack of risk diversification, especially among rural unit banks. White has also argued that "some form of branching contributed almost $330,000 to the average size of state banks"—not a negligible amount given their average half-million-dollar capitalizations in 1910.[154] Of course, the rural unit bankers comprised the most vehement opposition to branch banking: they "formed anti–branch-banking lobbies which successfully blocked increased branching at the federal level and in many states."[155]

State regulations, under attack from Populists and bankers themselves in the 1890s, constituted only half of the regulatory playing field on which banks operated. Laid over the unit-versus-branch network, the government had placed a two-tier system of national versus state banks. George Anderson, a partisan historian of Kansas banking, has noted that it "was neither national nor a banking system," but rather, "it was a loose organization of currency factories especially designed to meet the needs of industrial and commercial communities and confined by administrative decision almost entirely to the New England and Middle Atlantic states."[156] New federal legislation apparently discriminated against western states by giving preference to existing state banks in granting national charters. The Treasury emphasized this aspect of the system over that of establishing a quota for circulation in each state.[157] Clearly the South suffered from this system, for very few southern state banks survived the Civil War. In parts of the West, the shortage of national bank notes in circulation and the corresponding popularity of greenbacks gave rise to one strain of growing resentment against the newly created system, while in mining areas, the residents found bank notes of any kind unacceptable.

Congress recognized the problem by 1870, when it authorized additional western and southern circulation and a partial redistribution of existing circulation. Editorialists attacked national banks as gold gamblers, stock speculators, and oppressive, unscrupulous monopolists.[158] The president of the Kansas Farmers' Association called the national banking system "more oppressive than famine and more destructive than war."[159]

At the same time that Westerners rabidly denounced the national banking system, they often delicately avoided attacking their own local national banks. Even John Davis rarely singled out a specific Kansas national bank for criticism. Westerners knew better than to bite the hands that fed them credit, as national banks provided invaluable services. Thatcher's instructions to his cashier to accommodate existing customers even if it required the bank to violate the law, while seldom repeated in writing elsewhere, were universally followed in actual practice. That, in turn, drove examiners and regulators to the point of exasperation. A new struggle between the authorities and the banks appeared, made all the more ironic by the fact that in theory bankers supported regulation as a barrier to entry by competitors, but in practice they dreaded the incessant meddling by the comptroller and federal and state examiners.

One sticking point stemmed from the fact that some state examiners came from the ranks of ex-bankers from failed banks. The deputy bank examiner for Montana in the 1920s, Tom Messelt, recalled that the state also frequently appointed such men as receivers, with "the natural (if selfish) tendency . . . to make receivership last as long as possible. . . ." Messelt reported observing "much maneuvering" to get the ex-bankers appointed as receivers.[160] Whether such shenanigans occurred in earlier decades cannot be stated with certainty, but seems likely. Other areas of friction resulted in greater documentation by the bankers, including overdue loans: the comptroller of the currency, at the slightest sign of overdue paper, insisted that a bank call in its loans. When such an order went to First National Bank of Santa Fe in 1878, the cashier gently attempted to explain the vicissitudes of the New Mexico economy to the comptroller: "Banking in New Mexico is surrounded by many . . . trails by which banks in the East are free [especially having as customers sheep growers] who though perfectly good and solvent *and always pay in the end* are invariably in the spring of the year hundreds of miles away with their herds."[161]

First National's justifications to regulators notwithstanding, the bank attempted to reform its lending internally in the late 1870s, reflecting a trend throughout banks in the West. Even before the activities of Imbolden and Hill, bankers had become wary of "insider" loans. At First National Bank of Santa Fe, in August 1877, the board agreed to make no loans without the assent of three directors, and a year later it resolved to make loans only with "good collateral, or upon not less than one good security."[162] Rufus Palen, a director and cashier, refused one voucher for cattle as collateral and told an endorser that the bank considered some $28,000 in bills receivable held by the bank "worthless aside from your name."[163] While continuing to be tolerant well into the middle of the Great Depression, banks had begun subtle changes in their deposit, reserve, and lending policies.

Internal regulation came too late to derail the passage of state statutes. Most states decided that unregulated private banks, such as the Imbolden and Hill unchartered banks that still existed in droves, posed a threat to the entire system. Hugo Seaberg, a New Mexico capitalist, illustrated the flexibility and relative freedom from regulation such bankers had. A former clerk with the Springer Mercantile and Banking Company in New Mexico, Seaberg then worked in a law firm as a salesman. He moved into insurance sales, helped to plan a system of offices for the National Home Building and Loan Association in New Mexico, and in 1894 founded the Mills-Seaberg Company, which included among its work legal duties, buying and selling of property, lending money, and management of collections and loans.[164] Using the built-in advice of the law firm, the "bank" could float around the fringes of the law while dealing in real estate, lending, and railroad scrip operations. Seaberg's business remained profitable, but private banks such as his offered a tempting target when they failed, for customers had little legal recourse. As in Nevada, much of the legislation throughout the West came on the heels of other populist, then progressive, reforms. When one considers the source, the inconsistent and contradictory nature of the regulations makes more sense. Comments such as those of Colorado congressman John Bell illustrate the fuzzy thinking that characterized regulation efforts. Speaking before the House, Bell said "we have too many banks now," then continued with the self-contradictory conclusion "This is because of the enormous profits in banking."[165] Bell attacked the "bank power" that fathered financial legislation "made by the banks . . . for the banks alone."[166] Polemicists urged the masses to "dethrone the money kings," with the *Platte County [Nebraska] Argus* crying out against the "organized money power" and "their cruel, heartless mortgage on the industry and individual efforts of our countrymen."[167]

Local bankers were bewildered at the populist tirades against banks of any sort. According to one Nebraska banker, recalling the history of his own bank, the attacks "could not have been directed against Nebraska banks . . . for the same difficulties beset them."[168] Moreover, the anger of the populists and the resulting pressure on lawmakers fed irrational legislation. Consequently, the public heard statements from responsible state officials such as the Wyoming state bank examiner, who in 1921 stated: "Our department has felt *for some time* that there are too many banks in Wyoming" (emphasis added), after which the convention to which he spoke passed a resolution to "condemn" branch banking in any form."[169] Just three years later, Wyoming's banks would experience what one bank historian termed a "massacre," brought about largely because of the weaknesses of unit banking.[170]

Responding to the twin pressures of the populist/progressive reform on the one hand, and the federal encroachment in the regulatory arena on the other, both fueled by merger waves and the recurring panics, the besieged local bankers banded together in associations to lobby for their interests (see table 3.2). Nevada bankers in Virginia City formed an association as early as August 1863 for the purpose of establishing uniform methods of conducting business, although the group dissipated quickly. The timing of the creation of the Nevada Bankers Association in 1908 and its goals—to "secure uniformity of action" on legislation—suggest that the panic of 1907 was the last straw for Nevada bankers.[171] Similar concerns appeared throughout the West. The Arizona Bankers Association dedicated its entire 1908 annual meeting to the lessons of the panic, although its members demonstrated little agreement about what the "lessons" were. Virtually all states had professional associations by 1910, and the ten that

Table 3.2   Dates of Founding for Bankers'
Associations of Western States

Arizona	1903
California	1891
Colorado	1902
Idaho	1907
Kansas	1887
Montana	1904
Nebraska	1890
Nevada	1908
New Mexico	1908
North Dakota	1889 (Dakota Terr., 1884)
Oklahoma	1893
Oregon	1905
South Dakota	1889 (Dakota Terr., 1884)
Utah	1910
Washington	1889
Wyoming	1909

Source: Bankers Association of individual states.

were in existence before 1905 were able to marshall their lobbying efforts into shaping the seemingly inevitable federal legislation. Arizona bankers even received an invitation from the territorial bank comptroller to help shape the new state's legislation in 1911, a remarkable exercise of influence on the part of an association. South Dakota's Department of Banking had become so concerned with the influence of the South Dakota Bankers Association that it launched an investigation of the association. The investigation found "no dishonorable tactics of any kind practiced [by the SDBA]." The president of the association noted that the balance of the report "suggests that a vicious lobby was maintained and that bluffing, browbeating, cajoling, and predicting future results which may never occur were resorted to."[172]

How much state bankers' associations influenced national legislation is unclear, although many that were dominated by unit banks denounced branch banking. In 1894, the American Bankers Association decided to deliberate the Baltimore Plan to issue currency based on a ratio of bank assets, but in the subsequent informal discussions, dominated by the New York Reform Club and a number of powerful industrialists, few Westerners participated.[173] At least, few participated directly: a powerful pro-silver tract that "seemed to have become required reading in the West," *Coin's Financial School* by the itinerant speculator and miner William Hope

"Coin" Harvey, startled the Reform Club with its popularity and circulation.[174]

Western bankers were conspicuously absent from the National Sound Money League, created in 1897, although each state sent a "vice president" to the organizational meetings. Even at that, Montana's representative, Wilbur F. Sanders, was a lawyer for the Northern Pacific Railroad; Utah, New Mexico, and Arizona, which were still territories, did not sent "vice presidents," nor, inexplicably, did Idaho, Nevada, and South Dakota.[175] The executive committee had only one member out of eight from the West or South, and the original design and organization of the plan flowed from the New York Chamber of Commerce. Junius Sterling Morton, a Nebraskan, eventually succeeded to a one-year term as president, and in 1898 the league held its annual meeting in Omaha. Still, the league was dominated by nonwestern bankers.

Some of the original vice presidents, including John J. Valentine, Wells Fargo's president, also received appointments to the National Monetary Commission in 1897, but their small number only reflected the domination of other areas.[176] Hugh Hanna of Indianapolis, Robert S. Taylor, a patent attorney, and Lyman Gage, the president of the First National Bank in Chicago, illustrated the overrepresentation of the Old Midwest, the manufacturing South, and the border states to the exclusion of the West. Only three delegates came from the West as defined in this study, with two others from Texas. The commission itself had its roots in Indianapolis, where the Indianapolis Monetary Convention met in late 1896 with representatives from the West as we have defined it.[177] J. N. Dolley, the bank commissioner of Kansas, in a 1911 speech to other bank supervisors, supported the Sound Money League's goals of "co-operation, not dominant centralization" of the system and "full independence of the individual bank."[178] No clearer statement of antibranch sentiment could have come forth, and the domination of the unit-banking states ensured that branch banking, although recommended as an aspect of broader monetary reform, would not survive. While the Gold Standard Act, which eventually resulted from these and other meetings and lobbying, attempted to provide the West and South with more money by making the issue of notes by national banks more profitable, by 1902 "when it became clear . . . that country bankers would not tolerate branch banking [the consensus of the Indianapolis Monetary Convention] dissolved.[179]

While it is clear the "country" unit bankers doomed branch banking, the influence of western country bankers—and certainly their intentions— are less clearly understood. For example, monetary reform groups sprang up like summer weeds, but New Yorkers dominated the New York Chamber of Commerce Reform Committee, and another committee appointed by the American Bankers Association excluded bankers west of Iowa.[180]

As a result of those groups' efforts, national sentiment coalesced around supporting some type of central bank. But westerners' reasons for supporting such an institution were different from those of their eastern brethren.[181] National branch banking offered a solution to each criticism, but the obstacles in its path loomed too great. Critics—especially the Populists—sought to deemphasize New York's control over the nation's money supply, while easterners, exemplified by Thomas Woodlock, editor of the *Wall Street Journal*, and, later, Frank Vanderlip of National City Bank, blamed "country bank money" for the nation's problems.[182] Charles Dawes, who became comptroller of the currency in 1898, helped to kill a branch-banking bill otherwise destined to become a provision in the Gold Standard Act, and further promoted lower capitalizations for national and state banks. In turn, as Eugene White has pointed out, this created an army of new unit banks and "a more vigorous antibranching lobby. . . ."[183] It also ensured that there would be more small banks. White determined that in a vicious circle, antibranching sentiment helped to keep banks from joining the Federal Reserve system, and in turn these small banks were more likely to fail.[184] But if they survived, they would join the unit banks in opposing branching.

By failing to permit branching by national banking in any state, the government had predisposed potential bankers to avoid the benefits of the national system in favor of the otherwise more lenient state laws. Not only were capitalizations lower, but state legislation usually permitted real-estate lending on first mortgages and removed portfolio restrictions that national laws placed on banks. Panics persuaded state lawmakers to raise requirements so that by 1909 many states' reserve requirements conformed to the national laws (see table 3.3). The deposit guaranty laws that appeared after the panic of 1907 also created an advantage for state charters, and states "that adopted deposit insurance schemes saw their banking systems grow at a rapid rate while the national banks in their domain tended to stagnate."[185]

DEPOSIT INSURANCE

While many western states were content to let banks remain uninsured, others made compulsory insurance part of their reforms. Perhaps no state embraced the concept of deposit insurance more enthusiastically than did Nebraska. William Jennings Bryan had presented a bill to the U.S. Congress for a national deposit insurance fund in 1893, and Nebraskans lost no time after the panic of 1907 in passing a state deposit insurance law, aided by the efforts of state registrar Charles W. Pool. Nebraska had passed a widespread banking law in 1909 that "defined banking as a quasi-public business subject to regulation and control," and required all banks

Table 3.3   National and State Bank Reserve Requirements on Demand Deposits, 1895 and 1909

	County	Reserve City	Central Reserve City	
National Bank	15 (3/5)	25 (1/2)	25 (0)	

	1895		1909	
State Banks	Country Banks	Reserve Agent	Country Banks	Reserve Agent
Arizona	0	0	15 (3/5)	designated
California	0	0	15 (3/5)	designated
Colorado	0	0	15 (3/5)	designated
Idaho	0	0	15 (1/2)	designated
Kansas	20 (1/2)	designated	20 (3/4)	25 (3/5)
Montana	20 (1/2)	designated	15 (any)	designated
Nebraska	15 (1/3)	designated	15 (3/5)	20 (3/5)
Nevada	0	0	15 (2/3)	designated
New Mexico	0	0	15 (3/5)	designated
North Dakota	20 (1/2)	designated	20 (3/5)	designated
Oklahoma	0	0	20 (2/3)	25 (2/3)
Oregon	0	0	15 (2/3)	25 (2/3)
South Dakota	20 (1/2)	designated	20 (1/2)	25 (1/2)
Utah	0	0	15 (any)	20 (any)
Washington	0	0	20 (any)	designated
Wyoming	0	0	0	0

Source: Eugene Nelson White, *The Regulation and Reform of the American Banking System, 1900–1929* (Princeton, N.J.: Princeton University Press, 1983), pp. 30–31.

to obtain corporate charters.[186] Its most ambitious proposal, the establishment of a guaranty fund for depositors, represented the triumph of an idea that had met with defeat in 1897, 1899, 1905, and 1907 (plus Bryan's failed national bill). Nebraska followed the lead of its neighbor, Oklahoma, which had enacted a similar law in late 1907, although a court test case was pending at the time Nebraska acted (in 1911 the U.S. Supreme Court ruled that states did have the authority to enact such legislation).[187] Kansas, North and South Dakota, and Washington all followed suit with their own deposit-insurance laws (see table 3.4), although North Dakota bankers strongly resisted their legislation. Under the Nebraska law, the state guaranty fund assessed banks on the basis of capital for capitalization of the fund. It also authorized special assessments if the fund fell too low.

Table 3.4 Characteristics of Early State Deposit Insurance Systems

State	Date of Legislation	Participation	First Assessment	Annual Assessment	Deposits Insured	Payment	Captial Ratio	Limit on Interest Rates	Advertising
Oklahoma	1907	Compulsory	1% of deposits	To maintain fund	All	Immediately	None	3%	Permitted
	1909	Compulsory	1% of deposits	0.25% of deposits	All	Immediately	Deposits limited to 10 times capital and surplus	3%	Permitted but penalty for advertising state protection
Kansas	1909	Voluntary	$500 cash or bonds for each $100,000 deposits	0.05% of deposits	All	6% bonds provided until bank liquidation	Deposits limited to 10 times capital and surplus	3%	Permitted but penalty for advertising state protection
Washington	1917	Voluntary	$1000 cash or bonds for each $100,000 deposits	0.5 of deposits	All	Upon liquidation of bank's assets	Deposits limited to 20 times capital	Set by Guaranty Board	Permitted but penalty for advertising state protection
Nebraska	1909	Compulsory	1% of deposits	0.1% of deposits	All	When receiver determines deficiency	Investments limited to 8 times capital and surplus	None	Permitted
South Dakota	1909	Voluntary	0.1% of deposits	0.1% of deposits	All	When receiver determines deficiency	Deposits limited to 15 times capital and surplus	5%	No provision
	1915	Compulsory	0.25 of deposits	0.25 of deposits	All	Unchanged	Unchanged	5%	Limited
North Dakota	1917	Compulsory	0.05% of deposits	0.05% of deposits	All	When receiver determines deficiency	Deposits limited to 10 times capital and surplus	4%	No provision

Source: Eugene Nelson White, The Regulation and Reform of the American Banking System, 1900–1929 (Princeton, N.J.: Princeton University Press, 1983) pp. 210–211.

Later, another mechanism was established for dealing with failed banks so that the guaranty fund would not be tapped.

Certainly not all Nebraska bankers acquiesced in the creation of the fund. Silas Burnham of First National Bank of Lincoln, for example, vehemently criticized the plan. The Nebraska Bankers Association filed suit to challenge the constitutionality of the law, but failed in the aforementioned case. By 1926, the state referred actively to the fund in its "booster" material, claiming the fund had given the state's banks a new level of stability.[188] One option remained for the larger Nebraska banks if they wished to avoid the compulsory insurance: join the national system. Indeed, in some cases, the insurance fund only encouraged officers to close state banks or savings banks, or merge them into national institutions. This was the case with First Savings Bank of Lincoln, which merged into First National Bank in that city.[189] Kansas bankers also established a competing private deposit insurance fund, subscribed to by about one hundred banks, and South Dakota's law "was so formed that *it has not been used* [by 1914]" (emphasis added).[190] Like Kansas and South Dakota, Washington offered voluntary insurance, and thus "avoided these battles."[191] Washington's deposit fund never came close to meeting the liability of the members' deposits, and although it eventually paid off the $9 million in unpaid deposits that remained from banks that failed in the early 1920s, most member banks withdrew and the legislature repealed the law in 1929.

Most of the ill effects of the deposit insurance laws returned to roost with banks during the troubled 1920s, and thus we address them in the following chapter. Nevertheless, seen in the context of the birth of the regulatory era, the deposit guaranty funds represented important tradeoffs against other types of regulatory regimes. Legislators frequently viewed deposit insurance as a tradeoff against branching. The concept often prevented branching—indeed, reversed it in Washington's case—and otherwise helped weak banks to stay in business. The insurance schemes also encouraged weak new banks to commence operations. That was particularly true in Nebraska, where the State Department of Banking failed to oppose any new charters, and several new institutions joined the ranks in the already overbanked state. Finally, depositors no longer had an interest in good bank management, because they stood to get their money back anyway, and estimates put the losses under the Nebraska system at $20 million.[192] Deposit insurance could never solve the most pressing problem, "limiting the size of single risks," the problem branching met so easily.[193]

ADJUSTING TO REGULATION

As the era of regulation dawned, the frontier practices gradually disappeared. New attitudes predominated. No longer was the law to be avoided or deliberately broken; instead, bankers shifted from physical symbols of safety and their own reputations to a more ostentatious adherence to established public rules and procedures. In that way they continued to hold the public trust that had once been maintained only by reputation and symbol, although buildings and safes would remain as critical statements of a bank's condition well into the 1930s. Nevertheless, at an increasing rate, those troubled banks that did not take regulations in general and examiners in particular seriously found themselves under a barrage of threats.

Such a change is evident in the books of Utah Commercial and Savings Bank and in the letters of its president, William F. Armstrong. As early as 1905, the examiner had noticed executive overdrafts in the bank, writing Armstrong to "call [his] attention again to past due and overdrawn a/cs and notes. . . ." He concluded that the bank had between $60,000 and $70,000 in "bad loans," and insisted that "some changes must be made at once."[194] The bank's condition, in the eyes of the secretary of state, was so poor that he warned Armstrong and the board of directors that "an assessment of at least 25% upon the capital stock of the bank is necessary."[195] Moreover, by February 1906, the authorities grew irritated that the bank no longer responded to their letters. The bank collapsed soon thereafter, and a creditor wrote in June 1914 that, "As for the Utah Commercial & Savings account, there is absolutely no prospects [sic] at present of ever paying it."[196] Likewise, Colorado National Bank noticed the "after 1893, the bank examiners' reports began to be more critical. . .," a statement applicable to all western banks.[197] South Dakota banker William Pease, knowing that his bank would not pass an examination during the panic of 1907, "used to watch the train [arrive] to see if the bank examiners got off," while others, such as Andrew J. Davis, the president of First National Bank of Butte, Montana, took a more aggressive stance, telling a federal examiner who criticized the bank's paper: "If you do not like that paper we will throw in our national bank charter and start business tomorrow as a state bank."[198] Wyoming examiners harassed cashiers, trying to eliminate overdrafts. One Wyoming cashier, W. J. Thom of First National Bank of Buffalo, observed that a prohibition of overdrafts would effectively eliminate 25 percent of all the bank's customers.[199] Elsewhere, however, examiners found themselves severely constrained by their budgets. Montana examiner William Hodnell reported in 1902 that the examiners kept from exceeding their budgets only through "the courtesy of railroads in granting passes."[200]

Collecting, always the single most common problem in the routine of banking, grew even more serious under the watchful eyes of federal and state regulators. Loans to individuals whose credit and character had been without question suddenly came under scrutiny. Creditors so harassed debtors and receivers of the bank that one responded to threats by writing:

"Leave me alone and I will do the best that can be done. . . . I have sweat all the Blood over the matter that I am going to. . . ."[201]

Part of the increased emphasis on collecting stemmed from new organizational practices of larger banks, which by the early 1900s had become highly professionalized businesses. Utah banking house McCornick and Company paid its president, W. S. McCornick, a salary of $15,000 a year and its cashier $5,000.[202] In return for salaries such as these, bankers had to possess an increasingly greater level of expertise, experience, and training, much of it gained through apprenticeships of a sort. Professional people, receiving big salaries, had to make tough business decisions. Much of the style associated with one-man banks went by the boards. Increasingly, bank boards of directors, more than the president, set the lending program. McCornick and Company's directors' minutebooks offer an interesting look at routine meetings during less-than-routine times. Meeting in May 1910, the directors discussed "General conditions, both locally and throughout the country," and decided that "until the feeling of pessimism now prevailing . . . was overcome . . . the bank should *curtail loans as much as possible. This policy was urged upon the officers*" (emphasis added). Directors analyzed local conditions ("the scarcity of locally was accounted for largely by the fact that very little money had been received this year by the wool growers"), and real-estate transactions (purchase of stock in the bank's building). The officers, at another meeting, "read the new banking laws for the benefit of the directors." In compliance with the law, the bank appointed a loan committee, marking the first time the officers had come under special scrutiny. This committee regularly examined the loans and investments of the bank, and recommended that certain loans be charged off (i.e., written off as uncollectible), or that others be bolstered with additional security.[203] Elsewhere, bankers gradually learned the new rules of the game. At the Citizens State Bank in Chouteau, Montana, owners Freeman Johnson and Fred Althern paid dearly for their mistakes. In 1915 when farmers came to the bank to take care of their obligations, the owners told them to "pay all their other bills first, and if they had any money left they could pay the bank. If not, the bank would carry them over."[204] The following year, when the crops remained poor and the farmers could not pay, the bank closed. Many other bankers watched and learned, modernizing their practices in the process.

But the small-town bankers still hung on in many parts of the West. William Pease, of Wagner, South Dakota, typified the small-town banker at the turn of the century. He began work at First National Bank in his mid-teens at a salary of twenty-five dollars a month. His chores included work "on the remittance registers, presenting sight drafts, running errands and so forth." Pease moved to Wagner, where he "was installed as Cashier of the Commercial State Bank . . . on the munificent sum of $40 per month." He and his wife lived in temporary rooms in the bank. Pease decided to "learn as much as possible about banking, and I set about learning the business as thoroughly as I ever tried to learn anything. The salary didn't interest me. . . ." The assistant cashier was a woman, Rose Kaberna, and her pay as assistant nearly equaled that of Pease.[205]

The new cashier noted with some amusement that people "attributed to me more wealth than I had or ever though of possessing." This perception put Pease at a disadvantage "and made it hard . . . to meet the requests and demands made upon me in a personal way." Friends expected special favors, but to Pease, banking was strictly business: "I knew loans had to be made if the bank was to make money and I studied the value of the things our customers dealt in. . . . I knew from day to day the price of hogs . . . of various grades of cattle . . . and the value of land." Pease harbored no illusions about borrowers, and once on intuition refused a properly endorsed check from a stranger, learning a few days later that the man was a swindler. He still essentially ran a one-person bank, making lending decisions himself after obtaining information from his directors, and prided himself on the "caution of his inexperience."[206] (Such practices occasionally had bizarre results: according to a veteran Montana banker, local inexperienced bankers had somewhat arbitrarily set an interest rate of 12 percent because it was easy to compute at the rate of 1 percent per month. When one of them suddenly reduced his rate to 10 percent, it set off a scramble as bankers tried to obtain books with interest tables in them.)[207]

Much of the bank's business came from real-estate loans, which received a boost in 1903 when Congress passed the Inherited Indian Land Act. If an inheritor of Native American land had died, that land, after a trustee period of twenty-five years, went onto the open market, wherein non-Natives usually purchased it. As Pease noted, that meant business for land agents and brokers "which, of course, included banks." The president of Commercial State Bank, Albert Boynton, set out to handle these lands "for the double purpose of making money . . . and of getting the lands into the hands of people who would put them under cultivation. Indeed, Pease engaged in "farming by proxy" when he associated with energetic young farmers in remote spots of the state. Pease's bank had an advantage in these proceedings, because Boynton's father, Abraham, had been the U.S. Land Office registrar in Mitchell, South Dakota, and had passed his knowledge on to his son. Even so, the other bank in Wagner also did land business, and Pease admitted that "contrary to prevailing opinion at the time, the profit in handling the inherited Indian land was not large." The bank always had a customer before it purchased land, and the real long-term profits came from "getting the land into the hands of people who would cultivate it," including farmers from Nebraska. Pease vehemently denied any collusion to fix the price of land, but the bidders all understood the value of the land and bid accordingly. However, the superintendent of the Indian Agency often held the closed deeds and presented batches of them at one time for payment—"a nerve wrecking business for the two banks at Wagner."[208]

The bank also granted advances to Native Americans who had sold lands, but the government ruled that land funds needed to be deposited in designated government depositories, with the nearest one to Wagner being the national banks in Sioux City, Iowa. Consequently, banks that had loaned money had to obtain the approval of an Indian agent before they could collect, and in many cases found they could not collect at all. Inspectors sent by the government to see that banks were not swindling Native Americans added another layer to the examiners who scurried through the banks' records. Bankers claimed that perfectly good notes they had obtained from Native Americans to cash were being ruled fraudulent by the inspectors. Pease acknowledged that those doing business with Native Americans had not always treated them fairly, but he personally disclaimed any unfair treatment and steadfastly insisted that losses associated with such business offset gains.

Western country bankers, as epitomized by Pease, had a somewhat different role from that of their city colleagues. According to the South Dakota cashier, "A country banker is expected to be advisor, councillor, custodian, salesman and, above all, diplomat." Expected to know the law, the banker gave advice "on almost every financial and personal subject brought to him." Compared to the formalized proceedings at the city banks such as McCornick and Company, the affairs of the Commercial State Bank seem remarkably relaxed. Pease essentially ran the bank, making almost all lending decisions and even suggesting distribution of dividends. Most country banks would maintain this informal and comfortable atmosphere for at least three more decades. City banks had already undergone a transition, however, and their practices increasingly dictated the operations of independent country banks. Individuals such as Imbolden, Seaberg, and Pease were gradually being replaced by the Albaughs, Palens, and Millses. Pease, during his twelve years at Commercial State Bank, noticed these changes. A chain bank had moved into town, and he noted that the cashier "had practically nothing to do with making loans." The banker, he lamented, had been reduced to one who "did nothing but cash checks. . . ."[209] As a result, an impersonal board of directors slowly replaced the familiar cashier as the symbol of authority in banks.

While bankers learned the management skills necessary to operate in the new environment, and while they had seen their ranks professionalized in a number of ways, they still relied on some of the traditional symbols of safety that had sustained them for thirty years. As the nation lumbered toward the creation of the Federal Reserve system, the banking system, from the government regulators to the individual bank organizations, had developed a much more professional, bureaucratic, and removed air. Creation of clearinghouses had proved an insufficient stopgap to broader reform, especially widespread adoption of branch banking, and the growing influence of the bankers' associations in shaping western legislation illustrated the recognition on the part of bankers that the period of frontier banking had passed. Internal changes within the banks that governed lending and investments marked the final admission that western banking had entered a new era.

4

MAKING THE LOCAL BANKERS THE GOATS: REGULATION AND RECESSION, 1913–1939

Regulation that everyone looked to as a solution to the ills of the old system did not correct them or prevent the rise of new threats. Among the old problems that reappeared were unavailability of credit for a growing economy, and a system which proved helpless in the face of widespread bank runs. New problems included the financing of World War I, a rash of bank robberies facilitated by the advent of automobiles, and the appearance on the scene of overzealous and occasionally incompetent examiners. A more significant failure of the new regulations was that they exacerbated existing weaknesses that ultimately devastated the entire financial system of many western states.

With the creation of the Federal Reserve system, most Americans would have predicted a new era of stability and safety. Twenty years later they would not only look back to see the carnage of unprecedented bank failures, but also would find that institutions that once defied robberies now suffered a plague of them. Except for the patriotic boost bankers felt through their efforts during World War I, western financiers had few victories and numerous defeats from 1913 to 1939. Nevertheless, bankers survived the darkest period in their history and in the process produced leaders who shaped the direction of banking in the region, some of whom attained national prominence: A. P. Giannini, Marriner Eccles, George Wingfield, and Walter Bimson. Other western bankers who found positions of leadership at the regional and national level, include Lewis Douglas, Joseph Sartori, George Eccles, and Carl Bimson, although their impact cannot be compared to that of the "big four." Overall, the West entered the Second World War poised on the brink of unparalleled expansion, and the changes wrought by the Depression in no small way contributed to the financial rebirth of the West after the war.

Bankers especially retained and improved upon their chief symbol of safety, the bank building, in the early 1900s. Many major institutions entered the first decades of the twentieth century by constructing bigger and more elaborate facilities, all still characterizing the banks as stable and impregnable, and focusing on the vault as the ultimate guardian of depositors' money. Between 1900 and 1920, new banking houses were constructed by Wells Fargo (San Francisco, 1911), Colorado National Bank (1915), Farmers and Merchants National Bank (1905), the Bank of California (1908), the Bank of Italy (1908), Security Savings Bank and Trust Company (1906), First National Bank of Denver (1911), First National Bank of Lincoln (1911), Ladd and Tilton Bank, Portland (1911), and First National Bank of Portland (1916), to name a few.[1] According to one bank architect, banks needed to be large, especially the interior of the buildings, because "Every foot added means another foot in the public space [and] banks grow by increasing their contact with the public."[2] These buildings proved more elaborate and ornate than their predecessors, replete with huge columns and decorated facades on the exterior, and expensive art, murals, and fine furniture inside.[3]

They also showed some schizophrenia about placement of officers and teller. The traditional western values of democracy and openness placed an officer in the main lobby, sometimes in the very center. This floor plan detracted from the new image of a professional manager, and consequently a second general floor plan appeared with ever greater frequency, one in which the officers were physically removed from routine business. With the growth of deposit-box business, banks found it increasingly difficult to provide a public view of the vault and free access to the deposit boxes. Thus, another symbol of safety gradually received less emphasis, although common plans still placed the vault area to the back of the building, permitting at least some inspection by the public. Practicality forced some changes, with banks such as First National Bank of Portland moving their vaults to a basement location, but usually bankers followed the advice of Alfred Hopkins, a premier bank architect, who recommended that the vault be at "the point of highest visibility," even to the extent that a clock was put over it in one instance.[4] By 1913, bank buildings and vaults looked more impregnable than ever.

WORLD WAR I

World War I presented new opportunities and challenges for western bankers. Deposits increased by more than $40 million, and banks focused their energies on agricultural and farm loans. Increased agricultural prosperity caused deposits in Lincoln, Nebraska, to double during the war years. Other western banks played key roles in the U.S. war effort, especially in bond sales. Confusion, naturally, marked the period before the U.S. became involved. North Dakota bank examiner J. R. Waters warned the cashier of Bismarck National Bank: "There is a movement on foot [sic] solely on the part of some very few rabid men, to spread false rumors that the government intends to confiscate bank accounts of all Germans in case of war."[5] The cashier was also advised to protect against a run. Once the war actually began, banks embarked on an energetic program of selling bonds and war savings stamps, and lending to farmers or miners for increased production. These Liberty Loan drives always featured bankers in the forefront, and western states oversubscribed on a regular basis. During the second loan drive in 1917, Oklahomans subscribed to $35 million in bonds, helping to push the Tenth Federal Reserve District over its goal, while Montanans' total purchase of bonds exceeded the state's allocation by 50 percent.[6]

To facilitate bond sales, the U.S. Treasury established the Denver branch of the Federal Reserve Bank of Kansas City in 1918, as a concession to the Colorado and Wyoming bankers who wanted the Federal Reserve city to be Denver. Local bankers participated in the loan drives, with Harold Kountze chairing both the Denver and the state Liberty Loan drives and serving as treasurer of the War Works Fund.[7]

Some banks, such as Peoples Savings Bank of Seattle, saw the bonds as a valuable investment, purchasing over $2.39 million worth of government securities.[8] Arizona's economy, already booming from wartime copper demand, spread to the banks "a happy condition of prosperity."[9] The state's loan drives always succeeded to the extent that the government continued to increase Arizona's quota on each drive. Charles Woolf of Tempe National Bank was the chairman of one loan drive and Dr. Alex Chandler, who had founded the Bank of Chandler, leased ten thousand acres of his land to the Goodyear Company for its wartime cotton production.[10] Others had less shining credentials: Montana banker Charles Kelly, of the Daley Bank, headed the Montana Council of Defense, which saw its primary duty as seeking out traitors, and one of the councils' targets, A. J. Just, president of the Bank of Ashland, actually had to stand trial for violation of the Sedition Act of 1917.[11]

Three Arizona bankers got even more directly involved in the war by going to France as officials in the distribution network of the International Red Cross. William H. Brophy and J. S. "Rawhide Jimmy" Douglas, co-founders of the Bank of Bisbee and the Bank of Douglas, and Thomas Collins, an energetic investor in bank stocks, all worked in France until the end of the war, with Douglas developing a close friendship with French president Georges Clemenceau. Douglas even named a bank and a mining town after Clemenceau.[12]

New Kinds of Crime

The end of the war should have signaled western bankers that tough times lay ahead, but they hardly expected trouble to come in the form of bank robberies. Despite the appearance of security, to a greater extent than ever before banks proved susceptible to robbery, for the advent of the automobile gave thieves unprecedented advantages over lawmen. Easily followed horseshoe tracks gave way to invisible trails on well-travelled roads, and without prior knowledge of the direction of escape—something most criminals did not routinely discuss—the pursuing posses found that their adversaries had insurmountable head starts. Primitive radio communications could not offset the advantage of speed held by the robbers. Numbers of holdups soared: in Oklahoma, sixty to seventy-five banks were robbed annually in the 1920s.[13] Oklahoma banks suffered fifty-four heists in 1924 alone.[14] Not only did the numbers rise, but thieves attained an increasing level of publicity, which was exactly what the nineteenth-century bankers had dreaded, namely, widespread suspicion that banks were not safe. Some robbers even achieved notoriety to the extent that romantic legends developed, with Bonnie and Clyde in the 1930s topping the list. Robberies thus struck at the foundations of banking in three ways: first, they depleted the funds of the bank; second, they undermined the image of security that banks had worked so hard to cultivate; and third, they forced private insurers, with whom banks insured their deposits and buildings (against robberies only), to drive up prices.

South Dakota banks in the late 1920s complained about insurance rates with regularity, but Oklahoma bankers had witnessed drastic leaps in coverage. From 1924 to 1925, robbery insurance rates for Oklahoma banks jumped 100 percent. Then, from January to April of 1925, they shot up another 500 percent.[15] One insurance company demanded that full-time guards be placed in all the banks that his company insured.[16] Kansas, Oklahoma, and South Dakota, which had a particularly bad time protecting their rural banks, made a crusade out of stopping thieves, largely copying the programs adopted in Iowa. Eugene Gum, the director of the Oklahoma Bankers Association (OBA) not only hired special agents from the Burns Detective Agency, as well as other independent agents, but followed the Kansas Bankers Association in organizing vigilante groups. By October 1925, one-third of the counties in Oklahoma had fully armed rifle groups, some with over one hundred men in the ranks. Gum had researched the effect of such groups in Kansas and especially Iowa, where the statewide robbery rate fell to three per year and insurance rates dropped by three-fourths after the Iowa vigilantes were organized.[17] The program apparently worked in the Sooner State, which saw its robberies cut by two-thirds after Gum's efforts. Gum also helped develop the "town guard" network, whereby armed guards near a bank were secretly signaled electronically during robbery attempts. The guards prepared an ambush when the bandits left the bank. By mid-1929 only twelve "town guard" banks had been hit, and only two of those successfully.[18]

South Dakota banker Marcus P. Beebe, from Ipswich, who chaired the South Dakota Bankers Association's "protective committee," also single-mindedly sought to end bank robberies. In his state, ten robberies or break-ins had occurred in less than a year in 1920–21.[19] Often, however, he found his efforts ill-funded or not well received. The Burns Detective Agency, in response to Beebe's plea for help, urged the association to "protect [yourselves] by careful handling of the money," and further advised that banks ask nearby merchants to "keep a gun in their stores" and buy buckshot for their neighbor merchants.[20] (Nevada banker George Wingfield, at times a skinflint, insisted that all banks in his chain keep a shotgun "for instant use in the bank," and to that end he distributed shotguns and shells to every cashier, for which he later billed them.)[21] Beebe, whose extensive correspondence with detectives and law enforcement agencies betrayed his frustration at not being more actively involved, in 1921 had appointed sixteen additional police on behalf of the South Dakota Bankers Association and had standardized a system of reporting holdups. His committee put out a "protective bulletin" that detailed the comings and goings of known convicts, publicized recent con games operating in the area, and listed stolen bonds and bad checks.[22] Over the years, the con artists used a number of remarkable tricks: one gem involved a preacher who provided partners with information on targets, and another scam, reported by the North Dakota Bankers Association in 1930, involved a "bank bandit 'mob' " that used a unique scam featuring a legless advance man who used begging as a front to draw attention away from the entry of the thieves.[23] More important, the committee established rewards for killing or capturing bank robbers. South Dakota seems to have been plagued more than other western states. In 1928 an Idaho banker told a local newspaper that in the preceeding five years his state had averaged just one robbery per year. He compared Idaho to Iowa, where, he claimed, five times as many robberies had occurred over the same period, and South Dakota topped Iowa.[24]

Beebe's procedures achieved at least some measure of success. W. S. Gordon of Burns Detective Agency proudly reported that "more bandits have been killed in South Dakota during the past year than in any other state.[25] Yet bank heists continued to such a degree that as late as 1929 the South Dakota Bankers Association had adopted a thousand-dollar reward for information on robberies.[26] Ultimately, however, Beebe's committee balked at covering non–member banks, because the overall reduction in crime carried with it an obvious free-rider problem. So South Dakota continued to suffer. The crime increase, however, afflicted all western states, and few had more useful solutions than the South Dakota bankers, although occasionally attempts to suppress robberies succeeded with unexpected results. One bandit, his face covered with a burlap bag, yielded his weapon—a pitchfork—when confronted by a sheriff.[27] And in 1928, two brigands held up a bank in Clarksdale, Arizona, and during their escape had the misfortune to encounter seventy-year-old deputy sheriff John Roberts. In Dirty Harry fashion, Roberts pulled his revolver and blasted one thug in the head, then shot out one of the tires on the car, which swerved madly until it crashed and knocked the other bandit unconscious. Sheriff John calmly proclaimed, "wasn't nothin' to it."[28] Amusing as some aspects of these attempts may have been, they underscored the threat posed to the symbols of safety, and bankers scrambled for ways to recapture the image by installing warning buzzers, adding security guards, and even putting in tear-gas-firing guns above tellers' windows.[29]

Perhaps as damaging as bold-daylight robberies were to the image of banks, an equally insidious unseen enemy also was at work: white-collar crime. A typical incident involved the new assistant to the auditor hired in 1927 at Peoples Savings Bank (later PeoplesBank) in Seattle. This new assistant noted that the senior auditor conducted a great deal of after-hours work and became suspicious. Doing some after-hours work of his own, the assistant learned that over a period of several years the auditor had appropriated $75,000 for his own use. The enterprising auditor paid for his unauthorized loan with two years in prison.[30] A more sophisticated fraud, by officers of Northwestern National Bank in Portland, bled that institution of $800,000. And in addition to run-of-the-mill embezzling, shaving, and false bookkeeping, bank employees found that cohabitation with politicians offered unique and rewarding avenues for padding their income. One of the most famous episodes of a bank/political scandal occurred in George Wingfield's Nevada banking chain when one of his cashiers, H. C. Clapp of Carson Valley Bank, became involved in fraud.[31]

On April 27, 1927, George Cole, the former Nevada state controller, and Ed Malley, the current state treasurer, met with George Wingfield in Reno.[32] They disclosed that $516,322 in state funds was missing from Carson Valley Bank, which Wingfield owned, and that they and Clapp had taken the money, which they had sunk into a speculative oil venture. Wingfield had recently discharged Clapp for sloppy work related a drinking problem, and no doubt Clapp had wished to get even. It is also clear, though, that a year before the confession by Cole and Malley, Wingfield suspected the cashier was a risk (although he apparently never suspected him of criminal activity). In a letter to Wingfield dated well before the news of the defalcations became public, Clapp admitted he had fallen into heavy debt covering the overdrafts of a friend (as he claimed) when the two of them had invested in stocks. Wingfield may have doubted the existence of the friend, and he certainly had no sympathy for such activities on the part of one of his cashiers. Wingfield demanded weekly reports from Clapp "explaining the details of every loan made through the week. . . ."[33] The Reno banker received similar reports from his other cashiers, which already exceeded the information most bank presidents would receive, so he had not singled out Clapp. But it is clear that Wingfield had his eye on the Carson Valley cashier.

Cole, Malley, and Clapp had worked their scam on the state as well as on the bank, and had successfully perpetrated their crime since 1919, issuing fraudulent cashier's checks that Clapp paid out a little at a time. Regardless of the incremental disappearance of funds, the *Reno Evening Gazette* found it astonishing that "one-half million dollars of the peoples' money could be lifted . . . and replaced by paper which may prove worthless."[34] Of course, that was not the case, as Wingfield responded by personally depositing $600,000 in Carson Valley Bank to prevent a run, and his dollars were as green as the state's. Clapp turned state's evidence following his arrest, making Cole and Malley's chances for acquittal nil, despite strained attempts by the defense attorney (and political boss) Pat McCarran. In an ironic twist, McCarran's defense of Cole and Malley hinged on implicating the bank—especially Wingfield—but in the process McCarran exposed the unrelated corruption of Gilbert Ross, the bank examiner who had investigated Carson Valley Bank.[35] Under questioning, Clapp acknowledged that the bank allowed Ross some $6,900 in overdrafts, not because he was in on the plot but simply because he was the examiner. Wingfield's bank eventually agreed to pay 50 percent more than the law required—almost $155,000 against a required bond of $100,000—yet he earned the enmity of redistributionists who thought he should have covered the entire amount. It is ironic that while some historians (McCarran's biographer, for example) thought Wingfield schemed to avoid paying for the state's losses by not going beyond what the law required, the Reno banker won praise from other financiers, including important bankers outside Nevada, who correctly understood that he had prevented a major panic. Frederick Kiesel of California National Bank praised Wingfield's "magnanimous action" that protected Carson Valley Bank.[36]

The Carson Valley Bank episode exposed several problems with which western regulators had not yet come to grips. First, the public had increasingly been squeezed out as a regulatory force, and the emphasis instead on investigations by impartial examiners had made bank activities more than ever a "secret" business understood by only a few experts. Thus, ironically, regulations designed to make banks more open to public scrutiny actually removed them even further from view, while at the same time citizens reassured themselves that someone was watching the banks. Second, the process of public regulation inevitably made banking more political than ever before in the West. Regulators and examiners, political appointees, could not help but be influenced by party bosses. Third, as could be predicted, the regulators added yet another level to the gradually expanding layers of bureaucracy that separated the public from the bankers—a layer that itself proved in need of policing, as Ross showed. Yet examiners could no more expect to successfully police all banks in the 1920s than they could in the 1890s. The North Dakota Banking Board admitted in 1917 that reports to the examiners showed that many banks were "grossly violating" state banking laws.[37] L. Q. Skelton, the chief bank examiner in Montana in the 1920s, found that in 1921, out of 227 state banks, 181 had not undergone an examination in the last year. Worse, he did not have a sufficient budget to hire eight new examiners to replace those who resigned.[38] Thus, at the same time examiners in different areas could simultaneously demonstrate incompetence and oppressiveness, partisanship and scrupulous dedication. Those constituted the growing pains of any regulatory system. The more significant problems, however, emerged from public perceptions of banks once the regulators assumed responsibility for the system's safety, even in the crudest sense. In one sense, regulators and examiners joined academics as the new experts whose special knowledge of banks' conditions further added to the inability of the public to decipher bank reports.[39] In the citizen's mind, the bank reports took on an aura of mystery, further convincing depositors to leave them in the hands of the specialists. If the experts vouched for the institution's safety, then who could doubt it? Because the law required increased public access to bank information, the process had the unintended effect of making that very information increasingly less useful. Moreover, new temptations arose for examiners, depending on the current political winds, to find troubled banks solvent or vice versa. These factors combined to make the reports of examiners in the 1930s suspect, and the procedures instituted on the basis of those reports questionable. It was not the first nor would it be the last time that bank examiners responded to the prevailing political mood.

By the 1930s, almost every western State's banking system had already started to feel the brunt of the agricultural problems that had plagued the region for a decade, although almost every bank in the region had suffered losses in the 1920s. But, with the twenties roaring all around them, even troubled western banks had reason to expect increasing prosperity, and many joined in the boom. For example, U.S. National Bank of Oregon, thanks to the timber and shipbuilding business, entered an auspicious period of growth, taking over two banks that had failed.[40] In Washington, the acceleration of the merger movement pushed up the total bank resources, and the total number of banks would have grown except for the tight grip on new charters by the state regulators.[41] But while some bankers did well, others observed the farmbelt casualties with growing concern. Not only did they face increased crime and see their images of stability sullied by thefts and embezzling, but some areas had entered the worst wave of failures in their financial history. At first, they found it hard to believe that anything could interrupt their region's growth, for bankers optimistically expected farm loans to continue to turn handsome profits even after the war. They also had witnessed the entry and expansion of a powerful new California bank, A. P. Giannini's Bank of Italy. By the 1920s, its success in using California's branch-banking system offered tremendous encouragement to entrepreneurs and immigrants, and evoked considerable optimism about banking growth and stability. Less than twenty years old, the Bank of Italy crystallized new concepts in commercial banking.

Amadeo Peter Giannini, the son of Italian immigrants, moved with his parents to San Francisco in 1881. After his father was murdered, his widowed mother married Lorenzo Scatena, a salesman for a produce commission house. Giannini learned the trade from his stepfather, and even while a teenager excelled at soliciting new customers, who enjoyed working with the tall and energetic young man. The produce farmers learned to trust Giannini, and the firm—Scatena and Company—grew to such an extent that he was able to retire in 1901. The retirement was short-lived: a year later Giannini's stepfather died, leaving him as the manager of the family estate and a director in the Columbus Savings and Loan Society.[42] His opposition to the tight-fisted lending policies of the other directors spurred Giannini into resigning his position and left him with a determination to organize his own bank. The Columbus directors bought out Giannini, as well as his friend Isaias W. Hellman, the president of Wells Fargo, who had an interest in the institution.

Giannini's new venture, the Bank of Italy, which opened in October 1904, though certainly not the first western bank to view the "common man" or the "little fellow" as the bank's most important customer, proved by far the most successful. Over its first fifty or so years, it had a rate of growth of 40 percent compounded annually, or about 5,000-fold. Giannini wanted a bank to help Italians, with employees who spoke Italian. He insisted on broad stock ownership to avoid anyone's having a controlling interest, and designed the lending policies for many small borrowers rather than a few large debtors. By making loans available at lower rates, Giannini's bank stood in perfect position to attract new customers after the 1906 earthquake and fire. Giannini even accepted passbooks of other banks as collateral on loans—he would lend double the amount anyone had on deposit elsewhere if the borrower made a commitment to rebuild in San Francisco.

The bank also advertised heavily and unconventionally, even using door-to-door soliciting. Innovative and restless, Giannini constantly prodded the bank toward more daring ventures—highway construction, school children's accounts, and the staple of its lending, agriculture—while simultaneously forging a branch-banking network unparalleled in the West.[43]

Within its first year the bank had resources of over $1 million and in 1907 it opened its first branch. At the time, A. P. Giannini was only thirty-seven years old, but he single-mindedly pursued his vision of a stable banking empire built on branching. He conceived of a farm-lending institution able to shift its resources internally, according to the seasonal growing needs of different areas. Two years later, the first non–San Francisco branch opened in San Jose, but Giannini carefully avoided injecting the Bank of Italy into communities without some local ties. He therefore purchased existing institutions with well-known personnel. Moreover, even before he entered a new area, Giannini walked in rows beside farmers engaged in plowing or went to local merchants advertising the future benefits that the Bank of Italy would bring. The Bank of Italy offered several services that traditional banks did not, including insurance brokerage and property assessment. In the course of this expansion, however, Giannini encountered several foes.

Joseph Sartori, the Los Angeles branch-bank pioneer, and president of Security Trust and Savings, the largest bank in Los Angeles, strongly opposed the Bank of Italy's entry into the city in 1913. Sartori, himself a remarkable success story, had hoped to divide California into "spheres of influence" with the Bank of Italy. Giannini would have none of it. When Giannini looked for a local bank to purchase, he found Park Bank to make into a Bank of Italy branch. Sartori was unsuccessful at keeping Giannini out, but the state government almost prevailed where Sartori had failed.[44]

The California superintendent of banking, William R. Williams, who became Giannini's second-toughest opponent, had attempted to use traditional accounting procedures on the Bank of Italy's expansion. He maintained that a system was only as strong as its weakest branch office. But Giannini expanded so fast that normal procedures could not capture the resilience of his system. Throughout the Bank of Italy's expansion, Williams and other unit bankers raised the specter of a huge monopolistic bank charging high interest rates. In fact, branch banking brought uniformly low rates, as Giannini contended, and the superintendent, looking objectively at the evidence, ultimately agreed to the concept of statewide branching. Williams also gained Giannini's respect, and when Williams resigned from his state post, Giannini offered him the position of cashier at the Bank of

Italy, thus bringing an important legal perspective and administrative experience to the bank.[45]

PROBLEMS IN THE 1920s

The Bank of Italy profited from the agricultural boom generated by World War I, as did all western banks. But warning signs soon appeared on the horizon, and in many areas, business started to slip. The papers of Bismark National Bank reveal some distress in rural areas as early as 1918. One borrower, F. A. Little of Fayette, North Dakota, reported: "The Banks of this section practically cut out making loans last June and . . . collections were exceedingly poor as well as sales in the store. . . ."[46] Whether Little was just another debtor trying to repay his loans is not clear, although by late spring he deluged the board with inventive excuses for not paying his notes. First, he contracted "blood poison," then "Spanish Influenza . . . set all lines of work back for two months," and by 1922, he pleaded helplessness: "I certainly am at your mercy."[47] Parts of the entire northern tier of states suffered from 1918 onward, with the president of American National Bank in Helena, Montana, writing Bismarck National in the summer of 1918 requesting a $10,000 advance. Bismarck National agreed, but noted "money is very close . . . [but we] expect to get some wool money next month."[48] By the fall of that year, the vice president reported: "collections are at a standstill." To Continental and Commercial National Bank of North Dakota, Bismarck National pointed out that although that bank's balances did not qualify it for its requested $25,000 loan, the customer's account had a long solid history, and the loan was approved.[49] During the war, people had borrowed from banks to purchase war bonds, and banks lent freely. The banks tended to maintain this high level of lending after the war, mostly for agriculture. Consequently, even tiny banks such as First National Bank of Vermillion expanded their operations considerably during World War I.[50] But after the war, not only did American farmers continue to produce at wartime levels, their European counterparts soon joined them. Prices fell, and the agricultural sector plunged into depression, joined by mining, which had seen the wartime demand for ore similarly shrink. Except for some Pacific Northwest banks whose primary clients were lumber companies, virtually all of the rural and smaller Western banks suddenly found two groups of their primary borrowers in serious trouble. Sharp, periodic drops in the precipitation rate in several areas added to the woes of farmers and ranchers: two of Wyoming's worst periods of bank failures—1920 and 1924—correlate almost exactly with serious falls in precipitation rates in three principal agricultural regions. Without branching to shift funds from city to country, banks discovered themselves locked into a downward spiral of extending credit to cover farms and mines that were already heavily leveraged. Farm foreclosure rates per thousand owner-operated farms between 1926 and 1930 hit dramatic levels: 70.4 percent in South Dakota, 58 percent in North Dakota, 50 percent in Oklahoma, 42 percent in Arizona and Colorado, 38 percent in Nebraska, and 37.4 percent in Idaho.[51] Yet if the banks foreclosed, the property they acquired fell in value on a daily basis. Beginning in 1920, bankers in the West faced their toughest decade ever, with the early 1920s far worse than the years during the Great Depression itself. Indeed, for many states the period from 1913 to 1941 only set their banking system on a better foundation, due to changes in policy. In that respect, banking in the 1920s acted as a prelude to depression, as western bank failures contributed to the overall drop in the money supply.[52]

Western banks for the sixteen states included in this study numbered 8,092 in 1920. By 1932, there were only 4,036. Wyoming had particularly disastrous years in 1923 and 1924, when twenty-three national banks went out of business, ten of them failures. State banks fell from a total of 133 in 1920 to fifty-seven in 1927, and to 32 by 1936.[53] But each state seemed to have its own trough: between 1920 and 1926, 214 Montana banks went under, bankrupted by the eleven-thousand farms that had been vacated, despite the fact that the Federal Reserve Bank of Minneapolis consistently expanded its credit to Montana banks. From 1920 to 1922 end-of-the-month credit outstanding to Montana banks averaged over $7.5 million.[54] The state was not only the national leader in bankruptcies, it alone in the Union had a population decline. Oregon lost one hundred banks from 1928 to 1932. From mid-1920 to the end of 1921, North Dakota saw thirty-four banks fail, and in 1923 and 1924, over 260 failed each year.[55]

Although declining agricultural prices posed the greatest threat to the northern tier of western states, no one can deny that banks in each unique subregion of the West faced special problems seen in no other area. Montana's bank failures in the 1920s owed the failure of two of their number to the strange circumstances surrounding the Dempsey-Gibbons boxing match held in Shelby on July 4, 1923. The two banks, one in Shelby and one in Great Falls, had extended financial backing based on what appeared to be a guaranteed moneymaker. Indeed, the event proved too popular—with overflow crowds, mobs took over the seating area without paying. The "sure-thing" loans collapsed and with them, the banks. Another Montana banker, a minister, balanced his accounts through prayer, confident "the Lord would take care of him." Yet another Montana banker relied extensively on the deposits of local bootleggers.[56]

Such strange escapades affected the averages somewhat, but contemporaries saw the problem differently. One Federal Reserve Bank agent, writing several years later about the problems in the northern tier states, blamed two classes of factors for the problem: the collapse of agricultural commodity price, and the generous bank chartering policy. The latter afforded "men of inadequate banking training supervised by directorates which had an insufficient knowledge of sound banking principles" too many opportunities to enter banking. Nor did they "realize the end of the pioneer period had come. . . ."[57] Such analysis failed utterly however when directed elsewhere, for not only did small banks fail, but some of the most influential and important institutions, run by individuals of considerable banking acumen, also collapsed. In Oregon, for example, Northwestern National Bank's failure shocked the community. Organized in 1913 by Henry L. Pittock, the publisher of the *Oregonian* and controller of the Portland Trust Company, and his son-in-law Frederick W. Leadbetter, the bank seemed to have a solid capital base. Pittock and Leadbetter installed Emery Olmstead as president, a man whom Pittock had hired in 1910 to manage the Portland Trust Company. Olmstead's friends included the major figures in the Wilcox Investment Company, which by 1919 controlled Ladd and Tilton. He soon brought in James O. Elrod and John E. Wheeler to the Northwestern board, and before long the group maneuvered itself into a position of control. Pittock and his allies panicked: just as the Ladd family was identified with Ladd and Tilton in the public's eye, so Pittock was linked to Northwestern.[58] Not only did the Olmstead-Wheeler group cause concern among insiders, but other Portland bankers, such as Abbot Mills of First National and John C. Ainsworth of U.S. National, watched Northwestern warily. Privately, these bankers noted the poor investments and loans on the bank's books.[59]

At the root of the bank's weakness was Wheeler's McCormick Lumber Company, which had been thrown deeply into the red by the slump in the lumber market. Using Northwestern stock as collateral, he borrowed $100,000 from National City Bank of New York, and at the same time was over half a million dollars in debt to his own lumber company. Wheeler and Olmstead devised an intricate kiting scheme, which itself remained undiscovered for some time, but led to huge cash shortages that a bank examiner detected in February 1927. The examiner, threatening to close the bank immediately, forced the bank to come up with $1 million, all of it from the Pittock estate.[60] The board terminated Olmstead and information surfaced that at least one of the other directors knew about the scheme.

Word spread of Northwestern's weakness, and other Portland bankers expected to have to share at least some of the burden of bailing out the bank, which by March 1927 had $2 million in bad loans. On March 28, a run developed, with depositors "clamoring for their money . . . struggling for their money."[61] Ainsworth and Mills knew that they had to help take care of the $18 million in deposits at Northwestern and protect the $96 million in deposits at First National and U.S. National. Together, officers of the three banks took a steel-eyed look at Northwestern's true condition, and determined that it had $4.5 million in bad notes. The Pittock estate delivered another $2 million, while Northwestern director E. S. Collins and attorney O. L. Price put up another $2 million. The three banks then announced that they would guaranty all deposits, the runs ended, and Northwestern entered into a leisurely liquidation handled by E. C. Sammons of U.S. National. Ainsworth later referred to Price and E. S. Collins as "heroes," but in fact Ainsworth and Abbot Mills had jumped on the grenade, for without their support Northwestern would have failed before April.[62] Although U. S. National increased its deposit rolls by $8 million from Northwestern customers, the bank did not need to expose itself in order to attract depositors who would have eventually changed their accounts. As for the villains in the affair, Wheeler and Olmstead went to prison on fraud convictions.

Still other financial failures rocked Portland in the 1920s, the most serious of which included the Bank of Kenton and the brokerage house of Overbeck and Cooke. But some stabilizing influences appeared, too. San Francisco banker Herbert Fleishacker poured money into successes (a newspaper) and failures (Northwestern). Fleishacker also backed Julius L. Meier (1847–1937) in his purchase of Pacific Bancorp, a holding company of ten banks, in September 1929.[63]

Meier, a furniture merchant and partner in Meier and Frank Company, pioneered the use of outdoor signs in Oregon. An aggressive civic booster, he spearheadeed efforts to bring a world's fair to Portland in 1925. Despite his efforts, the fair did not materialize, in part due to the troubles at Ladd and Tilton. But it pushed Meier to the fore as a civic leader, and his control of Pacific Bancorporation further cemented that image. Frank served as chairman, with George Joseph as secretary, and in late 1929 Meier reorganized the holding company as American National Corporation, with resources of $12 million. He soon immersed himself in his successful 1930 gubernatorial campaign. During Meier's absence, the bank developed several trouble spots. By acquiring Columbia National Bank in 1931, American National became Portland's fourth-largest bank. However, its loan portfolio suffered from the depressed economy, and the acquisition of Columbia left the bank cash poor. By 1932, American National had sunk to the point that Meier needed extensive loans from his family to keep it afloat. Aaron Frank, Meier's nephew, put up most of the money and searched for a buyer, which he found in First National Bank in June 1933.[64] This consolidation enhanced the position of First National, a pioneer institution that bloomed as well as any bank could during the depression.

CONSOLIDATIONS IN THE 1930s

Like Northwestern National, several bank "failures" of the 1930s actually represented final liquidations of banks that were all but dead in the 1920s.

From 1922 to 1930 in Kansas, of 432 "failed" banks, 203 were either nationalized, voluntarily liquidated, or consolidated.[65] The Commercial Bank and Trust Company of Douglas, Wyoming, closed once in 1924, reopened as First State Bank of Douglas, and failed again in 1931. Likewise, Riverton State Bank had been in serious trouble since 1926, even though it did not close until 1932. "Failure rates" also reflected consolidations that tended to reduce the total number of banks. In Wyoming, for example, Wyoming Trust Company merged with Casper National in 1933; State Bank of Cokeville was consolidated with First National Bank of Kemmerer in 1932; Glenrock State Bank joined Casper National in 1934; First State Bank merged with Stockmens Bank in 1933; Kemmerer Savings Bank and First National Bank merged in 1931; the Bank of Hudson was absorbed by Lander State Bank in 1930; Hulett State Bank and Sundance State Bank joined in 1931; Security State Bank in Newcastle consolidated with First State Bank; American State Bank of Moorcroft consolidated with Sundance State Bank in 1932; and so on. Three other mergers occurred by 1939 in Wyoming.[66]

Perhaps the most important Rocky Mountain consolidation involved Deseret National Bank in Salt Lake City, which had the unfortunate luck of sharing a building with Deseret Savings Bank. When the latter failed, the natural reaction of its customers was to line up at the windows of the nearest bank, Deseret National, which was in no way connected to the savings bank. The run forced the otherwise solid bank onto the ropes. Marriner Eccles's First Security Corporation, in a series of secret negotiations, arranged for an affiliate of First Security, the National Copper Bank, to merge with Deseret National and operate as First National Bank of Salt Lake City. Thus, in an exercise of bank power, First Security had merely absorbed two competitors into its operation. Eccles, who disliked corporate branch banking as a policy, found chain banking acceptable and mergers a personally fruitful pursuit.[67] Among the other big chain banks, First Bank Stock Investment Company of Minneapolis acquired the two banks in Vermillion, South Dakota, and merged them into one.

Portland's oldest bank, Ladd and Tilton, also entered into a major merger. A private bank that in 1907 had incorporated in compliance with the Oregon Banking Act, it had recorded impressive growth rates in the early part of the century. By 1909, its fiftieth anniversary, the bank had assets of $14.7 million, or a 30,000 percent increase.[68] William Sargeant Ladd had achieved his goal of making Ladd and Tilton one of the most profitable banks in the West. Following his death in 1893, however, his son, William Mead Ladd, succeeded to the presidency, a position for which he was ill-suited in temperament and talent. Theodore B. Wilcox, the president of Portland Flouring Mills (which William Sargeant Ladd had also founded), emerged as the force behind important bank decisions, and still other local businessmen influenced bank lending. During the 1907 panic, William Mead Ladd needed to raise $2.5 million to reimburse depositors of another of the Ladd family's institutions, the failed Title and Trust Company, and sold 63 percent of the Ladd and Tilton stock to Frederick Pratt, a wealthy Brooklyn son of a Standard Oil associate and Ladd's brother-in-law.[69] Wilcox acquired and held this stock for a short time, and under his control the bank made several poor investments. Among other problems, the bank had purchased a considerable amount of notes in the Bankers Discount Corporation, a livestock loan company that made loans to cattle ranchers with their herds as collateral. R. S. Howard, an officer in both Ladd and Tilton and Bankers Discount, encouraged the former's customers to purchase the notes of the latter, and from 1918 to 1922 Ladd and Tilton lent $2.8 million to Bankers Discount. When Pratt, who resided in New York, decided to learn the precise details of the bank's investments, he hired E. B. MacNaughton, a partner in Strong and MacNaughton Trust Company, to infiltrate the bank and examine the books. Although Pratt gave MacNaughton a cover position as vice president, the officers knew his task was to investigate the Ladd and Tilton loans, and many of them treated MacNaughton as a pariah.[70]

The new vice president found debts more extensive than he or Pratt had imagined. In June 1925, MacNaughton concluded he could not save the bank, and that Pratt should sell it. Deputy state bank examiner O. B. Robertson agreed, telling MacNaughton that he had wanted to close the bank for some time, but refrained from doing so out of fear of disrupting the entire state banking system. When MacNaughton told Pratt of his recommendation to sell, Pratt asked, "How much will it cost me?" To reimburse all possible depositor losses, MacNaughton answered, "Fifteen million dollars on the outside." Pratt agreed, and MacNaughton discussed the sale with John C. Ainsworth of U.S. National Bank in July. Ainsworth convinced his board to merge Ladd and Tilton into its own structure, and on a Saturday afternoon U.S. National and Ladd and Tilton employees loaded gold and other bank assets on horse-drawn drays and transported them down the street to a newly completed wing of U.S. National. The unfortunate Ladd, whose family had led the Oregon banking community for decades, and whose father had been an original investor in almost every Portland enterprise, stood by, glumly "watching the whole bank go down the chute like a dead ox." The two banks had completed the deal without any participation by, or even notification to, the state banking authorities, who protested having been frozen out. Still, the regulators found themselves presented with a fait accompli. According to MacNaughton, who went on to great success as a Portland banker and civic booster, the Pratt family "deserved a monument" for "cleaning up a hopeless mess" and preventing a banking collapse in Oregon.[71] He did not mention, however, the role Ainsworth and U.S. National played. By taking a chance on the floundering institution, U.S. National became Portland's leading bank.

Several other Oregon and Washington consolidations occurred in the 1920s, led by the Anglo National group of twenty one banks and two other chains, Pacific Bancorp and West Coast Bancorp, as well as U.S. National. These four chains included forty-nine banks, and Anglo National at least had been formed in an attempt to counter the incursions by Giannini's Transamerica.[72] In Washington, Union Securities Company of Spokane formed the Old National banking group, reorganizing in 1929 as Old National Corporation, with twenty-two banks and combined resources of $44 million. Another growing banking company, John Price's Marine Bancorporation, acquired one of Seattle's largest banks, National Bank of Commerce, with its $21 million deposit base in 1928. John's son, Andrew, acquired a reputation as an important banker in the Pacific Northwest after that acquisition. (One of the directors of National Bank—Joshua Green—opposed the merger, but his own bank, Peoples Savings Bank, continued to grow.) Price's Marine Bancorporation emerged from the acquisitions in 1929 holding ten banks with combined assets of $50 million. Three other major banking groups joined into a combination that constituted the largest bank north of San Francisco and west of Minneapolis, First Seattle Dexter Horton National Bank. This combination featured Dexter Horton State Bank, Jacob Furth's Puget Sound National Bank, and Seattle's oldest bank, Phillips, Horton and Company, as well as Seattle National. The new bank had assets of more than $80 million.[73]

Consolidation sometimes indicates that weak banks are seeking salvation from embarrassment by soliciting takeovers, but not always. First National Bank of Vermillion had a succession problem and welcomed its merger, while First National Bank of Lincoln merged two other Lincoln banks, City National and Central National, into its structure in the late 1920s, largely in order to grow.[74] But a merger or a consolidation should not universally be viewed as a symptom of weak banking or insolvent banks, and insofar as reduced bank numbers reflected many consolidations, throughout the West, it is important to note that many special conditions shaped the overall numbers. In Arizona, where a decade-long reduction in the number of banks totaled thirty-five (of which three were consolidations), two of the banks that closed were voluntarily liquidated by the eccentric and volatile J. S. "Rawhide Jimmy" Douglas, who closed one of his solvent banks in protest of Franklin Roosevelt's economic policies, despite the fact that his son Lewis was Roosevelt's director of the budget.[75] Douglas labeled the New Deal "some sort of German Plot," and soon closed another of his banks because it was not as profitable as he thought it should have been, again owing, he thought, to the New Deal.[76] Yet except in the most tortured sense, these bank closings cannot be seen as casualties of the Great Depression itself.

Several independent banks became branches of existing banks, which did not necessarily decrease banking services. Indeed First National Bank of Ogden took over the liabilities of six troubled banks shortly after the branch-banking law in Utah was amended, and operated those banks as branches. At least one other Utah bank assumed a failing bank for conversion into a branch.[77] By 1936 in New Mexico, five branches existed along with forty-one banks, bringing total banking offices almost up to 1932 levels.[78]

As a result, the Depression acted as a blessing in at least this one respect—it forced many western states to reexamine their banking policies. Kansas, which had thought its 1909 bank deposit guaranty system insulated the state's banks against difficulties of exactly this sort, soon learned differently. The "crisis in agriculture led directly to a number of bank failures and indirectly to the collapse of the Deposit Guaranty System." Almost 80 percent of the banks chartered in Kansas from 1920 to 1930 had less than $25,000 capital, indicating they were almost all rural, agricultural banks. When that lack of portfolio diversification was combined in an increased number of banks in the Deposit Guaranty System (703 by 1922), it was obvious that difficulties in the agricultural sector would strain the Deposit Guaranty funds. Ironically, although the small farm banks kept the pressure on the system, the failure of a large bank, American State Bank in Wichita, threw the fund on the rocks by draining $5 million in guaranteed deposits. At the same time an increasing number of banks failed, thus draining cash from the guaranty fund, many still-solvent banks sought to escape by applying for withdrawal. By July 1926, only 225 banks remained in the system, which foundered with assets of $1.1 million and liabilities of $6.7 million; by 1928, no assets at all remained.[79] But Kansas bankers learned little from experience: they concentrated their efforts on more rigid examinations and limiting concentration, again ignoring branching.

Legislators in other states were not as hardheaded as those in Kansas when it came to branching. By embracing even voluntary deposit insurance and rejecting branching, the Kansas lawmakers had sown the seeds of banking destruction. According to a powerful study by Charles Calomiris, deposit insurance laws still in effect in the 1920s strongly correlated with the worst asset depreciation in the country and with excessive failure rates.[80] Calomiris found that states in the West with compulsory deposit insurance—North Dakota, South Dakota, Nebraska, and Oklahoma—had astonishingly low repayments from assets to total claims, even compared to neighboring states. North and South Dakota's ratios (17.2 and 24 percent respectively) stood at less than half those of most neighboring states that did not have compulsory deposit insurance: Montana (51.9 percent), Idaho (47.4 percent), Wyoming (53.7 percent), Colorado (68.1 percent), and Minnesota (48.2 percent). Likewise, Nebraska (35.4 percent) lagged far behind its neighbors Missouri (52.6 percent) and Iowa (53.6 percent), as well as Colorado and Wyoming. Oklahoma's deposit law influenced banking in the 1920s less because it lasted only until 1923. In addition, Oklahoma's ratios look somewhat better because it was bordered by two states with voluntary deposit insurance schemes, Texas and Kansas. Calomiris found that voluntary insurance states ranked below all other regulatory regimes except compulsory insurance, and that as a protective device, branching remained the best option.[81]

Calomiris also noted a difference in failure rates for four "state-chartered, insured banking systems relative to national banks operating in the same state." Those differences did not constitute "merely an artefact of different exposure to agricultural risk, due to different locational patterns . . . or more restrictive regulations on national-chartered banks—in particular, stricter limitations on real estate loans." Among other problems, he found that insured deposit systems usually faced interest-rate ceilings that kept them from competing for the accounts of large, sophisticated depositors, especially in rural areas, and that capital requirements constituted more of an impediment for risk-taking on the part of large banks than for smaller banks (in the case of voluntary systems). Moreover, in the West during the agricultural boom years, it had been precisely the insured banks that witnessed the greatest growth: of the sixteen state-bank systems to grow at a rate of more than 2.5 percent during the period between 1914 and 1920, seven were insured systems, including the banks ranking first, fourth, and fifth in asset growth.[82] Most of that growth came from increasing bank numbers rather than assets per bank.

Calomiris also compared uninsured state-chartered systems to insured systems and found that banks in the former tended to be larger, grow less, and have higher capital than banks in the insured systems. And in voluntary insurance systems, such as in Kansas, banks switched en masse to other state or national systems from 1924 to 1926.[83] But, as Calomiris reaffirmed, branching remained the best of all systems. Unfortunately, it took the deposit insurance failures of the twenties to discredit deposit insurance, even though today many laymen still believe that federal deposit insurance "saved the system" in 1935. As a result, serious attention to the antibranching laws did not occur until the pit of the Great Depression.

Utah's legislature in 1933 amended its antibranching law to the advantage of larger banks by permitting banks with paid-in capital of over $100,000 to operate one branch within the state for each $50,000 of paid-in capital. Whatever benefits this had in furnishing bankless towns with facilities, it was somewhat offset by the prohibition of branches in any town where a bank already existed (except Salt Lake City), thus discouraging competition. And although New Mexico refused to repeal its antibranching law, the state legislature had to make concessions to towns such as Carrizozo, Hobbs, Fort Sumner, Tularosa, and others left bankless by the Depression. By 1935, existing banks had skirted the law by establishing "paying and receiving offices" in bankless rural towns. The New Mexico legislature reluctantly permitted limited agency or office privileges, and five of these quasi-branches were in operation by the end of the year. At the end of 1939, seven branches conducted business, all in towns without other bank offices.[84] Aggressive expansionists, such as Pratt Thomas of Commercial Bank of Utah in Spanish Fork, moved to acquire banks at Heber City, Nephi, and Delta when he saw them in dire straits during the 1930s. These banks formed the basis for his branch system. Thomas also established "suitcase banks" in Eureka and Payson, Utah, two recently bankless towns. These agencies were created with thirty dollars in capital stock and accepted deposits, but did not make loans.[85]

The Pacific Northwest and Idaho also approved changes in their banking codes permitting branching. Washington's code required a bank to have $200,000 in capital for each branch, making the ante extremely expensive for a bank to establish de novo branches in small towns. For multicounty branch banking, $500,000 total capital was required. In March 1933, Peoples Bank and Trust won the approval for two branches, the first in the state, and it and other Washington banks began expansion, usually through acquisition.[86]

Idaho finally permitted statewide branching in 1933, but this move came too late to stem the rash of failures in 1932, which was instigated by the suspension of Boise City National Bank. This bank had received more than $181,000 in loans from the Reconstruction Finance Corporation, and historian James S. Olson views it as precipitating numerous other runs in "the Boise Valley, Southern Idaho, and Eastern Oregon."[89] Boise City's failure on July 30, 1832, placed extensive pressure on First National Bank of Idaho, which closed on August 31. First National in particular was trusted and had cultivated a reputation for stability. Its closing triggered a panic that shut the doors of nine other banks, all chain-bank affiliates of First National. The Reconstruction Finance Corporation (RFC), its reputation and effectiveness on the line, rushed a team of investigators to Idaho. They determined that four of the banks, including Boise City National Bank, would not be saved. They merged two other banks, and agreed to lend First National $2 million if it could raise $600,000 in capital. By November, the crisis in Idaho passed, but not before damaging the notion that limited bailout loans would work. Only massive infusions of cash could save many chains, and that meant the RFC had to pick and choose the institutions to which it tossed life preservers.

For the most part, the other chain-related banks, operating under the protection of the Eccles brothers' First Security Corporation of Utah, had few problems. The chain previously known as Anderson Brothers Bank was renamed First Security Bank of Idaho, after passage of the branching law. Headquartered in Boise, it operated fifteen branches in the state. Marriner Eccles engaged in a variant of interstate banking that compared to William Ralston's establishment of a Bank of California branch in Virginia City, Nevada, in 1864, some 120 years before any real interstate banking legislation existed.[88]

Branch systems fared well, and chains had somewhat better experiences than unit banks (with some exceptions, such as the First National Bank of Idaho chain). Chains offered several of the advantages of branching, although they lacked the critical function of being able to shift money from point to point on demand. For chain banks, loans and deposits still had to balance at each location, unlike branch banks, which theoretically could collect deposits at one branch to make loans at another. Chain banks, with common directors, gained liquidity by quick communication and loans to each other. This liquidity could also be gained by yet another arrangement. In Minneapolis–St. Paul, First Banstock and Northwest Bancorporation were bank holding companies that dominated much of the finance in the northern tier from Wisconsin to Montana. Northwest Bancorporation had member banks in Fargo and James River, North Dakota; Lead, Deadwood, Sioux Falls, Watertown, and Aberdeen, South Dakota; and Omaha, Nebraska.[89] The banks owned by the holding companies, according to Bob Hendrickson, a North Dakota banker who was president of First National Bank and Trust in Bismarck, had many advantages over independent banks. Hendrickson, who started as a teller in a tiny bank on the Canadian border, recalled that the First Banstock banks had independent boards of directors, but that the parent company watched their balance sheets closely, running its own audits and examinations. These, Hendrickson commented, "were tougher than [those of] the feds."[90]

Our understanding of western chain banks is somewhat obfuscated by the troubles in George Wingfield's twelve-bank chain in the 1930s, keeping in mind that economists have viewed chains as a best substitute for branching where branching is prohibited. The Wingfield drama, called by a historian of the RFC, James Olson, the "rehearsal for disaster," not only provides a chance to analyze the strengths and limitations of chains and branches, and constitutes a remarkable case study of the dynamics of the RFC's lending to banks, but it also offers a unique opportunity to explore the largest western chain failure of the Depression.[91] But the obvious conclusions—that chain banking failed; or that Wingfield was a poor manager; or that, due to serious political animosity, politicians in the state allowed his banks to fail—do not suffice to explain the peculiar dilemma of the Wingfield chain.

THE COLLAPSE OF THE WINGFIELD CHAIN

Wingfield settled in Nevada in 1896, and, after a brief fling with a gambling concession (he excelled at faro), joined George S. Nixon (later a U.S. senator from Nevada) in Reno to form the Goldfield Consolidated Mines Company in 1906. That company featured such renowned investors as Bernard Baruch, William Crocker, and Henry Clay Frick. He married Maude Murdoch, the daughter of a San Francisco millionaire, in 1908, and the following year moved to Reno. During the partnership with Nixon, he acquired an interest in the Tonopah Banking Corporation, bought two hotels, and established the flagship of his banking chain, Nixon National Bank (renamed Reno National Bank in 1915 or 1916).[92]

Wingfield fit the image of a westerner. When the International Workers of the World tried to suppress distribution of a local paper that carried an anti-IWW editorial by Wingfield's friend, editor L. C. Bramson, Wingfield strapped on two Colt revolvers and paraded the streets with the newsboys, riding "shotgun" on their deliveries.[93] As a banker, Wingfield was familiar with the details of his operations, demanding weekly reports from his cashiers, which he returned with considerable analysis of the loans, collateral, and bank balance sheets. At times, Wingfield's comments suggest that he knew each borrower personally, and he certainly identified problem debtors.[94] At one time, Wingfield thought the Carson Valley Bank's livestock loans needed improvement, so he brought in D. P. Malloy of Lake View, Oregon, a livestock expert, to evaluate all of the bank's livestock loans.[95] (At that time Wingfield may have sensed something wrong at Carson Valley Bank—where cashier Clapp engaged in embezzling—but likely thought the problems stemmed from poor banking practices, not dishonesty.) And Wingfield had no reluctance when it came to collecting: of one borrower, for example, Wingfield instructed Clapp to "get right after the Heinicke Construction Co. & make them settle up their balance . . . as I don't like the way that thing looks."[96] On another occasion, the Reno banker urged Clapp's successor to hire a new collector "who has no political friends to reward by going easy on them. . . ."[97] Wingfield also kept a close eye on cash accounts, ordering Clapp to reduce cash by $100,000 on one occasion.[98] Examinations on the bank's taxes paid to the U.S. government suggest that it usually did an accurate job of reporting, and the examiners even noted that loopholes existed that Wingfield had not exploited.[99] When another of Wingfield's banks underpaid its taxes, Wingfield strongly suggested that the bank finish them early and forward the forms to Wingfield's accountants and tax advisors for inspection.[100] More important, earnings sheets for banks such as Carson Valley Bank showed constant profits during the 1920s.

Indeed, nothing in Wingfield's management smacks of incompetence. He knew the position of all of his investments, most of which in the 1920s produced regular profits. He insisted on uniform reporting—right down to standardized forms for his weekly cashiers' memos—and demanded competence and loyalty from his employees. To a request for a vacation from the superior of one assistant cashier, Wingfield in exasperation replied that he would give all the employees a "permanent vacation" if they did not "pep up."[101]

Given the meticulous attention Wingfield lavished on his banks, it is interesting that it has long been assumed that mismanagement caused the collapse of Wingfield's chain in 1933.[102] Certainly there were warning signs: Carson Valley Bank's net earnings plunged by an average of $20,000 between 1926 and 1928.[103] In 1929, Wingfield owned outright or held a controlling interest in twelve banks of Nevada's forty one) spread through nine cities, which by 1932 held 65 percent of the state's deposits and made 75 percent of the state's commercial loans.[104] During the 1920s, even the weakest of the banks made noteworthy profits. Carson Valley Bank, where the corrupt Clapp was cashier, reported a profit of $9,344 to the Internal Revenue Service in 1920, and earnings for the yearly period ending in 1921 totaled $18,000.[105] A year later, net earnings passed $20,000 and profit reached $17,396, all from a bank whose cashier engaged in embezzling and which had not collected $6,000 owed by the previous examiner, Gilbert Ross![106] Although earnings dropped through 1927, when net earnings were only $3,597, so did losses charged off, which fell by 95 percent from 1926 to 1927. The bank, however, had again been struck by white-collar crime, this time at the hands of Irma Emmitt, an employee whose embezzling was discovered by an internal audit.[107]

While perhaps Wingfield should have known of those problems, he operated as thorough an auditing procedure as any other bank, probably more standardized than most chains or even some branch operations. He displayed constant concern with costs, especially items such as company autos (the cashiers frequently wanted luxury cars, while Wingfield demanded that they use no-frills passenger cars), yet he never hesitated to pay high wages, and he admonished the cashier of Churchill County Bank to hire a "better class of help than you have . . . even if you have to pay them a little more."[108] Wingfield always suspected trouble well before it appeared in internal audits or external examinations. He cautioned Churchill County Bank cashier E. W. Blair, who was inexperienced at agricultural banking, "this is somewhat a new line for you. After staying in a mining camp for 20 years, it is hard to break in as a farmer banker."[109]

All Nevada's economy was in trouble, with unemployment in the mining counties reaching 75 percent. The state suffered from overbanking, even under normal conditions. As James Olson pointed out, Elko, a town of fewer than five thousand people, had two banks. Moreover, "the banks in Nevada in general and the Wingfield banks in particular, suffered from a chronic inability to diversify their loans."[110] Wingfield especially had a soft spot for the Nevada sheep ranchers and farmers, hundreds of whom he kept in business: his banks held just over 50 percent of the assets in the state, and made up to 85 percent of Nevada's bank loans by 1932. During the 1920s, few questioned the Reno banker's strategy, as sheep worth eighteen to twenty dollars a head secured the ranchers' loans taken at four dollars a head. But when the wool market collapsed, the price of wool fell from thirty cents per pound to eight cents by 1932.[111] The drastic plunge in wool prices placed a huge demand on Wingfield's banks for renewals of existing loans or additional funds to keep the sheep alive. In 1932 alone, defaults in the Wingfield chain amounted to more than $3.5 million, and the ranchers still pressed for more loans. To refuse these requests not only ensured the demise of the sheep ranches but also would have forced the banks to take the sheep as settlement and attempt to sell them in a slow market. Even in a good market, the banks were not equipped to sell livestock on a regular basis. Yet Wingfield personally knew many of the ranchers, and compassion compelled him to extend their loans as much as possible. According to the auditor of Reno National Bank, Wingfield essentially sacrificed himself and his empire to save the Nevada livestock industry.[112] He could have permitted his weaker banks to fail, thus saving the bulk of his other banks and his entire non–bank-related fortune, including his own ranches and hotels.

Ironically, it may have been a rejected loan that sent the listing ship under. In July 1932, E. W. Blair noted that a disgruntled borrower had spread rumors about the bank's instability, and by October, "the run . . . had become a 'stampede'."[113] That year, Wingfield applied to the RFC for a loan of $2 million for Reno National Bank, and that request was soon followed by a request for another $1 million. In addition, Wingfield's other banks received over $2.1 million in 1932. Those RFC loans actually harmed the chain in that they carried relatively high interest rates (6 percent) and allowed only six-month maturity dates, meaning that the banks no sooner got a loan than they had to scramble to pay it back. Worse, the RFC demanded the best assets of the banks as collateral, claiming, for example, $3 million of Reno National's best securities for a $1.1 million loan in April 1932. The Henderson Banking Company, which received its first RFC loan in May 1932, for $150,000, asked for $55,000 in June, $200,000 in July, and $220,000 in September. For the May and September loans alone, the RFC demanded $1.3 million in securities. Banks had to liquidate their best assets just to keep the RFC happy. And the RFC undervalued the assets it accepted. For livestock held as security by the Wingfield chain valued at $15 million in 1928, the face value had plummeted to under $8 million in 1932. But the RFC valued it at only $3 million.[114] Finally, although the RFC pumped considerable sums into Wingfield's banks, it turned its back on him when several of California banks agreed to lend between $500,000 and $1 million to reorganize his empire under their control.

Wingfield appealed to Governor Fred B. Balzar for a bank holiday to allow liquidation of some of his personal assets for application to the banks' capital structures.[115] (Balzar had a special interest in Wingfield's banks, as they held all the state's public funds.) Balzar met with President Herbert Hoover on October 30, 1932, and the following day, after talking to RFC officials, telephoned his lieutenant governor, Morley Griswold, instructing him to enact a "business holiday" the following day, since the Nevada constitution did not permit, in his opinion, a specific bank holiday. Indeed, under the business-holiday edict, not all banks closed, with Wingfield's competitor in Reno, First National Bank, remaining open. But Wingfield shut his banks' doors on November 1. T. E. Harris, the chief bank examiner for the San Francisco district of the Federal Reserve, warned J. G. Moore, the cashier at First National Bank of Winnemucca, to "carefully review your assets and determine whether your capital structure is sound." The examiner noted his "experience with closed banks, as distinguished from banks operating under a holiday . . . [was that] the estimate [of the bank's ability to meet depositor demands] is usually too low and I advise you to be very careful . . . to see that your capital is intact and that you have sufficient liquidity to meet withdrawals. . . ."[116]

Appeals to Crocker First National Bank of San Francisco, to whom Wingfield already owed $850,000, were met with the standard rejection, claiming Wingfield was already at his limit (although Crocker without hesitation offered to participate in the reorganization plan).[117] Depositors, nevertheless, remained confident: according to Moore, "the worst element we have to contend with are those who have little or nothing in the bank. Their chief diversion is to stand around the corners and hang crepe."[118] On the other hand, one depositor offered the contents of her safe deposit box—$2,000 in government bonds. Federal examiners, meanwhile, actively inspected the books and loans of the national banks, and determined that the banks no longer had enough collateral to guaranty their solvency.[119]

As ever, politics figured into the banks' immediate condition. Wingfield's opponents in Stroey County presented county drafts during the business holiday, contending that the governor did not have the authority to close the banks.[120] After extensive examinations by both state and federal regulators, the banks then formally closed down on December 14, 1932. Moore told Wingfield that he would make a final check of the books "and then join the 'army of the unemployed.' "[121]

On January 6, 1933, the deteriorating condition of the Wingfield chain led the comptroller of the currency to levy an assessment of $700,000 on the stockholders of Reno National Bank.[122] Depositors committees, which had already begun to meet, demanded that any reorganization plans give the depositors sole claim to the banks' assets.[123] Wingfield asked for depositors to sign waivers on their deposits in which they immediately relinquished the right to withdraw 75 percent of their deposits, giving Wingfield and the other owners the authority to reorganize the banks. At that time, the comptroller would have to agree to the plan. Rumors spread wildly, with a "non-signing depositor"—believed to be Graham Sanford, editor or the anti-Wingfield *Reno Evening Gazette*—raising a list of unanswerable questions and asking for guarantees that no banker could make.[124] By February, Wingfield had agreed to a plan worked out with "a group of San Francisco financiers" that included formation of a mortgage company to take over the twelve closed banks, along with a $1.5 million RFC loan; a promise by the California bankers not to withdraw their deposits for three years; and an agreement (contained in the waivers) by which the depositors would accept 25 percent of their deposits in stock in the new bank.[125] The majority of the twenty-seven thousand held deposits of less than two hundred dollars, and the ready cash would be used to pay them before other depositors. What the plan did not state was that calls by Standard Oil and the Southern Pacific Railroad for $500,000 in new outside capital were rejected. The potential investors obviously did not want the RFC's stringent credit restrictions.

According to the plan, only one director would be named by the existing stockholders, twelve by the depositors, and three by the California bankers. Still, hatred of Wingfield by some was so strong that the *Santa Barbara Daily News* reported the plan with the comment that "thousands of people in [Nevada] regard [Wingfield] with high affection and esteem [but] thousands hate him."[126] A week after that editorial, W. J. Henly, cashier at Virginia City Bank, observed that "the majority of the larger depositors here are all for reorganization . . . [but there are] some who are very bitter and do a lot of shouting. . . ."[127] The *Reno Evening Gazette* continued to paint the situation in the darkest colors, arguing that Wingfield had already lost everything, and agitating depositors' committees to lobby for his total exclusion from the new bank.[128]

The Nevada legislature had introduced a bill that would have turned over all the closed banks to the depositors, essentially confiscating Wingfield's investments. Although the house passed the bill, the Nevada senate bottled it up in committee, producing a substitute bill allegedly written by Wingfield's attorney, George Thatcher, which the legislature passed instead.[129] It allowed depositors with over 50 percent of the majority stock to reorganize an insolvent bank, giving the original stockholders class B nonvoting stock and retaining for themselves class A voting stock. As soon as possible, the bank was to purchase the A stock and retire it, leaving the B stockholders in control after all the depositors received their money.

However, conditions for Nevada banks (as for banks throughout the West) had deteriorated since the reorganization plan had been submitted, and on March 1, 1933, the governor declared another business holiday. Without the authority to declare a bank holiday, Balzar requested a bill to give him that authority, then mysteriously sat on a slightly altered bill that contained essentially similar provisions. After considerable political pressure by pro- and anti-Wingfield forces, Balzar signed the measure. The legislature immediately convened a joint committee to investigate all closed banks in the state, and the committee's report concluded that the livestock loans had broken the Wingfield banks. The report also condemned the State Banking Board and the bank examiner for permitting the ongoing livestock loans.[130]

Wingfield, in accordance with the provisions of the new law, revised his reorganization plan with a mortgage company containing individual trust funds for each of the twelve banks, specifically to hold the slow-liquidating sheep loans. This plan required that depositors take some of their deposits in mortgage-company stock as well as bank stock. This, plus a $2 million loan from the RFC, would ease the immediate cash problems until the sheep loans could be liquidated.[131] A projected distribution of deposit liability per $1,000 in each of the twelve banks showed Riverside Bank, Wells State Bank, the Bank of Sparks, and United Nevada Bank to have the lowest levels of unacceptable loans (all below $255 per $1,000), while Wingfield's Reno National, Virginia City Bank, the Bank of Nevada Savings and Trust, and Tonopah Banking Corporation all had over $500 per $1,000 in unacceptable loans. But Wingfield had assumed the worst and the balance sheet of the proposed bank reflected hugh writeoffs, while he could point to some of the newly acquired banks as indicators that he was gradually restructuring with newer, more profitable banks.[132] By late March, six banks had received enough waivers to enable them to reorganize, including Tonopah Bank, Virginia City Bank, Sparks Bank, Henderson Bank, Carson Valley Bank, and First National Bank of Winnemucca, and by the beginning of May, only the stockholders from Riverside Bank, United Nevada Bank, and Churchill County Bank had not approved the plan. Ultimately, all but the depositors in Churchill County Bank signed the waivers.

Still, a number of hurdles remained. First, Wingfield faced the deadline of June 17, 1933, that appeared on the waivers. He applied for the $2 million RFC loan on June 13 and filed articles of incorporation on June 15, leaving virtually no room for error. All the while, he contended with a lawsuit alleging mismanagement, and in subsequent suits the plaintiffs requested an opinion from the comptroller of the currency, J. F. T. O'Connor, as to whether the comptroller's office would approve of the plan. O'Connor replied that his office would not approve any plan under which a depositor who had not signed a waiver was co-opted into the reorganization of the bank, thus effectively removing the two national banks from the entire reorganization proposal. Wingfield also received a setback from the courts, which ruled the Nevada Bank Act of 1933, under which Wingfield had proposed to reorganize the banks, unconstitutional.[133]

A final attempt at reorganization, with enough cash to buy out the nonsigning depositors, followed a two month trial in which a Nevada district court agreed with the comptroller that nonsigning depositors could not be forced into the reorganization. The court dealt another blow to reorganization when it added that state and county governments would not be permitted to hold stock in the banks, thus adding the public deposits to the nonsigners. In desperation, Wingfield obtained yet additional support from the San Francisco financiers, but the RFC refused to make any more loans, and in November the Nevada District Court, seeing the reorganization plans stalled, ordered a receivership for the state banks, following the lead of the comptroller, who had already appointed a receiver for the national banks. Wingfield's personal liability on the national banks alone totalled over $450,000, and the demands forced him into involuntary bankruptcy.[134] Since sheep prices later rose, the depositors would have fared better under the reorganization than under the receiverships.

Did this mean that the premier banker in Nevada's history was a poor manager? Or was he, as Clel Georgetta claimed, a victim of Franklin Roosevelt's manipulations of the RFC in Washington?[135] The best evidence that Wingfield's long term prospects were good can be found in the eagerness with which other banks rushed to grant him loans. In 1929, for example, Continental Illinois Bank and Trust offered Wingfield a substantial line of credit to help him acquire Washoe County Bank.[136] California bankers' willingness to lend Wingfield a total of $1.85 million in 1933 clearly reflected their estimation of his managerial and banking abilities. Had they not viewed him as a solid risk, or his sheep loans as ultimately recoverable, they would have abandoned him well before 1932. His reorganization plan was an ingenious attempt to keep the banks afloat, and would have restored them to solvency after sheep prices rose. Even in forced liquidation, all his banks paid approximately ninety cents on the dollar and Riverside Bank paid 100 percent to depositors. Such liquidity suggests that the RFC was delinquent in its refusal to keep the banks afloat.[137]

It is not clear why, if California bankers supported the plan, the Southern Pacific and Standard Oil refused to provide the $500,000 for the trust company, but it was likely more their internal situation than the weakness of the Wingfield plan that prevented the loan. Free-market advocates might well ask why any well-managed bank would need a "bailout," and posit that the consumer might be better served by allowing the banks to fail. In Wingfield's defense, however, the condition of banks across the country had made government aid commonplace, and the RFC existed for the purpose of extending such aid. What is so striking about this episode is the ease with which the banks got "hooked" on government support, which by its very conditions became addicting unto death. The ultimate culprit—Nevada's undiversified economy and the crippling conditions of the RFC loans—eluded even Wingfield's brilliant attempt to introduce a quasi-branching system.

But even statewide branching could not have saved an undiversified economy, and no bank could escape the oppressive nature of the RFC's lending without some growth in the national or regional financial picture. Ultimately only rising wool prices could have saved Wingfield. Interstate banking, from California's banks, however, could have absorbed the losses until prices rose, and the influence of the California bankers in the reorganization plan indicate that Wingfield appreciated the advantages of interstate branch banking. The records of the RFC suggest that this was exactly the case when the California banks not only absorbed parts of Wingfield's chain but paid off the depositors. Likewise, the RFC changed some of its policies, lending beyond the collateral offered by banks. But this all came too late for Wingfield's banks.

The situation in Nevada shocked neighboring California and triggered similar developments elsewhere in the West. The ripples spread rapidly: M. D. Cravath, a director of Stockmen's National Bank in Rushville, Nebraska, was at his vacation resort in Long Beach when he reported: "the Seaside National Bank of Long beach closed its doors last Tuesday . . . we had our money in the bank. . . ."[138] Drastic reductions in total bank numbers during the twenties and early thirties led to the absorption of many existing unit banks by larger banks for conversion into branches or, barring branches, into chain members. Many survivors added new offices and increased their overall size, taking advantage of the absence of banks in rural areas. Towns that would otherwise have been bankless emerged as winners in the process. Thus reduction in competition (i.e., reduced numbers of unit banks) was offset by concentration of assets and increased branching.

Although it was too late for Wingfield, Nevada joined Idaho in 1933 to correct its system by permitting branching. With the exception of the Idaho chain, reopened with an RFC loan, branching and chain banking had demonstrated considerable more flexibility than unit banking. Ironically, it was a branch-banking holding company that ended Nevada's woes related to Wingfield's failed chain. Unfortunately, some of the regulatory rearrangement that occurred in the West after the turbulent twenties was aimed at propping up the unit-bank systems. Wyoming had, in 1925, passed a new banking law that eliminated the lowest tier of capitalization for banks, raising the minimum capitalization for banks in the smallest of towns to $25,000. As a natural effect, small town banks disappeared, while banks in larger locations took up their business. Several of the larger banks in Casper and Sheridan increased deposits throughout in the 1930s.[139]

FEDERAL EXAMINERS TAKE A CLOSER LOOK

While the states' antibranching laws helped force the dissolution of dozens of banks, the federal government tried to stabilize banks through tougher bank examinations. Federal examiners, however, often lacked any sense of the territory in which they worked and had almost no knowledge of individual borrowers whom the banks knew intimately. The comptroller of the currency, based on examiners' reports, would demand changes from the banks, usually in the form of lower default rates on loans or fewer suspect loans, and would specifically cite individual debts that the government thought were bad.

These conditions can be seen in New Mexico through correspondence from First National Bank of Santa Fe—New Mexico's oldest—to the comptroller of the currency. Responding to weaknesses the comptroller found in First National's statement, the president of the bank, Arthur Seligman, noted that local conditions known to the board explained or justified a number of loans about which the comptroller had raised questions.[140] The bank, as of February 11, 1930, had surplus funds of $800,000 on the New York market. Specifically, the president reported on items the examiner had questioned: the loan to H. H. Chandler, Jr. had been reduced by $600, and (perhaps conveniently) one of the houses mortgaged to the bank as security had just been destroyed by fire, and $4,500 insurance was to be paid.[141] In some twenty other cases, individuals had either reduced their debts or put up extra collateral.

Equally interesting are the local market conditions described in notes of the board of directors as they prepared a response to the examiner's comments for the comptroller on many of the banks' other loans. In one case, they noted that it was "unwise to insist upon" a financial statement from Jose Ortiz y Pino, who had a long-term Treasury Certificate deposit.

It was, the secretary noted, his "Spanish conservatism" at work, and the board found it "absurd to change [the] valuation daily on [the] books." Listing several loans that the examiner challenged, the board found them "good loans" in which the borrowers had shown increasing assets and met their payments regularly. Local merchants frequently manipulated their books due to "Fear of [the] tax collectors." The directors emphasized character over financial statements and questioned the ability of examiners "who come in for a few days" to judge as accurately as the local bankers the worth of a particular loan.[142] The 1930 episode was not the first time First National had clashed with the authorities, with a 1929 examination infuriating Seligman so much that he was "thinking seriously of denationalizing."[143] In Montana, when one national examiner left, the entire town celebrated: "If he never returns," the local paper noted, "it will be plenty soon enough for a number of people . . . who had the pleasure of doing business with this bird. . . ."[144]

Many bankers shared the opinions of the Santa Fe directors, and state examiners were trusted slightly more than their federal colleagues. Anaconda Copper Company in Montana viewed the new state examiner, L. Q. Skelton, appointed in 1924, as "a blind partisan" with little banking experience, and politicians engaged in "much maneuvering" to get ex-bankers named as receivers.[145] But some harbored less hostile sentiments. George Becker, vice president of Ogden State Bank in Utah, recommended that "immediate and positive action be taken promptly to comply absolutely" with criticisms and suggestions made by state bank commissioner W. H. Hadlock.[146] Becker's approach—that the bank should put more effort into collections by adding attorneys and expanding the real estate department to foreclose mortgages—differed sharply from the attitudes held by Wingfield, Walter Bimson of Phoenix's Valley National Bank, or Paul Walter of First National Bank of Santa Fe, all of whom saw most of their customers as ultimately solvent. Becker, indeed, opposed loans "made in the hope of saving loss to the community and to the bank but nevertheless in excess of technical restrictions of the law and in excess of what [he] deemed wise."[147] Becker's views were shared by the Ogden State Bank board of directors, which elected him chairman in 1931.[148] It is possible that Becker was cowed by regulators, or, more likely, that his philosophy about banking was different from that of his contemporaries. But most bankers reflected the views of North Dakota banker John Davis, whose father owned First National Bank of McClusky. Davis recalled that examiners thought the officers were not "tough enough on collections." The federal officials, he added, did not understand the German and Russian immigrants who made up the majority of the bank's customers: "Most of them were eventually paid up."[149] A good example of different assessments of a bank's condition can be seen in the correspondence of Stockmen's National Bank of Rushville, Nebraska, in the early 1930s. While the letters between directors and officers indicate that they were quite satisfied with the condition of the bank, one director noted: "The [federal] Examiner has been with us and gave us the usual 'walloping' in charged off etc. . . . [but admitted] the bank is looking better. . . ."[150] A year later, M. D. Cravath, a director and later president, after examining the bank's statements and the examiner's report, calmly reassured an officer: "Deposits and loans are getting near the spread that looks about right . . . and you almost have to accommodate a good customer. . . ."[151] Cravath could have quoted Joseph A. Thatcher: for valued customers, if necessary, break the law and take your chances.

Although we do not mean to suggest that most bankers saw the regulators as a threat, neither did they view overextended lending to good customers as an unsafe banking practice. They did, however, increasingly view federal regulators as especially uninformed about local conditions, and almost universally considered their own judgement as to loan quality superior to that of the examiners.

Many western bankers increasingly saw the federal government as a non-neutral regulator to be viewed with suspicion. The examiners' reports contributed to the distrust; the seizure of all privately held gold deepened it. When Franklin Roosevelt authorized the secretary of the treasury to call in all the gold in March 1933, dozens of solvent western banks saw their major tool to avert panics and symbol to reassure depositors of the banks' liquidity carted out their doors in bags. One clerk at Colorado National recalled that the bank had over a million dollars worth of gold in its vaults at the time and had loaned gold in earlier panics to weakened banks.[152] Colorado National was given yet another reason to dislike the government when the RFC, based on the report of the examiner, recommended that control be taken out of the hands of the families that had founded the bank and had run it for decades, the Kountzes and the Bergers. The RFC proposed to reorganize Colorado National by purchasing a large share of stock, thus adding to its capital base. Reluctantly, in September 1933, the bank sold $1.5 million to the RFC, although $1 million in stock remained in the hands of the two families.[153]

The RFC also looked for opportunities to involve itself in banks, and RFC chairman Jesse Jones even pleaded with Peoples Corporation in Seattle, which had rejected RFC overtures, to accept RFC support. Whether the Fed and the RFC worked together is in question, but after Peoples acquired First National Bank of Renton to turn it into a branch, the Fed made the conversion contingent on an increase in capital by $600,000, made possible only by an RFC loan. Peoples ultimately relented and accepted the RFC funds to get its branch.[154]

In some cases, western state governments acted to buffer the federal government from the further antagonism of the banks and the public by bearing much of the hostility themselves for their imposition of the state bank holidays, which had already been imposed in every state except one by the time Franklin Roosevelt declared a national, anticlimactic bank holiday on March 6, 1933. Arizona's Governor Benjamin B. Moeur issued a statement closing Arizona's banks shortly after Governor James Rolph had shut banks in California. Walter Bimson convinced Moeur that the frozen interbank balances that Arizona's banks held in California would cripple many Arizona institutions if the latter decided to remain open.[155] Solvent banks, especially in Bisbee, revolted, promising to remain in business despite the order. J. S. Douglas, in particular, spouted defiance. Moeur had copies of his proclamation posted on the doors of the Bisbee banks, and, when one of them finally broke ranks, even Douglas capitulated, but only after he sent out large cash supplies to loyal customers who might have emergency needs.[156]

Now, the mantle of the federal government actually protected some Arizona banks from the governor's order. National banks were not required to close by state edict, and at least two national banks located in less populated areas remained open.[157] Otto Herold, the president of First National Bank of Nogales, stated flatly: "The bank is liquid. We have a large available cash reserve. . . ."[158] Still other banks evaded the rule by closing the head office but keeping their branches open. Arthur Clarke refused to cooperate with the bank examination and the authorities kept his Lewiston, Idaho, bank closed, although eventually all of his banks passed the exam.[159]

Whatever benefits the federal government offered to western banks, the disadvantages soon seemed to outweigh them. Having Uncle Sam as a daily business partner multiplied the banks' problems. Colorado National Bank, for example, was forced into a wholesale management turnover, with president George Berger, Sr., shoved aside by the new controlling partner, the RFC.[160] (The RFC permitted Berger to be chairman of the board, a ceremonial position there.) The bank had grown for twenty-three years under Berger, but in 1933 it lost over $280,000. That fact had hardly deterred small depositors, who held more than three-fourths of the bank's 43,791 accounts and four-fifths of its $31 million in deposits.[161] But in the RFC's eyes Berger had committed the unpardonable sin of being personally in debt. Harold Kountze took over as president and CEO, and pleaded with the Federal Reserve Bank to get the RFC off his back: "We have played the game in every way with the RFC . . . if they really have confidence in me they will give us at least a few months to work out our problems in our own way."[162] Kountze successfully staged a guerrilla war with the RFC until it relented. Still, according to Melvin J. Roberts, an assistant trust officer, the bank "did a lot of foreclosures—under pressure from the bank examiners—who panicked." Roberts noted that although the bank had disposed of Climax Molybdenum at $1 a share, during World War II it reached $160 a share.[163] Perhaps of greater import to most banks, the RFC published the names of borrowers. This alerted the public that a bank had borrowed money, but it also caused people to believe that by obtaining a loan from the RFC, the bank teetered on the edge. Depositors withdrew, exacerbating the difficulties, until the bank really was in trouble.[164]

To other western bankers it seemed that the federal government had embarked on a policy that would ultimately put private bankers out of business. J. S. Douglas, for example, liquidated his Bank of Clemenceau in 1933 and scheduled the closing of his Bank of Bisbee later that same year (ultimately closing it in 1934). Eventually, Douglas, after a fierce battle with former friend and partner Frank C. Brophy, lost control of the third bank in his chain, the Bank of Douglas. This loss, and his disgust for Roosevelt's New Deal programs, convinced him to move to Canada.[165] Frank Brophy later reopened the Bank of Bisbee, but also found himself at odds with what he termed "New Deal economics."[166] Even Walter Bimson, the undisputed leader of Arizona's bankers, voiced his concerns about the "competition of government loaning agencies" and questioned "whether the centralization of power and control of the government and industry [would] prove beneficial to the nation."[167]

Walter Reed Bimson, a blacksmith's son from Berthoud, Colorado, took over Valley National Bank on New Year's Day, 1933. He had worked as a janitor for $40 a month in a bank owned by his father, learned to keep books, and eventually received a job at Chicago's powerful Harris Trust and Savings Bank, where he specialized in negotiating farm loans. Like Giannini, he developed an appreciation for retail banking to a broad consumer market. At the time Valley Bank contacted him about assuming the presidency, Bimson headed the state unemployment relief program in Illinois, but he had handled important financing in the Salt River Valley and knew Arizona.[168]

The energetic and innovative Bimson replaced a dedicated mining expert, Dr. Louis D. Ricketts, who had become president in January 1929 and who had lost much of his personal fortune in a real-estate holding company while attempting to save Valley Bank from its agricultural loans. At the time of Bimson's arrival, the bank toiled with a high overhead and conservative lending policies aimed at hoarding the final cash reserves: the bank's deposits had dwindled from $18 million to $6.7 million, and four months prior to Bimson's arrival Ricketts had barely escaped closing the bank. Bimson flew into action, trimming payrolls while guaranteeing all employees their jobs. He then instructed the officers to "make loans," adding: "I want this period of automatic loan refusal to end and end now."[169] Valley Bank needed to go into "mass production" on small loans and managers, Bimson admonished, and should attempt to make more smaller loans, rather than a single large one. (At Harris, Bimson had proposed that management lease a closed bank in the Loop to form a "people's bank," a proposal the Harris executives turned down as "chicken feed".)[170] Unlike the Keynesian-oriented Marriner Eccles, Bimson had no wish to see the government expand its activities in the economy, but unlike Giannini, he carefully avoided exposing himself to undue criticism from the authorities until late in his career when the bank could afford the risk.

His attitude and confidence spread to the bank's depositors and to the entire community. Money poured into the bank: during Bimson's first ten days as president, the bank took in $200,000 net deposits. Perhaps even more important, less than one percent of the new borrowers ever defaulted, and the one percent figure was hit only once, in 1942.[171] Critics of the day challenged Bimson's lending policies as "immoral," which touched off a fuse in Bimson, who exploded: "Immoral!? Immoral to help an enterprising individual equip and start a new business on his own? Immoral to enable a teacher to go to summer school so she can earn more pay and teach better? . . . Nonsense." He personally negotiated and concluded a loan for $280,000 "on nothing more than a smile and a handshake."[172]

Indeed, Bimson, though ultimately more successful than Wingfield, had more in common with the Nevadan than he did with either the visionary Giannini or the humorless Eccles. Both Bimson and Wingfield embodied the traits that romantic western writers have attributed to the frontier mentality—a willingness to trust character more than physical assets, a commitment to their communities (occasionally at the expense of their institutions), and a determination to lend in the face of adversity. Bimson, however, had the good fortune to receive a wave of deposits, something the *Reno Evening Gazette* short-circuited in Nevada, and his friendly relationship with local lawmakers far surpassed that of his Reno counterpart. Still, the similarities are striking. Neither really envisioned the growth of his bank in the ways that Giannini did (or that Eccles feared). While they, to a degree, dominated the central financial institutions of their respective states, they looked no further than the state lines, and certainly never contemplated a national empire as dreamed of by Giannini. Wingfield kept a list of "principles of banking" in his Reno office that easily could have hung on the wall of Valley National Bank in Phoenix. Examples include: "Capital and Surplus is merely loose change with which to begin business. The real capital and the greatest asset is confidence." Or, "A chattel mortgage is of little value if the maker is dishonest," and, " 'I promise to pay' signed by an honorable person is a solemn obligation."[173]

Although these sentiments may have remained in vogue in the 1920s, certainly the 1930s marked the end of "handshake and a smile loans" for most of the West. Moreover, the imprint of each remained on their respective banking systems: in 1986, Valley Bank found itself the only major Arizona bank not involved in a regional network, while as a result of the collapse of the Wingfield banks, Nevada's financial institutions were marked by their conservatism and aversion to risk.

Bankers had a twofold mission during the Depression. First, as Bimson showed, they had to generate loans. Second, they had to go to unusual extremes to carry debtors. Bankers in the city of Okmulgee, Oklahoma, agreed to put a moratorium on all debts and mortgages, and devised a plan that involved a municipal improvement program that paid in scrip. The scrip, accepted by all the merchants, carried a $.03 tax per dollar, used for administrative costs.[174] Leonard Arrington's book on Tracy-Collins Bank in Utah details the intricate maneuvers the bank went through to close a sale of a specific property, including lending the buyer money, accepting a parcel of land from the buyer to use for a down payment, and convincing the sellers to pay the taxes.[175] Indeed, as long as a bank could collect the taxes on mortgaged properties, frequently it delayed collecting the principal, and, on occasion, even the interest. Some borrowers did not want to pay, but there is evidence that others, such as Preston Nutter, a farmer from Price, Utah, had the desire and ability to pay at least some of their debt, but were delayed by the RFC. Nutter had maintained a profitable ranching business since the 1890s, and in the Depression had the good fortune of obtaining interim financing from his friend and attorney A. L. Hoppaugh in Salt Lake City. By 1932, Hoppaugh had advanced Nutter over $3,900 in checks or loans to Continental National Bank and Trust Company and acted as an agent to sell his property. There is evidence in Nutter's correspondence to suggest that red tape associated with the RFC slowed liquidations so much as to cause individuals to lose money that they needed to repay bank loans.[176]

Small banks during the Depression found themselves severely tested. The correspondence of Stockmen's National Bank of Rushville, Nebraska, offers a frank account of the bank's business problems. Even as early as 1930, although director George P. Comer reported to fellow director and president M. D. Cravath that the bank was "in better shape now than it ever was so far as good notes and assets are concerned," the officers had other nagging headaches.[177] The most irritating of all was a stockholder referred to as Mr. Duncan, who, one correspondent noted, was "crazy," and acted like "some wild beast."[178] Duncan apparently lobbied for employment at the bank by persuading friends to threaten to withdraw their funds if the bank did not immediately employ him as a vice president.[179] He attended a meeting of the board of directors "and gave the board . . .

a fair sized cussing," and, according to some insiders, actually sought to gain control of the bank along with a Mr. Ellsworth.[180] Despite these distractions, the bank reported business "moving along in its usual course," but the episode demonstrated that even in troubled times, internal struggles often emerged.[181]

With Duncan out of the way, the bank continued to improve, and by early 1931, Coner noted: "[the bank] has passed through the worst part of the depression, and should, from now on amount to something."[182] By early March, Comer observed that "collections [were] slow," and that "the quiet depressed condition of business [seemed] universal." Still, he added: "We will . . . grow out of it."[183] He had chopped salaries and expenses at the first sign of trouble, and thought that it had paid off. As the depression wore on, Cravath recognized that most of the troubled notes the bank held should be charged off: "The security that the Bank did have has partly vanished."[184] Comer, too, admitted by early 1932: "The financial situation . . . is far ahead of anything that has ever been my pleasure to meet . . . [and there are] more people crying for bread than ever heard before in our time. . . ."[185] (Occasionally the bank had less pressing problems, including the "smoking nuisance" that proved "almost unbearable to some of the patrons.")[186] Typically, however, the bank officers and directors had far more important matters concerning them. A. N. Gehrt, president of the bank before Cravath, after another depressing visit from the examiner, reported "[he] only charge[d] off around $6000/oo . . . that makes a total of around $29,000/oo."[187] The problem, according to Gehrt, was that the bank's casher made loans "whenever & wherever" he pleased.[188] Still, usually the bank refused to make even the most common loans.

Even powerful Utah banks such as First Security and the Tracy-Collins Bank operated under extreme conservatism, although their cautious attitudes could not ensure liquidity at all times. Marriner Eccles had bluffed his way out of a major run on First National Bank of Ogden in the summer of 1931. Over a weekend, Eccles had heard that Ogden State Bank was not going to open the following Monday. In a famous scene, before the bank opened Eccles gathered his employees, along with those of the Eccles-owned First Savings Bank, which shared the same building. Eccles instructed the employees to give the theatrical performance of their lives:

> Go about your business as though nothing unusual was happening. Smile, talk about the weather, be pleasant, show no signs of panic . . . [the tellers' windows] must be manned at all times . . . no one can go to lunch. . . . You are going to pay [the customers]. But you are going to pay them very slowly . . . [and] look up every signature card. And take your time about it. . . . When you pay out, don't use any big bills. Pay out in fives and tens, and count slowly. Our object is to pay out a minimum today.[189]

When long lines formed, as Eccles anticipated, he decided to keep the bank open as long as depositors wanted their money. Bolstered by the arrival of Federal Reserve cash bags, brought in with great fanfare, Eccles climbed atop the black and gold marble counters to assure the customers that money had arrived and that there was more "where that came from," not bothering to tell the depositors that the bank had no claim on that extra money.[190] He even dragged the surprised Federal Reserve officer to the countertop for a similar statement of reassurance. The officer, likewise, announced that there was lots of money at the Fed office in Salt Lake City.

The lines never completely disappeared, but Eccles prevented a panic on the first day. On Tuesday, he changed tactics, opening the bank early, ordering the employees to pay out as quickly as possible, making certain no lines formed. His act worked, for by midmorning the bank was back to usual business. During the crisis, Eccles had convinced the other banker in town, Harold Hemmingway, to remain open and even loaned him $40,000 cash when Hemmingway's reserves dipped.[191]

Eccles's biographer, Sidney Hyman, attributed the banker's ability to remain open to his "strong nerves . . . inherited from his father and mother."[192] Marriner Eccles had in fact inherited a family history of poverty-turned-to-wealth; a business acumen based on thriftiness and initiative; and a wierd proto-socialist philosophy that typified Mormon concepts of collective welfare mixed with individual enterprise. His blind Scottish grandfather raised Marriner's father, David, in Glasgow's slums not far from where Adam Smith had penned his *Wealth of Nations*, (which none of the family read). David Eccles worked for pennies a day until the family moved to America in 1863, settling in Utah. A polygamist who fathered nine children by his first wife—Marriner being the oldest—and twelve by his second, David Eccles built a business empire that ranged in products from coal to milk, lumber to sugar, and, of course, banks. Marriner, born in 1890, was a high school dropout who never displayed any interest in books, but he voraciously devoured corporate reports and companies' financial statements.[193] He dutifully served his two-year Mormon mission, leaving for Scotland in 1910, and upon his return found himself richer in experience but sadly lacking in basic skills, so much so that he could not take notes in meetings of the board of directors. But by escaping to Scotland, Marriner avoided the unpleasant task of raising his eight siblings, and gradually eased himself out from under the shadow of his powerful father, of whom he lived "in mortal fear."[194] Marriner became legal guardian of his father's interests at the age of twenty-two when David died, and also inherited a long battle with his half brothers from David's other marriage over the businesses. Marriner emerged the winner, taking control of First Security Company, First National Bank of Ogden, the First Savings Bank of Ogden, and the rest of the family's interests. At first a devoted disciple of laissez-faire economics—the real theory of which he never really understood—Eccles tinged his version of capitalism with his own color of Mormon welfarism, a theological workfare that permeated Utah and other parts of the West where Mormon settlers resided.

Eccles came under the spell of a flawed, pre-Keynesian book, *The Road to Plenty,* by William T. Foster and Wadill Catchings, an odd couple who thought they had refuted Say's Law and found in government spending the salvation of industrial America.[195] Whether or not Eccles accepted the book's thesis wholeheartedly, he found the underconsumption aspect intriguing. As the depression deepened, so did Eccles's guilt, which ranged from his feelings of inadequacy as a money manager for his clients to melancholy over the victims of his collections. He got himself off the emotional hook by rationalizing that individual bankers were powerless to reverse the policy of credit stringency, and he soon adopted Foster's views of "collective action" by the federal government. Eccles called for an unbalanced budget and suddenly embraced government activism in the marketplace, surprising fellow Utah bankers and industrialists so much that more than one thought the general banking collapse had given him a nervous breakdown.[196]

Attracting attention as a Westerner who seemed to side with the ideas of Roosevelt's "Brain Trust," Eccles was invited to testify before the Senate Finance Committee in February 1933, an appearance that won him the support of Senator Robert M. Lafollette, Jr. He then met with Rexford G. Tugwell. During those meetings, Eccles gained a reputation as a banker with radical ideas. In 1933, Jesse Jones, the powerful Houston banker and head of the RFC, sought a Republican to serve on the three-person board of directors for the newly created Federal Deposit Insurance Corporation (FDIC), and Eccles's associate at First Security, E. G. Bennett, received the nomination. This, in turn, placed Marriner's younger brother George in charge of First Security. Marriner, meanwhile, was slated for bigger things, as Tugwell immediately sought to draw him into the administration. Henry Morgantheau, secretary of the treasury, soon heard of Eccles and extended a vague offer for him to "go to work in the Treasury Department." What this meant specifically, Eccles had no idea, but his brothers said they could handle the Utah banks and an associate convinced him that it was important "someone west of the Mississippi River had a strong voice in the Treasury Department."[197] That Eccles's views on government intervention hardly reflected those of most bankers—let alone western bankers—went unstated.

Eccles left for Washington in early 1934, having been appointed to the position of assistant to the secretary of the Treasury, essentially as a money-

and-credit troubleshooter. He was indeed the first western banker in the Treasury, but both Bennet and Lewis Douglas of Arizona, son of the irascible "Rawhide Jimmy" and later the president of Southern Arizona Bank and Trust, preceded Eccles as prominent western financial leaders in the Roosevelt administration. Douglas, in fact, opposed Eccles's plans to cure the depression with inflation. At one of the first meetings the Mormon banker attended in Washington, one blunt questioner asked Eccles how he was going to "get around Lew Douglas. . . ." And when the two men eventually met, Eccles concluded that Tugwell's description of Roosevelt's choice of Douglas—"awful"—was an understatement.[198]

But Douglas proved a formidable foe. He had won election as the single congressman from Arizona and had the power of his father's wealth behind him. As an "influential member of the President-elect's inner circle," Douglas was "one of the most persuasive men around Roosevelt during the formative months of the New Deal."[199] Even at the time his father's banking chain in Arizona was in the throes of a struggle for control, brought on in large part by J. S. Douglas's trepidation about the Roosevelt administration, Lewis Douglas had persuaded Roosevelt to cut jobs and salaries in government as proposed in the "economy bill." On the Thomas Amendment, a reflation plan involved a new issue of greenbacks, Douglas stood in firm opposition, but Roosevelt decided to accept the bill. Douglas and James Warburg managed to limit the total note issue, but Douglas sadly commented that the bill even in its revised form was "pretty discouraging" and that Roosevelt's unsound money policies marked "the end of Western civilization." Douglas insisted on balanced budgets and fought Roosevelt himself in acrimonious debates over the issue when the president began to waffle.[200] On banking, Douglas contended that Jesse Jones was a flop. But in the struggle over reflation, Eccles had more staying power than the Arizonan. Douglas resigned in August 1934, disgusted with the liberal thrust of Roosevelt's programs. The president nevertheless continued to respect Douglas's considerable talents and, more important, he needed them. In 1947, Secretary of State George C. Marshall convinced Douglas to accept the ambassadorship to Great Britain, a prestigious post in which Lewis Douglas distinguished himself before entering banking in 1949 (although he had served a short time as the president of Mutual of New York Life Insurance).

Eccles's star continued to rise, and in 1934 Roosevelt appointed him chairman of the Federal Reserve Board, essentially giving him the exact position he needed to produce the inflation he sought. Self-righteous, obsessed with politics—according to his biographer he was incapable of "small talk"—and, in his own mind, virtually immune to error when it came to the big issues, Eccles wielded exceptional power in the administration. He had Roosevelt's ear when he needed it on most subjects (with the curious exception of branch banking). But his positions rarely benefitted western banks, and he soon found that Lewis Douglas was not the only Westerner, or western banker, aligned against him. A. P. Giannini had supported some of Eccles's policies initially, hoping that he could count on Eccles's commitment to the idea of branch banking when the situation arose. Giannini soon learned otherwise.

BUILDING THE WEST'S BIGGEST BANK

The Italian-American financier had marched his Bank of Italy through the boom 1920s in California like a conquering army. He had emerged victorious in a battle with Henry Dawes, the comptroller of the currency, over the issue of branch banking. Dawes wanted to strengthen the national banks by prohibiting all branch banking, a position that threatened to strike at the heart of Giannini's dream. Dawes had his moments: in 1923 the Federal Reserve Board limited branching by state banks that were members of the reserve system, although the final legislation was watered down by Dawes's deputy, Charles Collins, who had visited California and seen the advantages of branching. Representative Louis T. McFadden of Pennsylvania, himself a banker, saw the benefits of branching but was powerless against the antibranch forces, who acted to prevent the spread of branch banks into nonbranching states. Fortunately for Giannini and California, Dawes retired, and the new comptroller, Joseph W. McIntosh, willingly entertained any plan that would stop the hemorrhage of national bank conversions into state banks. Moreover, McIntosh came to believe that one of his top priorities would be to bring Giannini's vast network of California banks into the national system. Giannini agreed, as long as he could merge his four branch systems and retain all branches as national bank branches, thus consolidating his four chains. McIntosh and chief examiner John W. Pole held meetings—negotiations, really—with Giannini and his representatives in Washington.[201]

Giannini and McIntosh still had to alter the McFadden bill, which the House had passed and with which the Senate now grappled. Senator Carter Glass of Virginia was lobbied by McIntosh to cooperate with Giannini to pass the bill without the antibranch provisions. Glass promptly agreed, changing the branch-banking sections to permit national or state banks to retain any branches they had on the date the bill became law. When he worked with McIntosh to alter the bill, Giannini's true purpose was to change the regulatory climate to allow nationwide branch banking.

To realize his ambition of a nationwide (or even worldwide) branch-banking system, Giannini had established several independent branch systems. Those systems had increased his flexibility in the face of the antitrust and antibranching sentiments of the 1920s. Giannini's first move out of California involved founding East River National Bank in New York in 1919, which required him to establish Bancitaly to hold the majority stock, and Bancitaly soon acquired an Italian bank and its branches. In 1921, the California state superintendent of banking suddenly blocked any further acquisitions by the Bank of Italy, and as a result this holding company started Liberty Bank in San Francisco to buy other California banks.[202] Giannini thus used Liberty Bank to build a branch system in northern California. In southern California, where Giannini's acquisitions and de novo branches faced formidable opposition from Joseph Sartori of Security National Bank, Giannini formed another holding company, Americommercial, to purchase the Bank of America of Los Angeles in 1924. An eighteen-month-old bank, the Bank of America had been founded by Orra Monnette, a Los Angeles banker since 1907, and Charles C. Chapman, a rancher who pioneered the marketing of Valencia oranges. At the time Giannini acquired it, the bank had two branches and sixteen-thousand depositors. Americommercial then purchased Commercial National. With Orra Monnette president and Bancitaly Corporation the owners, Americommercial faced no restrictions in acquiring southern California banks to add to either state or national banks in the system, depending on the regulatory climate. By the end of 1925 the two banks in the Americommercial system had a total of thirty-five offices. The Bank of America of Los Angeles moved into the hinterlands and Commercial National, with its federal charter, stayed within Los Angeles.[203] But to outsiders these banks appeared to be independent. A. P. Giannini chafed under this arrangement, and wanted the Bank of Italy logo on all his banks. Moreover, he thought that superintendent of banks Frank Johnson displayed considerable bias against him, because while he had approved fifty-four branch permits for Giannini's competitors in southern California, he had turned down all but one of the Bank of Italy's requests for de novo branches.

Meanwhile, the debate over the McFadden Act in Congress, which permitted state banks to join the national bank system and retain all their existing branches, had evolved to include a provision prohibiting them from opening new branches after they joined the Federal Reserve system. They nevertheless could keep any branches of banks they acquired after the passage of the act if the branches had been established before the passage of the act. Giannini saw that clause as a way to unify all his California banks, and he worked to incorporate into his system as many banks as he could before passage of the act. He had the Bank of America and Commercial National stretching the Giannini net across the southern part of the state, and Liberty Bank providing the branching system for the northern California area. When William Wood took office as the new California superintendent of banks in January 1927, Giannini thought the time opportune to combine all his systems. No sooner had Wood assumed his post than Giannini presented him with requests to purchase roughly sixty banks and to merge the Bank of America of Los Angeles and Liberty Bank. Overwhelmed, Wood asked how many branches the new system would request. The next day Giannini's representatives turned in a list of thirty-eight locations in Los Angeles, and notified Wood that they planned to add more in the days to follow.[204]

After seeking legal counsel, which informed Wood that no precedent existed for denying a merger between willing banks, Wood approved the merger of Liberty, the Bank of America, Commercial National, and the newly purchased Southern Trust of San Diego under the name Liberty Bank of America. The new system had 136 branches—sixty-one newly acquired—and won approval for nineteen de novo branches within the next few weeks.[205]

In the few months while Giannini maneuvered his banks into position, Congress continued to battle over the McFadden bill. Horror stories of the Bank of America's predatory behavior characterized the debate, and southern California bankers pleaded for stronger restrictions on branching to slow their rival's growth. Some legislators threatened a filibuster, and Senators Carter Glass and Burton Wheeler had a fist fight. Nevertheless, on February 16, the bill passed seventy-one to seventeen. Giannini, in return for a promise by the Federal Reserve to approve the merger of the Bank of Italy and Liberty Bank of America, brought almost all of his banks under the control of the Federal Reserve System. But once under the Fed's jurisdiction, the Bank of Italy could acquire banks only in San Francisco, thus limiting expansion. Two days after the McFadden bill passed, and the Federal Reserve gave its approval for the merger, painters started to change the signs of all the banks to "Bank of Italy." In that way, the Bank of Italy rose to the position of third-largest bank in the United States, behind New York's Chase National and National City banks, joining the Federal Reserve with resources of $675,000, more than $1 million in deposits (roughly one out of every five in California), and 276 branches in 199 locations. The Bank of Italy justifiably celebrated, with president James Bacigalupi inviting nine hundred officers to a banquet in San Francisco at which he preached the Giannini creed: "The Bank of Italy is essentially a bank of the people. . . ."[206]

Giannini still had not fulfilled his vision, however, for while all his banks were consolidated into the Bank of Italy, and while de novo branches could be added within San Francisco, the Federal Reserve system limited further expansion. So, he built a new state system, the cornerstone of which was the French-American Bank of San Francisco. One the stable early banks, it had $24 million in assets when Giannini used it to found French-American Corporation, a new bank holding company in 1927.

This holding company bought fifteen banks, including three Southern California banks with the word "security" in their titles. These he combined as branches of Security Bank and Trust Company of Bakersfield, and he also acquired other banks as branches. Acquisition of a bank in La Habra rekindled the opposition of Giannini's southern California rival, Joseph Sartori, who contended that the use of the word "security" in the title of Giannini's banks threatened to blur the distinction between his bank, Security Trust and Savings Bank, and Giannini's. Reluctantly, Giannini dropped the name, but complained peevishly: "Who has given Sartori exclusive right to the word security? . . . I see no reason why anyone should pick on us for the use of a name that we have purchased."[207]

In September 1928 Giannini began assigning the name Bank of America of California to his branches, starting with one small San Pedro bank. By 1930, that bank had 138 branches, including those of the former Merchants National, Isasias Hellman's bank (which Giannini had bought from Hellman's heirs), and the venerable Donohoe and Kelly Banking Company.[208] Thus the Bank of America of California pulled together some of the state's oldest names in finance.

As a condition of the consolidation of 1927, Giannini had agreed that Bancitaly would not own more than one-fourth of any other national bank in California. Therefore, combination of his banks required forming yet another new company, chartered in October 1928 and called Transamerica, a name that aptly fit Giannini's goal. Shares in the new company were traded for stock of Bancitaly, the Bank of Italy, and, by January 1929, the Bank of America of California, the Bank of America, NA, in New York, the Security banks, and the Hellman bank.[209] Transamerica soon became more than a bank holding company. To effect the purchase of a Sacramento bank, it acquired a casualty insurance company, and to diversify risk, Transamerica purchased other insurance companies. In April 1930, it further diversified by purchasing controlling interest in General Foods Corporation.

With the new holding company, Giannini pursued yet another consolidation, the last for some time, as the national banking system had started to slip into depression. On November 3, 1930, he brought together all the banks, with some regret at losing the name Bank of Italy, under the name Bank of America. To satisfy the McFadden Act, the Bank of America of California moved to San Francisco and merged with the Bank of Italy, retaining its national charter and taking the name Bank of America, National Trust and Savings Association. Giannini failed to get all the branches in under the grandfather clause, however, so he organized a state-chartered Bank of America. Also outside the network was his Bank of America in New York.[210]

Giannini's vision convinced other western bankers that his concepts of branching and forming holding companies had merit. Oregon bankers quickly copied his techniques. The twenty-three-year-old Peninsula National Bank and the five-year-old West Coast National Bank combined to trade their stock for shares in the newly formed West Coast Bancorporation in 1928. A Portland newspaper hailed the holding company combination as "the most modern development of banking." West Coast soon acquired U.S. National Bank of Salem, and by 1930 controlled five other Oregon banks and one Washington institution. That year, West Coast, in turn, was acquired by another holding company, U.S. National Bank Corporation, established out of the U.S. National Bank of Oregon. One impediment to efficient banking remained in Oregon, though, in that branch banking, outlawed in 1909, remained illegal until 1933, despite bills introduced in 1927, 1929, and 1931 to change the law. When the legislature finally legalized branch banking, U.S. National Corporation made many of its banks into branches of U.S. National Bank. By the end of 1933, the bank had twelve branches and assets of $83 million.[211]

Giannini had his eye on banks in the Pacific Northwest and in Nevada, but his march toward a nationwide branching system temporarily came to a standstill in the 1930s when the ailing Italian-American dynamo relinquished much of his official power to New Yorker Elisha Walker, who became chairman after the consolidation of 1930. In the face of the stock-market crash, Giannini's banks had continued to show deposit growth. However, as the depression deepened and the bank's deposits shrank and its bad loans mounted, Walker panicked. No longer concerned with adding branches, Walker faced the difficult task of saving the bank. But he could hardly have been more different than the fearless Giannini: Walker saw the potential liquidation of the bank around every corner, and sharply disagreed not only with A. P. but with A. P.'s son Mario Giannini, who resigned his position in the bank in protest of Walker's policies. When the elder Giannini heard of Walker's plans to sell parts of the empire he had so carefully constructed, he vowed to replace Walker and his board. A bitter struggle ensued, but when Giannini finally took the issue of control to the stockholders, they returned him to management by at least a six million vote margin.[212] Reinstated, Giannini set to saving the bank.

By late 1932, the Bank of America was finally turning a profit again, although its June 30, 1932, statement still showed an 11 percent loss (less than that of its four major national competitors) and the bank did not pay dividends in 1932.[213] But the bank had repaid loans to the RFC of $54.5 million, with just over $7 million remaining to be paid. On its way back to the top, Giannini's institution crossed paths with Wingfield's defunct banks headed the other direction. The Wingfield chain offered a natural opportunity for Giannini to expand into Nevada if state laws there would accommodate branching. Certainly the Nevada governor thought Giannini could rescue the Wingfield banks, as he requested that Transamerica take over the Nevada chain. However, the Nevada legislature displayed no hint that its antibranching laws would change, so Giannini declined.

The Banking Act of 1933 forced Giannini to reconsider the Nevada situation, as well as renew his interest in the Pacific Northwest. In 1930, just before expansion slowed, Transamerica acquired First National Bank of Oregon, culminating a Portland drama that had started unfolding in 1928 when Elliot Corbett, the descendent of Oregon banking pioneer Henry Corbett, suggested that E. B. MacNaughton merge his Strong and MacNaughton Trust Company with Security Savings and Trust, owned by First National. Not only had the Corbett and Failing families owned the bank for years, but prominent Oregon bankers Abbot Mills and C. F. Adams each had served as president of First National (Mills from 1903 to 1927, and Adams from 1932 to 1947). Strong and MacNaughton specialized in mortgage loans and real-estate transactions. MacNaughton had the inclination to accept the deal, but Strong refused, leading MacNaughton to leave the trust company and take a position with First National. He sensed that the competitors , especially U.S. National, merged into West Coast Bancorp, controlled far more banks than did First National. Moreover, the Corbetts had been extremely conservative, and they worried about the decline in their large holdings. They favored a sale, and Mac-Naughton handled the negotiations with Transamerica. The Portland banker earned Giannini's respect, and he was offered the presidency when Adams retired in 1932.[214]

Those successes led Giannini to again look at the closed Wingfield banks in Nevada. In 1934 Transamerica entered Nevada, taking over in many of the towns where Wingfield's banks—now in receivership—remained as empty shells. Indeed, Transamerica took over First National Bank of Reno, the Wingfield flagship. After two years, Wingfield's claim that a reorganization, a little more money, and a little time would save his banks appeared to be corroborated by Giannini.

Still, the 1933 law was only an emergency measure designed to fill the gap until more thorough and permanent legislation came along. In 1935, a new banking act superseded the older law, and this new bill in its draft form could have been written by A. P. Giannini, for it allowed branch banking on a regional basis across state lines. In this context, no sooner had Giannini's path crossed that of the declining Wingfield banks than he ran into the rising star from Utah, Eccles, who rapidly had gained prominence in the Roosevelt administration. The Utah banker claimed to favor regional branching at the time (and even took credit for the branch-banking clause of the bill), but used little of his political capital to see that branch banking remained in the new bill. The final version omitted the branch-banking provision. With the interstate branching provision removed, Giannini had reason to oppose the law, but instead he supported it, no doubt viewing it as a means of negating the influence of his major New York rivals. Thinking he could later count on Eccles' support, Giannini bided his time, and threw his weight behind the banking bill, for which Eccles expressed his gratitude. Giannini soon learned the value of that gratitude.

Both Eccles's and Giannini's biographers interpreted Eccles's actions before 1940 as supportive of interstate branch banking in general and of the Bank of America/Transamerica in particular. On closer inspection, however, Eccles hardly seems the stalwart defender of Giannini that Sidney Hyman and the Jameses have made him out to be. Eccles stood by idly while Giannini battled Henry Morganthau over examinations, despite his own considerable influence in the administration and his personal view that examiners were too conservative (a view he held, though, out of a desire for reflation rather than sympathy for the plight of the banks). Eccles's sudden change of attitude against expansion by the Bank of America or Transamerica after he became chairman of the Federal Reserve Board also reflects this interpretation more than the one offered by Hyman or the Jameses: he opposed Mario Giannini's attempts to expand, calling them a breach of the "gentlemen's agreement" that they had arrived at with Morganthau, even though the minutes of the meetings with Morganthau show no such agreement. Instead, Eccles had his own agenda, including centralization of the financial and credit system. A powerful independent branch-banking system that could not be co-opted posed a very real threat to such centralization.

THE TRIUMPH OF FEDERAL REGULATION

Moreover, during the mid-1930s, Giannini and other western bankers fought a war against the increasingly oppressive and extreme examinations by the federal regulators. Of the most widely shared of their complaints, namely the stiff and inflexible attitude of bank examiners toward loans, Giannini felt himself always the victim. Although he refused to allow the examiners' reports to stifle his lending, other western bankers, who lacked Giannini's massive reputation or huge deposit base, could not hope to prevail against federal regulators. Instead, they simply gave up: they refused any but the most traditional loans. In some cases, that meant they curtailed lending altogether. Colorado banks, which had taken more than their share of abuse from regulators, were nowhere near their limits on loanable funds. Some exceptions existed in New Mexico and Arizona, where the larger more secure banks found a ready market for loans, and a few, such as Walter Bimson's Valley National or Paul Walter's First National Bank of Santa Fe, actually expanded their lending during the crisis. But by and large, banks found themselves in a "squeeze play" by the government, where they were pressed to increase lending, but criticized for poor loans. Of course, once a depression has begun, most loans appear to be "poor."

Having a source of funds, of course, was a prerequisite for lending. Giannini solved this dilemma by always focusing on deposits and deposit growth. Valley National in Arizona generated deposits with its lending, although Bimson brought with him the "Harris pipeline," a conduit to his previous employer, the Harris Trust of Chicago, which had plenty of capital. Other banks, such as Albuquerque National Bank, had steered such a conservative course that they had accumulated loanable funds.

In August 1934, the comptroller of the currency instructed the chief bank examiners of each district to report the conditions in their regions. Among the questions they asked prominent bankers were:

Are banks in your section making all the loans that they can prudently make? If not, why are they refraining from lending?
Do you believe that banks have . . . refrained from making justifiable loans because of the fear of criticism by bank examiners?
What is your explanation of the fact that loans held by banks are at the lowest point for a number of years. . .?[215]

Paul Walter, the president of First National Bank of Santa Fe, replied that banks in his sector were making all the loans they could make, and banks took a more liberal position than usual in granting a lower rate of interest to desireable borrowers. Walter, however, noted that banks "are more cautious in making advances because of criticism by bank examiners."[216] The view that examiners had curtailed lending may explain why, despite very low interest rates, banks still hesitated to lend. The concerns about the bank examiner who visited Stockmen's National Bank has been noted, and by 1932 one of the officers of that bank observed: "We have not made a new loan in the Bank for the last six months."[217] Federal Bank Examiner William H. Donahue from Kansas City, after going through the books of Colorado National Bank, also commented on a reluctance to actively solicit loans.[218] Walter also reported that a number of what appeared to him to be good loans had been examined and criticized. Moreover, examiners did not seem to understand unique elements of New Mexico banking law and, just as important to Walter, local custom.[219]

First National Bank, for example, had carried borrowers who had collateral and paid the interest without requiring them to repay the principal. As a result of complying with the examiners' requirements, the bank reduced its indebtedness from $2 million to $750,000, which cost the bank $100,000 in annual interest payments. The bank board thought all the debts that the examiners had demanded be closed were in fact "perfectly sound."[220] Federal involvement in banking also led to bankers' turning down loans because of insufficient information. According to the minutes of the Utah Bankers Association, pressure from government competition caused bankers to speed up their loan review policies. As a result, there can be little doubt that decisions were frequently made without more complete information, which, given time, the banker might have obtained.[221]

Paul Walter also contended that the government's practice of taking over many banks' loans reduced their lending portfolios, which also meant, he warned, that the government would soon have "a residue of loans that [it could] not collect." Walter recommended turning the loans back over to the banks, although he wanted the banks to be able to choose the loans they wanted! And although conditions had "never been as prosperous" they were then, Walter admitted that much of this he ascribed to the $40 million expenditure by the U.S. government in New Mexico.[222]

The notion that all banks failed due to the poor state of the general economy or some inherent weakness in either the state regulatory structures or the operations of the Federal Reserve Board must also be qualified. Some banks, victims of graft, embezzling, or outright theft, found their ability to remain open completely eroded. An example can be seen in the affairs of First National Bank of Aurora in Colorado. The records of the bank's receivers, Hilliard and Hilliard, during 1933–35 show that the bank failed due to "the defalcations of [president] T. Frank Gilligan."[223] Reporting to the comptroller of the currency in 1934, the receiver from Hilliard and Hilliard, W. D. Hover, noted that no excess loans had been made, that no negligence existed on the part of the directors, and that Gilligan, since 1931, "maintained an extensive bookkeeping system of his own for otherwise he could not have concealed his embezzlements for so long." Gilligan had made fraudulent real-estate mortgage loans and also permitted back taxes on real estate to accumulate, apparently pocketing the tax payments himself. Gilligan so conned the depositors that a depositors' committee in 1934 concluded the bank's failure was "due to the depression." Hover, instead found, among the other problems, a $5,000 shortage Gilligan had "juggled and rejuggled" so that it escaped the bank examiners' notice for more than two years![224]

Not only did outright theft threaten western banks, but solvent operations often fell victim to relationships with insolvent eastern houses. Banks keep deposits in other banks for a number of reasons. Sometimes these deposits are used to assist a customer who needs funds in another city, say, a Kansas merchant purchasing goods in New York. Other times the funds are used in check processing and clearing operations. Most often, however, the funds serve as an investment by smaller banks in larger urban banks that earn interest for the depositing institution and provide funds to lend for the bank in which the money is deposited. Investments such as these facilitate interregional flow of funds across the nation and around the world. When good business opportunities, rapid economic development, or locally tight money conditions raise interest rates in one location, banks in other areas profit by diverting some of their investment funds to bank in that area. But as with all investments, a higher rate of return may instead signal higher risk, and for many situations the difference is hard to detect.

For example, some Idaho banks found themselves linked to the falling fortunes of Seattle banks, even though the Idaho institutions were healthy. Another example of the interstate deposit problem appeared in the relationship between Colorado National Bank, owned in large part by Charles and Herman Kountze, and the New York Kountze Brothers investment house. In October 1931 the Colorado Kountzes learned that the New York bank "was on its deathbed." The New York Stock Exchange suspended Kountze Brothers on October 31 for insolvency related to a drop in the firm's bond portfolios, and Kountze Brothers declared bankruptcy by the end of the year. Although Harold Kountze wired Thomas Davis (Herman Kountze's son-in-law and vice president of First National Bank of Omaha) that the New York bank's failure had not affected the Colorado bank's business, he later admitted that deposits in Omaha had in fact shrunk by $700,000. The relationship between the Nebraska bank and its New York correspondent was deeper than Colorado National's, and while neither failed, the Omaha bank suffered more seriously. Colorado National may have put itself at risk through its heavy investments in state, county, and local governments or agencies. According to Thomas Noel, the bank's historian, "CNB's loans helped many public . . . entities to survive the 1930s at considerable risk to the bank itself."[225]

One must take care, however, in assessing causal relationships either between crime within a bank or weak interbank balances and bank failure. Crimes, especially embezzlement, often provide the perfect "out" when a bank has sacrificed safety for high interest rates. Did the theft push the bank over the edge, or actually conceal even deeper troubles? Crime was an unavoidable part of banking, and one that was—and is—relatively unrelated to broader bank regulations (i.e., laws against fraud or embezzling are intended to reduce crime rather than to regulate). If it could be shown that western banks maintained excessive balances with particularly weak eastern or midwestern banks, then that would itself suggest an additional series of questions.

In other ways the states' regulatory structure occasioned a weakened banking system. For example, Nebraska had such high capital requirements for banks in towns of less than one thousand people—$25,000— that a chain of cooperative credit unions appeared throughout the state.

These credit unions were easy to start and the banks feared the competition. As a result, in 1935 Nebraska's legislature lowered capital requirements for banks in towns of less than one thousand to $10,000. In 1930 Nebraska had legislated against banks in yet another way by allowing collection of individual stockholder's liability, over and above the stock lost. This double liability lasted a decade, and helps to account for the absence of new starts after 1934, when the dustbowl crisis was at its worst. Overall, Nebraska lost almost three hundred banks from 1930 to 1940. Total state bank resources in 1939 ($79 million) had hardly changed from 1934 ($78 million).[226]

Of course, the agricultural situation and general depression tossed about unit banks in Nebraska, Oklahoma, Kansas, and other western states like so many autumn leaves. Oklahoma lost 174 banks from 1928 to 1932, most of those due to failing livestock loans. The state banking department implemented a moratorium plan to expedite the handling of insolvent bank assets and clearinghouses and "cash reserve associations" appeared.[227] All encountered at least some success before the reforms of the Roosevelt administration.

Pacific Coast states witnessed declines in assets and loans. Total assets and loans of existing banks in the Rocky Mountain region dipped from 1929 to 1939, although they recovered in the late 1930s. When comparing average bank size in 1929 with that in 1939, the effect on the states in the Rockies of Depression-era consolidation are evident. Arizona was probably the most striking case, with bank numbers dropping by thirty-five from 1929 to 1939 (73 percent), but assets fell by only 29 percent. Giannini's Transamerica acquired control of Phoenix National Bank, the Tempe branch of Phoenix National (formerly Tempe National Bank), and Phoenix Savings and Trust Company. Phoenix National was then consolidated, in 1937, with First National Bank, an earlier Transamerica acquisition.[228] These mergers left First National as the second largest Arizona bank, with resources of $16 million. By 1939 it held 20 percent of the state's assets, while the giant Valley Bank's $45 million in assets left it with 50 percent. Combined with Southern Arizona Bank and Trust, which held 11 percent, these banks controlled 81 percent of Arizona's banking assets.[229]

The pattern of consolidation in Wyoming, which accelerated during the 1940s, also revealed banking concentration, especially into holding companies. There, bank numbers fell by twenty-nine (34 percent) from 1929 to 1939, while assets fell only $16.2 million (28 percent). Clearly, Colorado and, to a lesser extent, New Mexico, saw their unit-bank laws restrain concentration. In Colorado, although bank numbers declined by 132 from 1929 to 1939 (48 percent), assets fell only $71 million (27 percent). New Mexico actually gained $800,000 in assets over the same period.

Overall in the Rockies, bank assets dropped from $725.2 million to $541.6 million, a change of 26 percent.

Loans fell dramatically as well, although again the decline did not keep pace with falling bank numbers. Only Wyoming and Colorado, two of the states that steadfastly refused branching, and Utah, which adopted a branch-banking law in 1933, witnessed a decline in their loan/bank ratios. All other states experienced an increase: Arizona more than doubled, and Idaho, Nevada, and New Mexico all significantly increased average loans per bank, especially after 1935. What explains the decline in Utah's ratio and the increase in nonbranching Nevada's? The Nevada Wingfield chain, which had been in receivership for almost two years, was transferred to Transamerica Corporation in 1934—too late for Transamerica's management to correct many of the Nevada chain's problems before the yearly report was due. However, by the time the Federal Reserve statistics again appeared in June 1935, the Nevada banks had begun their recovery. Utah, on the other hand, did not revive immediately after passage of its limited branch-banking law in 1933, showing returning signs of health only in 1935. By 1939, however, Utah banks had reached approximately 85 percent of their 1929 loan/bank ratio. If branching was a positive change, why did the Utah statistics not show a recovery similar to those seen in other states? One explanation may be that at least one large Utah chain had considerable interests in Idaho banks, and its management may have viewed the situation in Idaho as more serious than that in Utah. Indeed, by 1933, Idaho's assets had dropped by 54 percent and its asset/bank ratio by 25 percent, whereas Utah's respective declines had only been 43 percent and 2 percent! It seems likely that the First Security chain in Utah transferred funds to its Idaho chain relatives, although proof of this awaits examination of First Security's bank balance sheets, which at present are restricted. At any rate, by 1933 Utah's asset/bank ratio showed an 18 percent increase from 1929, somewhat below the regional average, but an increase nonetheless.

If, as bank examiners and regulators complained, lending had dropped in the early 1930s (and statistics show that indeed it had), one large potential lender remained to be tapped—Uncle Sam. Although the RFC had entered the lending arena by unburdening a host of western banks of their more questionable loans, bankers soon viewed the RFC as a competitor. When this competition combined with bankers' impressions that regulators and examiners were unreasonable, western financiers withdrew from lending in droves. What was needed was a federal program that encouraged lending by reducing risk, without the disadvantage of direct government competition. As a partial solution to this need (though certainly not the central focus of the program), the federal government enacted the National Housing Act in 1934 , which established the Federal Housing Administration (FHA) and the Veteran's Administration (VA) loan insurance programs. These agencies provided federal insurance for home mortgages and for home-improvement loans. Some bankers immediately grasped the potential offered by these programs, and their eyes lit up.[230]

Walter Bimson of Arizona's Valley National Bank, and his brother Carl, quickly appreciated the opportunities in lending offered by federally-insured mortgages. Carl had been instrumental in getting the act passed, and he actually embraced the concept more enthusiastically than Walter. Carl "made a crusade" of originating FHA/VA loans and Title I improvement loans.[231] Bimson's lending officers made over seven-hundred such loans in a single week, and Valley Bank made over $1 million worth of FHA-related loans in Phoenix and Tucson alone in a year.[232] Valley's success in originating these loans inspired the federal government to "lease" Carl from the bank and to use him as a spokesman in Arizona for FHA/VA loans.[233] From 1934 to 1935, using the Bimson's new lending philosophies, Valley National Bank ranked fifth in the nation in FHA loans, making over 3,348 during the year.[234] But the small bank soon bumped up against federal loan-to-reserves limits. The Bimsons quietly searched for ways around these constraints, and discovered that the bank could broker the loans to other western banks. Valley soon sold $1 million worth of FHA loans to Transamerica, which was the equivalent of a year's worth of such loans in Phoenix and Tucson, and the Bimsons could have peddled more to eastern insurance companies if not for the Easterners' fears that the government could not be trusted to actually insure the loans.[235]

Marriner Eccles, another western banker instrumental in getting the FHA authorized, emphasized FHA lending by his bank through his brother George, who ran the bank while Marriner was in Washington. According to Sid Nielson, whose job it was to process FHA loans for First Security, "We were hungry for loans and went to great lengths to secure them."[236] First Security even built parts of a model house in the bank's lobby to instruct customers on correct homebuilding methods. Even before passage of the housing act, First Security had already acquired Bankers Trust and Central Trust in 1930 and 1931, respectively, and these companies greatly facilitated First Security's mortgage lending. Due to the aggressive lending program at the bank, between 1936 and 1939 Utah ranked ninth in the nation in per-capita FHA loans, and overall lending in Utah, which by 1937 had increased from $16 million in the pit of the Depression to $23 million, reached $26 million in 1939.

Despite First Security's lending success with the FHA programs, it never reached the levels that Valley Bank attained and thus never faced the lending restrictions that Valley encountered. Partly because of these restrictions, Valley gradually moved out of FHA lending until, after World War II, the tiny A. B. Robbs Trust Company aggressively outhustled the larger bank for these loans, eventually becoming the nation's eleventh largest originator of FHA/VA loans, despite a capital only a fraction of that of Valley or other major Arizona banks, and minuscule resources compared to those of eastern banks.[237] Aside from the innovative exceptions such as the Eccles and Bimson brothers, most bankers chose to keep their lendable funds in the vaults, safe from regulatory criticism and relatively free from risk. They had diversified as much as state laws allowed and, having turned many of their troubled loans over the RFC, had no inclination to assume new, uninsured obligations.

As for the effects of state legislation, the overlay of chain-banking and branch-banking laws in Utah and Idaho make clear cut conclusions about this period more difficult. Nevertheless, it is apparent that many states in the West survived the rocky times of 1929–39 by permitting more extensive branch banking, allowing considerable consolidation, even to the point of encouraging interstate banking, and reducing overall lending. During this dark period, bankers frequently viewed state and federal regulators (more often the latter) as uninformed about local practices, lending conditions, and the character of individual borrowers. Through the RFC many banks unloaded questionable loans, then hesitated to initiate new lending programs. Brilliant initiative on the part of some bankers, along with the security of the FHA/VA loans, led to some expansion of lending. But the new federal programs, as with the RFC, came with strings attached, and before long bankers searched for avenues around various federal restrictions. In almost every case, government solutions rebounded with unintended effects.

World War II intervened before many of these undesirable effects bloomed, and the war itself offered new and different opportunities for banking growth. In many cases, the opportunities arrived just in time: the Dakotas lost 15 percent of their citizens in the 1930s, and Nebraska and Montana suffered similar population decreases. Wyoming's population fell by one third. Some of this movement consisted of farmers, tradesmen, and shopkeepers migrating further west, and these individuals brought with them talent and skills that proved particularly useful during World War II. Gerald Nash has argued that in many ways the West on the eve of war languished in a colonial status.[238] Certainly, even with the federal public works and water project expenditures during the Depression, the region had suffered through a miserable decade. This had not stopped some western bankers from emerging as national leaders in finance. Nor did it prevent them from laying the foundations for future growth and, in many cases, realizing that their personal, active involvement in boosterism was needed to make that growth occur.

5

BRASH BANKERS AND BIG BOOSTERS:
RECOVERY AND BOOM, 1940–1960

From 1940 until 1945, the United States had to make the transition from a peacetime economy in recession to a wartime economy at full employment. Lending opportunities were limited during the war, and bankers took on a new role—that of maximizing sales of government bonds. But the restrictive war years gave way to a postwar boom and some western financiers—but certainly not all—positioned themselves during the hostilities to surge at war's end. In the process, these bankers frequently became the West's biggest boosters.

BOND SALES

With the onset of World War II, bond sales comprised a natural activity for western bankers. The postwar boom involved the relocation in the West of rustbelt industries. Banks immediately recognized that opportunity as a chance not only to provide financing for those industries but also for the homes and cars needed by their employees. They also decided to use promotional efforts to retain both the businesses and their dependent populations after the war was over. The necessary expansion of the banking system was accomplished through a vigorous program of mergers and a new era of branching. Adept at packaging financial instruments for the public, bankers easily fit the government securities into their office paperwork pipelines. Most simply had the tellers sell the bonds, with one or more of the officers in charge of bond drives. The Federal Reserve Bank's Helena branch created seven Victory Fund committees in Montana, each headed by a banker. The drive easily oversubscribed its quota.[1] At First National Bank of Denver, Clarence H. Adams, president of the affiliated International Trust Company, chaired the war bond sales campaign, while John Evans, the bank's president, volunteered as chairman of the Colorado Victory Fund Committee.[2] First National of Denver differed from most western banks in that it created three separate departments to handle activities related to the war effort. Its Ration Department had the responsibility for overseeing all processing of government ration coupons; the Fitzsimons Army Hospital facility offered special banking services to army personnel or civilian employees on base; and the War Bond Department handled bond sales. Yet, even without such intricate institutional organization, western bankers found it easy to sell bonds. Oklahoma bankers exceeded the state goal of $108,000 in sales by 34 percent, with every Oklahoma county oversubscribing. Otis McClintock, president of First National Bank and Trust Company of Tulsa, besides investing heavily in war bonds with his own funds, gave out defense savings stamp albums to employees with the first dollar's worth of stamps already in place.[3] One Montana banker, Lee Ford, organized 350 people for a bond-sale breakfast meeting. Then they hit the streets, selling $1.8 million worth of bonds in a few hours.[4] George Eccles chaired the Utah war-loan drives as a "dollar-a-year man," and First Security's holdings of United States bonds and government securities increased by 500 percent from 1941 to 1945, at which time such securities represented 65 percent of the bank's assets.[5] Arizona banks' holdings of government bonds and securities soared 1,200 percent, and every bond drive was oversubscribed.[6] Fittingly, Walter Bimson served as chairman of the State War Finance Committee, which coordinated the activities of the Victory Fund Committee (created to sell securities to larger investors) and the War Savings Staff (to handle security sales to smaller investors). Montana's war savings-bond committee reported in 1944 that the sale of Series E bonds exceeded $104 million, or $219 per capita. This made Montana fourth among all states in per capita bond sales, and by the end of the campaign, the state's citizens had subscribed to over $461 million worth of bonds of all types.[7] Perhaps the most astounding feat by a bank was the sale of $21 million in war bonds sold in a ten day period around the state of Oregon by U.S. National Bank of Portland, with all expenses borne by the Bank.[8]

Of course, banks bought as well as sold bonds: Peoples Bank of Seattle had invested 53 percent of its total assets in U.S. bonds by the end of 1943, but still lagged behind most other Seattle banks in that respect. National Bank of Commerce, for example, had 62 percent of its assets in such securities, and Pacific National had 57 percent. Seattle First (Seafirst) matched Peoples' 53 percent, holding more than $273 million in government bonds and securities.[9] For the banks in the state of Washington, the total of government securities held increased from $126 million in 1940 to $1.3 billion in 1945.[10] A similar situation was found in New Mexico, where Albuquerque National held, by 1945, 80 percent of its assets in government bonds.[11] For all New Mexico banks, the holdings of government securities increased from $14.2 million to $132.7 million during the war years.[12]

In fact, as Sidney Hyman pointed out in his history of Utah's First Security Corporation, the banks themselves desperately wanted to purchase more government securities than the law allowed (a total of $10 billion for all commercial banks during the first two drives was permitted). The pricing system adopted by the Treasury encouraged this process. While the securities sold at only a small premium when offered, which encouraged oversubscription, the banks willingly lent money to buy the oversubscribed bonds. Securities purchased in earlier drives carried a shorter maturity than the later offers, and went at a premium. These premiums induced investors, then, to sell old securities and buy new ones, so though the drives led to subscriptions of $60 billion in securities, nonbank investors held only $19 billion.[13] Not only did the banks earn interest on the loans, but the securities expanded their deposit base, and in turn expanded their credit. Consequently, the banks bought six times more securities from nonbank investors than they sold.

For someone like Marriner Eccles, with his unbridled faith in the government's ability to stimulate or to control demand—hence, inflation—the banks' ease in finding a route around the federal regulators drove him to distraction. He and George were highly unpopular among rank and file bankers anyway, as they discovered at the 1935 American Bankers Association convention when they attempted to put E. G. Bennett of First Security in the line of succession to the presidency of the organization. Roundly denounced as an "Eccles stooge," Bennett faced a blistering personal attack, exceeded only by the assault on the Federal Reserve led by another Utah banker, Orval Adams, who was elected to the position Bennett had sought. No doubt many bankers, especially in the Utah-Idaho region, feared that First Security profited from inside information passing from Marriner to George, but genuine hostility to Marriner's quasi-socialistic schemes existed among more than a few country bankers, who had for years railed about the federal deficits as a threat to monetary stability. Suddenly, with the sale of war bonds, they had found a way to make inflation work for them, only to find that Marriner Eccles had "gotten religion" on the dangers of inflation. Both he and George published pieces, Marriner in *Fortune* and George in the local papers, warning that an inflationary boom lurked around the corner.[14]

Although George served as a "dollar-a-year" chairman of the Utah drives, he stressed getting the nonbank investors to retain their securities, a curious position given First Security's own numbers. In four war years, holdings of government securities rose sixfold, to the point that they comprised 65 percent of the bank's assets. George explained this in the annual report by pleading that conditions had forced the bank to change its policy.[15] He and Marriner had started to experience firsthand the difficulties associated with trying to use fiscal and monetary tools to fine-tune the American economy. It was one of the first encounters in the West with the Law of Unintended Effects, and for a man other than Marriner Eccles, it might have been a humbling experience.

SUPPORTING DEFENSE INDUSTRIES

In assisting the war effort, western bankers not only sold and purchased war bonds, but extended loans to defense-related industries. The government guaranteed the loans of large contractors, but not of subcontractors. Uncle Sam's preparations, even before Pearl Harbor, involved retooling and financing plant expansion, which threatened to choke off the growth of small industries that suddenly found their peacetime consumer base had evaporated. No one better understood the predicament of the small businesses better than did A. P. Giannini, who insisted on a "bits and pieces" approach that encouraged all plants to participate in the defense effort, and the government to extend contracts to these small shops. The Bank of America suggested that Governor Culbert Olson call a conference in Sacramento to organize the participation of small shops across the state. Receiving contractor status on loans occasionally required several small businesses to band together (such as San Jose Manufacturers, Inc.) to bid as a prime contractor. The bank formed an information service that aided small contractors in receiving 1,900 contracts totaling $42.5 million in just three months. Shortly before the United States entered the war, Congress passed a law permitting government contracts to serve as collateral for bank loans. Thanks to further efforts by Mario Giannini especially, Congress created the Smaller War Plants Corporation, and the Federal Reserve Board enacted Regulation V which greatly eased the qualifications for a plant to receive a contractor's loan. Rates on these loans dipped as low as 1.5 percent. Recipients of V loans included Norden Bombsight Manufacturers, for tachometers; Western Stove Company, for incendiary bombs; and Walt Disney Productions, for propaganda and educational films.[16]

Throughout the West, industries turned out war materials, including some sixty thousand aircraft manufactured in California alone. Workers, starved for jobs during the Depression, flooded the West. Population in Idaho and Utah rose 18 percent in the decade following Pearl Harbor, but employment in manufacturing industries in those states rose 96 and 93 percent, respectively. George Eccles noted that from 1941 to 1945 in Utah, investment in industrial capital exceeded $110 million, which equaled total capital investment in the state in 1939.[17] Besides the Geneva Steel Plant and a high octane gasoline plant, First Security financed a small arms plant, a facility to produce radio tubes, and several chemical-processing plants. Denver's population increased by over eleven thousand nonmilitary government personnel, added to the twenty thousand newcomers employed at Remington Arms Company and the fourteen thousand at the Rocky Mountain Arsenal. Altogether, the Queen City's population shot up 20 percent during the war years.[18] Idaho also attracted many war-related industries and military bases. Farragut Naval Training Base at Lake Pend Oreille, established in 1942, trained forty-five thousand recruits at a time. First Security officials in Pocatello secured the establishment of a large naval ordinance plant with 225 foot-long lathes and two-thousand-square-foot buildings. The Boise area's population grew with expansion of Mountain Home Air Base, while the town of Mountain Home saw its population quadruple.[19]

The Golden State experienced the greatest absolute growth related to the war. By 1943, employment in California airplane plants alone had soared by 227,000 over prewar levels. Reuben H. Fleet's Consolidated-Vultee Aircraft in San Diego, which experienced a boom in government orders with its successful B-24 Liberator bomber and its PBY Catalina flying boat, drew on a bankers' pool for a $200 million loan. The Bank of America contributed $15 million to the pool, equaling the amount contributed by its powerful eastern competitor, Chase.[20] Consolidated-Vultee's San Diego plant expanded from 1,500 employees before the war to 44,673 during peak war production, operating the first continuously moving assembly line for aircraft production in the world. The Bank of America also floated a $20 million loan to Lockheed Aircraft as part of a $175 million total package, and accounted for 25 percent of a $55 million loan to Brewster Aircraft, a Buffalo company plagued with delivery problems during the war.[21]

As important as aircraft were to the war effort, the navy in the Pacific theater required huge numbers of ships, and again California was the obvious choice for new yards. Although the state lacked merchant ship-building yards between the wars, suddenly more than $430 million in capital for shipbuilding flowed in to construct plants in San Francisco, Stockton, and Napa. The western shipbuilding achievement, which completely overwhelmed Hitler's U-boat production with a sea of Liberty ships and destroyers, could be credited to Henry J. Kaiser, who never built a ship until the war. He ran seven shipyards in California, Oregon, and Washington that turned out an astounding 1,490 ships during the four years of war, almost 35 percent of the U.S. total.[22] His plants used radical prefabricating and welding techniques that made use of assembly lines. Ships rolled down the ways in record times, usually less than two weeks for total construction, and the *Robert E. Peary* appeared in four and a half days.[23]

Giannini had introduced Kaiser to Franklin Roosevelt after Kaiser's companies won the contract for Boulder Dam, and over the course of the Roosevelt administrations, Kaiser oversaw construction on the Parker, Grand Coulee, and Bonneville dams. With a $7.5 million loan from Giannini's bank, Kaiser built the world's largest cement plant to supply cement for Shasta Dam. This same plant provided most of the sixty-five thousand barrels of cement for the restoration of Honolulu's bombed-out airfields.[24] Kaiser, although relying primarily on government loans, held the largest single line of credit with the Bank of America, $43 million. His magnesium plant turned out eighty-two million tons for incendiary bombs and another twenty million tons for airplane parts. He built a $112 million steel plant to provide steel for his shipyards. His activities eventually led the administration to turn down one of his contract bids, as the government officials could not believe that Kaiser could possibly take on even one more project. It is little wonder that Paul Johnson, the lucid chronicler of the modern world, who remarked that the war had "put back on his pedestal the American capitalist folk hero," specifically referred to Henry Kaiser.[25] But the war had not restored the image of industrialists only, for all of California's shipbuilders and most of the West's defense efforts, aside from government's obvious contributions, were financed by bankers from the region.

Little question exists that the federal government's massive investment in the West during and after World War II provided an important boost to the economies of the western states, although cities such as San Diego and San Francisco had carefully laid the foundations for establishment or expansion of military facilities after World War I. Besides "special piers, docks and other facilities [that] added to the sailor's convenience," Oakland, Los Angeles, Long Beach, Vallejo, and other California cities "moved progressively toward a kind of military welfarism."[26] Newly established military bases brought thousands of personnel to places such as Tinker Air Force Base in Oklahoma City; Davis-Monthan Air Force Base in Tucson; Point Mugu Naval Air Station, Long Beach; and the San Diego and San Francisco Seventh Fleet Naval Bases in California. Areas around Great Falls and Glasgow, Montana, boomed, with federal funds in excess of $25 million flowing into the state.[27] New Mexico's military personnel alone rose from fewer than one hundred in 1940 to forty-six thousand by 1944.[28] Not only did the government build new bases, it expanded existing ones at Wichita and Junction City, Kansas; Omaha, Nebraska; and Lawton and Enid, Oklahoma. To service the additional personnel, banks or branches in these new boom towns had to extend their hours, add personnel, handle war coupons, and conduct other business at previously unknown levels. The Richmond branch of the Bank of America handled ten thousand customers a day.[29] Where military personnel located, so appeared civilian service economies around them. New Mexico's civilian employees, for example, more than doubled to sixteen thousand by 1945.[30] And where military bases existed, defense-related industries sprang up, especially in sunbelt regions of the West—Albuquerque, Las Cruces–El Paso, Phoenix, San Diego, and Los Angeles—where the climate enhanced year-round production and the lack of humidity attracted electronics companies.[31]

Portland and Seattle also were the sites of extensive military buildup and both supported defense-related industries, especially those related to ships and aircraft. In the first years of the war, over seventy-two thousand workers arrived in Portland. Henry Kaiser, who recruited in the East and South, brought workers in on special trains to Portland. These workers wanted to stay in the area, as seen in a 1944 survey by the Kaiser company in which 52 percent of those questioned showed a willingness to remain in the city after the war. When asked about any particular condition that caused inconvenience, over half had no criticism.[32] Likewise, Boeing Aircraft Company's employment expanded the payrolls in Washington State, including half the 166,000 women in the Washington work force. The Department of War even requested that Peoples Bank install a branch at the Boeing aircraft factory at Renton, with its three-shift work force of forty-one thousand. Although, when the bank requested permission to open a branch office near Todd shipyards, the comptroller rejected the application because control of the bank rested in one family, the Greens.[33]

Sometimes, the war only intensified previous efforts to lure government investment. First Security and other Utah banks, in this respect, had begun attracting government and defense work to the area even before the bombing of Pearl Harbor. First Security, infused with Marriners Eccles's view that the government should stimulate demand, had champed at the bit to entice federal investment. George Eccles and other Ogden bankers "promoted Ogden as a logical site for a major military installa-tion."[34] In 1920 the War Department had chosen Ogden as the site of a munitions depot, and the Ogden Arsenal opened in 1931. In the late 1930s the government spent $3.5 million to modernize this facility and from 1940 to 1942 spent still another $6.1 million on the site. Other Utah bases included Hill Field, which employed twenty-two thousand, and the Defense Depot of Ogden, built in 1940, which eventually employed seventy-seven hundred. Other important wartime sites included the Tooele Army Depot and the Naval Supply Depot at Clearfield, which employed seven thousand.[35]

The war could serve only to expose many of these service members and new workers to the West; it could not guarantee they would stay after the fighting had ended. Indeed, Wyoming received 10,700 Japanese Americans interned in a $5.5 million camp near Cody, a site constructed by three thousand workers, yet after the war virtually all of the internees and workers left permanently.[36] Arizona and Idaho, as well as inland areas of California, also provided sites for large internment camps that housed upwards of 100,000 each, which were completely dismantled after the war ended. Other areas had better luck retaining the wartime transients, and in those areas the communities themselves and the business leaders had to encourage the visitors to remain, usually with bankers leading the way in creative financing that cemented western urban growth.

Bankers recognized almost at the outset of the war that they had a unique opportunity—perhaps once in a lifetime—to impress the multitudes of soldiers, sailors, and civilian contractors with the tremendous advantages of the West. That not only meant impressing the temporary population while they worked in the West, but financing their permanent residence there if possible, and the astonishing accumulation of wartime deposits by western banks provided the capital pool. Surprisingly, North Dakota banks led the entire nation in the rate of increase in deposits. Between 1939 and 1947, deposits in the state's banks increased by 664 percent, and over three-fourths of North Dakota's banks reported increases of more than 900 percent during the same period. As a result, "by 1945, North Dakota had only two banks with deposits of under $500,000 . . . [and] average bank size had increased from about $145 in 1920 to about $2 million in 1945."[37] Rapid City National Bank in South Dakota, which had already seen enough growth that it laid plans for a new bank building, also experienced a boom in deposits. Over two years, the bank's total deposits almost doubled. An army air base outside town brought in more than deposits, with new residents applying for GI and FHA loans in record numbers.[38]

Rocky Mountain states witnessed rapid deposit growth as well. Wyoming's bank deposits tripled from 1940 to 1945, and total assets increased to an average of $5 million per bank, while New Mexico's deposits, bolstered by a 20 percent employment increase and a per-capita income gain of 150 percent, quadrupled during the same period.[39] A similar deposit growth occurred in Colorado. When the war in Europe started in 1939, Denver's ten largest banks had deposits totaling over $205 million. By 1945, deposits exceeded $619 million, which permitted loans to increase by 150 percent during the war. First National of Denver experienced the greatest growth both in actual dollar terms and in percent.[40] Colorado National Bank's deposits rose from $40.2 million to $109.3 over the same period.[41] Montana's banks showed less deposit growth, but still notched impressive gains, causing Fort Benton banker R. M. Lockwood to remark:

"There is not a great deal we can do with these funds, but it is nice to have them anyway."[42] Whereas all U.S. bank deposits rose 190 percent from 1939 to 1945, Washington's banks showed a 340 percent increase.[43]

Armed with the means to generate new loans at record levels, some bankers simply relied on the natural beauty of the West for "selling" visitors. That strategy worked fine in some more temperate areas, or in spots such as Denver and Albuquerque, with their picturesque mountains and winter sports. Persuading visitors to relocate on the Great Plains when the war ended proved a more difficult task. Such states as South Dakota never experienced the rapid growth of other Western states. For boosters in those areas, creating any kind of boom took more than exposing short-term visitors, such as servicemen or defense workers, to the natural advantages of the state. Boosters in those areas did not lack hope: they soon learned that they had to promote actively their region and generously extend credit for commercial development instead of agriculture, a process that ran against the grain of their entire history. From 1945 to 1962, South Dakota's percentage of commercial and industrial loans compared to all bank loans hovered at 15.5 percent, never rising above the high of 16.5 percent in 1962. Nor did the state make up in bank numbers for the overemphasis on agricultural lending: in 1940 the state had less than 1 percent of all banks in the United States, and by 1962 it had only barely surpassed that percentage.[44] Its sister state, North Dakota, as late as 1960 had only 35 percent of its population in urban centers.[45] Clearly, some areas faced a more difficult challenge in retaining wartime populations, whether civilian workers or servicemen.

Other states saw in the soldiers and sailors a natural postwar population base, and some bankers, such as Valley National's Walter Bimson, enacted programs specifically aimed at service members. Valley Bank, for example, featured a "300 Club" that granted automatic three-hundred-dollar loans to air force members trained at Arizona bases to use as travel money for visits home before they left for points overseas.[46] After the war, U.S. National Bank of Portland recruited a corps of young service members to process GI loans for housing, while the Bank of New Mexico opened branch offices at Sandia Base, the testing facility for the Atomic Energy Commission and the nation's nuclear weapons program, and at the bustling Kirtland Air Force Base.[47]

Oklahoma bankers had also begun a shift during the war, moving from agricultural to industrial loans, establishing the first industrial-development foundation in 1940, the Industries Foundation of Oklahoma City. First National Bank of Oklahoma City, at the request of the city's chamber of commerce manager, Stanley Draper, financed the acquisition of land for an army air corps base and supply depot. As a result of this seed money, underwritten by an additional $294,000 for loans pledged by other city bankers, the War Department put Tinker Field in Oklahoma City.[48] It did not hurt Oklahomans that Fred Jones of Fourth National Bank of Tulsa was on the regional board of directors of the War Plans Association. Oklahoma businessmen received $4.6 million worth of contracts from 1943 to 1947 and received loans from Oklahoma bankers totalling $6 million.[49] Officers of Fourth National Bank of Wichita played a critical role in the decision to bring a Boeing Aircraft plant to Wichita. The Fourth "through the late 1940s and continuing into the 1950s, became the financier for the Wichita division of the company."[50]

POSTWAR BUILDING BOOM

Retaining defense workers after the war proved easier, as they had lived in the temperate or scenic climates for several years, whereas the servicemen had often been stationed at a base for only a few months. The bankers accurately perceived the primary need of those defense workers: homes. Most western city bankers had familiarized themselves with the advantages of the FHA lending program, and no western bank had greater success in this program than Valley National Bank. Walter Bimson dispatched employees in a door-to-door campaign to sell loans, and the bank even ordered house plans from architects and obtained cost estimates from building contractors, then offered the houses—plans, estimates, loans, and all—to the public. The aggressive program adopted by the bank proved so effective that by 1935 this relatively small institution ranked fifth in the entire nation for dollar volume of FHA loans. In the first year after the program started, the bank made $1 million worth of loans in Phoenix and Tucson alone.[51] Walter Bimson's brother, Carl, realized that Title I of the Federal Home Loan Act applied to appliances inside or attached to homes. Equally important, the appliance loans could total as much as $2,500, and they needed no security. These consumer loans brought in borrowers who had never before used a bank. Valley National made seven hundred Title I loans in a single week.[52] The success of the bank soon caught the eye of government officials, who persuaded Valley Bank to lend Carl to the government as a salesman for the FHA program: he toured the country touting its advantages at parks, country clubs, and auditoriums.

A wise friend once suggested that those things that a society values can be determined by looking at the structures it builds. Medieval society valued religion, and the cathedrals proved it. Modern America treasures money and cars, and without doubt the most prominent structures in any American city are its banks and freeways. It is important to note that almost all autos are bought on time, thanks to loans from local banks, and that most urban buildings are made possible by bank financing (or, at least, pools). In Oklahoma, for example, Tulsa and Oklahoma City, the two cities that contained one fourth of the state's population, witnessed tremendous growth after World War II. During the 1950s, Oklahoma City's population rose 30 percent and Tulsa's rose 39 percent. As early as 1947, the state's banks loaned $30 million for residential building. Such growth obviously showed up in residential housing. In Oklahoma, lending for real estate purchases rose 94.4 percent from 1945 to 1947, and total loans on residential properties rose 92.1 percent.[53] World War II had a boom effect on the Colorado economy also, and after the war, housing demand shot up. According to Charles De Belle, vice president for commercial loans at Colorado National Bank, "Denver couldn't handle all the demand." The bank shipped mortgages east to Boston, New York, and Chicago, as well as west to San Francisco. De Belle recalled that "about a third of our CNB loan portfolio went for housing in the 1950s." Because new construction loans were "risky," De Belle made personal auto trips around the Denver area, "checking out our construction sites."[54] The Bank of New Mexico, noting "a sharp increase in construction throughout Albuquerque in 1967," intensified its lending on construction and housing.[55] Even in sparsely populated South Dakota, A. E. Dahl, president of Rapid City National Bank, reported that in 1947 "the building boom continued. The city was spreading out in every direction." Rapid City National Bank, already the largest originator of mortgage loans of any bank or other lending institution in South Dakota, began to package FHA and other mortgage loans for sale to other banks and insurance companies.[56]

Once a city begins to expand, the most visible sign of growth—the skyline—often reflects the level of local financial involvement. Bankers in several western states eagerly provided high-level finance for downtown office buildings. First National of Denver constructed its $16 million, twenty-eight-story skyscraper by selling stock to the Murchison brothers (John D. and Clint, Jr.) of Dallas.[57] Although the deal did not rely on completely local financing, it did suggest that the area beyond the Mississippi had rapidly approached the point where it could generate its own capital for real-estate lending. By the late 1960s, Arizona banks had provided funds for most of the major skyscrapers in Phoenix and Tucson, occasionally drawing on their credit lines in Denver, Los Angeles, or San Francisco.[58] Of course, the banks themselves frequently owned or occupied the largest buildings in a city. Among them was the Wells Fargo building at 420 Montgomery St., completed in 1960, and the Guaranty Bank Building—Arizona's first skyscraper—completed in 1961. When the Denver National and U.S. National banks merged in 1958, they occupied the twenty-five-story Mile High Center, which had been completed four years earlier. In Los Angeles, the first wave of high rises were completed in the 1960s and included Crocker Citizens Plaza, the Union Bank Building, the United California Bank Building, BankAmerica Tower, and Security Pacific National Bank. In San Diego, United States National Bank moved into its twenty-five-story building in 1963, and in 1961, the Bank of New Mexico occupied the $4 million building constructed by Dallas financier Trammel Crow.

Financing these huge towers of steel and glass offered impressive avenues for banks to advertise their lending achievements. But the grunt work, and the steady revenue stream, still came from the residential loans. A major source of residential loan capital—eastern insurance companies and savings banks—had not really been tapped by the western banks as of 1950, despite the inroads made by Colorado National Bank. The story of the breakthrough in this area of lending bears note because it is the story of one entrepreneur who outhustled the local giants, especially Valley National Bank. By the late 1940s, Valley Bank had lost its hold on the residential lending market in Arizona. Remarkably, even after making so many FHA loans in 1935 that it ranked fifth in the nation; even after pioneering the use of FHA mortgages in much of the West; and even after in 1945 selling $1 million worth of loans to California-based Transamerica, Valley National Bank still had not tapped the Arizona development boom. In stepped A. B. Robbs, Jr., who, through a contact at National Life of Vermont, saw an opportunity to make an "end run" around the lending limits that constrained Arizona banks.[59] Robbs and his father created a trust company that vigorously acquired mortgage funds from eastern investors. An agency capitalized at $50,000 thus found itself servicing $12 million worth of mortgage accounts from 1947 to 1950.[60] In a remarkable arrangement, the trust company generated the Arizona business, the investors (mostly insurance companies, such as John Hancock or Paul Revere Life, or savings banks, such as Brooklyn Savings Bank or People's Savings Bank) provided the cash, and Uncle Sam insured the operation. By 1953, the Robbs Trust Company lent more than $30 million, generating more residential-construction money than the entire state of Oklahoma had just six years earlier.[61] Development exploded, especially since Robbs personally worked with a host of influential young developers, including Del Webb, John F. Long, Ralph Staggs, John Hall of Hallcraft Homes, and especially David Murdock, who would emerge as one of California's premier real-estate developers in the 1970, following his move from Arizona.[62]

Robbs' connection and friendship with Murdock proved exceptionally rewarding for Phoenix's downtown development. David Murdock founded Murdock Development Company in 1946, and, using money from Robbs's trust company, he built Phoenix's first skyscraper, the Guaranty Bank Building. Another skyscraper was later used by Murdock as equity valued at $1 million in a deal to establish a comprehensive mortgage-related financial company called the Financial Corporation of Arizona, which sought to handle all aspects of the real-estate business.[63] Robbs supplied $20 million to Murdock by 1961 for construction of nineteen buildings, and by 1963 the two men had founded or acquired two banks. Robbs and Murdock both served as founding directors on Guaranty Bank, but although they also had founded the Financial Corporation of Arizona together, Robbs sold his stock in that operation and moved on to other enterprises.

Murdock remained the driving force behind the Financial Corporation of Arizona, but the company collapsed when a vice president embezzled $1 million from a subsidiary. Murdock purchased all of the corporation's outstanding stock after its value plummeted, moved the headquarters of Murdock Development to Los Angeles in 1969, and rising from the ashes, created a powerful development company there.[64] By 1987, his vast empire included Murdock Development Company, Pacific Holding Company in Los Angeles, Goettl Air Conditioning in Phoenix, and Murdock Hotels Corporation (with the Hay-Adams in Washington, D.C., the Cornhusker in Lincoln, and the Harbor Court Hotel in Baltimore). He also was the CEO of and major shareholder in Castle and Cooke, a prominent Hawaiian food-processing and real-estate company which owns Dole Foods, besides extensive real-estate developments through Oceanic Properties.

Well before Murdock hit the development scene in California, real-estate lending in Los Angeles had hit boom levels. This was somewhat surprising, given that only a few of California's biggest banks plunged into the mortgage market. During the 1940s, when the state's population soared from 6.9 million to 10.6 million, banks had shifted from holding war bonds to issues that would strengthen the state's superstructure, especially school and utility bonds.[65] From 1950 to 1960, Los Angeles grew 54 percent, on top of the addition of four million people in the previous decade. FHA loans again facilitated the growth of residential housing. California banks saw their lending for nonfarm, one- to four-family homes increase 120 percent from 1946 to 1950. These loans were dominated by A. P. Giannini's Bank of America, which by 1948 had $600 million worth of FHA loans outstanding (44 percent of California's total and 10 percent of the national total). The bank lent Paul W. Trousdale, a Los Angeles developer, FHA Title IV money to build two houses a day, seven days a week, and at one time he had three hundred houses underway every day. Other California banks lent on residential property as well, to the tune of almost ten times the amount that the Bank of America had. Whereas Giannini had personally emphasized home lending, and had even appeared in branches to ask managers for justification when homeowners' mortgage applications were rejected, the "old man" had been reluctant to lend to developers, and was not alone in this attitude among his fellow

California bankers. Still, bankers were not inhibited in their lending to individuals for mortgages, especially A. P.'s son and the bank's president during the 1940s, Mario Giannini. During the war, Giannini's bank advanced Trousdale nearly $8 million. When Henry Kaiser's wartime shipbuilding methods were applied to homebuilding in southern California, the Bank of America lent more than $50 million for six thousand homes. The Bank of America supplied San Francisco builder Henry Doelger, who began with a credit line of $110,000 in 1936, with $75 million for west Los Angeles tracts in the 1950s.[66]

Despite racking up some impressive numbers, California bankers never approached the legal limits for real-estate lending in the 1940s and they cooled to all types of lending to real-estate developers in the 1950s. Real-estate prices began to level off in 1949 and stayed flat for roughly three years. At the same time, government bonds offered increasingly more attractive investments. In addition, a temporary disturbance in the secondary market for government-insured mortgages caused by the dissolution of the RFC further eroded bankers' confidence. A gap developed between the RFC's discontinuation in July 1947 and the October 1949 authorization for the Federal National Mortgage Association to buy VA mortgages in large quantities from a single lender. A distinct drop in new VA mortgages corresponded with that three-year gap. Although the state-chartered banks had no limit under law on the total amount they could invest in real estate, and although they could have doubled their total real estate-loans outstanding for 1946–51 and still not have exceeded the federal limit for non–government-insured loans alone, they did not increase real estate lending, opening the market to a new group, the California savings and loans (S&Ls).[67] In 1949, California S&Ls held $870 million in mortgage loans, making its S&L industry third in the nation, behind the traditionally strong S&Ls of Ohio and New York.[68] By 1954, this number had increased to $2.3 billion, and assets of California S&Ls had increased by $512 million.[69] Where neither the banks nor the S&Ls could supply enough local capital, they imported it from insurance companies, whose mortgage loans increased 319 percent in the 1950s.[70] By 1960, 13 percent of all real-estate loans made by insurance companies were in California, and most of that (77 percent) represented a transfer of out-of-state funds, especially eastern and midwestern money.[71] By 1949, S&Ls' lending on real estate (for loans of $20,000 or less in Los Angeles County) exceeded that of banks, and was almost double bank real-estate lending by 1951.[72]

Commercial banks were not squeezed out of mortgage lending by these intruders. On the contrary, from 1956 to 1959, when the housing boom revived, commercial banks annually financed $700 million in new construction in California. Over the same period, California commercial banks' holdings of FHA/VA loans increased by $400 million.[73] Thus, while overall lending by banks on real estate increased (but decreased as a portion of all lending on real estate by financial institutions), some banks aggressively continued their real-estate lending. Wells Fargo Bank alone saw its real-estate lending leap from $272 million in 1959 to $2.26 billion in 1975.[74] The percentage of real-estate loans among total loans went from 20 in 1959 to 38 in the mid-1960s.[75]

Although its numbers were dwarfed by those of California bank lenders, Utah, spearheaded by Salt Lake City's banks, witnessed a similar competition between building and loan associations and banks. The state's building and loans (B&Ls) grew from $51 million to $255 million in assets from 1932 to 1962, while banks grew from $152 million in 1935 to $1.2 billion in 1962.[76] From 1950 to 1965, eleven banks were organized in Salt Lake City, of which four were "bank and trust companies" especially oriented toward mortgage lending.[77]

Dating from the creation of the FHA under the National Housing Act of 1934, Utah banks had maintained a special appreciation for the lending possibilities under the act. Marriner and George Eccles had seen First Security Corporation grow into a powerful Utah bank holding company. Unlike other Utah commercial banks (but like Valley Bank in Arizona and the Robbs Trust Company), First Security knew exactly how to react to FHA insured mortgages: the management "seized every chance to make FHA loans." It had already acquired the Ogden Savings Bank, active in the mortgage market since the 1920s, and by 1945 it shot ahead of other Salt Lake City (and Utah) banks in mortgage lending. The postwar boom period only increased the demand for home loans in Salt Lake City. Mormons held a deep-seated belief in large families and stressed home life. When combined with the wide open spaces of the intermountain West and the absence of densely packed urban areas, "since the last decades of the nineteenth century the proportion of families in [Utah and Idaho] that owned their own homes was among the highest in the nation." Not only did First Security possess an active mortgage-lending department, but its affiliate, First Security Trust Company, managed to tie into the same eastern sources of capital that were financing Phoenix's growth through the Robbs Trust Company, including National Life of Vermont and Prudential Insurance. Financing homes for war production workers in the Wasatch Front region (and its newly established Geneva Steel Mill) the banks established a policy to always find mortgage-loan funds, no matter how completely its subsidiary banks were "loaned up." In 1955, First Security offered an insurance plan at a rate of ten dollars per thousand, to pay off a home loan if the owner died before repaying the loan. Since, however, the regulations controlling national banks permitted them to engage in insurance business only if they were located in a community of five thousand or less, First Security established an out-of-state subsidiary corporation, First Security Life Insurance Company of Texas, to handle the insurance.[78]

Robert Hemingway of Commercial Security Bank in Ogden took an even more direct approach to providing homes to families that had moved in during the war. In 1954, he arranged the sale to homeowners of Washington Terrace, a housing area built by the federal government for employees of its bases. The bank, under Hemingway's leadership, obtained from Washington money to buy thirteen hundred houses, as well as pay for general rehabilitation of other buildings.[79] And the FHA–home mortgage boom extended to small western cities, too. Rapid City National Bank in South Dakota, under A. E. Dahl, so embraced FHA lending that by 1949 it handled 84 percent of all the FHA loans in the city. Dahl's bank did such a booming FHA business that he directed the organization of a separate trust company for mortgages. He succeeded, creating Rapid City Trust Company in 1952; yet, the state later complained that Dahl had fooled the commissioners, and that they had not known that he had applied for a bank with trust powers, despite the presence of the word "bank" in the articles of incorporation in at least four places. The state attorney general brought suit in 1953, and the governor intervened by persuading the banking commission to withdraw the suit in return for a change in the trust company's bylaws prohibiting commercial banking activities. Since South Dakota had no such law, a subsequent challenge by a stockholder led to the prohibition's being overturned. Dahl had won, getting the trust company back to its original status.[80]

BANKERS AS BOOSTERS

Virtually every western boom city had its Hemingway, Eccles, Dahl, or its Robbs. Denver's powerful First National Bank had Gerald Hughes and John Evans. As chairman of the board, Hughes saw that the postwar population explosion around Denver presented a chance for expansion of the bank's trust activities. He offered the job of heading the trust department to Denver judge Charles Kettering, who had handled probate and trust cases for fourteen years. John Evans, the fifth president of the bank, who served from 1928 to 1959, and who from 1928 to 1932 simultaneously presided over the affiliated International Trust Company, had lobbied extensively and successfully to get the United States Air Force Academy established in Colorado. Operating under the same assumptions as the Bimsons—namely, that once the servicemen and women saw the West, they would eventually return permanently—Evans and other bankers promoted Colorado to the scores of defense-related companies, such as Hewlett-Packard, IBM, Anaconda, Shell Chemical, and Martin Company. Employees from these companies, along with former service members, combined to cement the Trust Company of the First National Bank as the largest in the Rocky Mountain area. It merged into the bank in 1958, with total assets of $70 million.[81] Together, the two companies issued $5 million worth of new stock—much of it again taken by the Murchisons, a Dallas Texas family famous later for owning the Dallas Cowboys—and by December 1958 the condensed statement of condition showed over $300 million in assets.[82]

Despite this remarkable success, First National eschewed FHA lending, preferring consumer installment lending to residents who obtained mortgage financing elsewhere. Part of this may have been due to the low asset base of Colorado's banks, which could in turn be traced to its anti–branch banking law. The number of banks increased in Colorado from 140 in 1945 to 212 in 1965, but assets rose only from $1.14 billion to $3.18 billion. In other words, by comparison, in 1954 when California's banks had $1.6 billion in assets, its S&Ls were lending $2.3 billion on mortgages alone. First National followed the merger route in attempting to expand its capital, most notably through a 1958 merger with International Trust, giving the bank assets of $300 million.[83] The role of individual bankers in advancing western real estate development is underscored by their dual function as local boosters. Oklahoma bankers successfully lobbied for state aid to establish the Oklahoma Industrial Finance Authority. Governed by a seven-member board including bankers, the authority's goal was to assist the work of industrial development foundations. Developers had to put up only 25 percent of a project's cost, with the authority putting up 25 percent, and the remaining 50 percent being provided by a bank with a loan secured by a first mortgage. Bankers then lobbied for creation of the Oklahoma Business Development Corporation, which "encouraged industrial growth by providing new businesses with short-term and intermediate funds for working capital and equipment purchases."[84] Commercial banks in Oklahoma pledged $5 million of their capital and surplus to this corporation.[85]

Ogden's chamber of commerce, encouraged by George Eccles, one of its members, had in 1936 and 1937 directed private funds toward the purchase of the decayed Ogden ordnance facilities, which it then outright donated to the government for construction of a munitions plant. This plant brought nearly $10 million into the Ogden economy in four years. When the naval supply depot at Clearfield outlived its usefulness after the war, boosters, led again by George Eccles, attempted to create the Freeport Center for private industry on half the property, but were outbid by a California surgical supply business.[86] (The government converted the other half of the massive facility into the supply center for the western states division of the General Services Administration.)

Bankers' activities in other areas made the efforts at boosterism in Utah and Oklahoma seem mild by comparison. Phoenix's story has been well documented by Michael Konig, but it bears retelling in part because seldom were the links between a city's goals for growth and the participation of the local bankers so clearly documented. Konig noted that "bankers were the catalyst" that brought together private enterprise, municipal-industrial public policy, and federal government expenditures. The Phoenix Chamber of Commerce, especially its active front organization, the Phoenix Thunderbirds, actively publicized the amenities of the city. Thunderbirds, with prominent bankers such as the Bimsons, Wesley Montgomery, Frank Brophy, Hugh Gruwell, and others, met at the airport representatives from prospective companies that were considering relocating in the Valley of the Sun. These bankers often "personally contacted and 'sold' innumerable industrial visitors on the advantages of Phoenix."[87] Arriving at the airport in their high-necked blue jackets, with their thunderbird neck chains and silver-and-turquoise belts, looking like a cross between Navajos and Shriners, these business leaders ushered the representatives to the best hotels, golf courses, and restaurants. They bombarded their guests with powerful arguments for the growth of Phoenix and advanced innovative fiscal ideas. Despite the Thunderbirds' somewhat silly appearance, they convinced most of their visitors. Although bankers hardly dominated the group by their numbers, they wielded an extraordinary amount of influence, as seen by the appointment of Patrick Downey, a Valley National Bank executive, as the primary traveling representative of the chamber of commerce. The chamber reimbursed the bank for Downey's time and assumed his expenses.[88]

Downey's efforts paid off. Between 1948 and 1960, 290 new manufacturers located in Phoenix, which found its employment surging. Bankers exercised their personal contacts to bring Motorola, AiResearch and scores of electronics firms to Phoenix in the 1950s. And the Phoenix bankers did not simply rely on Downey or their personal contacts: they pioneered the use of advertising tools such as *Arizona Progress*, a small, densely packed statistical volume that tracked employment, manufacturing, and population. Although it was a Valley National Bank publication, it carried no specific bank advertising. It was the best single piece of promotional material in Arizona's history. Because of this local drumbeating, Arizona received endless attention in national publications. The September 30, 1961, issue of the *Saturday Evening Post* featured Robbs, Murdock, and developers Long, Hall, and others in an article entitled "The New Millionaires of Phoenix," and a 1954 issue had featured Walter Bimson in an article called "The Brash Banker of Arizona."[89]

Of course, Arizona bankers did not invent boosterism. As early as 1876, Colorado congressman Thomas M. Patterson boasted that the "topographical and geographical situation of Denver, its centrality to the mining sections of the Rocky Mountain regions with reference to its railroad system, developed, completed, and under construction, establish the fact that the mint at Denver is an essential element [of the national banking system]." He further argued that "Denver is the true entrepot of all [the Rocky Mountain region]," and that "Arizona and New Mexico, Wyoming and Montana, and Utah are by nature . . . tributary to it. . . ."[90] Denver, however, and more broadly, Colorado, had suffered from a number of problems in the early 1900s in its bid to become a Federal Reserve city, and few other Rocky Mountain cities—especially those destined to fall into the Denver district had the city won its Federal Reserve status— shared Denver's view of its leadership position in the West. So in some ways, Colorado boosters found themselves starting anew in the war years. They lobbied for defense industries and government offices harder than ever, but even then they encountered resistance from so-called "establish-ment" figures, one of whom commented that industrializing Denver would bring "low-brows, foreigners, and dirt into a respectable city." During the wartime influx of workers, Denver's longtime mayor, Benjamin Stapleton, remarked: "If [after the war] these people just go back where they came from, we wouldn't have any problems here."[91] Some Oregonians expressed similar feelings regarding Portland's wartime immigrants. Many boosters simply favored new industrial development over low-cost public housing. The issue took on racial overtones because much of the public housing was occupied by blacks.[92] As frequently as not, the established families viewed any sign of a growing population (of any race) with concern. California's Governor John G. Downey, a merchant who established an early bank in Los Angeles, while predicting that his state's commercial position, resources, and climate would "always guarantee to California a respectably numerous [population]," hinted that he held sentiments simi-lar to Stapleton's by adding: "We never hope for a dense population, such as will swarm the great northwest."[93]

But these attitudes hardly typified those of most western bankers. Whether they even permeated a significant minority of Denver's elite, for example, is questionable. Most Colorado bankers, including prominent Denver financiers, disagreed. Harry Kountze, Jr., commenting on Colo-rado National Bank's postwar development, noted that the rise of the bank's public relations department constituted the "most significant" change in the bank, and he observed that other Denver banks had seen similar growth in their marketing departments. This, he thought, gave them the "opportunity to discard the small-town outlook and branch out into many new lines of finance and enterprise."[94]

John Evans of First National rejected Stapleton's view. Evans, as a founding member of the Air Academy Foundation, lobbied successfully to get the Air Force Academy located in Colorado Springs.[95] But long before he was involved in the Air Force Academy, Evans played a crucial role in the reorganization of the Denver and Rio Grande Railroad. Evans's father and grandfather had worked with Denver railroader David Moffat to make Denver the port of entry for the region, and his father had proved instrumental in completing the Moffat Tunnel in 1928. When the railroad received extensive RFC loans in the early 1930s, it did so with the understanding that it would deposit as security Colorado National Bank shares equal to all outstanding minority shares. A further reorganization, in 1934, brought John Evans into the picture. He sought ways to recover control of the railroad's stock from the RFC, which held the line in trust until the Denver and Rio Grande could pay the entire $10.75 million in loans it had received from the RFC. Within a six-month period, Evans persuaded a syndicate of Colorado and Utah bankers to buy $1.65 million worth of trustees' certificates. Besides Evans's First National and the International Trust, other participants included Colorado National Bank, Denver National, First National Bank of Colorado Springs, and First National Bank of Pueblo. After the railroad recovered somewhat, Evans led the "Denver group" in a bid to recover the railroad from the "New York group" of insurance companies. Over a twelve-year period, the railroad was modernized through the infusion of $73 million. In 1947, the Reorganization Committee held a stockholders meeting, following federal approval of the recapitalization of the line, and the committee elected Evans chairman. It had survived—and celebrated its hundredth anniversary in 1970—largely due to Evans's boosterism and determination that a locally capitalized and owned railroad could succeed.[96] By 1959, Evans had attracted such attention as a banker and booster that *Life* magazine ran a nine-page story on him and his family.[97]

Other Denver boosters paved the way for the U.S. Department of Defense to open the Rocky Flats Nuclear Weapons Center and the headquarters of the North American Air Defense Command, with its invincible facility located inside Cheyenne Mountain. One of the largest federal bureaus in the West, the Denver Federal Center, was constructed on the grounds of the Remington arms factory shortly after the war. By 1948 it employed ten thousand, and by 1970 over thirty thousand. Nevertheless, the Colorado boosters shared a trait common throughout western booster organizations—they avoided overtures to "dirty" industries, especially heavy manufacturing and steel, for several reasons. First, the value added to high-tech electronics and plastics surpassed that in the smokestack industries. Second, without doubt, the new western regions wished to avoid large migrations of blue-collar workers and the unions they seemed to bring. Finally, and perhaps most important, the environmentalist streak in the West mitigated against these pollution-intensive sectors, which also seemed always to require exceptional amounts of precious water.

Boosters recognized the significance of retaining the wartime industries and of attracting other new residents. They especially concentrated on convincing defense contractors to remain in place or to relocate to Colorado. Peter Grant, president of Colorado National Bank since 1975, recalled that the bank had formed important relationships with Auto-Trol Technology, Martin, Beechcraft, Lobe Laboratories, and Mastercraft Industries.[98] Other businesses enticed to open regional headquarters or major branch operations included Remington and Dow Chemical during the war, and, eventually, IBM, Ampex, Honeywell, Johns-Manville, Eastman-Kodak, Sunstrand, Anaconda, Western Electric, and, in Colorado Springs, Hewlett Packard.

Not all bankers became civic boosters, with some seeing greater growth coming from improved efficiency, not from an expanding local population. Montana banks, for example, launched into new advertising campaigns and bank-personnel training programs, but showed no interest in moving beyond the agricultural/mining focus of the state. When the mining and railroading business base declined, the bottom fell out of Montana's economy. In 1950, the state had the twelfth-highest per capita income in the country, but by 1968 it had dropped to thirty-first and remained at that level (roughly 90 percent of the national average) throughout the 1970s.[99] Some areas had to work hardly at all to attract new postwar business and population. In Washington, for example, the natural corollary of the housing boom elsewhere translated into lumber and logging jobs, with employment in forest products hitting an all-time high in the 1960s. To some extent, then, boosters in Washington's case would have been redundant if they focused only on forestry. And, of course, not all boosters succeeded. In one case, a booster group in Portland actually drove a major industrialist to Tacoma. The group was led by Henry Corbett, the grandson of the pioneer banker, a civic booster, and a politician cursed with a "lack of charisma." Corbett arranged a luncheon conference with the president of Brown Boveri, who considered locating a plant in Portland, and a group of local business leaders. Among those present was E. C. Sammons, the president of U.S. National Bank of Portland, although everyone on the Portland side of the table assumed that Corbett would control the closing of the deal. Instead, Sammons interrupted, rudely cross-examining the visitor as if he had applied for a loan at Sammons's bank. Obviously, Sammons had even less charisma than did Corbett, and the industrialist scratched Portland off his list. Despite such blunders, Portland grew at a rapid rate—125 downtown blocks had been sold between 1943 and 1946—and realtor Chester A. Moores observed: "There has never been so much activity in the entire 100 year history of the city [as in the postwar years]."[100]

It is also important to note that Portland's boosters actually launched their major drive shortly before World War I, and continued it in the decade following. The major booster organization, the Realty Board, had organized itself in 1906. Realty Board president Frank L. McGuire declared: "One way to make money—one sure way—is to invest in Portland real estate and to become foremost in the maelstrom of activity which is inevitable."[101] From 1905 to 1915 Portland, according to a city biographer, "experienced its most explosive population and construction boom."[102] The Realty Board had been organized for promoting growth, "the fulfillment of the city's destiny."[103] Among the activists were bankers E. B. MacNaughton and Frederick H. and Robert H. Strong. The estate of William Sargeant Ladd, the preeminent early Portland banker, had Portland real-estate holdings of $5 million by 1909.[104] After the war, the Realty Board continued its booster efforts. The sons of pioneer bankers, including William Mead Ladd, with newly arrived bankers, such as E. C. Sammons, combined with MacNaughton, John C. Ainsworth, and Julius L. Meier to form a solid front of boosters.

After World War II, these boosters split over the types of industry, and therefore the types of residents, they wanted to attract. Though a boom mentality influenced the construction of major downtown highrises, such as the *Oregonian* Building (financed by First National and the Bank of America), and important business facilities, such as the Fred Meyer warehouse and shopping centers, and the addition of a new NABISCO cracker factory, problems remained.[105] Portlanders feared the creation of another Vanport—the predominantly African-American city on Portland's outskirts created to house wartime workers. Whenever possible, the environmentally oriented Oregonians sought to attract clean service and high-tech industries to their region in place of the traditional heavy manufacturing.

The collective and often unconscious decisions by the boosters about the types of residents they wanted to attract resulted in the arrival of many newcomers from the ranks of engineers, managers, technicians, professionals, and other white-collar workers—in short, people very much like the bankers themselves. This made advertising campaigns even easier. Then, together they formed new alliances to further encourage emigration of other suburbanites. Urban specialist Carl Abbott, for example, has noted that "new suburban business interests . . . emerged in many sunbelt cities . . . with their own programs for investment in suburban service and promotion of suburban growth."[106] Abbott observed similar developments in Portland, San Jose, Long Beach, and other western cities.

POSTWAR CHANGES IN BANKING STRUCTURE

Still, bringing in new customers constituted only part of the equation, because their deposits increasingly went to suburban banks. In branching states, that mattered little. In restricted unit-bank states, despite the inflow of businesses, urban banks faced a serious deposit drain. Meanwhile, the suburbs boomed. Such was the case in Colorado, where the large urban banks, unable to branch, lost deposits to suburban banks in Aurora, Arvada, Englewood, Lakewood, and Cherry Creek. To solve the suburban flight problem, Colorado banks established separate banks with common shareholders. While this satisfied customers' demands for continuity, it could not solve the problem of real-estate financing that required much higher capital and asset bases. For all Colorado banks, the only alternative to branching was an inefficient holding-company structure.

The flaws in the Colorado bank legislation have caused some critics to assume that "Denver's fate [was] linked to the movement of outside capital," and that "Colorado and the whole West were a province or possession of the [eastern] money centers." Nothing could be further from the truth. Just as New York and Boston had developed financial systems independent of London; just as Chicago in turn created a system free of New York, and Minneapolis a system free of Chicago; just as Los Angeles and San Francisco, and ultimately Phoenix and Oklahoma City found ways to generate their own capital, so, too, could Denver. A large part of the difference between Denver and those cities lay in poor legislation, as Colorado constantly battled an antiquated, constraining unit-bank law. As a result, Denver bankers had to watch idly as New York's First National Bank financed a multimillion-dollar expansion bond for the Gates Rubber Company in the late 1940s.[107] They also proved far less willing to lend than were banks in Salt Lake City, Albuquerque, Portland, or Los Angeles. Denver journalist and financial critic Gene Cervi noted that Denver banks typically lent only 30 percent of their deposits, while those in other money centers lent 40 to 50 percent. He "was so angry that [he] hardly ever went to press without a blast at the restrictiveness of . . . [this] repressive banking."[108]

Nevertheless, Denver financiers, especially those at First National, provided most of the capital for the initial conversion of sheep pastures into the ski resort at Vail. They financed the Mount Werner ski complex at Steamboat Springs and Winter Park. In addition to energy and mining loans, Colorado banks found their niche in capitalizing the state's tourist trade.[109]

In contrast to the weakness of the Colorado multibank holding companies was Transamerica, which in 1956 bought three Colorado banks, just before the national Bank Holding Company Act took effect. This prohibited bank holding companies from crossing state lines unless expressly permitted by state law, and Colorado lacked such a law. Thus Transamerica got in under the wire, and with its vast resources, it could direct funds from its member banks to areas of high demand. Since the company existed solely in the West, and since most of the rest of the West had entered a boom phase, Transamerica directed its resources elsewhere. While it could have taken advantage of Colorado's structure, the state antibranching regulations still make holding Colorado banks less attractive than those in other states.[110]

As the ultimate western bank holding company, Transamerica represented the vehicle through which A. P. Giannini had envisioned building an interstate empire. By the mid-1940s, Transamerica owned a diverse selection of companies, including General Metals foundries; Enterprise Engine and Foundry; Aerco and Adel (manufacturers of airplane parts); California Lands (property management); Columbia River Packers Tuna Company; and a variety of financial companies that sold life and casualty insurance and provided consumer financing. It was the banking division that caused problems for the empire by the end of the decade. The Federal Reserve Board, in 1945, asked Attorney General Thomas C. Clark to investigate Transamerica for antitrust violations, but Clark reported that "no persuasive evidence" of antitrust activities existed.[111] Undaunted, the FDIC, the comptroller, and the Federal Reserve all continued to seek restrictions on Transamerica, and the Fed went ahead with its own investigation, based on an internal legal brief. In June 1948, Transamerica was charged with antitrust violation for its ownership of the Bank of America and banks in Arizona, California, Oregon, Nevada, and Washington.

That decision to some degree pitted Marriner Eccles, chairman of the Federal Reserve Board, against the Gianninis (although A. P. died the year after the government launched the suit). Eccles had previously supported branch banking, but his support apparently did not extend to practice. He frequently argued for banking reforms that permitted branching—and also for massive centralization of the banking system in the hands of bureaucrats. However, Congress always excised the branching provisions of the various bills. The Transamerica case offered the first opportunity Eccles had, as chairman, to defend an existing branch system against attack. To that end, he failed miserably. According to his biographer, Sidney Hyman, Eccles said: "There was no way on earth to prevent the Bank of America from expanding."[112] But did Eccles really want to prevent the bank from expanding? Apparently he did. In contrast to all previous episodes in his political life, when Eccles decided one of his principles was under attack—his demand-side pre-Keynesianism or his pursuit of greater regulation of the banking system—he waded in unreservedly, using all his personal contacts (including Roosevelt, when necessary) to achieve his goals. On the Bank of America matter, Eccles all but faded into the shadows, perhaps because he sensed the government had no case.

Eccles thought that without national branch banking, Transamerica was too large a competitor, a circuitous line of reasoning at best. He also by then had adopted a "big government" approach to the marketplace, and saw a regulated solution to most problems. He rarely mentioned the advantages of the marketplace after he joined the Roosevelt administration, only the threats it posed. On a more personal level, Eccles thought Giannini had on one occasion attempted to bribe him, and on another gone back on his word.[113] Thus, at a point when one man of the West had the opportunity to aid another in removing the single greatest source of instability in the American banking system, he dropped the ball. The government's case, although far from airtight, convinced Transamerica to divest itself of the Bank of America and leave banking altogether in order to gain greater freedom to grow in the insurance industry and in other directions. After the case had dragged on for five years, Transamerica won the lawsuit, but by then it had separated from the Bank of America, leading one scholar to call the case "victory from defeat" for the Federal Reserve Board of Governors.[114] In 1950 Transamerica tried to sell all of its other banks to the Bank of America, but the Federal Reserve—Eccles, again—spiked that plan. By 1955, the Bank of America existed as a separate legal entity with branches all in California. The remaining Transamerica banks, numbering approximately two hundred, were sold as Western Bancorporation, which included First Western Bank and Trust Company (with fifty-seven branches in California), First National Bank of Portland (with seventy branches), First National Bank of Arizona (with twenty-one branches), Southern Arizona Bank and Trust Company (with seven branches), National Bank of Washington (with fifteen branches), First National Bank of Nevada (with seventeen branches), and the Bank of Nevada (with four branches). In the following year, branches were added in Colorado, Idaho, Montana, New Mexico, Utah, and Wyoming. Then, on May 9, 1956, the system's expansion came to an abrupt halt when the Bank Holding Company Act restricted the expansion of holding companies across state lines.[115]

Even without the full power of this interstate giant available, banks in the West facilitated the growth of urban areas through boosterism, direct investment, enhanced consumer lending, and channeling funds from outside sources. The individual state's legal framework dictated the strategy the bankers took. Even those laws stood only as short-term deterrents to financiers' long term goals. (In Texas, the unit-bank law had only encouraged mergers and holding companies, which, by the mid-1970s, had grown large enough to finance real-estate development without outside funding.)[116] North Dakota, for example, introduced a device to expand banking services in its rural areas, yet not fully adopt branch banking. The legislature in the early 1950s warmed to a quasi-branch arrangement by allowing "paying and receiving stations" to open. These agencies received deposits, cashed checks, issued travelers checks, and handled collections, but did not make loans or provide the full range of bank services. Even these, perhaps, were unnecessary, as North Dakota by 1950 had a ratio of one bank per 3,603 people, the fifth highest such ratio among all fifty states, and well below the national average of eight thousand people per bank.[117] Buoyed by the wartime deposit boom, many of these banks experienced a somewhat artificial prosperity in the early 1950s.

Banks in the Pacific Northwest also entered a period of branch expansion after the war. Peoples Bank, National Bank of Commerce, and Seattle-First National ("SeaFirst") all rapidly acquired banks for branch purposes. In the 1950s, Seattle-First acquired twenty-eight, National Bank of Commerce twenty, and PeoplesBank eight banks as branches. The state's economy boomed with the postwar expansion, which slowed after 1957 but gained momentum in the 1960s.[118] Washington's neighbor Oregon witnessed similar growth. The state's population had increased by almost 40 percent from 1940 to 1950, yet bank density had fallen from one bank per 4,305 people in 1930 to one bank per 9,191 in 1946. The state attempted to keep pace by chartering new banks (some thirty-seven between 1944 and 1963), and in 1947 the state's new banking law encouraged branching, causing the number of branch banks to grow. Not only did the new law reduce the required capital for banks in communities of more than twenty-five thousand, but the superintendent of banks also granted more branch applications and rejected fewer. The expansion and encouragement of statewide branching came as a reaction to the aggressive branching of First National and U.S. National. Both witnessed significant growth in the postwar period. U.S. National engaged in mergers with twenty-five banks with deposits of $42.5 million, and from 1933 to 1940 over half its growth resulted from mergers.[119] These merged banks became new branches. The bank's holding company, U.S. National Corporation, even purchased dwelling units in the towns where the new branches resided, which it leased to branch managers. In 1949, U.S. National had established twenty-nine branches (twenty-five of them from merged banks).

Even so, it could not keep up with the growth of its major competitor, First National. As early as 1934, the advisory board of First National's then-associate, Transamerica Corporation, suggested that First National "should start negotiations for the purchase of banks in favorable locations in Oregon, such purchases to be financed by a subsidiary of the Transamerica Corporation" at the earliest opportunity.[120] O. N. Hood, a Portland broker, acted as the above-named subsidiary, through which, from 1933 to 1945, First National acquired thirty-nine banks with deposits of more than $73 million.[121] In 1938, Transamerica purchased First National outright, although the regulatory authorities refused to sanction the conversion of the acquired banks into branches. Transamerica continued to acquire Oregon banks, even though they could not be converted into First National branches, and operated them as affiliate banks.

While by the 1950s the restraints against Transamerica and Western Bancorporation temporarily halted Giannini's dream of true interstate banking, well before that all but a few of the most hardheaded western bankers had failed to see the benefits of branching. Some states, such as New Mexico, with its limited branching arrangement, witnessed tremendous growth in bank numbers after the war. Fourteen new banks opened in New Mexico in the late 1940s. That number was dwarfed, however, by the sevenfold gain in branches, and by the end of 1959, there were as many branches—forty-eight—in operation as the total of branches and main offices operating in 1945.[122] Colorado bankers tried repeatedly to persuade lawmakers to pass a probranching law. Montana bankers had faced a branching ban since 1927. But in 1967, banks in Anaconda and Butte took advantage of a 1931 amendment that permitted consolidating banks in neighboring counties to keep them open. Both the comptroller of the currency and the state attorney general approved, and branching had its foot in the door. Unit bankers rapidly mobilized to oppose the concept, and in 1969 they succeeded in getting the 1931 amendment repealed, leaving Montana as one of only eleven states to prohibit branching.[123] Montana banks, like those in North Dakota, thus tended to have small capitalizations, and as a result they fell prey to mergers and takeovers by holding companies, especially the "big three," First Bank and Northwest Bancorporation of Minneapolis, and Western Bancorporation (later, First Interstate). By the late 1950s, twenty-two of Montana's 112 banks were chain banks controlled by out-of-state holding companies.[124] Local bankers argued that oppressive taxes on banks (the highest in the nation) had contributed to the problem by causing low capitalization. In 1957, after heavy lobbying by bankers, the legislature passed the "Better Banking Bill," Montana Senate Bill 15, which reduced taxes on bank surpluses up to the total amount of capital. Following passage of the bill, capital accounts rose $5.2 million, and by 1963 aggregate capital accounts topped $75 million, up from $41 million in 1956.[125]

FINANCING FARMERS

Like banks in other western states, the financial institutions in North Dakota and Montana participated in the postwar land boom, more in agriculture than in urban development. North Dakota banks increased their mortgage debt from $727,000 in 1945 to $5.78 million in 1954, although they still trailed well behind life insurance companies and Federal Land Banks and their holdings comprised only 7.3 percent of the total.[126] Still, insurance companies had slightly decreased their holdings of farm-mortgage debt since the war, and the Federal Land Banks, established in 1917, had lost more than half their farm-debt holdings, falling from $35.7 million in 1945 to $16.5 million in 1954.[127] Montana bankers also sought ways to revive the predepression agriculture industry, a feat that the war greatly aided. In 1941, then again in 1942, Montana farmers set records for production. Oklahoma bankers similarly searched for new ways to make farm loans, and expanded lending to agriculture by one-third in the first year after the war ended. By 1943, Oklahoma agricultural lending had increased by 48 percent over prewar levels. By 1954, Oklahoma bankers had lent over $90 million to farmers, and by 1962 that total had risen to $152 million. Led by W. H. Patten at Security National Bank in Norman, banks opened new agribusiness departments. Most banks expanded their interest in special farm projects, Future Farmers of America, 4-H, and other educational programs related to agriculture. Perhaps the greatest push came in funding new programs to end soil erosion by cooperating with the Soil Conservation Department of the United States Department of Agriculture.[128]

Utah's First Security developed a profitable relationship with J. R. Simplot, the Idaho potato farmer who invented the process for freeze-drying potatoes and onions. Simplot then sold his product to the genius behind MacDonald's hamburger stands, Ray Kroc.[129] The Utah bank also made extensive loans to U and I Sugar. Although Arizona banks too backed sugar enterprises, especially sugar beets, luring a large Spreckels Sugar factory to the Chandler area, most of the agricultural lending there focused on cotton, alfalfa, sorghum, soybeans, and hay. Arizona banks also financed livestock ranches. Valley National Bank led the lenders, at once becoming the nation's fifth-largest agricultural lending bank.[130] California, too, witnessed a brighter picture for agriculture, although it had begun the recovery in the 1930s. As of 1938, California banks had $80 million in agricultural loans outstanding. During the war, these numbers increased rapidly. The Bank of America alone made over $20 million in agricultural loans in a single year, and by 1952 its farm loans topped $159 million. The bank emerged as the nation's number one wine bank, and invested heavily in irrigation bonds and other water-district offerings. Among the numerous canals it financed, the All-American Canal made possible $125 million worth of Imperial Valley crops in 1952, some thirteen times greater than the return in 1938.[131]

Expansion of agricultural production during and after the war concealed an important fact that bankers who had the "booster" mentality perceived: quite often agricultural expansion came through mechanization. Montana's agricultural work force, for example, declined by almost 50 percent from 1950 to 1964. Not all bankers could diversify their lending—Montana provides just such a case—but elsewhere by the 1950s, bank lending had expanded into almost every activity in the West. Petroleum, motion pictures, gambling, and even new automobiles received financial support from western bankers. Oil had been known to Oklahoma's Native Americans long before Edwin Drake drilled his Pennsylvania oil well, and one of the earliest wells in the state, sunk in 1886, turned out a half barrel per day.[132] Other early wells were capped for lack of demand, but demand in the 1950s pushed the new industry to the forefront of the Oklahoma economy. The most noteworthy of the Oklahoma petroleum lenders, National Bank of Tulsa, earned the nickname "Oil Bank of America." It maintained a petroleum engineering department, and its share of oil loans as a percentage continued to increase. First National of Oklahoma, also a large petroleum lending bank, emerged as the largest bank in the state.[133] The oil boom hit Denver and Wyoming as well, although in a somewhat later period. In the early stages in Denver and Cheyenne, local banks found that they could provide necessary capital for the independent oil companies. However, by the 1970s, when bigger sums were needed, the unit banks found themselves unable to participate.[134]

POSTWAR BRANCH BANKING IN CALIFORNIA

Such was not the case in California, where the strength of the branch system enabled banks such as the Bank of America, Wells Fargo, Security, and First Interstate to lend generously to agricultural sections on the one hand, and to extend credit to motion pictures, petroleum, and autos on the other, because of the diversification of its portfolio. California had already entered a period of branch expansion in the 1950s, with the total number of unit banks shrinking by 101 in the decade (see table 5.1). Meanwhile, the total number of branches grew from 979 to 1,676 between 1950 and 1960. This growth continued almost without interruption. The controller kept a wary eye on de novo banks that might cause excessive competition where branching existed. The comptroller reasoned that a branch could always open in a city in which a unit bank existed. Therefore, mergers occurred more in branching states than in nonbranching states.[135]

Predictably, the Bank of America National Trust and Savings Association led the way. Even while Bank of America awaited the outcome of the case against its parent, Transamerica, it added more than thirty branches.[136] Many of those branches represented acquisition of farmers' unit banks. In most cases, these were small-town banks with the stock held by family members or their friends. These banks had several attractive features, including low loan-to-deposit ratios and capital makeup that often featured high retained earnings. As J. W. Hellman, the grandson of the founder of Farmers and Merchants Bank of Los Angeles, recalled, his family sold its

Table 5.1 Number of Banks and Branches in California, 1950–1960

Year	Number of Banks Unit	Number of Banks Branch	Number of Banks Total	Number of Branches
1950	156	46	202	979
1951	151	50	201	1004
1952	147	52	199	1036
1953	148	58	206	1058
1954	117	54	171	1121
1955	96	54	149	1212
1956	85	55	139	1304
1957	74	58	128	1387
1958	69	62	124	1466
1959	57	65	115	1566
1960	55	66	117	1676

Source: Federal Deposit Insurance Corporation, *Annual Report* from 1950 to 1960.

bank because they could no longer provide leadership or offer a proper pension plan for the employees.[137]

Usually, a few large banks took the initiative. In addition to the Bank of America, other large California banks acquired small suburban unit banks. California Bank of Los Angeles (later itself acquired by United California Bank, which became First Interstate) actively expanded, purchasing five banks in 1955 and another eight by the end of the decade. The Bank of California acquired four banks in 1955. Security First National Bank of Los Angeles bought nine banks in the late 1950s, including Isaias W. Hellman's Farmers and Merchant Bank and another institution that itself had just acquired three banks. Finally, Crocker First National Bank and Anglo California National Bank, which merged in 1956, acquired ten banks between 1955 and 1960.[138]

The characteristic activity among California banks involved big banks getting larger by merging and expanding into the suburbs. California banks, while always large, tended to be toward the top range of U.S. banks (see table 5.2). More than 30 percent of California banks had total resources of more than $15 million, and more than 22 percent had resources in excess of $50 million, compared to fewer than 5 percent of U.S. banks.[139] The Bank of America topped the list of big banks, holding 45 percent of the state's deposits in 1959, with Security First National a distant second at 13 percent.[140]

This flurry of acquisitions and mergers hardly stifled de novo branch creation, which accounted for three times as many branches as mergers

Table 5.2 Size Distribution of California and U.S. Banks, 1960

Size of Bank Total Resources ($million)	% of Banks	
	U.S.	California
less than 1	6.8	3.1
1–2.5	23.7	7.8
2.5–5	24.8	13.3
5–15	27.6	30.5
15–25	6.7	13.3
25–50	4.9	9.4
more than 50	5.6	22.6

Source: Richard E. Towey and Robert Lindsay, "Liquidity of California Banks," p. 149.

(see table 5.3).[141] Of course, as the decade ended, the number of desirable banks thinned considerably. Nevertheless, all of the statewide branching available, even in as large and diverse a system as the Bank of America's, could not have financed a new automobile company in the 1940s. Henry Kaiser, the wartime industrialist who had expanded his empire to include fifteen plants making over a hundred products by 1945, with total sales above the half-billion-dollar mark in 1952, wanted to create an entirely new auto to challenge Ford, General Motors, American Motors, and Chrysler. Of all the entrepreneurs in the country, Kaiser had the qualities and resources to pull it off. He had experience producing steel and mass producing ships; he had aluminum plants; and he had a trained workforce. The Bank of America agreed to back Kaiser's initial effort with a $12 million line of credit.[142] The Kaiser-Frazier automobile resulted from that loan.

Although Kaiser turned an initial profit and repaid the first Bank of America loan by 1947, a failed stock offering quickly led him to request an additional $10 million, which he received. The company continued its efforts to expand, negotiating for the purchase of Willys-Overland in 1953 for more than $60 million, of which Giannini's bank put up one-third. Transamerica, Giannini's other company, also played a role in the Kaiser financing, purchasing $15 million of the car company's stock.[143]

It is not clear if the Gianninis knew that Kaiser-Frazier was drifting toward serious trouble, but it seems unlikely. They were experts on agriculture, branching, and small business, and although they had no experience with autos, the point man for the Kaiser account, Fred Feroggario, knew the situation intimately. According to David Halberstam's account, Kaiser repeatedly was cautioned by Feroggario: "Henry . . . your cash position is weak," to which Kaiser replied, "Fred, why don't you get

Table 5.3   New Banks and branches in California, 1951–1962

Year	New Banks	New Branches de novo	New Branches Converted
1951	1	25	2
1952	4	17	5
1953	11	20	3
1954	5	27	39
1955	8	63	29
1956	2	83	12
1957	4	69	15
1958	0	79	4
1959	1	80	10
1960	5	118	3
Total	41	581	122
1961	11	115	5
1962	11	173	4
	63	869	131

Source: David Alhadeff, "Banking and Competition," p. 189. Compiled for the author by the Research Department of the Federal Reserve Board of San Francisco.

a record of that so you won't have to waste your time telling me the same thing again and again?" In 1949, when Kaiser's son Edgar went to the Bank of America for another loan, Feroggario replied, "I'll lend you money on anything except Kaiser-Frazier."[144] Even Henry Kaiser himself seemed baffled. By the 1950s, the company had degenerated into a capital sinkhole, swallowing over $100 million, as Kaiser dourly noted, "without a ripple" in the industry. Although it never advertised the fact, it is likely that the Bank of America had to write off significant losses related to this ill-advised project.

FINANCING DIVERSIFICATION

But not all auto companies suffered the same fate as Kaiser's. The Mack Truck Company, aided by a $30 million line of credit provided by a syndicate that included Peoples Savings Bank, thrived. Peoples also approved a $450,000 line of credit to the Kenworth Motor Truck Company.[145] Locally, most banks extended loans on a regular basis to car dealerships, and nationally the auto industry grew rapidly, with auto installment loans making up a larger portion of banks' total portfolios. Indeed, installment credit soared to $28 billion by 1956, leading Carl Bimson to question the

liberal lending of banks—the type his brother Walter had once encouraged. Just as the Eccles brothers had championed federal monetary expansion as a way out of the Depression, but did an abrupt about-face after the
war, the Bimsons, too, expressed concern about credit growth. As chairman of the Installment Credit Committee of the American Bankers Association, Bimson warned that credit "might be getting out of hand."[146] Still,
the economy continued to roll, given another boost by the Korean War,
which had revived the aviation and shipping industry on the West Coast,
especially the huge Boeing plants in the Seattle region. Along with military
aircraft, the burgeoning civilian aircraft industry needed aluminum. This,
in turn, generated business for the aluminum mines in Washington.

Still, the conclusion that defense, per se, spurred western growth leaves
much to be desired. By 1962, one study suggested, California, Washington, Utah, and Colorado (of the western states in question) were "highly
dependent" on defense-related income as a percentage of exogenous income. However, it called the others either only "slightly dependent" or
"moderately dependent." The author's model for the states in our study
(plus Texas) also suggested that a hypothetical redistribution away from
defense income would only seriously hurt Colorado, Utah, Kansas, Washington, and California. Meanwhile, such a hypothetical redistribution
would have improved per capita income in ten western states, among
them Idaho (by 14 percent) and Oregon (by 10 percent). The combined
military payrolls of the Pacific and Mountain regions that encompass most
of the West did not equal the payrolls of the South Atlantic region of the
country in 1962. The combined defense wages for civilians in the two
regions fell short of those in the South Atlantic region.[147] Finally, despite
California's position as leader among states receiving defense dollars over
the period, it should be noted that the Golden State started its boom well
before the "military-industrial complex" ever appeared. Defense industries surged into California because its other advantages—harbors, oil,
climate, and investment conditions—made it attractive. Similarly, the
ominous predictions made by experts after World War II ended—that a
depression would soon follow—seemed to overemphasize wartime industries as a source of employment. For example, Oregon newspapers announced thousands of job cancellations in a single day, and shipbuilding
centers in Washington and Oregon, employing 128,000, swiftly closed
down. Even so, the "all but insatiable demand for all kinds of raw and
industrial materials, from lumber to steel to nylon," dispelled such concerns.[148]

Other new areas of finance unrelated to the military-industrial complex
demanded capital in the West. For example, the gambling industry in Las
Vegas, which did not attract traditional bank financing because of its seamy
underworld connections, resorted to innovative methods to obtain bank

capital. Several prominent Las Vegas investors, including real-estate promoter Nate Mack, Beverly Hills attorney Sam Kurland, and a transplanted Utah banker, E. Parry Thomas, explored the possibility of creating a bank specifically for the purpose of financing the hotel and gaming industry. In 1954, Thomas and his superior, Walter Cosgriff, of Continental Bank in Salt Lake City, worked out the terms for a new bank, the Bank of Las Vegas. The decision to consummate the deal resulted in no small part from the support of the Las Vegas Mormon community, which had already concluded that the area was ripe for growth. The Bank of Las Vegas (later called Valley Bank of Nevada) financed the remodeling or expansion of the Sahara, the Desert Inn, the Sands, the Dunes, the Stardust, the Riviera, and several other hotels and casinos. Thomas and Cosgriff also convinced officials at First Security Corporation in Salt Lake City to participate in these loans, although the Utah bank kept its role as confidential as possible. Still, even into the 1970s, "Nevada banks [were] reluctant to lend to gaming establishments though they [were] willing to accept their deposits."[149] The state entered a period of remarkable growth—at times leading the nation in percent increases—and Nevada's banks grew along with it. But Nevada had neither the diversification nor the wartime investment of other states, and banks there, by limiting their participation in one of the three major industries, necessarily restrained their growth. Perhaps most important, no new Wingfield emerged to lead Nevada's financial institutions.

In this ironic way, Nevada underscored the importance of aggressive leaders in other states such as Washington, where the Green family had developed a powerful family-controlled bank. As a boy, Joshua Green, Sr., had a deadly eye with a slingshot, to provide wild game for his family. After moving to the West Coast in 1888, he cut brush as an axman, and moved into finance when he noticed that among the construction crews, one who quit or was given his "walking papers" prior to payday received a voucher that was not redeemable until payday. If a worker needed money immediately, local saloons and merchants accepted the vouchers, but only after charging a discount. Green quickly started a similar service, charging lower rates. He then moved into steamboating, working as a purser on the *Henry Bailey*, where he learned to navigate.[150]

Convinced of the opportunities for steamboating, Green and some friends formed a partnership and received a loan from Jacob Furth's Puget Sound National Bank. His company prospered, and eventually merged with the Puget Sound Navigation Company. In the new operations, Green stepped up to the presidency. For many years, he had acquired stock in Seattle-area banks and in Marine National Bank, and in 1906 he was named a director in the National Bank of Commerce.[151]

After selling his steamship interest in 1923, Green, who certainly was

not ready to retire, acquired stock in a small Seattle savings bank, the
Bank for Savings, founded in 1907 by his friend Daniel Kelleher, chairman
of Seattle National Bank. These two banks joined First Seattle Dexter
Horton Bank in 1928, and Green sold his stock at that time. He retained
his interest in finance, however, and looked for another bank to acquire.
His eye landed on Peoples Savings Bank, as did the eye of another legend-
ary Seattle banker, Andrew Price, then the head of Marine National. But
the Seattle banking community considered Price an upstart—not a "real
banker"—and Green was offered the stock. He purchased controlling
interest, and held a seat on the board. He immediately recapitalized the
bank by five times its previous capital, stocked the board of directors with
respected community leaders, bought a new building, and moved his own
officers into positions of power in the bank. The bank grew, and in 1923,
Green moved into group banking by incorporating Peoples First Avenue
Bank. By 1930, the company had $17 million in deposits, although it
started to show losses resulting from the depression. The bank run in 1933
reduced deposits by $2 million, but by the late 1930s the bank had entered
another period of expansion, and in 1937 it became a national bank.
Within two years, deposits reached $26 million; during the war that figure
doubled, and by 1945, deposits had increased 425 percent to $160 million.

Green served as chairman of the board while able presidents ran daily
operations. Meanwhile, Joshua Green, Jr., who had attended Harvard,
worked an early job with the bank, then joined the U.S. Navy during
World War II. When he returned—"a changed man . . . a different person"—he progressed through several jobs until, in 1949, he became president of Peoples.[152] Under Josh Green's management, Peoples Savings
Bank embarked on rapid expansion through acquisitions and branching.
The bank was the largest family-held bank in the state and, despite Josh
Green's conservatism (a trait that he shared with his father), by 1960 net
earnings exceeded $1 million annually and deposits topped $205 million.
In 1962, Josh Green was elected chairman, and Joshua Green, Sr., then
ninety-two years old, moved to the position of honorary chairman. Remarkably, Joshua Green, Sr., lived until 1975, when he died at age 105.
Joshua Green, Jr., replaced his father as honorary chairman in 1979 after
his son, Joshua "Jay" Green III became acting chairman. Three generations
of the Green family had developed a small savings bank into a major
Northwest financial institution.

The Green family, the Eccles brothers, the Bimsons, A. B. Robbs, Jr.,
John Evans, and, of course, A. P. Giannini constituted a group of bankers
who wielded influence in national financial circles and in critical monetary
issues disproportionate to the size, population and wealth of their growing—but still relatively small—region. This group, almost all of whom
came from lower- or middle-class families of a traditional bent, against a

backdrop of conservative Republican politics, pioneered several radical investment practices and, in general, supported creative, but sound, financial and banking concepts, such as branching. Although some of them occasionally championed the use of government involvement in the economy, especially in the area of credit and monetary expansion, in truth, they demonstrated the value of the "vital few," and, above all, exemplified the critical role that individuals play in forging powerful businesses and regional economies. While they understood that the population boom associated with the postwar period was critical to urban growth in the region (again, with the exception of Eccles, who in his later years developed a deep fear of increasing population), they made the industry of growth itself their own arena. And in that, even Eccles ultimately participated, becoming a strong proponent of Utah's economic growth. Pulling in residents with their aggressive policies and relentless boosterism, they changed a temporary phenomenon into a permanent, powerful consumer base and an asset. Without their abilities and aggressiveness, the West might well have been dotted with temporary military bases, Indian reservations, a few mining camps and farms, and little else.

6

THE ASIAN INVASION: NATIONAL EXPANSION TO INTERNATIONAL COMPETITION, 1960–1980

As in the 1960s the United States entered one of the more chaotic periods in its history, Western banking changed dramatically, along with banking nationwide, due to new technology, a wave of mergers, a revival of branching, and the entrance of women into management. Many of the giants had passed from the scene: A. P. Giannini had been dead more than a decade, and his son Mario had died in 1952. George Wingfield, his banking empire destroyed in the Depression, began a remarkable comeback in hotels and mining, but never returned to banking, and died in 1959. Although some of the important figures of the 1930s and 1940s remained active in banking or politics (including Walter Bimson, who retired as chairman only in 1970, and Marriner Eccles, who continued to make policy speeches as late as 1972), they had made their marks on their banks, and a new generation of business-school educated, corporate-groomed managers stepped forward to change the face of banking. Except for a host of entrepreneurial-minded bankers who created small and highly profitable "niche" banks, the new group generally had a "managerial" mentality. Several of them presided over remarkable expansion, and indeed Tom Clausen, the man who oversaw the growth of the nation's largest bank, the Bank of America, led it to quadruple its size. Yet in many cases, the rugged individuals had given way to faceless bureaucrats, intent on preservation, focused on stability. Exceptions could be found—Joshua Green, Sr., and Joshua Green, Jr., at Peoples Bank in Seattle provided colorful and well-known figures. But the majority of the sixties and seventies generation of western bankers found themselves more than ever responsible to thousands, or even millions, of stockholders, enmeshed in regulatory restrictions on their activities, and even under assault by college students for "corporate greed" and general insensitivity.

The West differed little from the rest of the nation in experiencing the change caused by new technology, mergers, branching, and the entrance of women into bank management. However, most of the western states, as a part of the growing Sunbelt (or what Kirkpatrick Sale called "the Southern Rim"), found themselves expanding faster than were other parts of the country.[1] That growth fueled renewed competition, and western bankers, already operating in a marketplace with thrifts, savings and loans, and building and loans, faced one challenge that did not reach bankers in other regions: the Asian invasion. Western banks thus entered a new era of international competition not seen since New York had displaced London as the financial capital of the world. No sooner did the Bank of America rise to challenge New York's power, than a new foreign presence—Japan— sought to seize financial leadership of the world from the United States. By the end of the 1970s, a new xenophobia swept into America, fueled initially by anti-Arab feelings after the oil crisis of 1973 and the late 1970s, then by anxiety over losing ground in manufacturing and finance to the Japanese.

CONTINUED EXPANSION

In fact, however, the same laws that had made possible the prosperity of the California banks also made the state attractive to foreigners. But it was not just California that lured investment—all the West had proved fertile ground due to its phenomenal growth. While much of the rise of the West can be rightly credited to government support dating from World War II, to defense industries, to energy, and to tourism, the financial infrastructure in some of the fastest growing states profited from branch-banking laws. California had witnessed the expansion of its already impressive branching system to new levels in the 1960s, as did Arizona. A new wave of branching and bank creation swept the entire West in the decade, thanks to the 1960 Bank Merger Act, which required review by the appropriate banking agency before any bank could purchase the assets of another. Several legal suits brought in 1961 and 1962, including one against Valley National Bank of Arizona, the state's largest, showed that the government intended to subject banks to antitrust legislation and thus restrain their acquisitions. Valley Bank, which had experienced a surprise federal investigation in 1957, thought it had emerged unscathed because the government filed no charges. Then, suddenly, the bank signed a consent decree in which it agreed to eschew takeovers and mergers. In fact, however, Valley had already decided not to pursue branching, and had passed up opportunities to take over some banks in the 1950s.

Partially as a result of this refocus on Valley's part, new banks found an open field in the Arizona boom market. A. B. Robbs, Jr., for example, while witnessing gains in the trust and mortgage financing department that were nothing short of astounding, nevertheless decided that a more diversified portfolio would be advantageous. The boom years, he knew, often gave way to recession. In 1953, a building recession resulted from the construction of about two thousand "speculative homes" in the Phoenix area.[2] A sharp recession also hit Arizona in 1963 and 1964. While the cyclical recession of 1959–60 convinced Robbs to lend in areas other than real estate, he had experimented in banking before that. First, he joined with the society-minded James Minotto, a wealthy dairy farmer, to create the Bank of Phoenix in 1957, possibly the first "boutique bank" in the state's history. Minotto, by insisting on a minimum deposit of $10,000, ensured that the bank would not grow. Although Robbs convinced him to lower the minimum deposit to $5,000, that amount still was too high for the average depositor in the 1950s, so Robbs resigned from the board of directors in 1958. Frustrated, he sought support for another bank from his personal and social friends, including developer David Murdock. Murdock and Robbs had joined forces on several of Murdock's projects, with the Robbs Trust Company providing the financing on many of the large developments. Along with ten other investors, Robbs and Murdock put up a total of $3 million for a new bank, called Guaranty Bank, and these twelve became founding directors. Robbs, who wanted control of the bank, mysteriously refused to be made chairman, and he supported a bylaw that limited the percentage of stock any individual could own. He attempted to exchange shares of his much more valuable Robbs Trust Company for a 40 percent ownership in the bank, but president Jim Simmons and the other directors balked.[3] Robbs then determined to create yet another bank.

In 1962 Robbs and Murdock had joined forces to put together the state's first full-fledged financial network, Financial Corporation of Arizona, which included the Bank of Phoenix, Home Savings and Loan, and Stewart Title and Trust Company. Murdock contributed the equity in one of his large buildings, the Security Building, later renamed the Union Title Building.[4] Although the company was an instant success, a vice president in Union Title (as Stewart Title was renamed), in an elaborate scheme, started to embezzle what eventually became $1 million of the company's $1.2 million in capital. When the company officials discovered the crime, it was too late. Financial Corporation of Arizona was ruined. Robbs had sold his shares almost a year earlier, in 1963, and Murdock had to fight off bankruptcy alone, buying back the near-worthless stock at huge losses.[5] Nevertheless, he managed to stave off total liquidation and later relocated to Los Angeles, where he started a new empire.

Robbs meanwhile set out to create the bank he had envisioned: a full-service institution that retained the profitable mortgage business in which he and his staff had their expertise. In 1963, he organized Continental National Bank, in which he exchanged shares of the Robbs Trust Company for bank shares.[6] The Trust Company then transferred to the bank its valuable mortgage-servicing contracts, worth well over $1 million.[7] This one-of-a-kind exchange gave the bank a built-in mortgage business, called by one vice president a "money machine."[8] The young bank acquired $11 million in assets in five months and continued to grow, becoming the state's sixth-largest bank by the mid-1970s, and during the 1970s consistently held the distinction of being the most profitable bank in the state.[9]

Arizona's market, opened by the restraint on Valley Bank and First National, saw other banks created besides Continental. One bank, established in the growing suburb of Glendale, got it start when Valley Bank failed to successfully replace a popular branch manager there. Local businessmen, wanting better service, created Thunderbird Bank in 1964. Like Continental, Thunderbird soon found a niche. Whereas Continental specialized in mortgage lending, Thunderbird emphasized small-business loans. It soon became Arizona's seventh-largest bank and vied with Continental for the distinction of being the state's most profitable bank.[10]

The boom of the postwar period continued in the 1960s in states other than Arizona. New Mexico's banks' resources rose by $87.5 million in 1961 and 1962. Despite this, one economist, writing at the time, proclaimed "the end of the great postwar boom in New Mexico."[11] In fact, the state continued to show strong growth, so much so that urban historian Bradford Luckingham included Albuquerque in his study of four booming sunbelt cities.[12]

California, of course, led the way in the new branch movement, although there was a subtle shift in emphasis among California banks. Beginning in the early 1960s, banks gradually started more de novo branches and acquired fewer existing banks to turn into branches.[13] In addition, new banks received charters at an increasing rate, partly as a result of the new comptroller of the currency, James J. Saxon, who took over in 1961 and immediately implemented a liberalized charter-approval policy. In his first year, only 11 percent of the applications for national charters were rejected—the lowest rate in four decades. State authorities followed his lead and soon even put pressure on Saxon to reverse his policy by their own liberal chartering. As a result, by 1965, Saxon announced that Los Angeles, Oakland, San Francisco, San Diego, and Orange County (essentially the metropolitan centers of California) "which are patently well banked at this time" would be closed to new banks.[14] Again, state regulators followed Saxon's lead and the number of new state banks declined sharply after 1964.

Other factors contributed to the increase in California bank charters, including investors' growing enthusiasm for holding bank stocks. Part of this enthusiasm was based, not altogether incorrectly, on investors' perception that smaller banks that merged with larger banks offered significant returns. Certainly shareholders of banks that had merged in the 1950s experienced more than a satisfactory return on their investments, both in appreciation of capital stock and in returns from dividends, with some rates "phenomenal." Indeed, among insured banks, those in California had a higher rate of net profits to stockholders' equity than the national average, and their earnings, according to one analyst, exceeded those of other corporations in the postwar period.[15]

This keen interest in new banks changed the character and shape of California banking in the late 1960s. Most of the new bank owners, although they were relatively unsophisticated investors who owned no other stock, nevertheless took an active part in bank management. They demanded quick returns and waited impatiently for big tender offers from the major banks. As a result, their marketing strategies shifted more toward enticing merger partners or advertising themselves for sale than toward attracting a new customer base or retaining their existing customers. With dozens of banks "on the market," larger purchasers had their pick. Still, many succeeded in merging or being acquired: of the banks opened between 1960 and 1965, 57 percent merged within ten years. In 1964, of the thirty banks that opened, more than 40 percent were acquired within five years and 63 percent within ten years (see table 6.1). The following year saw forty-eight banks open, of which 64 percent were merged or acquired within a decade.[16]

California was not the only state whose number of banks rapidly expanded. From 1950 to 1969, fifty-nine new Oklahoma banks opened. All but twelve of those were founded in the 1960s, with the major population centers, Oklahoma City (plus Norman, forty miles away) and Tulsa accounting for twenty-four of these banks.[17] One of those banks in particular would change the shape of banking more than all the rest put together: Penn Square Bank, NA, in Oklahoma City.[18]

Throughout the West the 1960s saw an army of smaller banks check the rising dominance of the big ones. From 1960 to 1979, forty-five new Wyoming banks received charters, with 38 percent concentrated in the seven largest cities and towns. The trend reflected concentration even in sparsely populated Wyoming, with many towns that had banks in the 1920s finding themselves without one in the 1970s. The state's financial centers had also shifted with the economy: in 1900 the two largest banks were in Cheyenne, with two of the top five in Rawlins and Evanston. By 1920, the latter cities had dropped off the list, replaced by banks in Casper and Laramie. With the development of the coal industry in Gillette, that town placed a bank in the top five by the 1980s, and Laramie dropped off. The new growth and realignment of the state's banking system occurred without a failure in the period from 1960 to 1980.[19]

Table 6.1   Acquisition of Banks Opened in California, 1960–1965

Year	Number of Banks Opened	% Acquired within 5 years	% Acquired within 10 years
1960	6	16	50
1961	10	0	50
1962	11	36	45
1963	30	43	63
1964	48	35	64
1965	13	30	38
1966	1	100	100
Total	118	33	57

Source: Based on information from Gerry Findley, *Mergers and Acquisitions*, pp. I–2 to I–5.

The large banks in Idaho also took advantage of newly legalized branching to buy smaller banks. By 1960, it seemed that First Security, Idaho First, the Bank of Idaho, and Idaho Bank and Trust would eventually absorb every independent bank in the state, but by the 1970s many of those banks were operating successful branch systems of their own, with the result that the state was served by an unprecedented number of bank offices.[20]

Likewise, in Arizona, the eight largest banks in 1951 held almost 90 percent of the state's deposits, and in 1960 that number rose to over 93 percent. Five years later, however, the percentage of deposits held by the large banks had fallen to below the 1951 levels.[21] But the founding of Continental Bank and Thunderbird Bank in the mid-1960s marked a major change. On January 1, 1968, Saguaro Bank of Scottsdale, Central Arizona Bank of Casa Grande, First Security Bank of Mesa, the Bank of Yuma, and Guaranty Bank formed United Bank, the state's fourth-largest institution (and, behind Continental and Thunderbird, the most profitable over the decade of the 1970s). Another merger joined the Bank of Phoenix, the Bank of Scottsdale, Pioneer Bank of Arizona, the Bank of Tucson, and First Navajo National Bank into Great Western Bank and Trust Company. This institution suffered from the weaknesses of one of its merged entities, especially Navajo National Bank, as well as a generally poor loan portfolio. Despite its position as the fifth-largest Arizona bank for most of the 1970s, industry experts expressed concern about its ability to continue competing.[22]

Along the Pacific Coast, new entrants somewhat buffered the expansion of the two major bank holding companies and their branches, U.S. National Bank and First National. As of 1965, Oregon had 283 banks with debits (the dollar value of checks drawn against the deposit accounts of individuals and businesses) rising at a rate of 7 percent per year.[23] U.S. National reacted to this growth by introducing a bank credit card, acquiring of a mortgage company, and forming an international division. That diversification suited the comptroller of the currency, James Saxon, who continued to remove restrictions on banks, but the Federal Reserve Board's attitude toward varied bank activities remained skeptical. To forestall problems, U.S. National, along with many other banks, formed a one-bank holding company, known as U.S. Bancorp.[24]

Even Colorado, which seemed at a disadvantage in the postwar boom because of its limits on branching, witnessed growth spurts among its major banks. United Banks, United California Bank, and Colorado National Bank all underwent expansion programs. All three had also created holding companies in the 1960s out of the need to acquire and establish subsidiaries and out of their failure to change the Colorado unit-bank law. In December 1968, First National Bank of Denver incorporated First National Bancorporation, and to do so had battled its way out of an attack by hostile shareholders. The episode had its origins a year earlier when the descendants of Mahlon D. Thatcher, who had started First National Bank of Pueblo in 1871, insisted on receiving greater representation on the board. The group at the time held some 25 percent of the bank's stock, and wanted six of the twenty-five seats on the board. Management at First National resisted, so in summer 1968 the Thatcher Banking Partners made a cash tender offer that eventually reached almost twice the market value of the shares before the offer. William White, Jr., the leader of the "raiders," timed the offer to prevent an 80 percent exchange of Bancorporation stock for bank stock, possibly depriving the shareholders of significant tax advantages. A compromise gave the Thatcher group four seats, and First National Bancorporation came into existence. It quickly acquired First National Bank of Denver, First National of Southglenn, First National of Northglenn, and First National of Bear Valley. The holding company also sought to move into Greeley, in northern Colorado, but the Justice Department filed suit to block the acquisition of First National Bank of Greeley. Eventually, Bancorporation won the suit, and acquired or formed thirteen banks, insurance companies, mortgage companies, and leasing companies by 1981.[25]

In 1964 United Banks of Colorado was created by merging Denver National Bank and United State National Bank. The merger joined the third and fourth largest banks in the city and resulted from the initiative taken by Arthur Johnson, the major shareholder in U.S. National, and Chris Dobbins, who represented the interests of the powerful Boettcher family. As one observer recalled, the two banks were "right across the alley" from each other and had a similar customer base.[26] Stewart Cosgriff of First National assumed the position of chairman for a short time until Dobbins replaced him in 1960. The bank formed a holding company, Denver U.S. Bancorporation, in 1962. Colorado National Bank was the third Denver bank to form a holding company, Colorado National Bankshares, in 1967. Even the holding companies, however, could not get around the antibranching law. In 1980, despite the support of the major bank holding companies, a referendum on branching saw the measure defeated by a vote of 3 to 1 after the anti–branch-banking forces successfully painted the contest as one of big banks versus small banks. One group that benefitted from the antibranch referendum, the suburban banks, stepped into the breach. Newcomers with unique services, such as Mountain States Bank, which had opened as the state's first drive-in bank in 1947, in the 1960s steadily cut into the larger banks' market share. By 1975, suburban banks numbered eighty-five, with over $125 million in deposits, while the downtown banks had lost deposits totalling more than $96 million.[27]

Inspired by the powerful Norwest Banks and First Banks holding companies in Minneapolis, the Denver bankers realized that without branching, group banking was the only way they could assure themselves of the portfolio flexibility they needed. They, like the California bankers, found an ally in comptroller of the currency Saxon. And precedents existed from Colorado's early history as well as from World War II, when the Treasury Department granted special requests by banks to open facilities at Lowry Air Force Base and other installations. This encouraged Colorado National Bankshares to absorb the subsidiary banks that it had already opened in the suburbs (and which retained their own boards of directors), and to let them adopt the corporate logo. It soon added several other subsidiaries and a mortgage company, as well as an insurance company.[28]

Most western banks also entered a new era of construction. The facilities that had served them well during the 1950s and 1960s had become quite overcrowded. The decisions to build new structures reflected none of the concerns about image or the symbolic preoccupation with safety that had characterized the first wave of building in the West. But they did reveal a new set of issues—issues that had not existed when the major banks built their downtown headquarters from the 1930s to the early 1960s. The flow of funds to the suburban areas reflected a new reality of the downtown areas. Many metropolitan centers, including Phoenix and Denver, had deteriorated or simply aged since the war. Newer western cities, especially, had witnessed dramatic building growth in their downtown areas as they boomed. Twenty-five years later, the population had abandoned the inner-city areas for suburbs, taking much of their business with them. When the major banks made their decisions to build new corporate homes, they confronted the problem of remaining downtown. To do so meant a massive commitment to the city, but it also meant having corporate headquarters well removed from the majority of the customers. Moreover, guessing wrong on the ability to fill offices in the buildings, or about the relative value of downtown property, could have disastrous consequences.

In Arizona, the Valley National Bank board and officers, still listening closely to Walter Bimson, considered relocating outside the downtown area. Most of Phoenix's growth had come to the north and east, and new groups of skyscrapers dotted the northern lengths of Central Avenue. Nevertheless, in 1971 First National announced plans to construct a new structure for its home office in downtown Phoenix, a move hailed at the time as courageous by civic boosters who had seen some banks take their headquarters outside the downtown area. Two years later, Valley Bank committed itself to building a forty-story downtown skyscraper, and soon Arizona Bank followed suit. Likewise, in 1971 Colorado National Bank laid plans for a $26 million, twenty-six-story office tower in the central city area. First of Denver (formerly First National), found its 1958 skyscraper filled to capacity in the mid-1960s, and had rented space for its own use. In 1969, the bank acquired surrounding lots to construct a thirty-two-story adjacent tower fronted by a plaza for public gatherings.[29] In Tulsa, the Bank of Oklahoma constructed a massive structure downtown in 1975.[30] In Oregon, the northern part of Portland was given a needed boost with the purchase of a large lot by U.S. Bancorp for a second downtown location.[31] And in California, the skylines of Los Angeles and San Francisco were heightened by numerous new bank buildings.

ASIAN INVASION

By the late 1970s, a new competitor had appeared on the horizon—in this case, on the western horizon—Japan. Concerns that so often were voiced about big corporations and concentrations of financial power had diminished during the decade as Americans grew increasingly anxious over foreign competition in products from autos to textiles. Of course, such concerns were nothing new in U.S. economic history. Americans have always expressed considerable anxiety over foreign control of native companies. Much of this merely was a remnant of the Revolution and hostility toward British control of trade. Certainly by the 1830s, Americans had modified their views considerably. States and private corporations routinely sold bonds to raise capital, with the vast majority of these going to foreigners, and the largest share of the bonds sold overseas went to the English.[32] No doubt the plethora of bridges, harbors, railroads, canals, banks, and other improvements the Americans receive tended to reduce their opposition to foreign investments. Nor did it hurt that, on occasion, when states or territories defaulted on their bonds, the foreigners suffered the greatest losses or were the last to be paid.[33] Nevertheless, overseas investors pulled back only temporarily, and usually brought their money back into the United States whenever it offered the best combination of safety and return. By the 1970s, the British, although still ranked as the largest single foreign-investor nation, were joined by several other groups, including the Saudis, the Swiss, the Dutch, the French, the Kuwaitis, and the Japanese.[34] Britain remained by far the largest investor nation, but as a group, British investors kept a low profile. Besides, as one observer noted, "names like Bayer, Shell, Nestle, and Phillips don't sound . . . ominously *alien*."[35] Others made their purchases more openly and even invited publicity. As a result, a new xenophobia sprang up. This coincided first with concern about Arabs, whose treasuries suddenly swelled with petrodollars, which needed an investment home. A common fear was that the Arabs had secretly purchased all the best American farm land. (As with most xenophobia, this variant had little basis in reality: by the mid-1980s Arab purchases of American farmland totaled less than 1 percent of all U.S. farmland. At that rate, the Arabs would have indeed owned all farms in the United States by the year 3488!)

Although foreign banking was not new to the West, the 1970s brought a large number of new foreign-owned banks to the area. Most of these were owned by Japanese, a few by British, and several by various other Asians. The trend originated out of the strength of the trade relationship between the Pacific Coast states and Asia and the trade surplus Asian countries had with the United States. Westerners referred to this dramatic change as the "Asian invasion."[36]

As early as 1840 the Bank of British North America received a charter to operate in the West, and probably represented the first foreign-owned bank to do so. Associated with the Hudson's Bay Company, it operated in San Francisco and probably in the Puget Sound region. Other foreign-owned banks soon followed: the Bank of British Columbia (1862); London and San Francisco Bank (1865); Swiss-American Bank in California (circa 1870); Anglo-California Bank (1873); London-Paris National Bank (before 1900); London, Paris and American Bank (1885); and the Canadian Bank of Commerce (1901).[37] The Bank of California, Donohoe-Kelly, and other larger banks in California maintained correspondent relationships with Hong Kong and Tokyo banks to support trade between the two areas. Lumber and furs came from the Pacific Northwest, while Asian imports included pottery, rugs, silk, and "*nenkeng*" (literally, "low quality goods," or "junk"). Silver from the Comstock Lode went into Japanese coins, and William Ralston sold, and provided financing for, railroad cars from his California company to Asia.[38] Ties between Japan and California grew stronger when Yokohama Specie Bank of Japan came to the Golden State in 1899. Other Japanese banks followed this lead, with two opening in

California in 1906 (Japanese Bank and Japanese-American Bank), followed by Kimmon Ginko Canton Bank—described as "purely Chinese"—the next year.[39]

Of the first fifteen members of the San Francisco clearinghouse, which opened in 1876, four were British-owned, including the Bank of British North America, Davidson and Company (agents of the Rothchilds of London), the London and San Francisco Bank, and the Swiss-American Bank. Lazard Freres, the venerable French bank, joined in July 1877 after operating in the area for some time. (Indeed, francs had circulated in the city since in the 1850s.)[40]

Foreign banks, therefore, were well established on the coast, especially in San Francisco. Still, growth remained slow until the 1970s, although by then both Sumitomo Bank of Japan and Lloyds and Barclays of England had established subsidiaries in the Golden State. In 1972, the Federal Reserve Board found over one hundred foreign bank operations in the United States.

Four years later, foreign-bank business loans accounted for 20 percent of all business loans in the country. By 1980, the Federal Reserve counted 339 foreign bank entities in the nation, of which nineteen had their headquarters in Los Angeles or San Francisco. Of course, California represented the western center of foreign banking growth in the region, with seven subsidiaries of foreign banks operating in 1970, and eighteen in 1979. These subsidiaries accounted for 35 percent of all corporate loans.[41]

Under California law, foreign banks were allowed to open banking offices or to form a subsidiary bank incorporated under state charter. Offices or agencies of foreign banks, while prohibited from accepting deposits, could make loans even in other states and had to meet no capital requirements. In fact, California treated these subsidiaries much as it did other banks in the state. They had the right to branch freely within the state and had to have FDIC insurance. In addition, they needed U.S. citizens as directors and were subject to the same capital requirements as domestic banks. Often the banks' names reflected their foreign ownership, for example, Sumitomo of California or Lloyd's Bank of California. Other names, such as National Bank of Long Beach (a subsidiary of Danish Actibanken), however, were not noticeably foreign.

While most of the foreign banks concentrated on wholesale or international business, Barclays Bank of California, Lloyd's Bank of California, Sumitomo, and California First Bank (owned by the Bank of Tokyo) all had extensive retail branch systems. Barclays, Lloyd's, Sumitomo, and California First built their systems mostly through careful expansion, but some growth occurred through quirks in American law. When the $800 million deposits of Southern California First National Bank were available for purchase in 1974, antitrust laws prevented some of the U.S.-based potential purchasers from bidding, allowing the Bank of Tokyo to buy it, change the name, and jump to the position of eighth-largest bank in the state. Similarly, when the Bank of California retrenched, Sumitomo bought sixteen of its branches.[42]

The growth of foreign banking in California was not accidental, but rather was due to the oddities of U.S. banking laws. Many of the foreign banks entered the market or expanded by buying into American banks, with the American institutions usually experiencing some weaknesses. With strict interpretation of antitrust laws and enforcement of the laws against branching across state lines, finding prospective buyers within the United States proved harder. These prohibitions actually made the Asian invasion particularly welcome. But as the decade unfolded, the rapid growth of foreign investors caused concern, especially from the "I-earn-American-dollars-I-buy-American-made" crowd. Even though the Japanese, in particular, ran their local enterprises with local talent, their competitors wondered whether their access to parent banks' capital gave them an unfair advantage. In fact, Japanese banks tended to have fewer high-risk loans than their American counterparts, and thus they operated with more leverage. While American banks were required to have $1 of capital for every $15 in assets, the Japanese banks needed only $1 for every $40 of assets, resulting in a lower cost of doing business. Critics also raised the protectionists' favorite hue and cry, that the Japanese sacrificed profit to gain market share.[43]

In reality, other factors made the cost of doing business higher for the subsidiaries of Japanese banks. When raising money to lend, these banks tended to rely less on low-cost demand and savings deposits and more on funds acquired in the impersonal financial market. The foreign-owned banks managed to improve the profitability of the banks they acquired, but their profits remained lower than those of other California banks.[44] This concern about the possibility of an unfair advantage prompted the passage by Congress of the International Banking Act in 1978. Under this law, state and federal regulatory authorities had to jointly approve foreign-bank entry or expansion. The act prohibited foreign banks from opening interstate branches or maintaining agencies in more than one state unless states specifically allowed interstate or regional branching, and made all branches and agencies subject to Federal Reserve Bank requirements.[45] They also had access to the services of the Fed on the same basis as did domestic banks.

The Computer Revolution

Banking in the 1960s and 1970s was also shaped by technological change, especially the development of automatic teller machines, plastic credit cards, and paperless bookkeeping on magnetic tape. In 1968, California banks formed SCOPE, the Special Committee on Paperless Entries, a group that worked toward developing the legal, operational, and technical framework for "preauthorized paperless entry," or a "checkless" society.[46] The system went into operation in 1972 and processed its first entries. Within a year eighty-nine banks representing 95 percent of California's banking offices that participated had formed the California Automated Clearing House Association to administer the system. They intended to reduce the amount of paperwork, especially checks, that traveled through the system by making possible multiple transfers of funds into or out of an account by the execution of a single written authorization by the depositor. This permitted wages to be automatically deposited, utility or mortgage checks to be automatically paid, and savings to be automatically withheld.

Like similar systems, the California system put requests for a particular transaction, say, automatic deposit into a specific account, onto magnetic tape, transmitted by the person's (or company's) bank given the authority to conduct the transaction through the clearinghouse to the depositor's account for credit. The Federal Reserve Bank of San Francisco and its branches acted as clearinghouses for the California Automated Clearing House Association. Initially, the SCOPE committee estimated that of the 2.2 billion checks written in the state in a single year, 650 million were suitable for conversion to the paperless system.[47]

Another major change in consumer banking involved the widespread use of plastic bank credit cards, namely VISA (at first called Bankameri-card) and MasterCard (once Master Charge). Department stores and oil companies had had revolving charge cards for many years, but these traditionally carried either a provision that the cardholder pay the entire balance at the end of the month or, in the case of department stores, required that the cardholder use the card only in that particular store. VISA and MasterCard offered consumers a nationwide—indeed, soon, worldwide—network to purchase goods and services and to receive cash advances. Introduced by the Bank of America in 1959 as strictly a California service, this bank credit card swept through the country. The BankAmeri-card system offered licenses to banks in other states beginning in 1966. To join, banks had to pay an initiation fee of $25,000, and the Bank of America retained tight control over minimum-credit standards and operating procedures.[48] Within a decade of its inception, BankAmericard had 29.5 million cardholders. Responding to the success of BankAmeri-card, in 1966 a group of banks in Pittsburgh, Milwaukee, Seattle, Phoenix, and California formed Interbank under the leadership of Marine-Midland vice president Karl Hinke. That system, too, took on a decidedly western flavor and its ultimate success was made possible only by the strength of the

Mastercard network.[49] An association formed in October 1966 composed of the Bank of California, Crocker-Citizens National Bank, United California Bank, and Wells Fargo Bank and Trust Company had conducted a feasibility study for launching the new credit-card system, and, concluding they could compete with BankAmericard, launched Master Charge in 1967. The move was, as Gary Hector noted, a "defensive response . . . to create an alternative [to BankAmericard], for fear that Bank of America might capture the entire market."[50] A year later, Denver banks entered into a joint venture by forming the Mountain States Bankcard Association to market Master Charge in the Rockies. By 1969, more than 3,800 banks across the nation participated in Master Charge. It is notable, therefore, that both MasterCard and VISA, the two most popular multiuse credit cards in the world in the 1980s, originated in California.

Both systems had early problems that were inherent in the credit card business. Many individuals abused their cards and debts piled up. Collections proved difficult, and the cards hardly promised the return that their originators had envisioned. But the cards quickly shifted into the black, with returns of 5 percent common (compared to 3.5 percent on installment loans). Competitors left out of the two networks scrambled to offer their own packages for regular customers with special credit lines, interest rates, or "designer" cards. The designer cards went full circle: in the late 1970s banks issuing VISA and Master Card obediently covered their entire cards with the appropriate logo, placing their own bank's name in an inconspicuous spot. But by the mid-1980s, banks returned to placing their own logos more prominently on the cards, and by the end of the decade everything from scenery to the symbols of National Football League teams covered the cards. Even airlines participated, applying frequent-flyer miles to a cardholder's account every time the card was used. One early innovation allowed individuals to use their credit limit as a reserve account for their checks: if they overdrew, the bank automatically charged their VISA or MasterCard account and transferred the money into their checking account. Essentially, people had instant loans available through their credit-card accounts, and expectedly the number of troubled borrowers increased. Although most individuals learned to manage their money, some abuse continued. Before long millions of borrowers had piled up previously unheard-of debts.

Banks made debt even easier by allowing individuals to use their cards in yet another way, as a means to gain access to another developing technology, the automated teller machine (ATM). Introduced in June 1967 by Barclay's Bank in England, the first American-made automated tellers were installed by Chemical Bank in New York in 1969. They experienced several difficulties typical of any new technology. The tellers "ate" cards, broke down frequently, and failed to release cash or accept deposit envelopes. The earliest machines proved extremely expensive. Citicorp, which in the 1970s had committed itself to putting two of the machines at each of its retail branches, spent hundreds of millions of dollars and dropped Citicorp's profits below those of the Bank of America, which had avoided the machines. A similar scenario played itself out in other states.[51] Arizona Bank, the state's third largest, introduced the state's first ATM, which it advertised as "The Ugly Teller," in 1973. One of the big obstacles noted by Arizona Bank officials (and virtually all other bank officials who observed customer behavior) was the reluctance on the part of customers to interact with a machine. Many customers found the machine and its buttons imposing, and the necessity of remembering code numbers proved daunting to more than a few. Moreover, mistakes made by a machine seemingly offered little recourse, while one could return to a human teller to discuss an error. But several factors combined to bring customers into the modern age. On a daily basis, whether through personal calculators, videocassette recorders, or microwave ovens, people interacted with technology on a rapidly increasing level. And the ultimate advantage of the machines—twenty-four-hour withdrawal on an account—gave people instant cash and freed them from meticulously budgeting for weekends or from using credit cards. ATMs also gave account information on demand, and, should an individual find an account overdrawn, the machines accepted deposits. Obviously much cheaper than even the smallest branch operation, ATM locations appeared in shopping malls, grocery stores, and in freestanding booths in parking lots, providing banking services where none would exist otherwise.

Led—or in this case, restrained—by the Bank of America, California remained a foot-dragger where ATMs were concerned. According to a 1979 *ABA Banking Journal* report, bank-watchers saw the state "bringing up the rear" in ATM installation. As of mid-1979, Wells Fargo had nineteen ATMs installed; the Bank of America had five; Security Pacific had only three; and California First had none. Only the highbrow City National, of Beverly Hills, and Crocker had any significant number of ATMs, with forty-eight and forty-five, respectively. Several reasons existed for California banks' tardiness in adopting ATMs. First, Californians had "worked out a modus vivendi with their banking system" that took some of the urgency out of adding new conveniences, especially the supermarkets' practice of cashing checks at almost all hours.[52] The cost of ATMs hovered at levels still too high for many banks to justify their expenditures on such machines, and the machines themselves constantly suffered from technological glitches. But while other banks rapidly recovered, the Bank of America's reluctance to enter the ATM market haunted it in later years, when it had to spend millions to catch up with banks it once considered its inferiors. At that point, Citibank's earlier investment gave it an important edge over the Bank of America.

However, with the exception of the ATMs, at least until the late 1970s, few banks kept up with the technology better than did the Bank of America. It was the first commercial bank to use a computer to help process checks. This machine, designed by Stanford Research Institute and built by General Electric, put the Bank of America in the forefront of bank computer technology.[53] Others soon copied the Bank of America: First Security Corporation in Utah purchased its IBM Computer Magnetic Tape System shortly after the Bank of America did, but tested it and conducted preliminary installation procedures for three years. First Security became the first bank in the intermountain region to computerize, and by late 1961 the system handled, on a nightly basis, transactions for seventy thousand checking accounts, forty-two thousand installment loans, and fifteen thousand mortgage loans in roughly five hours.[54] First National of Denver also joined the computer revolution at an early date, establishing a separate computer center in 1961. It also "was the first bank in the nation to utilize a computer for processing checks and deposits for correspondent banks. . . ." In 1970, the bank pioneered an on-line central information system as a computer service for correspondents. Eventually the programs provided personal trust records and commercial and mortgage loans.[55] Even banks in "backwater" areas automated. A. E. Dahl's American National Bank and Trust in Rapid City, South Dakota (with resources in 1964 of $59 million) purchased a major IBM computer system in 1965.[56] More important than the rapid bookkeeping—although that certainly revolutionized many banking tasks—the computer allowed an integration of the financial system only dreamed of in the nineteenth century. It made its presence felt in the credit-card arena by linking together banks in credit-card systems. Powerful regional banks joined BankAmericard's system, as seen in First Security's decision in 1966 to participate with nine other banks in an interstate BankAmericard network. First Security's BankAmericard holders expanded so rapidly that by 1968, one in four families in the Intermountain region had a card, and by the end of the decade the number of cardholders in that region alone neared 300,000. By 1977, gross sales on First Security's BankAmericard amounted to $153.2 million.[57]

THE ROOTS OF REGIONAL BANKING

But the success of the important regional banks—First Security (both the Utah and Idaho variants), Valley National Bank, U.S. National, and so on—served to reinforce the overall position of First Interstate, Security Pacific, and the Bank of America. And, for First Interstate and Security

Pacific's successes, in the 1970s, no western bank better captured the image of growth and prosperity than its San Francisco competitor. The Bank of America, in many ways, symbolized much of how banking had changed since the frontier period. From 1970 to 1981, Tom Clausen led the bank—only the fourth to do so since Mario Giannini's death. He could not have been more different from A. P. Described as "demanding and humorless," subject to fits of temper and "callous disregard for junior officers," Clausen was neither a "charismatic leader, nor a globe-trotting figure." The son of a newspaper owner from Hamilton, Illinois, Clausen had worked his way through school, eventually earning a law degree from the University of Minnesota. He took a job at the main Los Angeles Bank of America branch counting cash, but expected to be offered a position as an attorney for the bank. When that failed to materialize, Clausen decided to dedicate himself to a banking career, and worked in corporate lending, where he made a singular impression: "no pluses and no minuses."[58]

Clausen, the first chief executive not hired or trained by either A. P. or Mario Giannini, had in his early years established a reputation as a decentralizer, which he abandoned as soon as he took the reigns of power. He brought in specialists who had made their careers on large corporate loans designed to compete with the New Yorkers—Morgan Guaranty and First National City Bank. Clausen inherited a bank that still drew two-thirds of its profits from the California division, and the character of the institution still emphasized small businesses and local depositors. Such small potatoes had little to interest Clausen's corporate lenders, known to those inside the bank as an elite, arrogant group of "Prussians." Still, no one could argue with success: under Clausen, the Bank of America went from $25 billion in assets to more than $100 billion, expanding its overseas operations, which alone brought in almost 40 percent of the bank's total profits.[59]

Among the other strategies adopted in the 1970s by the Bank of America, it avoided Real Estate Investment Trusts (REITs), which enabled banks to borrow heavily to finance real-estate development. With the borrowed funds, the banks sank millions into office buildings and skyscrapers, counting on the real-estate boom to continue. It did not: during the oil crisis of 1979, many banks lost millions. Some New York banks reported losses of up to 5 percent of their loan portfolio. But not the Bank of America. It had avoided REITs, and in fact Clausen had limited the bank's lending growth to 10 percent a year. However, although Clausen limited the total growth in percentage that the bank could lend, he changed the character of the loans, increasing the largest loan that could be made in the field by four times its previous limit. This attracted large corporate borrowers, frequently of the kind A. P. Giannini had avoided. In addition, the bank pushed out into international lending, with its World Banking Division becoming "the darling of the company."[60] A rift developed between the California division—still the biggest profit maker in the company and its heart and soul—and the overseas division.

These changes certainly did not seem to hurt the Bank of America. In 1977 it passed Citicorp as the world's most profitable bank, earning $395 million. From 1975 to 1979, the Bank of America averaged 19 percent a year in earnings. Such numbers could not help but impress even the most flinty-eyed pessimist. While small Arizona banks such as Continental and Thunderbird hovered at around 22 percent return on equity, they hardly had the incredible scope of operations or sheer dollars that the Bank of America had. It seemed only fitting: California, by the end of the decade, stood as the *world's* seventh-largest economy. (By the mid-1980s, despite troubles at the Bank of America, California verged on overtaking Italy in the sixth spot!) Despite prognostications to the contrary, there seemed to be no end in sight for the California boom. Santa Clara, one of the densest concentrations of innovative industry existing anywhere in the world, had more than eight hundred scientific companies and 150,000 employees—"an innovative ferment on a scale without precedent in industrial history."[61] As Kirkpatrick Sale noted, the emergence of the Silicon Valley proved particularly interesting because, aside from Hollywood, "it mark[ed] the first time that a major new industry was located largely for climatic and social amenities, with no regard for the old established commercial and trade centers."[62]

The emergence of the Bank of America as the nation's largest bank further underscored the growth of the entire West for those who had issued a declaration of independence from Wall Street. In truth, the declaration was not even necessary: Wall Street had lost whatever control it had over the West decades earlier. But for quasi-Marxist academics, who still interpreted events in terms of "control" and "exploitation," the burst of expansion in the West drove the final nail in the coffin of "colonization." Even Kirkpatrick Sale, who tended to view growth of the West and South as the result of expenditures from the federal treasury, noted:

. . .the issue of Yankee money in cowboy corporations is one of some importance, since there have been those who hold that if a corporation is owned by people in New York, it is a part of the Yankee power complex no matter where it may be located. [But] a company has more overall effect where its plants are located than where its stockholders are located. If a New York–based group owns a mine in Arizona, a percentage of the profits therefrom will certainly be going back to New York—but an even greater percentage of the profits, and virtually all other money, will stay right there in Arizona, in the form of plant and equipment, reinvestment and expansion, salaries for labor and management, exploration, maintenance and the like; that money, moreover, is creating a ripple effect in the local economy. . . .[63]

Sale's choice of Arizona as an example is interesting. It underscores, whether intentionally or not, the fact that while the Bank of America remained the most powerful bank in the West, the financial institutions in the rest of the region had hardly stood still. Arizona, not laden with the anti–branch-banking laws that encumbered other states, had witnessed the growth of the twenty-seventh–largest bank among fourteen thousand American banks, Valley National.[64] In addition to being the state's largest—it held 42 percent of all deposits in banks in Arizona—Valley National remained extremely profitable. It ranked second in the nation in return on equity among banks its size in 1980, and its president, CEO, and later chairman, Gilbert Bradley, received *Financial World's* accolade as one of the nation's top three CEO's in 1979, a year in which he also received an appointment to the Federal Advisory Council of the Federal Reserve Board.[65] Arizona also had—in the state's second-largest bank, First National—a part of the interstate network that once belonged to Transamerica and remained conscious of the possibilities of interstate banking. In 1980, anticipating interstate banking on at least a limited level, First National joined twenty-one other banks in eleven western states in a simultaneous name change to "First Interstate Bank of . . ." followed by the appropriate state.[66] These banks were all members of Western Bancorporation, a regional holding company. The transition included installing seventy-eight hundred new signs, issuing five million new bank cards, and embarking on a massive advertising campaign to reassure western customers that they would continue to receive personalized service while receiving many advantages associated with larger banks.[67]

Utah's First Security had also established a network of seventeen banks in Texas, Colorado, Wyoming, Idaho, Washington, Oregon, Nevada, New Mexico, Arizona, and California, with 138 total offices. It maintained insurance or mortgage companies in ten western states. By 1978, First Security's average return on equity was 16.8 percent over three years. As of 1977, the total resources of the First Security system totaled $2.8 billion.[68]

These interstate networks served to undercut yet another criticism of western banking in the 1960s and 1970s, that the region's financial concentration was unhealthy. The concentration in Arizona, mentioned earlier, which caught the eye of regulators, was indeed high, but hardly stifling.[69] Critics raised similar complaints in New Mexico, despite much lower concentration rates. Four of New Mexico's top ten banks, including the top three—SunWest Bank, First National, and the Bank of New Mexico, all located in Albuquerque in 1980—held 31 percent of the state's $5.4 billion worth of assets. The rising financial concentration among New Mexico's banks had brought out the antibank lobbies in the 1970s. One group published an "expose" in 1980 complaining that the high number of bank holding companies stifled competition (a contradictory position). Western Bancorporation, formed by Transamerica in 1956, combined the Bank of New Mexico, Santa Fe National, Roswell State Bank, First State Bank of Gallup, and New Mexico Bank and Trust. In 1958, First New Mexico Bankshare, formed around Albuquerque National, acquired controlling stock in nine state banks, and in 1969 Bank Securities (originally headquartered in Alamogordo, but relocated to Albuquerque) was formed around American Bank of Commerce. New Mexico Bancorporation (later called NM BanQuest), based on the state's oldest bank, First National of Santa Fe, held three banks, while Southwest National Corporation not only included the Southwest National Bank of Hobbs and the Southwest National Bank of Albuquerque, but through stock of its owners, the Levinson family, this holding company also tapped the resources of the Bank of Las Vegas (New Mexico) and Carlsbad National Bank. The state also had two chains (one was the Levinson chain mentioned above) controlling a total of fifteen banks. Combined, the six holding companies and chains controlled 54.1 percent of all the deposits in New Mexico, and "the top four control[led] 47.2 percent of all deposits—almost one half.[70]

One critic contended, then, that a "functional monopoly" prevailed in New Mexico and that the concentration in Albuquerque of the flagship banks of the holding companies meant that "Less and less of New Mexico deposits [were] available for reinvestment in the communities where the deposits originated." Of course, financial concentration did not mean that at all. In a modern economy, New Mexico banks extended loans for the same purpose they always did, to make a profit. By that standard, New Mexico's banks showed impressive growth. The Bank of New Mexico's deposits rose $6.3 million in 1978, while Western Bancorporation, its parent holding company, saw its 1979 assets reach $29.6 billion, an increase of $3.7 over the previous year, while First National Bank of Albuquerque had net earnings increase by 19.9 percent from 1978 to 1979. Moreover, six holding companies competing for just over half the bank assets in a state hardly constituted a functional monopoly, especially when banking had entered a new era of telecommunication and interstate competition. It presented depositors and borrowers with greater choices and options, and meant that the "little old lady" in Carlsbad no longer had to be satisfied with whatever the local banker gave her. And on top of internal competition, a powerful savings and loan industry, with $1.2 billion in assets in 1979, also offered stiff competition.[71] Finally, the best argument for the holding companies was the miserable track record of the small rural banks or banks relegated to local mono-economies. Those essentially unstable, inefficient banks had simply been replaced with systems that offered better portfolio balance and easier capital mobility.

Nor was concentration without other advantages: one of the present authors has contended that the dominance of Phoenix over Tucson came primarily because of its ability to concentrate the major bank headquarters there.[72] Los Angeles surged past San Francisco in much the same way when, in the 1970s, it "surpassed San Francisco as the West Coast's financial center," and its deposit totals rose steadily.[73] More importantly, many observers perceived Los Angeles as "more vibrant" than its northern sister.[74] Its ability to lure foreign banks, with their huge cash holdings, contributed to that image. Perceptions fueled reality, though. When junk-bond trader Michael Milken of Drexel Burnham Lambert established himself as an important factor in the bond market, he immediately moved his headquarters to Beverly Hills.[75]

While concentration through holding companies or branching often fueled urbanization, banks in states where the unit banks remained the dominant power in financial politics had to compete as best they could. In Kansas and Nebraska, for example, that required the development of extensive correspondent banking. Correspondent banking dated to the earliest days of the western frontier, when small institutions established correspondent relationships with banks in financial centers, usually New York, Chicago, or San Francisco. Small banks placed some of their deposits with the larger banks in order to gain more rapid check clearing, the financial advice of the big banks' research staffs, and other services, such as data processing, trust services, and safekeeping facilities. The large banks acquired additional deposit funds to lend. Correspondent accounts did not, especially in modern times, need to reach all the way to New York. Wichita banks in 1967 held over $60 million worth of correspondent deposits. Through them, the smaller correspondents had the potential to invest more than $53 million in earning assets that year. The largest two or three Wichita institutions valued their correspondent accounts at just over $3 million.[76] The survival of the six hundred Kansas unit banks depended on the correspondent system.

The most significant of the Wichita banks, Fourth National Bank, developed into an important statewide and regional institution during the 1960s and 1970s. Becoming one of the nation's top three hundred banks in 1964, Fourth National added a real estate loan division purchased from a local company, and saw its mortgage lending rejuvenated. In the early 1970s, the bank announced plans to construct a "massive financial center" in downtown Wichita, and took the opportunity to have Skidmore, Owings, and Merrill, the architectural firm that designed the U.S. Air Force Academy Chapel and the Sears Tower, design a 386,000-foot L-shaped building with an enclosed courtyard featuring a remarkable mobile visible from the outside through the front glass. Completed in 1974, the new center symbolized the bank's steady growth, for, even with a two-year regional depression from 1972 to 1974, the Fourth more than doubled its assets in the 1970s.[77] Until Kansas banking legislation was liberalized somewhat in 1985, the state's banks created holding companies to circumvent the antibranching laws (which permitted branching only by merger) and Fourth National laid the groundwork for future expansion by creating Fourth Financial Corporation in 1969. That holding company immediately started purchasing minority interests in other Kansas banks.[78]

Still, with the exception of the very powerful unit-bank constituencies in a few states—especially Colorado—the accumulation and mobility of funds through holding companies and branching allowed banks in most western states to take advantage of important shifts in the economy, such as that attributable to the growth of the energy industry in the 1970s. Energy had contributed to a second boom in Wyoming, New Mexico, Oklahoma, and Colorado, and it remained an important part of California's economy. Banks in the oil and gas centers of Hobbs and Roswell, New Mexico, grew rapidly, with three banks based in those towns ranked in size among the top banks in the state.[79] Activities related to energy accounted for as much as 19 percent of Denver's economic base in 1979, an increase of 30 percent over the previous decade. Denver, as a hub city, served as the regional headquarters for Amoco, ARCO, Conoco, Amax, and Union Pacific, as well as a major regional air terminal. Because of the state's anti–branch-banking law, Denver banks had struggled to participate in the huge financial packages that energy required. The state's laws left them on an unequal footing with other western banks, and most energy loans quickly fell into the hands of First Interstate Bank, Wells Fargo, the Bank of America, or Texas's Republic National Bank. Indeed, local bankers expressed increasing concern about the numerous California and New York loan-production offices in the state, and Colorado found that much of the financing of the small energy companies flowed from the issue of penny stocks.[80] Indeed, it was the demand for outside financing of energy that led a little bank in Oklahoma City, Penn Square Bank, to package energy loans to larger buyers, including Continental Illinois and SeaFirst Corporation, the parent of Seattle-First National Bank, Washington's premier bank.

Some Colorado banks nevertheless managed to fill the market for lending to smaller energy companies and related industries. United Banks of Colorado led the way in these loans. United had evolved from a holding company created by Denver U.S. National Bancorporation in 1962 (which in turn was formed by Denver U.S. National Bank—itself a union of Denver National and U.S. National—and which at the time of its 1958 merger was the second-largest bank in Colorado); First Bank of Aurora, in a growing suburb; and Arapahoe County Bank of Littleton.[81] The new company began operations in 1964 and by the end of the year had $405 million in assets. This holding company acquired seven banks by 1970, at which time its name changed to United Banks of Colorado. By 1974, the company had fifteen banks with well over $1 billion in assets. Its foray into energy lending no doubt looked promising in 1974 after energy prices rebounded from a "disappointing" 1973, in which net income fell 15 percent.[82] But by the end of the decade, energy companies—particularly oil companies—had not recovered as hoped and United Banks started to feel the pinch. The consistent growth in the 1970s, however, led United Banks to plan a fifty-story tower, completed in 1983, called One United Bank Center.[83]

WOMEN IN BANK POSITIONS

Other developments of a very nontechnological nature changed the face of western banking in the 1970s, not the least of which was the expansion of the role of women. From the 1940s to the early 1970s, women had held clerical and teller positions, and had a reputation for "neatness, deft handling of money and papers, tact, and a certain intuitive judgment."[84] Bank management seldom considered them for executive jobs, although there were some exceptions. Carrie Tucker at Oakly State Bank in Idaho was named cashier in the early 1900s, a position second only to the president at the time, and Mabel Kasiska served as cashier of Lava Hot Springs State Bank in Idaho in 1933. She went on to assume the presidency of that bank in 1960.[85] When her uncle, then the president, died in 1913, another Idaho woman, Ina A. Anthes, took over the presidency of Citizen's Bank and continued in that capacity until 1924. As of 1928, *American Banker* reported that two thousand women held executive positions, but most of these were operations officers, a position with authority only over tellers and clearly inferior to lending officers who were training for vice-presidential and presidential positions.[86] Even before the Second World War western banks had added women's departments, with Fourth National of Kansas one of the first in the West to do so. Beginning in 1923 (and well publicized at its opening), the Fourth's Women's Department featured three teller windows for women exclusively, although they were free to use the other lines as well.[87]

The world wars changed the gender of banking positions incrementally. During World War I, women assumed many of the back-office clerical assignments previously handled by men, but in World War II they moved onto the teller lines for the first time. As one bank historian noted: "many a 'Thelma the Teller' began to appear" alongside the "Rosie the Riveters," giving them contact with the public on a regular basis.[88] The president of U.S. National Bank of Oregon noted in 1943 that the bank had "temporarily" replaced men absent for military service with young women "who . . . are rendering excellent service."[89] In Seattle at Peoples Savings Bank, for example, by 1943, 151 of the bank's 221 employees were women, and in 1944 the board elected its first female officer. But changes came slowly. As of 1970, only 15 percent of Peoples' officers were women, and by 1974 only 33 percent were female. In 1975, Peoples was hit with a class-action sex-discrimination lawsuit, and the bank responded by naming thirty-one women among its forty-seven new officers. Minorities and women made up 45 percent of the officers by the end of the year.[90]

But lawsuits did not change attitudes. Female loan officers found that male commercial customers simply did not like discussing business needs with them. As one female branch officer recalled: "men enjoyed discussing their financial needs with us about as much as a trip to a lady proctologist." Another noted: "it was impossible to take a male customer to lunch and pick up the tab. . . . We used to make special arrangements with restaurants . . . to avoid the discomfort of trying to arm wrestle them for the check." And another simple fact was that, despite important and highly publicized promotions—Anna Foster of Valley National Bank in Arizona, for example, was the bank's first female vice president and the first woman president of the American Institute of Banking—most banks of any size had been started by men, and, when possible, they had kept the bank in the family through male heirs. Again, some exceptions existed, such as Ladd and Bush Bank of Salem, which had two female directors between 1913 and 1940, both related to male founders.[91] At First National Bank in Albuquerque, two sisters of George Maloof, the major shareholder, were vice presidents in Maloof's other businesses and, consequently, held positions on the board.[92] Some women acquired large blocs of bank stock, and therefore board positions, through marriage, as with Mrs. Frank Mapel at New Mexico Bankshare Corporation, who inherited her 8 percent share after her husband died; and Ruth Martin of Home Interstate Bancorp, Long Beach, who found it necessary to move into the fifth-floor office of the chairman of the board after her husband's death in 1986. She directed the growth to almost $500 million in assets by 1991.

But entrepreneurial women who headed their own banks were extremely rare, and in 1986 no major bank in the West had a female CEO, chairman, or president who attained her position through other than inheritance. A few banks had female directors, such as Claire Giannini Hoffman, who inherited both her father's name and his public relations role with the bank. She thus served on BankAmerica's board (the holding company for Bank of America) but "never became a part of the inner circle of management," and she resigned in protest of bank policies in 1985.[93] First National of Denver invited two women to join the board in the 1970s, including movie star Audrey Meadows Six, the wife of Robert Six, who had founded Denver-based Continental Airlines.[94] Of the dozens of entrepreneurial bankers with whom we have had discussions in the 1970s and 1980s, virtually none considered training a daughter to follow in his footsteps, although Sherman Hazeltine, the son of Arizona's Bank of Prescott cashier and president Moses Hazeltine, had a daughter, Cynthia, who attained the rank of vice president after the bank became First Interstate.[95]

Women could effect changes more quickly as consumers: First Women's Bank of New York opened in 1975 and set a precedent for a bank aimed at female consumers. The Women's Bank of Denver followed this lead, and 80 percent of its new accounts were opened by women.[96] Still, many of these women's banks were short-lived, for the bottom line of any business is money and service, not gender or race. Indeed, to many male and female customers such banks smacked of discrimination, and repelled them.

Although aggregate statistics captured some of the shifts in women's roles as bankers, they also conceal some of the interesting stories. Ruby Nelson, for example, began as a bookkeeper for the A. B. Robbs Agency when Robbs, Sr., realized that she had not only kept up her own work but had helped out a male employee who had failed to do so. The agency promoted her, and A. B. Robbs, Jr., made her an integral part of his trust company, first as bookkeeper, then, as the trust company became Continental National Bank, as an officer. She eventually attained the rank of executive vice president and comptroller, a powerful and influential position in the Robbs network. Often keeping the intricacies of the bank's finances in her head, she proved invaluable to the unceasing wheeling and dealing on which Robbs thrived. At the time of her retirement, she was in all likelihood the wealthiest woman in Arizona banking (whose wealth was not inherited) and easily was one of the best-paid female executives in the state. Moreover, she had reinvested much of her considerable salary in the bank, which, when it sold to Chase in 1987, brought her premiums on her stock the equal of or superior to those of many other male executives of similar tenure and rank.[97]

Robbs's trust company gave another brilliant female executive her early training. Lilymae Penton, who held a rank that roughly approximated that of Nelson in the organization, had quite different talents. Whereas Nelson specialized in numbers, Penton learned the law. She had worked on many of the financing projects involving David Murdock. When Murdock moved his operations to Los Angeles in 1969, he asked Penton to join his organization. She accepted, and her skills in mortgage and property law continued to grow. By the late 1970s, without a law degree, she stood as the ultimate legal authority in the organization, and held the rank of senior vice president for Murdock Development. But her training had come from the small bank in Arizona.[98]

The changing face of banking that put women into management in the 1970s also saw competition force a quantum leap in new marketing techniques and expanded advertising. No longer could banks wait for depositors to walk in. They had to actively solicit accounts and promote banking services. Personnel, especially in the area of lending, who all their careers had practiced conservatism, suddenly had to meet quotas as car salesmen did. The change exacted a particular toll on the Bank of America, where the loan officials in foreign and domestic offices pushed loans in a frenzy.[99] The bank made billions of dollars worth of Latin American loans whose likelihood of collection was questionable at best. In foreign lending, the Bank of America was not alone: Security Pacific, First Interstate, Arizona Bank, and Valley National Bank all had significant amounts tied up in Mexican loans.[100] Only Wells Fargo managed to avoid excessive foreign lending in the 1970s.

Competition also led to higher levels of advertising than banks had ever produced in the past. Marketing campaigns included billboards, television, and public relations promotions. Some of the marketing activities revived the boosterism of the 1950s. For example, First National Bank of Denver financed the purchase of the Denver Broncos National Football League team and the Denver Bears minor-league baseball team by Allan and Gerry Phipps.[101] By and large, however, banks had grown extremely sophisticated in their marketing efforts, relying heavily on television and print media. Charitable giving or funding of arts, always a part of western banks' community service, suddenly required publicizing the staging of benefits or galas; support of 4-H and other agricultural activities; funding of high school or, more typically, university scholarships; sponsorship of dance, orchestra, opera, and other fine arts; promotion of events such as football games, basketball tournaments, and golf tournaments; and support of United Way and other charities. Banks made certain their names received proper display or notice in connection with each event. Increasingly they made use of television and radio spots, emphasizing their services more than their safety or size. Employee newsletters, once merely a source of internal communication, turned into full-color glossy productions designed for customers. Fourth National Bank of Wichita's *IV Front* exemplifies the public relations aspect of such newsletters, but virtually every large organization had such an internal organ designed for external consumption. Large banks even used their centennials as opportunities to hire historians or journalists to write official histories of the banks. While certainly those have had great value to subsequent researchers, they also constituted transparent works of self-congratulation. Nevertheless, western banks could afford such back-patting, both literally and in the eyes of the community. They had come through a decade of stagflation apparently uninjured; they had transformed the West with their mortgage lending and boosterism; they had started powerful efforts to eliminate restrictive banking legislation; they had seen one of their own rise to challenge the powerful eastern giants for the position of largest bank in the world; and they had financed the energy booms in half a dozen states. They deserved their victory cigars and savored them, at least for an all-too-brief moment.

7

From Deregulation to New Frontiers: 1980 and Beyond

Not since before the Great Depression had banks had the freedoms they exercised in the late 1980s. During the decade, many of the competitive shackles were removed from commercial banking, and in 1990, the government even started to permit commercial banks to engage in limited investment-banking activities for the first time since the Glass-Steagall Act of 1935). Certainly, deregulation constituted one of the major themes of the 1980s. At the same time, financial instability reached all time highs in parts of the West. The S&L crisis threatened not only to eliminate many of the western banks' strongest competitors, but to spill over to many of the banks themselves. Real estate, identified by Kirkpatrick Sale as one of the "six pillars" on which the West based its growth and a safe haven for any excess loanable funds, suddenly turned sour.[1] When combined with the fall in energy prices in the early 1980s, which struck hard at banks in Wyoming, New Mexico, Colorado, Oklahoma, and even Washington, a number of banks found themselves in trouble. The problems of the S&Ls and troubled banks that had overinvested in energy or real estate in energy-dependent cities comprised another of the decade's major themes. And because the Bank of America, at the outset of the decade the largest bank in the United States, found itself in severe difficulties related to each of these problems, its decline and pending revival constituted the third theme of the decade.

Troubled Times

Since the creation of the Federal Deposit Insurance Corporation (FDIC), historians and economists had credited the government with stabilizing the banking industry and with providing a way for banks to dissuade depositors from starting a run. After 1980, the FDIC insured all individual deposits up to $100,000, meaning that the average depositor had assurance that his money was safe. Only in the 1970s had some economists, mostly of the growing libertarian stream, begun to challenge the concept that government deposit insurance enhances stability. Rather, they argued, it allows banks to take risks they otherwise would not take.[2] In 1990, Henry Gonzales, chairman of the House Banking Committee, announced a plan to lower FDIC coverage, sell additional coverage and limit the number of accounts that could be insured. Those reforms would be too late to save the S&L industry. Some warning signs had appeared in the 1970s. First, S&Ls, mutual savings banks, and other financial institutions were all perceived by the public as covered by insurance. Some of those institutions, occasionally called "thrifts" and frequently having the word "thrift" in the title, were covered neither by insurance nor by banking laws. (The term became even more confusing in the 1980s when most major newspapers and magazines started referring to S&Ls and mutual savings banks as "thrifts," and yet further confusion developed when many finance companies—lending companies that charged high interest—used the term in their names). Even so, depositors who had money in institutions such as thrifts always assumed that the FDIC, the Federal Savings and Loan Insurance Corporation (FSLIC), or some government-sponsored institution covered those deposits. More important, they assumed that examinations ensured the safety of the investments. In fact, as the collapse of a western multistate thrift in 1972 showed, those institutions faced few of the restrictions that regulated banks.[3] In that case, Lincoln Thrift, headquartered in Arizona but with banks, thrifts, and other business (both financial and nonfinancial) in Colorado, New Mexico, and Hawaii, failed when the elaborate pyramid scheme that Robert Fendler used to finance his empire unraveled. Fendler went to jail, and Arizona changed its laws, but many caught in the scam developed a suspicion of banks in general.

Fendler's activities across several states should have alerted regulators to the difficulties of patrolling the banking and financial industry. Determined criminals routinely plied their trade. Internal bank mechanisms usually could control such activities, but when the culprit owned the bank, outside regulators had a harder time. In the late 1960s, for example, C. Arnholt Smith started to use his San Diego–based U.S. National Bank to finance his many business ventures, and continued successfully until the bank went into receivership in 1973. Early investigations failed to reveal that most of the loans the bank made went to businesses that Smith himself controlled—often through tortuous legal routes. Although regulators suspected that problems existed, they discovered the full extent of the damage only when they forced Smith out and brought in their own management team. Ironically, just at the time that the regulators took over, the bank collapsed. Smith went to jail, and Crocker Bank, in a heated bidding war with Wells Fargo, took over U.S. National. (That affair also shook Valley National Bank in Arizona, which restructured itself due to loans that had been packaged through Smith's bank.) Other major collapses had occurred in the 1970s, but often it took a complete failure before the regulators caught up with the infractions.

Another dangerous trend had started in the 1970s. A host of competitors, including many nonfinancial businesses, saw opportunities to move into banking. They lobbied their legislators, and their efforts paid off. The high interest rates of the inflationary decade prompted the formation of "money-market mutual funds." Those funds, organized by larger brokerages such as Merrill Lynch, sold shares in a pool of Treasury Bills and other assets, shares that could be converted to cash simply by filling out one of the checklike order forms provided. The public quickly realized those funds offered a profitable alternative to passbook savings accounts. As money flowed out of banks and S&Ls, pressures grew to deregulate banking and to allow payment of interest on checking accounts. The crisis came in 1979. For some years, a group of S&Ls in New England had been allowed to pay interest on a type of account that could be accessed by "negotiable orders of withdrawal," checklike orders for bank payment to another party. In 1979, the U.S. Court of Appeals for the District of Columbia ruled that U.S. regulatory agencies had exceeded their authority in allowing those interest-bearing accounts. The court also threatened the existence of credit-union checking accounts and telephone transfers of funds from saving to checking accounts. Congress was given until January 1, 1980, to pass enabling legislation for those practices. As a result, the Depository Institution Deregulation and Monetary Control Act of 1980 was passed.

That act repealed Regulation Q, which limited the rate of interest paid on deposits. However, Congress phased the ceilings out over a period of six years, and until the ceilings ended, the rates paid on deposits remained relatively low. Congress intended, by instituting a phased end to ceilings, to protect the banks from suffering at the hands of the majority of depositors, who generally held under $100,000 and who tended not to move their deposits as readily as holders of larger deposits in response to fluctuations of the interest rate.

Thus, like any regulation, the ceiling phase-out spawned a search for loopholes. One way that banks evaded the interest ceiling was to pay deposit brokers for deposits. The deposit brokers emerged in the early 1980s and offered to solicit potential customers with small amounts of money to deposit with the promise of higher interest rates coupled with the absolute safety of insured investments. They accomplished that by packaging the small deposits into $100,000 bundles that, under the phase-out, qualified for higher interest rates. Some institutions relied on inside

brokers as well as outside brokers using telemarketing to sell large certificates of deposit (CDs) to institutional investors. That practice made possible by a ruling that those accounts were insured to $100,000 per participant
in the institution. The brokers received a competitive fee for bringing
those bundles to a bank, while the bank had extra deposits, and the
customers received higher interest than they otherwise could have received on insured deposits. Although it appeared to be a no-lose situation,
a serious problem arose because the deposits proved extremely volatile.
If outside brokers thought they could get higher fees at another institution,
or if they sensed trouble brewing, they withdrew all the deposits. Banks
found they could not rely on the stability of the money.

Heritage Bank, in Orange County, California, demonstrated the flaws
of the brokered deposit system. The bank had grown spectacularly using
brokered deposits in the early 1980s, paying a higher yield to the brokers
than did its competitors. It accomplished this by letting each account
exceed the $100,000 insured limit, thereby saving some of the insurance
premium. It seemed a safe practice in view of the fact that up to that point
the FDIC had covered *all* deposits when a bank had failed, regardless of
insurance status. When Heritage's astounding growth leveled off, the
brokers quickly shifted their deposits elsewhere, causing the bank's demise. The FDIC surprised everyone, especially Heritage Bank depositors,
by deciding not to pay off all depositors with more than $100,000 in
their account, and the resulting repercussions substantially moderated the
practice of depending on brokered deposits for growth. Most western
banks had not engaged in brokered deposits in a large way, nor were they
as pressed by the regulatory two-step of the phased-out ceilings, which
affected the S&L industry in particular because S&Ls traditionally financed their long-term lending, which produced higher rates, with short-
term deposits paying low rates. In 1981, however, the yield curve reversed
into an abnormal pattern, and suddenly interest rates on short-term investments exceeded those on long-term investments. The S&Ls suddenly
found themselves with the majority of their assets in twenty-five to thirty-
year, fixed-term interest rate mortgages with relatively low interest rates.
Meanwhile, money-market mutual funds and other competitors paid high
interest, and attracted deposits away from banks and S&Ls and into more
direct investments. That process, known as disintermediation, forced the
S&Ls to borrow money at higher interest rates to replace the lost deposits
that they had already loaned out. Therefore, on the other end, the S&Ls
also had to make new investments at higher interest rates to maintain their
profits. This practice was encouraged by the Garn-St. Germain Act of
1982, which permitted more latitude in the type of investments that S&Ls
could make. High rates involved high risks, and, increasingly, investments
that did not pan out. In addition to those problems, the higher interest

rates of the 1980s created a lull in the real-estate market, which in turn adversely affected the value of S&Ls' chief asset. Many borrowers who had acquired property in anticipation of appreciating value suddenly had to let the lenders foreclose. With idle real estate added to the S&Ls' burdens, the only way they could unload those properties was to lower the prices and take a loss, which, in turn, forced real-estate prices lower still.[4]

Political cronyism in the S&L industry, especially in Texas, where Speaker of the U.S. House of Representatives Jim Wright, who had investments in many Texas S&Ls and whose friends ran others, further destabilized the system.[5] Wright was accused of using his Washington influence to impede investigations into failing S&Ls, and blocking FSLIC examinations whenever possible. Although the House of Representatives eventually indicted Wright on numerous ethics charges, those charges did not include his activities in the S&L industry. Most outside observers agreed that he had acted improperly, to say the least, but Wright was not alone. By 1989, the S&L mess had soiled the reputations of politicians of both parties, much of it through California's Lincoln Savings and Loan, which the press predicted "will probably turn into the biggest savings and loan bailout on record."[6] Lincoln's chairman, Charles H. Keating, Jr., made use of his political influence to delay federal investigations long enough to add perhaps $1 billion to the U.S. taxpayers' final bill while he invested in junk bonds, luxury hotels, and Arizona desert. Indeed, Senators John Glenn, Don Reigle, Alan Cranston, Dennis DeConcini, and John McCain all had ties to Keating. Most had accepted large campaign contributions from him, and McCain had even used Keating's private jet to take his family on vacations in the Bahamas. In April 1987, Cranston, DeConcini, Glenn, and McCain met with Edwin Gray, then chairman of the Federal Home Loan Bank Board, on Keating's behalf in an effort, as Gray said, to "subvert the regulatory process."[7] They asked Gray to withdraw an investment regulation that Keating opposed, and in return Keating would increase Lincoln's home loans. Gray refused, but within a week the same four senators and Riegle met with four top regulators from the San Francisco Federal Home Loan Bank, again asking them to withdraw the rule. They refused. A month later, the San Francisco Federal Home Loan Bank overseeing Lincoln's parent company recommended seizing the thrift, but Washington regulators overruled their recommendation. American Continental Corporation, Lincoln's parent, filed for bankruptcy on April 13, 1989, and regulators took over Lincoln the next day. The new chairman of the Federal Home Loan Bank Board, M. Danny Wall, had overruled the recommendations of the San Francisco examiners to close Lincoln. Meanwhile, evidence mounted that Keating had given jobs to several of Glenn's political aides, and had made donations to the five senators. Keating went to jail, unable to meet the $5 million bail, when he was charged with misrepresenting Lincoln bonds sold to bank customers who apparently thought the bonds were just another type of insured bank account and the senators faced their colleagues in an investigation.[8] In February 1991, Alan Cranston was accused by the Senate of violating ethical standards.

Another western gunslinger to gallop off on a California S&L was Charles W. Knapp. His Financial Corporation of America grew explosively to $33 billion in assets by hawking large-denomination certificates of deposit nationwide. He invested funds in real-estate and construction loans, which, as the market slowed, deteriorated rapidly. Financial Corporation gobbled up other businesses as well, including American Savings and Loan, while the Securities and Exchange Commission questioned Knapp's accounting. Knapp was deposed and the Bass Group in December 1988 rode in to save the failing institution by taking its good assets and renaming it American Savings Bank.[9]

By 1989, at least eighty-one western S&Ls had been taken over by the government or declared insolvent (see Appendix, table 4), including five in Arizona (among them, two of the three largest, with the third in serious trouble as of this writing); twenty-five in California (including Keating's infamous Lincoln Savings, Knapp's Financial Corporation, and the $12-billion Gibraltar Savings in Beverly Hills; and seventeen in Kansas (including the $2-billion Peoples Heritage in Salina). But the failures appeared in pockets, with Idaho, Montana, and Nevada having no S&Ls insolvent or under government control in 1989, and the Dakotas, Oregon, Wyoming, and Washington combined possessing six insolvent S&Ls. Usually, the troubled S&Ls existed in the high-growth areas, where they faced stiff competition for deposits. Overall, the S&Ls' day had passed, and the trends in the late 1980s suggested few would survive, even under the government's restructuring program.[10]

Rising interest rates in the late 1970s and early 1980s, followed by falling real-estate prices in some parts of the West, spilled over from the S&Ls to the banking industry. Banks in areas whose economies had surged around real-estate growth, such as Los Angeles, Denver, Phoenix, Oklahoma City, and Tulsa, suddenly (but often temporarily) saw their growth slow to a crawl.[11] As a consequence, in a 1990 list of forty banks in trouble, the FDIC included fourteen in Oklahoma City and Tulsa, five in metropolitan Phoenix, ten in Denver, and nine in the Los Angeles area. Other than Louisiana and Texas, Arizona was the only state west of the Mississippi to show a negative return on assets. It had more "problem assets" (as a percentage of capital and reserves)—70.7 percent—than had any state except Texas, which had 83 percent. More than 3,100 banks in the west made the FDICs "troubled" list with Arizona's Citibank branch the largest on the list. California banks had $323 million in assets in troubled institutions, almost double the total assets of Texas's troubled banks.[12] To put matters in perspective, by 1990 more than 13,100 banks remained open nationwide, and held $3.5 trillion in assets. Bank failures, while rising in the West and in Texas, had dropped from 221 in 1988 to 207 in 1989.[13]

Real estate–related problems caused Arizona's bank performance, which had generated tremendous profits for the major banks in the 1970s, to fall to forty-eighth in the nation in 1989, behind only energy-loan plagued Texas and Alaska.[14] Nonperforming loans in Arizona's banks amounted to 6.45 percent, compared to less than 1 percent in Hawaii and six southeastern states. Ironically, however, the banks that had fallen into the hands of Easterners faced the worst: Chase and Citicorp were among the top four banks with nonperforming loans, Chase with a whopping 24 percent. Chase of New York reported an $85 million Arizona-related real-estate loss, and its New York rival, Citicorp, also reported large Arizona losses. Critics charged that Robbs had contributed to the poor performance, but the evidence does not bear that out. Under Robbs, Continental Bank continued to grow through three equally severe recessions in the late 1960s and 1970s, all related to real estate. More likely, the new management, which made substantial changes in the bank's policies, destroyed the finely tuned machine that Robbs left. But regionally owned and locally owned Western banks also experienced troubles. Security Pacific's Arizona division lost $109 million in the third quarter of 1989. Valley National Bank fell into the real-estate "bog," reporting a $90 million second-quarter 1989 loss, much of it due to $180 million put in reserve for loan losses. By the third quarter it had announced another $72 million loss and suspended its dividends.[15] First Interstate estimated its 1989 losses at $400 million, again due almost entirely to the real-estate market. Los Angeles–based First Interstate reported that it had to declare a third-quarter $16 million loan loss due to its Arizona unit.[16] The insolvency of western S&Ls pushed land values even lower, and a huge former S&L, Merabank (which, despite its name, remained a thrift), verged on collapse. Its holding company, Pinnacle West Capital Corporation, had wrangled for months with regulators about Merabank. The land that speculators bought at $90,000 an acre in the 1970s and early 1980s sold in 1989 at $25,000 per acre.

Rural states such as Nebraska did not avoid the real-estate problems of the 1980s either. However, there the failures could be "traced directly to the high farm net income during the 1970s and the steadily increasing farm exports from 1977 to 1981 . . . [which] encouraged. . . . farmers to expand their acreage and convert marginal lands to crops." Those farmers "ran up enormous debts," and following the 1981 peak in agricultural exports and total net income of Nebraska banks, both indicators started a steady, followed by a precipitous, decline. As a University of Nebraska study found, the bank failures occurred in an area of "marginal agricultural value." In 1976, Nebraska's Guaranty Fund was created to guaranty the deposits of member credit unions and cooperative credit associations only. That fund failed in 1983, when, six years after the legislature expanded it to include industrial loan and investment companies, it overextended its coverage. Even so, Louis Jeffries, who authored the University of Nebraska publication, continued to propagate the myth that the "unwillingness of the State Department of Banking to refuse charters" played a major role in the failures of the 1980s while he absolved deposit insurance rather than pointing to the absence of branch banking.[17]

Among the solutions to the problem of losses caused by the real-estate downturn, western banks examined the idea of forming "bad banks" in which to discard their problem loans. An idea born of Drexel Burnham Lambert's investment bankers in 1986, it came to the attention of First Interstate Bank of California shortly thereafter. In 1988, First Interstate Bancorp organized a "bad bank" to take all the problem loans in a separate subsidiary.[18] The "good bank" kept only the good loans. At some point, in theory, the "bad bank" would sell off the bad assets or completely liquidate. Presumably, investors could choose between the safer investment and the "bad luck," whose relatively low stock price could make it highly profitable. The market has yet to render a verdict on that concept.

Weakness in the real-estate sectors would not have posed quite the problem it did had some of the same areas not felt the simultaneous hardships of rising interest rates and falling energy prices. No western areas suffered more from the deregulation of energy, and the subsequently low price of crude oil and gas, than did Oklahoma, Wyoming, and Colorado (especially Denver), where problems were more localized. Energy had provided the basis of some of the most rapid banking growth in the nation during the 1970s. Not only did banks make whopping profits, but their stocks soared, and a market for the securities of energy-related western banks itself became a market.

The most phenomenal growth was associated with a small, store-front operation in Oklahoma City called Penn Square Bank. It had tapped the energy skyrocket and quickly learned to package risky energy loans to drillers for other banks, pocketing a fee. From 1977, when Penn Square caught onto the packaging concept, until 1982, when it failed, the bank's worth had grown from $62 million to $520 million.[19] But through loan "participations," as the players called them, Penn Square had farmed out more than $2 billion, of which Continental Illinois took half. No sooner had Penn Square made a reputation as a hot new sales institution than the energy skyrocket fizzled. Many of the drillers failed to find oil or gas, and then falling energy prices compounded the problems. According to Irving Sprague, then Director of the Federal Deposit Insurance Corporation, the comptroller's office had watched Penn Square for some time, but even so, it had not been prepared for the extent to which other banks were exposed through Penn Square. Among the large exposed banks, only Seafirst, the holding company for Seattle-First National Bank, with more than $300 million in Penn Square–packaged loans, was in the West. Regulators came in two waves, first the examiners (instructed to be as unobtrusive as possible), then the liquidators. When word leaked to the press, the scene stood in marked contrast to the skill with which the Eccles banks had dealt with their crises. Penn Square had to issue cashier's checks because it had no cash. Although the Federal Reserve had promised to have cash ready, the bank could not pry any loose. After sorting through the bank's books, the FDIC and comptroller's office concluded that the bank fell outside the protection owed to a bank "essential to the community," as more than thirty-six banks conducted business in Oklahoma City, and thus they decided to let it die. As a result, the government had to pay off the depositors an amount estimated at $465 million, making it the fourth largest insured bank bailout in history. After a struggle between government agencies as to the proper procedure for closing the bank, on July 5, the FDIC closed Penn Square. The government took possession of the few assets available to the bank, and sued fifteen directors (but not insiders) for malfeasance, settling out of court for $2.5 million. It brought other cases against insiders as well. According to Sprague, Penn Square destroyed the myth that the government would never bail out a large bank, and also started to reveal the dangers posed by deposit insurance.[20]

Still, the West stayed in the forefront of growth in the decade and boasted some of the largest banks in the nation (see Appendix, table 3). The Bank of America ranked second, First Interstate fourteenth, Security Pacific eighth, Crocker sixteenth, Wells Fargo twelfth, and Valley National thirty-second. Most western banks continued to grow, and the majority remained healthy except in Oklahoma and Colorado.

BANKING BECOMES NATIONAL—OR INTERNATIONAL—INDUSTRY

Growth and prosperity also encouraged foreigners to take advantage of the strongest business climate in the world. Between 1970 and 1986, twelve new foreign-owned banks opened in the United States, with more than seventy-four branches in California alone. The International Banking Act of 1978 failed to stop completely foreign competitors in the American banking market: in 1982 the Industrial Bank of Japan bought more than 5 percent of Wells Fargo, and in 1983 Mitsubishi bought the bank William Ralston built, the Bank of California. By 1988, however, sensing the importance of an American name, Mitsubishi consolidated its California banks under the Bank of California name and the presidency of O. Yamada, making it the state's sixth-largest bank. Nor did foreign acquisition end there. Eighty-eight branches of the British-owned Lloyds Bank of California were sold in 1986 to Golden State Sanwa, making it the state's eighth-largest bank. And from the Los Angeles executive offices of First Interstate Bank, California's second-largest bank, the name of the world's largest bank, Dai-Ichi Kangyo, on a nearby highrise dominates the view. (Despite impressive expansion, Dai-Ichi Kangyo's profits did not keep pace, and in the late 1980s the Tokyo giant publicly grumbled about its flat earnings.) In 1989, an interesting reversal developed when Security Pacific contemplated the purchase of 20 percent of Mitsui Manufacturers Bank, a Los Angeles–based subsidiary of Tokyo giant Mitsui Bank.[21] In 1990, the Japanese stock market was far below its peak, and the rising cost of capital in Japan forced a reevaluation of these investments.

In the early 1980s, however, the threat appeared far more dire. First, Japanese banks had taken over the top spots on the list of the world's largest banks. Second, the Japanese continued their siege of foreign financial markets. Japanese insurance companies alone had $31 billion in foreign securities, and the Tokyo-based Nomura firm emerged as the largest securities firm in the world. Foreign direct investment in the United States climbed 60 percent in 1988 to $65 billion, and despite the fact that the British remained the largest investors, the Asian invasion most concerned Americans. It resulted in a flood of new editorials raising the question "Who Owns America?"[22] Critics pointed out that foreigners owned more than 60 percent of downtown Los Angeles real estate. Foreign ownership of plants, property, and equipment in the West appears in table 7.1. Overall, the troubles of the United States and its banks were greatly overstated. The nation had maintained a remarkable economic recovery, beginning with the implementation of Ronald Reagan's economic programs, and stood poised to push into the "Third Century" (of America's growth) as Joel Kotkin and Yoriko Kishimoto termed it.[23] Others, such as Henry R. Nau, flatly rejected notions of American decline.[24] While many Americans viewed foreigners—the Japanese especially—as invincible, foreigners actually had experienced some setbacks in their American investments. In Nevada, for example, Japanese sank millions of dollars into casinos, including the famous Las Vegas gambling houses the Aladdin and the Dunes. Many of these casinos, which the Japanese bought as failed businesses and tried to revive, have continued to lose money, even in the midst of an economic boom in the city. As of April 1989, the Aladdin faced $3.95 million in unpaid withholding taxes, and although the casino raised that amount, according to Nevada gaming officials, it remained on the brink of bankruptcy.[25]

Table 7.1   Foreign Ownership of Plants, Property,
and Equipment in Western States in 1989

State	Amount ($ billions)
Arizona	4.06
California	37.01
Colorado	4.88
Idaho	.38
Kansas	2.15
Montana	1.59
Nebraska	.40
Nevada	1.30
New Mexico	2.13
North Dakota	1.36
Oklahoma	5.17
Oregon	1.67
South Dakota	.39
Utah	2.62
Washington	3.39
Wyoming	2.84
Total	71.34

Source: Washington/Baltimore Regional Association, cited in Jack
Anderson, "Who Owns America? *Parade*, April 16, 1989.

If foreigners had occasional problems in the American economy, many western entrepreneurs did not. Enjoying the longest peace-time economic boom in history, small businesses staged a dramatic surge in the period from 1986 to 1988, heralding the emergence of a "New West." According to a study done by Cognetics, "the ground swell of small business activity" in fourteen western states (not counting California) had created jobs at two and one-half times the rate of large businesses.[26] The New West identified by the researchers, even excluding California, with its varied and high-tech economy, was characterized by a more diversified economy not dependent on large, nonlocal businesses such as oil, mining, and lumber. The western states witnessed impressive income growth between 1979 and 1989, with Arizona (152.4 percent), Nevada (150.4 percent), California (130.5 percent), and Colorado (112.6 percent) all exceeding the national average (112.0 percent). Washington (108.6 percent), Utah (107.6 percent), and New Mexico (107.2 percent) tailed only slightly. Those findings, however, promised to be dwarfed by an even more fundamental change in the economy, the ascension of the "microcosm" economy described by George Gilder. Essentially, in an economy of information and ideas, in which matter and physical resources grow increasingly less valuable, the information-based service industry of banking can emerge a winner only if its entrepreneurs remain faithful to the dream.[27] On a more specific note, bank-watcher and financial guru Alex Shushenoff predicted the Southwest would revive after shaking off its speculative excess in the area of real-estate lending. He seemed on firm ground: Arizona ranked seventh in national "business climate" in all states in the union in 1987, and, despite its troubles, held the same rank when rated against low-density states two years later. Grant Thornton, who conducts "the oldest [survey] that measures manufacturing climates," found that western states dominated the top ten in business climate, holding seven of the top spots in 1987. The low-density/high-density division of the country made evaluating the overall placement of states difficult, and obscured the desirability of the West compared to other regions in 1989, but South Dakota, North Dakota, and Nebraska, which held the top three positions for best business climate in 1989, had held the same spots (in somewhat different order) in 1987.[28]

The growth climate of the 1980s that brought in foreign investment had marked a sharp change from the late 1970s, which ended with a president who instructed Americans to tighten their belts and who later observed that a "malaise" had descended on the country. Many citizens indeed questioned whether the nation at that time had reached its limits. Stagflation had brought economic growth to a crawl, while unemployment and inflation chopped away at the economy from different directions. In many ways, though, banks found themselves insulated from those pressures, for, to some extent, they could always compensate for inflation through higher interest charges, and in the 1970s unemployment had only started to touch the industries that depended on commercial banks. Moreover, banks started to see the fruits of their strong lobbying efforts in Washington pay off. Those efforts culminated in 1980 with the DIDMCA (Depository Institutions Deregulation and Monetary Control Act), called by Senator William Proxmire the "most significant banking legislation since [passage of the Federal Reserve Act in] 1913."[29] It consisted of eight sections, which dealt with truth in lending, state usury laws, and other issues. As Richard Timberlake pointed out, its "first two titles contain the principal substance of the act as well as its contradictory implications: Title I greatly extends the Fed's powers and regulatory scope [while] Title II significantly relaxes restrictions on freedom of economic activity for the rest of the banking and financial system." Under Title II, nonbank institutions were permitted to issue demand deposits and banks were permitted to pay interest on their demand obligations. But Title I expanded the Federal Reserve

Board's powers and imposed reserve requirements on all banks, Fed members and nonmembers alike.[29]

In addition to DIDMCA, other regulatory changes gave a different look to western banking and softened the blow of the S&L collapse. One of the first cracks in the protective edifice of state borders against outsiders occurred in South Dakota. Citibank in the late 1970s had bumped up against New York's interest rate ceilings of 18 percent for balances over $500, and 12 percent for balances under $500, but itself faced a prime rate that moved constantly upward. The bank lost 5 or 6 percent on its credit-card transactions and New York law even prohibited imposing a service charge. Based on a 1978 ruling, *Marquette National Bank of Minneapolis* v. *First Omaha Service Corporation* (439 U.S. 299), if a bank holding company could find a state willing to invite it as a home bank, the bank could export its new "home" interest rate to other states (if it was a national bank, which was immune from state regulation). Citibank conducted a search and determined that Nevada, Hawaii, Missouri, Rhode Island, and South Dakota all offered prime choices for such a "home," and South Dakota and Missouri were the most attractive choices based on their usury ceilings. Overall, South Dakota represented the most advantageous choice. In February 1980, Citibank contacted Governor William Janklow, who explained that South Dakota had no intention of becoming "the Panamanian Registry for banks," and bluntly posed the critical question, as far as his state was concerned: "How many jobs?" Citibank officials promised to move jobs that did not need regulatory approval, such as customer service centers, collection, and traveler's-check processing. But at that time, South Dakota was considering legislation to exempt "certain regulated lenders" from all usury limitation in the state, a law about which Citibank claimed it was totally unaware. Despite concern by the bankers' association, which feared unfair competition, Citibank won the members over. At one meeting, Bill Dougherty of the Sun Bank of Sioux Falls said: "I'm the littlest bank in Sioux Falls and I don't fear [Citibank] at all."[30] On March 3, 1980, the South Dakota Bankers Association approved the proposal to extend an invitation to Citibank. The *Argus Leader* editorialized that South Dakota "now had a chance to export [its] interest rate" just as it exported crops.[31]

The legislature approved the enabling law on March 12, and Citibank only awaited approval from the federal regulatory agencies. Meanwhile, Citibank representatives visiting Sioux Falls to look for sites implied that the bank would provide between three hundred and five hundred new jobs. Governor Janklow expressed shock, for his own negotiations had led him to think that the entire credit-card servicing division, representing twenty-five hundred jobs, would move to South Dakota. Citibank officials explained that they had no plans to move collections from its Atlanta base, or New York repossessions from New York City. Janklow objected, but in two publicly released statements he had already agreed in principle to the move. Other Citibank officials hastened to soothe Janklow's worries, and, although leaving the number of jobs temporarily undetermined, they indicated that it would far exceed three hundred. At the hearings before the State Banking Commission of South Dakota, Professor Dennis Hein, who had received a contract to study the impact of Citibank's move to South Dakota, reported that the bank would generate $18 million in the local economy and pay $2 million in taxes. (In fact, the credit-card operation paid six million dollars a year in taxes to the state!)[32]

During the hearings for the comptroller of the currency, however, the issue of interstate banking arose for the first time. A Nebraska banker suggested that the South Dakota base offered a convenient expansion point in the Midwest if the barriers to interstate banking came down.[33] No one else raised the question, and the comptroller's office ignored it when giving its approval in November. Walter Wriston, Citibank's chairman, well understood the significance of the development. In March 1980 he had noted that regulations against doing business across state lines applied only to "those corporations . . . unfortunately chartered for the purpose of doing a banking business."[34] He was correct: quietly one more brick in the wall prohibiting interstate banking had toppled.

In February 1981, Citibank South Dakota (NA) opened, bringing with it a base of 5.8 million VISA and MasterCard account holders, 81 percent of whom already lived outside New York. The city of Sioux Falls held a South Dakota/Citibank Day on June 10 to celebrate the new partnership and the anticipated growth. By September 1983, Citibank operations in the state already exceeded one thousand personnel, with another two hundred jobs created in related or support areas, and the city's unemployment rate fell to one of the lowest in the nation. Sioux Falls in just two years reaped a $50 million windfall (with landscaping for the Citibank building alone costing $100,000), and Citibank-related mail constituted almost one-third of the city's total. Scholarly evidence that eroded previously held assumptions about the dangers inherent in interstate branching continued to appear. Charles Calomiris and others have shown conclusively how the absence of branch banking and interstate banking contributed to the Great Depression.[35] Richard Nelson concluded that there is "no reason to suspect that major changes in industry structure would occur if interstate branching restrictions were relaxed."[36] The regional agreements that met with success in the Southeast failed to reveal any harm in allowing banks to cross state lines.

Seeing the handwriting on the wall, in the 1980s regulators in seven western states—Kansas, Nebraska, North Dakota, Oklahoma, Oregon, and Utah (plus Texas)—broadened the ability of banks to expand geographically through branching.[37] Additionally, Kansas, Oklahoma, and Washington permitted geographic expansion through multibank holding companies. By the mid-1980s, all but five states in the nation permitted interstate banking, but three of those—Kansas, Montana, and North Dakota—were in the West. By the late 1980s, California, which had made state-by-state reciprocal agreements with its neighbors, passed a unique agreement that allowed banks of any state that permitted California banks to compete. That agreement will give the nation's largest banks free range in each other's markets by 1992.

Twelve western states allowed unlimited branching by the 1980s (three of these, though, by merger only), while New Mexico permitted limited branching. Only Colorado, Montana, and Wyoming remained glued to archaic unit-bank laws. But the pressures from states that had adopted branch banks was undeniable, and Wyoming and Colorado responded by permitting multibank holding companies.

Wyoming provided a good example of the impact of those holding companies. Excluding the one-bank holding companies (those that by law may hold stock in only one other bank, but may hold other related or nonrelated businesses, such as insurance, trust companies, etc.), by the early 1980s eight Wyoming corporations controlled at least two banks. Of those eight, two owned only two banks, and First Security (Marriner Eccles's bank) owned several, but only one in Wyoming. The four other holding companies owned forty-six of the state's one hundred and eight banks, including the two largest, accounting for roughly half of Wyoming's bank deposits.[38] In 1987, the five largest firms held 52.4 percent of bank assets in the state, but had shown only a modest gain of 4.2 percent since 1976.[39] First Wyoming Bancorporation held twenty-three banks, and Affiliated Bank Corporation held eight. Both expanded aggressively in the 1970s and early 1980s by organizing new banks: First Wyoming established ten between 1971 and 1982, while Affiliated mixed three new organizations with purchases of two existing banks, one of which itself held three banks. As one observer put it, "It is an expensive way to circumvent the unit banking rule."[40]

Likewise, the unit-bank problem essentially killed Denver's hope of becoming the "Wall Street of the Rockies." There, repeated efforts at changing Colorado's antibranching law essentially ended with a referendum in 1980. Instead, "Wall Street of the West" had emerged only in the last twenty years in southern California, as Los Angeles surpassed San Francisco as the banking center of the West. The metropolitan area of Los Angeles itself was remarkable: its population of 12.6 million and its rapid growth alone suited it for establishing a powerful financial center. Los Angeles's 1987 production of more than $250 billion worth of goods and services (making it the eleventh-largest nation in the world when measured by GNP), the fact that it has greater retail sales than does New York (a city roughly one-third larger), and its phenomenal employment increase—from 5.9 million in 1984 to an estimated 8 million by the end of the century—made the city a natural for financial leadership.[41] Since 1980, the deposit totals in Los Angeles rose by $75 billion (including S&L deposits), making it second behind New York, whose deposits have slightly declined. Out-of-state and foreign competitors anxiously wanted into the Los Angeles market, and in 1986 both Citicorp and Chase had their name on high-rise California headquarters in the downtown section. It was obvious that the Japanese had recognized the potential of the region when Japan's largest banks started to move to the United States, with five of its twelve largest institutions establishing their U.S. banking subsidies in Los Angeles, not New York. Richard Hanson, publisher of the Tokyo-based *Japan Financial Report*, joked: "They went there for the same reason they went to Pearl Harbor. It was close and easy to reach. And there were a lot of Japanese there."[42]

The dominance of Los Angeles, though, only underscored a more important trend, namely the rising financial power of the West as a whole. San Diego has witnessed increased growth, and Arizona and Utah remain significant regional financial centers. But many eyes stay fixed on San Francisco, whose two major banks, the Bank of America and Wells Fargo, have survived rough times and appear, as of 1990, to be rebounding.

TROUBLED TIMES AT BANKAMERICA

BankAmerica, the holding company for the Bank of America, saw its assets fall from $120 billion in 1984 to $95 billion in 1988. However, just as some started to predict its demise, the corporation had "risen and begun to accelerate," reported Tom Clausen in a 1989 USA Today interview.[43] From 1985 to 1987, the bank lost $1.8 billion on bad loans, and Third World debt still accounted for 80 percent of the bank's $4.2 billion worth of problem loans in 1989. BankAmerica's story, although recounted in Gary Hector's Breaking the Bank, bears summarizing here because less than a decade before, it was the world's largest bank, and appeared invincible.[44] Like many banks, in the 1970s it had expanded rapidly, and poured loans into foreign countries that seemed to have plenty of oil income. When oil prices suddenly shifted, BankAmerica's loans became worthless. In fact, however, many banks got burned by shifts in energy demand, and the true story of the decline of BankAmerica involved much more than a single sector of the economy.

Under Clausen, the bank had operated on a thin capital cushion, frequently putting less into loan-loss reserves in order to keep the stock prices high by paying regular dividends. Under Clausen the bank, as did all banks, faced the problem that the interest it had to pay depositors had gone up relatively more than the interest the bank received on its loans— the same mismatch that had driven the S&Ls to the wall. Clausen refused to cut expenses or to add to retained earnings. He also approved the acquisition of an Argentine bank for $150 million, beating the next closest bid by $100 million, just weeks before the Argentine government devalued its currency, thus destroying the entire value of the bank. Clausen had postponed the installation of new technology, giving competitors an important edge in automation. In several questionable accounting moves, the bank continued to show profits through the end of 1980.

When Clausen left BankAmerica to assume the presidency of the World Bank in November 1981, he left what appeared to be a healthy institution, although it had deep problems. Stepping into the leadership position of the bank came Sam Armacost, who had landed a job with BankAmerica as a credit trainee in 1961. After arranging a complex $250 million loan to a British company, RTZ, to finance an open-pit copper mine on the island of Bougainville, Armacost shot up the corporate ladder, heading the London office in 1972, then revitalizing the European affairs of the bank.

Armacost expanded the bank with several moves: in 1983, BankAmerica bought discount broker Charles Schwab and Company, a reliable money-maker, eventually selling it back to its founder for a profit, and in 1982 purchased the troubled Seafirst Corporation. Seafirst, which had acquired $366 million worth of oil and gas loans from Penn Square, was the first major casualty when the little Oklahoma storefront bank failed. At the time of the acquisition, Seafirst was a $9.6 billion corporation. Many thought the acquisition only added to BankAmerica's bad loans (although in the long run Seafirst looked like a better investment). [45] In the regulatory environment of the early 1980s, however, the only way a bank could acquire a large bank in another state was if no in-state buyer were available and if the bank to be acquired faced failure. As Hector noted, "Seafirst was that sick." When the new chief executive of Seafirst, Richard Cooley, took over in 1982, what he found appalled him. A talented and respected banker who had come from Wells Fargo Bank, Cooley had delayed retirement for the opportunity to rescue Seafirst, which he thought needed only a little time and some good management. But he found a mess. A lending officer at Seafirst, John Boyd, had traveled to Oklahoma City and hooked up with Bill Patterson, the head of Penn Square's oil and gas division. Patterson and Boyd worked out a risky package of energy loans that even other Penn Square clients had rejected. Boyd snapped them up and "In a two-month burst of optimism in late 1981 . . . doubled the size of Seafirst's loan portfolio by buying $350 million" of Penn Square loans. When Cooley took over, the company had $1.2 billion in oil loans, and he immediately announced a $91.4 million loss for 1982. Capital short, Cooley tried to raise the money to save the bank, but realized that he had only one option: sell Seafirst. Sam Armacost met with Seafirst officials, who portrayed the Seattle bank as basically a healthy one with a group of bad energy loans. Armacost came up with a plan in which BankAmerica offered $125 million in cash and $125 million worth of a special preferred stock that would be shrunk in 1990 based on loan losses. That ingenious plan ultimately knocked roughly $115 million off the price paid by BankAmerica.[46]

The Seafirst deal required different interpretations of FDIC rules. Like Penn Square, the regulators could not call Seafirst "essential" in its entanglements with other banks, but they did agree that the market might perceive that all of the Penn Square participants might face disaster if one went down. Washington-state legislators passed a bill permitting an out-of-state acquisition.[47]

Continued low capitalization plagued BankAmerica in the early 1980s. The board raised capital by selling the Bank of America headquarters building in San Francisco—an act that caused the founder's daughter, Claire Giannini Hoffman, to resign from the board in 1985—and by closing hundreds of branches. BankAmerica also put its Los Angeles Bank of America/ARCO towers up for sale, with the twin fifty-one–story buildings worth between $500 million and $800 million. Still, the bank kept falling into questionable—if not scandalous—deals that produced massive losses. For example, from 1984 to 1985 BankAmerica became involved as an escrow agent and trustee in the National Mortgage Equity Corporation scam that exposed the bank to potential loss of more than $130 million. It eventually escaped, due to falling real-estate prices, at somewhere between $27 million and $95 million (Armacost cited the lower figure to the board, but then requested the higher figure for loan-loss reserves).[48] Cumulatively, the losses ate away at the heart of the bank's reserves: in 1981 BankAmerica had $1 in reserves for every $2 in problem loans on its books, but by 1983 it only had fifty cents for every two dollars in bad loans.

The problems at BankAmerica soon led raiders and traders to assume that it was "in play." Major investment banking houses contemplated the mechanics of a takeover of BankAmerica. Joe Pinola, whose story is detailed later in this chapter, saw an opportunity to reunite First Interstate Bank with its one-time corporate parent. Pinola, Tom Clausen's former deputy, recognized the challenge of trying to take over BankAmerica, a corporation three times larger than First Interstate. In a meeting with First Interstate officials, Armacost seemed resigned to allowing Pinola to take over the reins of a merged institution. But suddenly the momentum for a merger halted. Because First Interstate wanted the takeover to remain friendly, it tolerated an exceptional amount of stalling while Bank-

America looked for ways out of its cash-flow dilemma outside the merger arena. By 1986, "the merger . . . looked far less attractive [to BankAmerica] than it had in late 1985." BankAmerica's stock had fallen and First Interstate, while realizing that BankAmerica had serious problems, had not seen the depth of the damage. The negotiations with First Interstate, however, were meant for only two purposes: to prevent a hostile takeover by Wall Street financier Sanford "Sandy" Weill (associated with Shearson Lehman), and to save Armacost's job. Weill had offered to raise $1 billion in new capital of the board named him CEO. In a somewhat staged board meeting, Armacost and his supporters shook off the Weill proposal and deliberately refused to raise the First Interstate offer. Without the specter of a hostile takeover, BankAmerica had no use for First Interstate, and that deal died too.[49] Yet BankAmerica was far from finished. Defying many predictions, the bank staged a turnaround. In 1988, it reported profits of $726 million, and in 1989, $1.103 billion. After the first two quarters of 1990, it reported a profit of $545 million, with a second-quarter profit higher than that of any other banking company. Net branch openings had again risen, thanks in part to the acquisition of sixty-seven of troubled Western Savings and Loan's branches and fourteen Nevada S&L branches purchased from the Resolution Trust Corporation (RTC—formed by the FDIC to sell assets of failed S&Ls). Third-world loan defaults remained unacceptably high, but had declined, as had other nonperforming loans.

THE BATTLE OVER BRANCHING CONTINUES

Despite the apparent demise of small competitors, entrepreneurs were alive and healthy in western banking, if for no other reason than the forthcoming interstate banking. DIDMCA accounted for part of the renewed interest in interstate banking. Another impetus to reactivate discussion of the McFadden Act, which seemed to limit branches to those allowed by state law and prohibit branches out of the state, was the increased competition presented by the money-market mutual funds. Those accounts were organized as mutual funds where investors pooled their money to buy liquid financial assets, but no geographic boundaries limited their ability to open brokerage offices to solicit funds, and customers could write checks on their balances. Major brokerage firms, such as Merrill Lynch and Dean Witter, met with great success at encouraging customers to open accounts with amounts as little as $1,000. Competitors such as the brokerage houses, with their new financial instruments, posed enough of a threat to banks, but when Sears acquired Dean Witter in 1981, it opened the vision of a bank in every Sears department store across the nation! Ironically, it also rejoined banking to the mercantile business from which it sprang in the West, but banks saw none of the historical charm of such a development, and clamored for the same flexibility.

The battle on branching erupted all over again. Small, independent banks, concerned that the giants would invade their territory, echoed past arguments: Kenneth Guenther, executive director of Independent Bankers, insisted that the battle was over "increasing financial concentration," and predicted that nationwide branching would cause the demise of most banks. But both the Carter and Reagan administrations had voiced their support for the concept, and twenty interstate mergers of faltering S&Ls had made news. When large banks in small markets grew troubled, acquisition by a local bank presented problems of antitrust combinations. For that reason, federal regulators allowed Citicorp to buy Fidelity Savings and Loan in California and allowed the Bank of America to buy Seafirst Corporation.[50]

Inevitably, bankers found the loophole in the McFadden Act that allowed them to accomplish their goals. In the southeastern states, several larger regional bank holding companies realized the benefits of moving across state lines, but feared that real interstate banking would merely attract the big New York banks. Since the McFadden Act (1) allowed holding companies to retain any banks in other states acquired before the act was in place, (2) applied to holding companies only for branches acquired after 1956, and (3) allowed branches if they did not violate state laws, the banks' assorted legal counsels determined that an agreement between states that allowed branching or holding company acquisitions only within specific states would meet the letter of the law. By the mid-1980s, banks in any of the southeastern states could move into any of the other states, but no bank from outside the region was permitted in. That turned the region into a healthy banking area, and brought unprecedented success to banks such as the North Carolina–based First Union Bank of Charlotte, which earned 18 percent on equity in 1986.[51]

Other regional agreements followed while regulatory officials argued about the legality of such arrangements. Arizona, Washington, and Oregon quickly bowed to the continuing intrusion of California banks by forming reciprocal agreements to let banks past state lines. California banks responded. In 1987, Security Pacific Corporation purchased Rainier Bancorporation, Oregon Bancorporation, and Arizona Bancwest. Nevada reluctantly followed its neighbors, letting California in by 1989. Security promptly also acquired a position there, with the purchase of Nevada National Bancorporation.

Security's race to neighboring states resulted from its desire to strengthen the bank's customer base before the biggest of the interstate banking agreements took effect: in 1991 a reciprocal relationship would begin that allowed any state's bank into California if similar privileges were granted to California banks. The most significant branching would occur between the nation's major money centers, New York and California.

Security remained the only West Coast giant to stay almost completely within the state, working on achieving excellence in retail and commercial banking in that large and growing market. Indeed, before the California–New York agreement passed, Security's chairman, Richard Flamson III, claimed he "wouldn't trade two square miles of the Bakersfield retail bank market for all of Manhattan."[52] Among the major California banks, Security had a unique position. In the 1980s, the holding company formed Security Pacific Brokers and acquired nearly a dozen brokerages and mortgage companies. When BankAmerica had to close branches by the hundreds to stay solvent, Security Pacific National Bank managed to hang on to most of its six hundred branches by cutting staff and converting to more sophisticated integrated computer systems (which, unfortunately, caused the closure of all their ATMs when a large earthquake rocked the San Francisco Bay area in 1989).[53]

Flamson, an unusual chief executive in the days of intense public relations (and a world apart from Clausen and Armacost), hesitated to take credit for Security's success in difficult circumstances, although the company's diversification has resulted from his personal efforts. "Brilliant. That isn't me," he said in an interview with *Executive* magazine. "A good manager knows how to motivate people to be good over both the short and the long term. We must encourage people to see where the market is going—we don't drive the market. It is not so much brilliance [that developed the strategy of diversification], but developing a spirit of being willing to try things, and understanding the risks involved. But we are never going to bet on one aspect of the business alone."[54] Flamson's own career, however, has not reflected a belief in diversification. He spent his entire thirty-year banking career at Security, in spite of the fact that the institution had the reputation as a training ground for other banks' executives. A graduate of Claremont College, just south of Los Angeles, he has lived in southern California ever since.

FIRST INTERSTATE BANK

Another southern California banker whose vision guided a powerful banking company, Joseph Pinola of Western Bancorp, headed a holding company that included twenty-one banks in eleven western states. Pinola came to Western Bancorp from the Bank of America, where as a member of the top management team reporting to Tom Clausen, he stood in line for the presidency. But in 1975, promotion to that position seemed, to him, infinitely delayed. So when Western Bancorp's United California Bank offered him the presidency, he found the opportunity to run the bank irresistible. United California Bank, ironically, had strong historic ties to the Bank of America, although they competed as rivals. When the Justice Department went after Transamerica in its 1948–52 case, Transamerica sold all its banks, and combined twenty-two that it could not sell into a new bank, First Western Bank, which Transamerica owned. The government's attacks continued, however, and in 1956 the Bank Holding Company Act forced Transamerica and other companies holding 25 percent or more of the stock in two or more banks to choose between keeping their banks or keeping their other businesses. Having anticipated passage of the bill by purchasing banks in eleven states to create a viable new holding company, Transamerica chose its nonbank businesses. The board transferred all directly held shares in majority-owned banks to the newly created First America Corporation in exchange for stock. Transamerica shareholders received the eleven million shares of stock created.[55]

One of the eleventh-hour acquisitions was Walker Bank and Trust Company, headed by an astute banker named John Wallace, who was put in charge of the Transamerica bank group. One of the first bankers to realize the potential of the newly created banking system, Wallace also realized that a real weakness existed in the management of the former Transamerica banks and in the lack of a base in southern California. His bank could solve both problems through a merger with a strong Los Angeles bank, and, therefore, in April 1957 Wallace opened discussions with his old friend Frank King, president of the $1 billion California Bank of Los Angeles. King agreed to a merger, if he could remain president of the combined bank, and after extended negotiations, the two completed the merger. The federal board reviewed the merger, as required by the new law, and gave its approval, but unexpectedly the Justice Department gave notice that it intended to charge FirstAmerica with restraint of trade if the merger went ahead to completion. Nevertheless, FirstAmerica went on with the deal and on April 9, 1959, acquired 97 percent of California Bank. Through an agreement with the Justice Department, the two organizations operated as separate entities while legal negotiations continued.

The Justice Department expressed concern over the decrease in competition that it contended would occur when branches of two banks in the same town merged. Parties finally reached an agreement in which the Justice Department approved the merger if a new bank, called First Western, formed by spinning off $500 million in deposits from the merger, was created to handle this problem. First Western acted as a retail bank, focusing on the needs of households rather than businesses. The merger parties also agreed to add more offices to the original proposal.

Although the Justice Department had satisfied itself that it had preserved competition, in reality FirstAmerica lost the chance to launch a real competitor to the Bank of America, and at the Bank of America, old timers expressed disgust to see banks purchased by Transamerica for eventual merger into that institution set up as competitors in a new statewide branching system. The Independent Bankers Association filed a complaint charging that the solution had resulted in less competition, while the Bank of California objected to California Bank's using the word "California" in the northern part of the state. By 1961, the various complications had been put to rest and the two banks were finally launched. First Western Bank, with sixty-five offices, was sold first to GreatAmerica Corporation in Texas in 1963, then to Jimmy Ling to add to his conglomerate. After the Justice Department blocked First Western's sale to Wells Fargo, it was purchased by World Airlines, and finally lost its own name when it merged with Lloyd's Bank (which was submerged into Sanwa in 1988). FirstAmerica's bank, with 134 offices, the twelfth-largest bank in the country, took the name United California Bank. First America also retained the banks outside California, and to satisfy the Bank of America, changed its name to Western Bancorporation.[56]

When Joe Pinola became United California's fourth president, the bank had just survived the most difficult period in its history. Once the bank had resolved the antitrust problems, Frank King expanded it statewide and overseas. While most acquisitions brought new customers and wider recognition, one purchase came to embarrass the bank. After opening branches in Belgium, Greece, South Korea, Lebanon, the Bahamas, Nicaragua, Spain, and Thailand, an office in Switzerland seemed a necessity. United California Bank officers thought themselves fortunate in 1969 to acquire Salik Bank, in Basel, Switzerland, with its management team intact. Paul Erdman led the team. Erdman, holder of an American M.B.A. and a Swiss doctorate, had built Salik Bank with the express goal of serving as a link between U.S. and European businesses. United California Bank found later, after its name had been changed to United California Bank of Switzerland, that Erdman had already directed his genius toward doctoring the books. The Basel bank engaged heavily in commodity and foreign-exchange speculation, often on margin. As deals went bad in 1968 and 1969, Erdman's group speculated even more heavily with borrowed funds, hoping to make up the losses. United California Bank's acquisition helped the Basel office gain even more access to credit.

Only after 1970 did United California Bank officials discover the extent of the problems. Swiss law required the use of local auditors for banks: the audit report in 1969 was in German, of course, but Erdman translated, and it looked very good. Ken Graham, a retired branch manager, served as the bank's only representative at the Swiss board's meetings, and the home office gave him no indication of any trouble. On his own, however, he grew increasingly uncomfortable with the Basel managers. He compared the English version of the audit with the German, and although he did not read German, one item caught his eye. "Due from banks . . ." read the English copy, but bank is "bank" in both German and English, and that word was not in the audit report. Instead, he found that the line read "Due from brokers." A subsequent investigation soon revealed massive losses.

With the United California Bank name over the door, and the names of many prominent individuals on the notes Erdman had signed on behalf of the bank, bank officials felt obligated to absorb most of the losses. Erdman and seven other employees visited the Swiss jails, although this was not an altogether unproductive time for Erdman, who wrote his best-selling novel, *The Crash of '89*, then. Frank King flew to Basel with a team of experts to calculate the damage. King promised to pay all the debts, even those which neither Swiss nor American law required the bank to cover. Losses amounted finally to about $40 million.[57] In the long run, paying off the losses proved a wise decision, as United California Bank developed an unparalleled reputation for standing behind its name. Still, the stress of paying the unforeseen debts was apparent when Pinola arrived in 1975.

Pinola found that not only the international division faced difficulties. A credit crunch in 1973 and 1974 had hurt the California real-estate and construction industries badly and United California Bank, which had invested heavily in those industries, saw its nonaccrual loans rise to 4 percent of total loans. (Nonaccrual loans are those accounts in which little or none of the interest is paid for more than ninety days, and the recovery rate is low. The bank, therefore, records as income only the interest received.) In addition to the nonaccrual loans, the bank held a large collection of foreclosed property.[58] At first, Pinola stuck to predictable changes in the bank: he cut expenses, engaged in aggressive loan write-offs, sold unprofitable divisions, and used stricter controls to evaluate new loans. Those changes, and a rapidly improving real-estate market in the inflation-laden last years of the 1970s, moved the bank into a profitable position, and brought to Pinola the chairmanship of Western Bancorporation.

In 1980, Pinola realized the unique position of his bank holding company. *Time* magazine characterized the banking industry as "[as] disjointed as the hamburger stand business before the advent of McDonalds."[59] But if interstate banking were to be legalized, Western Bancorporation could combine the twenty-one banks it owned into one large bank that covered the entire western United States. Pinola sought to exploit that position, and decided that the best way to do so was to give the banks a common name. He made his suggestion to the board, which quickly agreed, and set June 1, 1981, for the target date to convert all the names.

A committee reviewed more than forty-five thousand names and symbols, although once it made its decision, the answer seemed obvious: "First Interstate Bank" stressed the corporate goals perfectly. The change itself, however, proved more difficult. Some of the banks involved had a great deal of local history. For example, Walker Bank, First National Bank of Portland, and First National Bank of Arizona all had long and rich traditions in their areas. The bank had to educate both customers and employees on the advantage of the name change. (In Arizona, the campaign took on the somewhat silly theme of "Hank's Bank," wherein the bank attempted to assure the customer that it would remain the bank of the average person.)[60] On June 1, 1981, the banks at nine hundred offices proceeded to change six thousand signs.[61]

Despite the problems, the change met with unqualified success. People quickly adapted to the new name, and in fact overestimated the degree of integration between the various First Interstate Banks in different states. Legally, each remained a separate entity, and had the words "of (state or town)" as part of the legal title to distinguish it from other Western Bancorporation banks. Two other states soon saw the First Interstate logo on their banks when Western Bancorporation developed a unique franchising system for banks it did not own. While those franchises never achieved the success of McDonalds, by 1989 the First Interstate system covered twenty-one states.[62]

EFFECTS OF BRANCHING

Uncertainty over the exact nature of interstate banking had other effects. For instance, it put a premium on small but well-run banks. No state showed this more clearly than Arizona. In 1985, Thunderbird Bank, long one of the state's two most profitable banks, was sold to Marshall-Ilsley Trust Company of Milwaukee at more than 2.7 times book value. Shortly thereafter, Security Pacific acquired the Arizona Bank (with $3.55 billion in assets as of June 1985) at roughly the same price (2.63 times book value), while Union Bancorp purchased United Bancorp of Arizona (with $1.9 billion in assets as of June 1985) at 2.66 times book value. The big New York and Los Angeles banks soon moved in, with Citicorp purchasing Great Western (the weakest of the major banks—some insiders advised that Citicorp was desperate to get into Arizona to have purchased Great Western). Finally, A. B. Robb's Continental Bank (with $490 million in assets as of June 1985), long the state's most profitable, went to Chase for more than 2.84 times book value. First National, as noted above, had already established an interstate link through the First Interstate system. Thus, in a touch of irony, only Arizona's largest bank, Valley National, was left out, too big and expensive to buy, but not big enough to compete in the event of full interstate banking.[63]

With the rise of those powerful empires, the expansion continued in the Northwest pacing the powerful U.S. Bancorp, parent holding company for U.S. National Bank. On February 8, 1988, U.S. Bancorp and Peoples

Bancorporation, the holding company for the Greens' Peoples Bank, announced that the Portland-based company had acquired the Seattle bank.
That acquisition followed U.S. Bancorp's acquisition of Old National Bancorp. The combined assets of U.S. Bancorp totaled $12 billion and ex-
panded its influence into Washington, making it the largest independent
banking institution in the region. In the course of a year and a half, U.S.
Bancorp acquired Mt. Baker Bank in Bellingham (worth $180 million in
assets), Northwestern Commercial Bank in Bellingham ($104 million), the
Bank of Goleta in northern California ($150 million), and Auburn Valley
Bank of Auburn, Washington ($46 million).[64]

The awesome potential for expansion under interstate banking never
stifled the founding and success of dozens of small banks throughout the
West. Small, independent banks continued to appear at healthy levels.
"Niche" banks remained especially viable. While the story of the entrepreneur who founds a bank that rises to compete with the major institutions
is indeed rare in the 1980s, competition is fierce in the markets for
consumer loans, real-estate and development loans, and for loans for small-
to medium-sized businesses. Concentration ratios have fallen in many
western states, and have increased only modestly in many others between
1976 and 1987 (see table 7.2).

Surprisingly—and contrary to what unit-bank advocates have consistently argued—concentration fell in states such as California, Arizona,
Idaho, and Oregon, and increased only slightly in Washington, Utah, and
New Mexico, all of which had branch-banking laws (although New Mexico
had only limited branch banking).[65] Concentration *increased* in Nebraska,
and showed significant increases in Kansas, Wyoming, and Colorado,
which had unit-banking laws. Only in South Dakota did branching correlate with substantially increased concentration, and only in Montana did
unit banking not correlate significantly with increased concentration.
Thus, by the end of the 1980s, not only had the advantages of branching
been vindicated and accepted in most of the West, the corresponding
weaknesses of unit banking grew even more apparent. Further, the proponents of unit banking had to consider the possibility that the outcome of
their century-long battle against branching—concentration—was actually
more likely under their system than under branching.

It was not the first time legislation had achieved results far different
from those intended. The market repeatedly found ways to work around
legislation until, as in the case of branching and interstate banking, the
legislation itself changed or until critics found their own arguments co-
opted within the legislation. For example, the Community Reinvestment
Act, which served as the culmination of a decade of criticism about corporate responsibility, failed to achieve many of its goals when activists pur-

Table 7.2 Staate Concentration Ratios, 1976–1987

	Concentration Ratios (Five largest Firms)		Change since 1976
	1976	1987	(%)
Nevada	96.5	91.0	(5.5)
Arizona	94.6	89.2	(5.4)
Oregon	85.3	88.0	(2.7)
Idaho	88.6	87.2	(1.4)
South Dakota	50.9	77.7	26.8
Washington	75.2	77.2	1.7
Utah	73.5	75.0	1.5
California	77.9	66.9	(11.0)
Colorado	57.2	62.9	5.7
New Mexico	60.7	61.9	1.2
Wyoming	48.2	52.4	4.2
Montana	56.2	51.4	(4.8)
North Dakota	50.2	38.7	(11.5)
Nebraska	30.3	33.2	2.9
Oklahoma	31.6	28.3	(3.3)
Kansas	14.1	19.3	5.2

Source: Dean F. Amel and Michael J. Jacowski, "Trends in Banking Structure Since the Mid-1970s," *Federal Reserve Bulletin*, March 1989, 131.

sued them through conventional government regulatory processes. The story is relevant to western banking, and perhaps even had its roots in the burning of the Bank of America in Isla Vista during the height of the Vietnam War protests in February 1970.

Protestors had struck the bank office next to the campus of the University of California, Santa Barbara, not because of any connection the Bank of America had with the war itself, but because it was for them symbol of "corporate irresponsibility" and the "arrogance of wealth."[66] Part of the legacy of that generation's agenda, an attempt by American society to reallocate wealth or, at the very least, to improve opportunities for lower-income groups, was the Community Reinvestment Act (CRA), passed in 1977. It sought to force banks to "meet the credit needs of the local communities in which they are chartered" and to try to meet the credit needs of "low- and moderate-income neighborhoods."[67] Federal banking agencies had to review records of the more than nineteen-thousand lending institutions under their jurisdiction to try to ensure compliance, and had the power to turn down charter requests when they decided banks had not cooperated. The act established hordes of bureaucrats who faced the hopeless task of judging local lending situations.

Community groups used the act to file suits to compel banks to invest "in areas they [had] long shunned." These groups—at least the successful ones as of 1989—have all operated in the eastern cities, and certainly the activist groups have used government as a vehicle to achieve their ends. However, they quickly learned—just as the early western bankers learned—that government enforcement processes were extremely slow or notoriously ineffective, or both. More telling, however, was the fact that their rationale for involving community groups and citizens as an enforcement agent harkened back one hundred years to the western frontier days of pioneer banking. With only a few exceptions (and none to speak of in the West), the government has not yet wielded the "stick" of denying any branch charter applications because of violations of the Community Reinvestment Act. Even so, the banks "have often responded to community-group pressure quickly and, frankly, beyond the expectations of the groups themselves."[68] One example of how a successful and profitable bank had to at least attempt to comply with the pressures of the act, and to mollify the citizens' groups, can be found in the records of Continental Bank in Arizona just prior to its sale to Chase. Continental officials (all of whom left the bank after Chase purchased it) openly admitted that they had no intention of changing their lending policies because of "demands" from a community group (in that case, the group was called ACORN, or Arizona Association of Community Organizations for Reform Now). Instead they made the appropriate public statements and continued to lend where they thought safe and profitable. In fact, at the time, Continental took ACORN's public pronouncements seriously only because of the sensitivity of the negotiations to sell the bank to Chase.[69]

The community-activist groups, however, discovered that "In banking, as in so many regulated sectors of the economy, the regulators and the regulated are birds of a feather," and that bank examiners "are neither prepared nor inclined to get their hands dirty" discovering if the loans in urban areas are for legitimate low-income housing or for "triple-deckers." Moreover, those groups realized that "the door to promotions in the federal bank regulating agencies [was] still open widest to those most adept at traditional 'safety and soundness' examinations. . . ."[70]

One activist noted that political conservatives "could well have some difficulty discrediting a regulatory approach that places substantial discretion with local citizen groups in determining the direction of the regulatory process." While calling for "financing grassroots organizations and empowering them to participate in the regulatory process," that process characterized what had worked on the frontier West in the 1800s, except that no public agency funded such groups.[71] No one needed to. They acted in their own self interest, and bankers did the same. They knew their local markets, they created images of stability and safety, and they realized that ultimately the consumers were the regulators of last resort. After 140 years, their appreciation for the checks and balances of the market seems even more astute.

STRENGTH OF THE WEST

Despite the spate of recent troubles afflicting western banking, its prospects for the future appear unlimited. One advantage of the West is its geographical placement on the Pacific Rim in close trade proximity to Japan, Taiwan, Korea, Singapore, Hong Kong, and China. Western banks had for decades participated in the Oriental markets while stodgy Easterners deliberately eschewed them. (Even J. P. Morgan thought the Far East too risky a region for investment, and, perhaps in his time, he was correct.) In the twenty-first century, the historical ties and the geographic proximity can only benefit western financial institutions.

Second, the geographical proximity to the largest city in the world, Mexico City, and the natural and historical ties to Mexico, can only further cement financial relations there. Mexico's credit record hardly qualifies it for a "good borrower" star, but far more important forces may be at work. For example, if, as George Gilder and Walter Wriston have suggested, national borders will become increasingly less important; if computers can beam money and information from the heavens within seconds from around the globe; if the natural common sense of capitalism penetrates even into Mexico (which of this writing threatens to lag behind the Iron Curtain countries in accepting the fundamental soundness of a deregulated economy), then western banks will have positioned themselves better than anyone to reap the harvest of millions of new accounts.

Finally, both Gilder and Wriston have identified powerful trends that will increasingly favor all banks, but probably grace those in the West the most, namely, the quantum revolution of the microcosm, the computer. When linked with the natural desire of most humans to avoid extreme temperatures, especially cold, the freedom from geography for individual workers made possible by computer technology can only cause a resurgence of the sunbelt shift. Florida offers strong evidence for such a prediction. Except for those in agriculture, people remain in congested cities or in freezing climates because of their jobs. As those jobs shift inexorably to services that can be tied to headquarters in New York or Boston or San Francisco or Los Angeles by computer telephone networks (as with South Dakota's Citibank), strong incentives will arise for individuals to seek warmer climates and less populated regions. Attempting to stop the population hemorrhage in the Rustbelt by reviving heavy industry will sound the death knell for the Midwest. Indeed, only those areas that have successfully moved into "high tech"—the Boston region and the Cincinnati-Dayton regions, for example, will survive. But even then, the lure of temperate climates will pose an insurmountable problem for retaining population in most rustbelt cities, and evidence already exists to suggest that the "revival" of the Rustbelt never really occurred at all. As one author notes, "unfortunately for the region, however, there is little substance behind the bright claims of snowbelt advocates."[72]

Unexpected world conditions also played to the advantage of the western region. In 1990, Iraq launched an invasion of Kuwait. The subsequent war and resulting destruction of wells and refineries pushed oil prices up. That held out the possibility of a revival in the energy industries of Wyoming, Colorado, New Mexico, Oklahoma, and Texas. Equally important, the revival of land values in these states promises to bolster the portfolios of banks such as First Interstate, the Bank of America, and Valley National.

Yet even if energy prices fail to stay at 1970s levels, and the S&L industry continues its disappearing act, the western states will continue their growth. Along with them, western banks will grow as never before. The resurgent banks will find themselves awash in borrowers and lenders. Money will again flow south, to Latin America, or, if those countries cannot manage their economies, east, to those who can. In that eventuality, western banks, bolstered by their new populations, will supplant once and for all most of their competitors in New York and Philadelphia and Boston, and will turn toward Japan or Europe to face their new competitors.

But this is not a book about the future, it is a book about the past. Regardless of where western banking will be in a decade, or where it is going now, no one can deny the remarkable growth of banking in the West. Emerging from tiny frontier outposts or mining camps, banks financed the rise of a powerful—some would say dominant—economic and political region within the nation, and perhaps even the world. Throughout their history, western banks have led in regulatory innovations, the most important of which was branch banking, which in turn accounted for much of the financial growth of the region. But regulations provided only structures. Individuals remain the driving force in shaping any industry, and in that regard western banks have had more than their fair share of trendsetters and heroes (with a villain or two thrown in). The story of those financial heroes is a legacy appropriate to the vitality and dynamism of the American West.

APPENDIX

Table 1 Number of Banks by State, 1876–1987

Year	AZ	CA	CO	ID	KS	MT	NB	NV	NM	ND	OK	OR	SD	UT	WA	WY	Total
1876	2	126	41	4	122	10	45	16	5			8		6	4	5	394
1877	2	128	42	4	127	12	50	17	7			8		7	4	7	415
1878	3	135	43	4	130	10	62	19	7			11		11	5	7	447
1879	3	122	43	5	156	11	83	15	7			11		12	5	7	480
1880	7	126	71	5	190	15	114	14	13			13		13	8	7	595
1884	8	123	80	15	352	26	308	12	19			30		16	25	12	1026
1885	8	153	79	16	448	26	358	12	17			32		16	28	15	1208
1890	14	252	142	21	707	48	662	12	23	104	51	95	238	36	138	23	2515
1895	13	311	142	32	553	57	573	12	21	107	79	80	191	50	120	24	2337
1896	12	281	115	33	511	56	558	12	13	101	76	78	181	37	109	24	2200
1897	12	281	115	29	482	50	509	11	13	99	89	73	184	35	104	24	2097
1898	12	287	124	31	465	52	497	11	13	110	124	73	190	37	101	26	2118
1899	13	281	116	34	468	56	500	9	13	129	156	78	195	37	104	30	2187
1900	21	287	118	40	487	56	516	10	14	153	256	82	205	39	107	33	2320
1901	23	296	129	46	528	59	540	10	20	168	367	92	215	37	110	32	2551
1902	23	315	140	53	581	66	584	10	26	210	447	97	272	40	121	36	2936
1903	35	342	152	71	636	73	631	12	30	270	506	108	303	41	140	37	3317
1904	37	418	160	81	689	82	655	12	34	289	563	135	326	43	172	40	3652
1905	34	492	176	90	742	87	683	21	39	333	625	164	345	52	191	47	4030
1906	40	562	191	112	817	98	745	26	46	451	687	155	395	61	340	53	4726
1907	42	598	203	134	928	115	799	31	59	515	803	201	459	70	285	66	5146
1908	42	618	248	152	957	130	837	40	67	552	855	199	501	76	291	76	5591
1909	48	632	259	167	989	147	865	40	71	557	917	225	547	82	318	77	5853
1910	50	640	292	200	1062	189	902	39	81	671	913	245	599	94	348	85	6394
1911	52	655	316	196	1075	198	915	34	86	707	917	250	630	99	343	87	6551
1912	51	682	322	184	1110	212	938	34	85	715	924	255	627	99	363	87	6676
1913	56	720	319	192	1132	236	955	33	86	752	917	258	619	101	376	97	6853
1914	60	735	330	189	1144	287	977	31	84	765	909	260	631	113	373	104	6998
1915	59	733	328	181	1159	295	1015	31	85	783	889	259	601	113	357	109	7018
1916	66	721	340	182	1198	306	1038	31	94	817	895	258	622	118	362	115	7158
1917	70	712	349	194	1231	362	1081	31	107	853	920	260	632	123	361	125	7384
1918	78	696	358	204	1271	403	1137	33	117	858	926	265	642	123	362	136	7596
1919	81	700	371	208	1304	418	1169	33	113	882	960	277	655	125	370	148	7768
1920	87	717	403	222	1349	431	1225	35	123	899	982	285	679	133	394	160	8092
1921	83	726	399	216	1379	420	1211	35	126	855	934	277	700	129	400	155	8101
1922	80	718	381	198	1364	400	1177	35	110	847	905	277	695	121	392	146	7875
1923	75	693	367	182	1334	363	1150	35	101	832	809	277	687	119	391	134	7645
1924	64	668	342	177	1293	243	1125	34	76	688	809	277	553	116	379	116	6960
1925	58	653	336	161	1277	235	1111	34	66	659	774	279	526	115	365	96	6745

Table 1 Number of Banks by State, 1876–1987 (continued)

Year	AZ	CA	CO	ID	KS	MT	NB	NV	NM	ND	OK	OR	SD	UT	WA	WY	Total
1926	48	612	311	156	1254	220	1082	34	63	600	739	272	474	112	364	93	6434
1927	47	535	299	144	1180	210	1049	35	59	531	698	253	417	107	358	88	6010
1928	46	487	287	140	1114	202	929	35	58	490	670	243	412	105	352	86	5656
1929	48	445	280	137	1077	198	872	35	58	434	651	235	396	105	344	87	5402
1930	47	427	272	137	1051	185	796	35	53	367	600	228	374	102	333	84	5091
1931	39	401	252	131	975	166	749	33	52	303	552	215	320	96	317	82	4683
1932	28	353	223	112	880	151	632	28	49	238	512	170	257	71	259	73	4036
1933	21	285	151	86	783	124	400	11	42	194	406	108	212	69	183	64	3139
1934	19	273	167	64	748	125	447	10	43	212	417	105	212	60	202	63	3167
1935	17	265	165	61	728	118	442	10	41	204	408	105	206	59	204	59	3092
1936	16	257	159	56	719	121	445	10	41	206	406	94	195	59	185	58	3028
1937	15	229	153	53	699	117	440	9	41	192	403	80	181	59	179	58	2909
1938	13	222	149	52	687	114	435	11	41	182	400	77	175	59	153	58	2826
1939	13	219	148	50	680	113	434	11	41	171	398	75	166	59	146	58	2782
1940	13	216	150	50	671	112	429	11	41	162	393	74	165	60	142	58	2746
1941	13	213	149	50	660	111	426	12	41	162	392	73	162	57	138	57	2719
1942	13	207	148	50	651	111	419	12	41	160	391	72	162	57	135	56	2690
1943	13	202	146	46	633	110	413	10	41	160	387	70	162	57	133	56	2643
1944	13	199	146	46	623	110	416	8	41	154	384	74	164	59	127	56	2616
1945	13	201	145	46	618	110	417	8	41	151	382	71	165	59	126	56	2610
1946	12	199	147	46	614	110	418	8	42	151	383	71	168	59	125	55	2609
1947	13	201	147	46	612	110	417	8	46	152	386	72	170	55	125	55	2616
1948	12	201	147	45	609	112	416	8	48	153	383	70	170	55	123	55	2613
1949	11	203	148	43	610	111	416	8	50	150	387	71	170	55	124	53	2613
1950	11	202	152	43	610	111	418	8	51	150	386	71	169	54	121	53	2610
1951	10	202	157	40	608	110	418	8	51	150	386	71	169	54	121	53	2616
1952	12	201	159	38	604	110	416	8	51	151	386	70	169	54	122	52	2611
1953	13	201	160	37	604	109	419	8	51	153	386	69	169	54	119	55	2609
1954	14	200	161	36	600	109	420	8	52	154	384	51	170	54	115	55	2588
1955	12	161	163	33	598	111	420	6	52	154	384	50	171	48	111	53	2542
1956	10	139	170	28	595	114	421	6	52	154	386	55	171	49	93	53	2503
1957	7	128	175	28	593	115	421	6	52	154	387	51	172	49	88	53	2481
1958	8	124	181	31	593	115	423	7	53	155	387	56	172	49	89	52	2491
1959	9	115	186	32	593	116	426	7	52	156	388	54	173	50	91	53	2499
1960	10	117	192	32	587	121	426	7	55	156	389	51	174	50	87	55	2509
1961	12	121	195	31	590	123	425	7	57	156	388	49	174	49	91	55	2525
1962	11	129	205	31	593	123	426	7	60	157	392	49	171	52	92	56	2551
1963	13	155	227	24	593	125	429	7	61	159	401	52	173	52	97	63	2631
1964	16	200	246	24	594	129	432	8	63	163	417	51	173	55	97	68	2736

Table 1 Number of Banks by State, 1876–1987 (continued)

Year	AZ	CA	CO	ID	KS	MT	NB	NV	NM	ND	OK	OR	SD	UT	WA	WY	Total
1965	18	199	250	25	599	131	436	9	64	169	421	52	170	56	104	69	2772
1966	17	187	215	25	599	131	433	9	64	164	419	49	166	55	94	69	2696
1967	17	172	217	26	600	132	433	9	64	166	421	47	165	55	94	69	2687
1968	13	156	219	26	600	134	435	9	63	166	423	48	164	54	93	70	2673
1969	12	148	223	26	602	135	437	8	64	166	425	49	163	51	91	70	2670
1970	12	152	270	24	601	140	441	8	66	169	433	50	161	48	100	70	2745
1971	13	152	278	24	603	144	443	8	68	169	435	47	159	50	101	71	2765
1972	22	165	291	24	607	147	446	8	72	170	436	46	159	53	99	71	2816
1973	22	185	302	24	612	151	449	8	74	170	447	47	159	54	96	71	2871
1974	25	198	324	24	613	153	453	8	77	171	455	50	158	55	101	74	2939
1975	23	216	346	24	616	156	453	8	81	172	462	48	158	64	106	77	3010
1976	24	225	359	24	616	158	456	8	83	171	469	49	157	67	100	78	3044
1977	25	235	372	24	617	160	458	8	84	173	483	56	158	73	105	82	3112
1978	28	244	394	24	617	163	459	9	87	174	485	65	156	68	112	88	3173
1979	27	257	410	27	620	165	461	9	87	175	496	82	155	76	120	94	3258
1980	35	263	442	27	619	165	464	9	90	178	503	82	153	77	119	94	3321
1981	37	332	483	27	624	167	466	14	89	179	501	95	154	68	111	109	3451
1982	41	387	524	27	624	169	471	14	93	180	509	99	153	63	113	112	3579
1983	48	443	554	26	628	169	482	15	94	181	525	90	146	63	114	112	3686
1984	46	453	446	25	624	167	473	16	95	177	539	72	141	60	102	117	3557
1985	52	481	469	25	628	169	453	17	96	177	535	67	137	59	99	115	3575
1986	54	484	471	24	613	169	437	18	94	176	520	59	135	61	94	106	3515
1987	49	483	459	23	600	169	428	17	94	173	487	54	137	55	90	101	3419

Table 2 Assets of Banks by State, 1896–1987 ($)

Year	AZ	CA	CO	ID	KS	MT	NB	NV	NM	ND	OK	OR	SD	UT	WA	WY	Total
1896	2512	303935	49339	4638	56407	31906	65270	2480	4003	12000	5013	19540	13563	15185	26199	4331	616321
1897	3213	302489	52200	6838	58492	24618	64982	2445	5093	11201	5567	18819	13583	14953	26179	4566	615238
1898	3850	330129	58884	6081	67674	26509	78994	2999	5185	12676	8447	27290	15233	19744	33753	5125	702573
1899	4552	357274	71786	7683	72685	29697	89607	3468	6056	14299	10404	27953	19018	23202	40339	6241	784264
1900	5881	384747	83670	7980	83862	34105	101557	3966	7721	15816	14077	33751	21004	28153	47290	7589	884969
1901	7678	426934	91246	12408	105715	40839	114262	4495	7991	16931	28197	33612	25832	33341	51787	8657	1009925
1902	8592	475610	103049	13819	109127	45940	123283	5498	9677	25050	36579	45546	35870	35561	68425	10332	1151958
1903	11033	551877	103597	15734	124036	48323	128754	7275	10621	31072	45833	49444	37597	33676	83928	11100	1293900
1904	12084	595543	110256	20754	139773	49021	136851	9105	10874	32356	48155	61728	39604	34876	95183	10849	1407012
1905	13648	683196	129530	23778	152084	52855	153877	13675	13120	39287	60984	63102	45118	43591	98128	13057	1599030
1906	17602	838257	141638	27664	171675	61949	180687	17843	15858	50659	74589	76913	55951	54419	162453	16489	1964646
1907	22602	889653	157649	35705	203347	73060	206033	28611	19992	59840	96266	90079	69926	62865	187512	20387	2223327
1908	18290	812704	150366	36970	199808	76163	205387	24740	19777	61328	98133	108429	72606	56689	179518	20824	2141732
1909	20971	842971	163926	42739	230018	81551	231037	23586	23008	78247	125837	113888	93022	63841	199866	23005	2357513
1910	23934	969936	178331	53375	236032	92907	246010	22473	25330	94942	136828	138252	105688	70713	233711	26689	2655151
1911	26872	1042441	172332	46078	228516	89319	249470	23132	26196	86374	143183	143001	102937	68517	221578	26271	2696217
1912	29185	1149773	181537	53375	232256	95683	277537	22797	26161	94625	139629	151807	100833	79368	236349	27230	2898145
1913	38344	1203787	185365	51434	261320	111402	277899	23455	30055	111039	163458	158040	111124	80606	253847	28979	3092984
1914	41890	1220702	186822	51728	248883	115485	274509	22174	31925	114804	172565	162372	118467	85024	256996	30856	3130870
1915	40636	1239308	190600	53487	293493	114743	303368	22992	32358	123251	180932	154578	123950	87407	252538	31366	3244807
1916	53985	1408047	227823	66839	324020	148836	355807	26382	39693	158282	231435	162372	148211	107164	274786	40331	3774013
1917	68951	1626176	280004	89872	423079	200573	495982	31709	51296	181000	317449	206503	184401	129368	331761	56071	4674195
1918	71819	1823455	290498	100688	475699	202322	538181	34248	58311	196595	392931	233236	229907	133359	392611	65612	5239472
1919	79783	2025476	321097	126424	537920	223742	598614	39946	59628	244561	446040	277877	303166	156074	449840	85564	5975761
1920	100565	2487131	374372	156862	602064	234940	642126	41917	71600	280145	593388	337496	321377	166966	507343	98089	7016381
1921	88032	2449895	335471	123168	553518	210094	530759	37745	67668	234697	498793	288127	270964	151336	425776	89427	6355470
1922	85720	2603759	335207	106551	533386	197631	543015	38031	65231	230932	479216	281033	280448	138765	412093	82216	6413234
1923	81341	3020563	357444	96752	535769	187646	568272	39559	62123	233790	483324	305326	286967	151212	452250	88984	6951322
1924	80795	3149930	354135	95057	495825	147160	546514	40993	41629	199769	435406	310780	216396	156662	463796	81529	6814576
1925	82389	3454949	367884	91868	555933	160583	607817	42678	37004	219493	495830	322875	219525	162100	487278	66495	7372701
1926	79616	3684063	341966	97908	546426	165200	586777	45209	39213	216600	517167	333828	193662	171223	514470	67204	7600532
1927	83791	3804152	338903	96203	541455	170389	555894	46469	41297	193069	523736	326706	158640	175893	520026	68289	7644912
1928	98298	3988061	348544	103705	543602	191027	580855	49015	48214	192243	534602	336544	179234	186822	553302	72898	8006966
1929	108137	4128945	347429	100421	538683	190486	528565	53677	51257	177016	544818	327926	177214	194441	570335	74637	8113987
1930	98773	4194520	342773	100715	503505	176674	464556	48419	52592	156685	517363	325322	168906	195640	583519	71337	8001299
1931	84789	4003510	328934	92521	453833	157887	428661	46272	45972	140512	438777	310843	140256	184924	567585	68202	7493273
1932	56396	3480617	271528	69489	367452	124246	302879	40680	36924	114022	358774	241158	105079	130253	426948	56289	6182734
1933	53122	3290460	242428	52846	342084	109308	240146	14120	26237	94179	322921	207615	83407	129464	356811	49895	5615043
1934	57981	3564211	272759	63821	386654	115289	319457	18369	35625	101702	368507	229441	86868	123356	418935	52755	6215730
1935	63690	3746788	303873	78279	415678	129173	341068	24754	44768	115258	400029	251786	95536	138719	449728	59499	6658626
1936	77852	4241001	337294	91260	448565	144253	372815	31080	52181	116550	468070	289137	102620	154147	521192	65450	7513467
1937	90191	4322760	354397	103763	456803	147946	353031	35351	59655	112140	496764	311141	99482	164151	566664	66088	7740327
1938	91732	4406215	337911	98030	439796	143875	339037	36672	61796	102617	500513	308031	94881	159448	545172	66145	7731871
1939	95520	4581189	362128	102075	455843	151587	353365	40102	64757	102447	516837	328821	101901	169466	597237	72406	8095681
1940	101949	4897685	382274	111132	464836	161766	366930	46957	68271	111322	526210	363039	110758	181531	657873	75797	8628330
1941	112146	5355118	410571	123970	522469	173766	402120	50863	75540	127303	571742	423768	121065	198712	759174	82486	9510813
1942	131751	5805858	474730	139077	637083	187302	497399	68203	89250	160087	644393	511547	149147	233279	937433	89599	10756138

Table 2 Assets of Banks by State, 1896–1987 ($) (continued)

Year	AZ	CA	CO	ID	KS	MT	NB	NV	NM	ND	OK	OR	SD	UT	WA	WY	Total
1943	217055	8151603	653234	213011	972769	272157	791559	93936	144289	249237	929938	804713	225629	352226	1389664	120207	15581227
1944	263958	10005481	780345	279178	1177116	351257	983383	110867	176517	343854	1136453	1053564	275277	408666	1814943	146607	19307966
1945	339493	12091093	950066	348823	1449439	433123	1157720	136827	228512	413650	1410351	1255753	328125	491517	2133850	176744	23345086
1946	399280	13645097	1110480	417673	1590293	505587	1296933	166469	276291	511593	1599539	1389659	430586	556223	2305773	213950	26415426
1947	410113	13259417	1063863	414718	1566345	514564	1335894	168695	268340	553836	1580088	1338151	490855	539225	2170773	217119	25891996
1948	437869	13780380	1105079	426658	1622868	535688	1303689	175457	289770	600919	1699502	1380732	514561	557132	2166772	235513	26832589
1949	439541	13517312	1114896	429861	1656005	559616	1278580	164865	304477	624522	1645587	1324733	503081	562164	2144107	242667	26512014
1950	455514	14341649	1197551	427587	1718438	563249	1318366	179205	351248	579039	1757501	1400115	509120	583313	2219388	255047	27856330
1951	519972	15132567	1277349	437563	1713158	553475	1406072	191503	366705	565273	1769740	1487567	511290	612565	2371239	268341	29184379
1952	600908	14688660	1360427	488761	1934809	620333	1482650	219020	419442	626545	2032968	1626119	552371	680685	2450499	293991	31858188
1953	648845	17300289	1444319	509565	2023183	635108	1534597	245374	453876	622986	2052585	1672202	553504	723089	2550325	309060	33278907
1954	686411	18207433	1534403	516339	2095518	672943	1570345	285869	471191	640654	2260670	1737853	576727	765417	2651875	324535	34959082
1955	780395	19837093	1644948	541577	2130968	695836	1562576	304546	523513	643646	2302670	1903838	611461	810909	2796760	332815	37423551
1956	932642	21553896	1786902	592669	2261257	777877	1640761	331677	609622	709130	2517002	2024690	640018	910324	3041824	372742	40703033
1957	994158	22762419	1856279	613873	2273928	809104	1605910	357260	637218	764975	2597632	1995113	684222	916788	3078683	393964	42341526
1958	1136499	24863552	2044864	686149	2457581	874318	1827314	401919	714332	832160	2799478	2194142	787641	993727	3287438	432977	46344091
1959	1285244	26066466	2097797	695027	2509976	874202	1792096	444802	749702	839891	2851632	2249263	789676	1037140	3395557	442475	48120946
1960	1417593	26893130	2228009	707834	2661407	906837	1868907	481598	776476	839141	3000895	2281504	822168	1101762	3449869	462173	48993303
1961	1616348	29849910	2547819	746169	2873393	944848	1986602	540444	837159	857006	3297462	2443541	883664	1164356	3715656	498893	54733270
1962	1767448	32349060	2631384	788270	3070629	1017722	2133294	626916	879165	960874	3351914	2628099	961771	1259891	4016819	518320	58961576
1963	1947922	34864832	2832957	831385	3215160	1081988	2265614	680895	979602	1024474	3221450	2790822	1021740	1322130	4172710	559524	63113205
1964	2214156	37736109	3044734	906263	3495062	1142346	2439714	725358	1003917	1087352	3899022	3040512	1084197	1410808	4526999	597849	68354398
1965	2356694	39853102	3246563	984159	3744472	1233253	2567360	776954	1047094	1176165	4267579	3341908	1163544	1561149	4939208	616747	72875951
1966	2516375	42648582	3360060	1037827	4053855	1311842	2760119	813488	1107012	1123565	4577943	3429893	1231306	1635537	4670632	657978	76936014
1967	2843906	46693507	3729907	1154493	4486900	1425432	3113712	956754	1218144	1232283	5085581	3729907	1336232	1721002	5259829	706806	84770458
1968	3258854	52600949	4337380	1271603	4920462	1571761	3473198	1064057	1358712	1393458	5454715	4289223	1476043	1900074	5819655	790575	94980719
1969	3521642	53798162	4609656	1378816	5266950	1680207	3784034	1135282	1471045	1481833	5629988	4376882	1610695	1900853	6041048	834199	98521292
1970	4062907	58628728	5044999	1526670	5733180	1857146	4083490	1297517	1724653	1598168	6513316	4617159	1759117	2115792	6871048	917919	108351609
1971	5236275	67508147	5801410	1733779	6547796	2117044	4736882	1535532	2087963	1799776	7381545	5168341	1981928	2433709	7376098	1051092	124497317
1972	6216946	77030436	6943627	2100072	7439238	2442078	5369174	1753898	2508286	1995055	8610818	6016490	2250632	2855728	8372629	1244046	143149153
1973	7056939	88157078	7821665	2434242	8573975	2735051	6302351	1974756	2848160	2293330	9693537	6636664	2639083	3169913	9735464	1439679	163511887
1974	7084402	96897187	8336324	2768851	9283790	2994011	6791073	1997427	3057621	2550008	10803518	6949076	2920713	3409757	11051408	1631991	178527157
1975	7597214	104269061	8765211	3027698	10199760	3343371	7256703	2136249	3408282	2950073	11801124	7748097	3271281	3918446	11883529	1870411	193450510
1976	7551800	146961083	9688244	3302747	11126867	3569264	7701682	2372489	3698846	3135917	12976920	8470271	3558907	4293731	13917831	2099297	244746596
1977	8737781	124810166	11551269	3776880	12478768	4007008	8577883	2718936	4303607	4002649	15144982	9921139	3825188	500643	15942255	2425007	232724161
1978	10181089	191914025	13374211	4296691	13568762	4458263	9562484	3286806	4905028	4435241	17036048	11589899	4216179	5848372	20124059	2711701	321508658
1979	12156670	219253018	15145608	4609205	15289420	4891111	10502865	3631507	5422714	4870638	19718871	12615598	4675392	6335578	22146002	3082501	364342698
1980	13364300	237991600	16615000	5106100	16598700	5318700	11509100	3761300	6106600	5332900	22841800	12966400	5085100	6744200	23639000	3449900	396430700
1981	14702960	262382700	18281257	5477396	18162005	5732065	12899109	4055412	6800544	5225112	27768178	13960762	7992949	7552640	25710709	3789171	440492989
1982	16656730	275445871	20285434	5883914	19619042	6207417	13965089	4584294	7766268	5783955	29636063	14214829	8782850	8230102	26333959	4107921	467503738
1983	18997700	276101500	22254200	6438000	21045300	6881000	14651400	4999400	8432100	6355700	30671700	15612300	10433900	8912100	26260200	4297800	482344300
1984	21471000	279216000	24254000	6824000	22638000	7140000	15609000	5514000	8674000	6627000	32127000	16614000	13274000	9874000	29027000	4535000	503418000
1985	24556000	294272000	25957000	7209000	23812000	7187000	16190000	7568000	9376000	6859000	31953000	17684000	16047000	10234000	31446000	4544000	534894000
1986	27655000	292659000	25997000	7064000	24567000	7252000	16647000	9141000	9868000	6932000	29250000	18909000	18205000	11195000	33114000	4380000	542835000
1987	27682000	282832000	24978000	7171000	24714000	7277000	16804000	10053000	9763000	6991000	27063000	18617000	20536000	11063000	33077000	4205000	532826000

Sources for Tables 1 and 2

1876–81: *The Bankers' Directory of the United States and Canada* (Chicago: Rand McNally & Co.).

1882–95: *The Bankers' Directory and List of Bank Attorneys* (Chicago: Rand McNally & Co.).

1896–1955: Federal Reserve Board of Governors, *Federal Reserve All Bank Statistics, 1896–1955* (Washington D.C.: Federal Reserve Board, 1959). Figures are for the end of each year.

1956–65: Federal Deposit Insurance Corporation, "Assets and Liabilities of Operating Banks in the United States," in *Annual Report* (Washington D.C.: FDIC, annually, 1956–65). Figures are for the end of the year.

1966: Federal Deposit Insurance Corp., *Annual Report, 1966* (Washington, D.C.: FDIC, 1966). Figures are average for the year and include only insured banks.

1967–76: Federal Deposit Insurance Corp., "Report of Condition for Insured Commercial Banks," in *Operating Statistics* (Washington, D.C.: FDIC, annually).

1977–79: Federal Deposit Insurance Corp., "Number, Assets and Deposits of all Commercial Banks in the United States," in *Annual Report* (Washington, D.C.: FDIC, 1977, 1978, 1979). Figures are for the end of the year.

1980: Federal Deposit Insurance Corp., "Number and Domestic and Foreign Assets and Deposits of all Commercial Banks in the United States," in *Annual Reports* (Washington, D.C.: 1980). Figures are for the end of the year. Assets are reported to the nearest $100 million.

1981: Federal Deposit Insurance Corp., "Report of Condition for Insured Commercial Banks," in *Bank Operating Statistics* (Washington, D.C.: FDIC, 1981).

1982–83: Federal Deposit Insurance Corp., "Number and Domestic and Foreign Assets and Deposits of all Commercial Banks in the United States," in *Annual Reports* (Washington, D.C.: FDIC, 1982, 1983).

1984–87: Federal Deposit Insurance Corp., "Number, Assets and Deposits of FDIC-Insured Commercial Banks in the United States," in *Statistics on Banking* (Washington, D.C.: FDIC, 1984, 1985, 1986, 1987).

Table 3 Largest Banks in the West
1970

State	Name	U.S. Rank*	Resources ($ thousands)
Arizona	Valley National Bank, Phoenix	39	1,651,834
	First National Bank of Arizona, Phoenix	74	929,757
	Arizona Bank, Phoenix	161	440,090
California	Bank of America National Trust & Savings Assn., San Francisco	1	23,353,366
	Security Pacific National Bank, Los Angeles	10	6,958,960
	Wells Fargo Bank, NA, San Francisco	11	5,743,152
	Crocker-Citizens National Bank, San Francisco	13	5,735,473
	United California Bank, Los Angeles	15	5,176,006
Colorado	First National Bank of Denver	114	586,462
	United Bank of Denver, NA	125	543,628
	Colorado National Bank, Denver	212	299,064
Idaho	Idaho First National Bank, Boise	135	500,741
	First Security Bank of Idaho, NA, Boise	170	425,914
	Bank of Idaho, Boise	392	157,603
Kansas	Fourth National Bank & Trust Co., Wichita	217	289,067
	First National Bank, Topeka	351	179,417
	First National Bank, Wichita	364	170,808

State	Bank		
Montana	First Security Trust & Savings, Billings	**	89,869
	First Bank, NA, Great Falls	**	79,061
	Midland National Bank, Billings	**	72,067
Nebraska	Omaha National Bank	169	427,981
	First National Bank & Trust Co., Lincoln	282	244,100
	First National Bank, Omaha	318	198,301
	United States National Bank of Omaha	349	181,360
Nevada	First National Bank of Nevada, Reno	113	599,322
	Valley Bank of Nevada, Las Vegas	334	186,993
New Mexico	Albuquerque National Bank	237	267,014
	First National Bank, Albuquerque	295	214,038
North Dakota		**	
Oklahoma	First National Bank & Trust Co., Oklahoma City	134	501,843
	First National Bank & Trust Co., Tulsa	151	458,031
	Liberty National Bank & Trust Co., Oklahoma City	163	435,410
	National Bank of Tulsa	186	359,837
Oregon	First National Bank of Oregon, Portland	35	1,766,850
	United States National Bank of Oregon, Portland	40	1,614,348
South Dakota	National Bank of South Dakota, Sioux Falls	339	183,105

Table 3 Largest Banks in the West (*continued*)

1970

State	Name	U.S. Rank*	Resources ($ thousands)
Utah	First Security Bank of Utah, NA, Ogden	115	584,863
	Walker Bank and Trust Co., Salt Lake City	215	290,768
	Zions First National Bank, Salt Lake City	233	272,307
Washington	Seattle First National Bank	24	2,144,338
	National Bank of Commerce of Seattle	45	1,433,433
	Peoples National Bank of Washington, Seattle	162	438,070
Wyoming		**	

* Ranked by resources as of June 30, 1970
** Not ranked by Rand McNally

Sources: Prepared by Nen Kheng Hay from "Four Hundred Largest Commercial Banking in the United States," in *Rand McNally International Bankers Directory* (Chicago: Rand McNally, 1970).

The source of assets for Montana is the Montana State Department of Commerce, Financial Division.

Table 3 Largest Banks in the West
1980

State	Name	U.S. Rank*	Resources ($ thousands)
Arizona	Valley National Bank, Phoenix	33	5,404,566
	First National Bank of Arizona, Phoenix	59	3,168,000
	Arizona Bank, Phoenix	105	1,932,028
California	Bank of America National Trust & Savings Assn., San Francisco	1	103,570,233
	Security Pacific National Bank, Los Angeles	10	24,222,996
	Wells Fargo Bank, NA, San Francisco	11	20,593,124
	Crocker National Bank, San Francisco	13	16,020,668
	United California Bank, Los Angeles	14	15,339,602
Colorado	First National Bank of Denver	132	1,645,871
	United Bank of Denver	136	1,625,609
	Colorado National Bank, Denver	222	936,036
Idaho	Idaho First National Bank, Boise	127	1,678,520
	First Security Bank of Idaho, Boise	174	1,226,168
	Bank of Idaho, NA, Boise	366	540,527
Kansas	Fourth National Bank & Trust Co., Wichita	240	853,357
	First National Bank in Wichita	**	461,254

Table 3 Largest Banks in the West (*continued*)

1980

State	Name	U.S. Rank*	Resources ($ thousands)
Montana	First Security Trust & Savings, Billings	**	89,869
	First Bank, NA, Great Falls	**	79,061
	Midland National Bank, Billings	**	72,067
Nebraska	Omaha National Bank	169	427,981
	First National Bank & Trust Co., Lincoln	282	244,100
	First National Bank, Omaha	318	198,301
	United States National Bank of Omaha	349	181,360
Nevada	First National Bank of Nevada, Reno	113	599,322
	Valley Bank of Nevada, Las Vegas	334	186,993
New Mexico	Albuquerque National Bank	237	267,014
	First National Bank, Albuquerque	295	214,038
North Dakota		**	
Oklahoma	First National Bank & Trust Co., Oklahoma City	134	501,843
	First National Bank & Trust Co., Tulsa	151	458,031
	Liberty National Bank & Trust Co., Oklahoma City	163	435,410
	National Bank of Tulsa	186	359,837
Oregon	First National Bank of Oregon, Portland	35	1,766,850
	United States National Bank of Oregon, Portland	40	1,614,348

South Dakota	National Bank of South Dakota, Sioux Falls	355	563,763
	Northwestern National Bank of Sioux Falls	463	432,880
Utah	First Security Bank of Utah, NA, Ogden	129	1,675,796
	Zions First National Bank, Salt Lake City	164	1,291,378
	Walker Bank and Trust Co., Salt Lake City	290	706,521
Washington	Seattle First National Bank	20	9,256,703
	Rainier National Bank, Seattle	38	4,672,873
	Washington Mutual Savings Bank, Seattle	93	2,210,836
Wyoming		**	

* Ranked by resources as of Dec. 31, 1980

** Not ranked by Rand McNally

Source: Prepared by Nen Kheng Hay from "Five Hundred Largest Commercial and Savings Banks in the United States," in *International Bankers' Directory*, 60–63.
The source of resources for Montana is the Montana State Department of Commerce, Financial Division.

Table 3 Largest Banks in the West
1986

State	Name	U.S. Rank*	Resources ($ thousands)
Arizona	Valley National Bank of Arizona, Phoenix	32	9,643,338
	First Interstate Bank of Arizona, Phoenix	60	6,116,937
California	Bank of America National Trust & Savings Assn., San Francisco	2	106,156,000
	Security Pacific National Bank, Los Angeles	8	44,850,904
Colorado	United Bank of Denver, NA, Denver	125	2,918,706
	First Interstate Bank of Denver, NA	167	2,352,632
	Colorado National Bank of Denver	231	1,518,352
Idaho	Idaho First National Bank, Boise	131	2,869,341
	First Security Bank of Idaho, NA, Boise	211	1,770,174
Kansas	Fourth National Bank & Trust Co., Wichita	236	1,476,668
Montana	First Bank, NA, Billings	**	378,475
	First Interstate Bank of Billings, NA	**	298,468
	First National Bank of Great Falls	**	261,450
Nebraska	Northwest Bank Nebraska, NA, Omaha	239	1,464,644
	Omaha National Bank, Omaha	290	1,213,205
	First National Bank & Trust Co. of Lincoln	311	1,109,697
Nevada	First Interstate Bank of Nevada, Reno	129	2,878,160
	Citibank (Nevada), NA, Las Vegas	217	1,667,689

State	Bank	Rank	Resources
New Mexico	Sunwest Bank at Albuquerque, NA	232	1,516,952
	First National Bank in Albuquerque	326	1,068,044
North Dakota[1]	First Bank of North Dakota, NA, Fargo	**	274,762
	First National Bank & Trust Co. of Bismarck	**	216,131
	First National Bank in Grand Forks	**	207,501
Oklahoma	Liberty National Bank & Trust Co. of Oklahoma City	159	2,383,342
	First National Bank & Trust Co. of Oklahoma City	196	2,006,710
	Bank of Oklahoma, NA, Tulsa	207	1,783,523
Oregon	United States National Bank of Oregon, Portland	46	7,386,176
	First Interstate Bank of Oregon, NA, Portland	63	5,792,887
South Dakota	Citibank (South Dakota), NA, Sioux Falls	38	8,355,589
Utah	First Security Bank of Utah, Ogden	137	2,760,536
	Zions First National Bank, Salt Lake City	141	2,711,638
Washington	Seattle First National Bank	29	9,925,229
	Rainier National Bank, Seattle	41	7,761,215
Wyoming	First Interstate Bank of Casper, NA	**	291,011
	Norwest Bank-Casper, NA	**	260,840

* Ranked by resources as of June 30, 1986

** Not ranked by Rand McNally

Source: Prepared by Nen Kheng Hay from "Five Hundred Largest U.S. Banks," in *The Rand McNally International Bankers Directory* (Chicago: Rand McNally, 1986), 104–9.

The source of resources for Montana is the Montana State Department of Commerce, Financial Division.

[1]Supplied by North Dakota.

Table 4 Savings and Loans Taken over by Government or Insolvent in 1980s

National Rank	Institution	City	Assets ($ millions)	NW% 3/31/89	NW% 9/30/88
		Arizona (5)			
2748	Southwest Savings	Phoenix	2,109	-5.96	.91
2671	Sun State Savings	Phoenix	1,047	-2.48	4.13
2689	Western Savings	Phoenix	5,655	-3.27	1.98
2934	Security Savings	Scottsdale	568	-82.18	-50.49
2856	Universal Savings	Scottsdale	81	-21.45	-5.39
		California (25)			
2756	First Fed	Bakersfield	126	-6.36	-4.35
2609	Guardian Fed	Bakersfield	29	-.79	2.70
2586	Gibraltar Savings	Beverly Hills	12,133	-.33	.84
2603	Sierra Fed	Beverly Hills	49	-.66	2.49
2858	Pacific Savings	Costa Mesa	1,080	-22.07	-18.32
2729	Security Fed	Garden Grove	74	-4.65	-4.04
2618	Cabrillo Savings	Hayward	72	-1.00	1.92
2436	American Interstate	Los Angeles	27	1.61	3.71
2884	Founders Savings	Los Angeles	135	-32.65	-32.99
2046	Lincoln Savings	Los Angeles	5,252	3.51	4.66
2761	Southwest Savings	Los Angeles	897	-6.96	-.83
2926	Westwood Savings	Los Angeles	315	-71.01	-65.19
2707	Royal Oak Savings	Manteca	34	-3.91	-1.40

2920	Unified Savings	Northridge	35	−41.16
2906	City Fed	Oakland	20	−44.03
2905	First California	Orange	161	−40.88
2909	Arrowhead Pac	San Bernadino	60	−33.23
2594	First Fed	San Bernadino	130	4.65
2939	Gateway Savings	San Francisco	73	−73.90
2917	Perpetual Savings	Santa Ana	19	−29.45
2636	Viking Savings	Santa Monica	24	1.59
2718	Washington	Stockton	67	−2.75
2652	Independence	Vallejo	440	.93
2725	City Savings	Westlake Village	33	−3.42
2604	Westco Savings	Wilmington	188	.91
		Colorado (12)		
2843	American Fed	Colorado Springs	720	1.30
2822	First Fed	Colorado Springs	326	−.38
2842	Otero Savings	Colorado Springs	512	.05
2831	Equity	Denver	4	−7.11
2851	Colorado Savings	Englewood	46	.12
2648	Mesa Fed	Grand Junction	114	−1.79
2703	Modern Fed	Grand Junction	70	−2.91
2937	Valley Fed	Grand Junction	78	−88.85
2883	Sun Savings	Parker	229	1.09
2776	Alpine Fed	Steamboat Springs	54	−5.01
2628	Colorado Fed	Sterling	13	−.51
2845	Rocky Mountain Savings	Woodland Park	17	−10.33

Table 4 Savings and Loans Taken over by Government or Insolvent in 1980s *(continued)*

National Rank	Institution	City	Assets ($ millions)	NW% 3/31/89	NW% 9/30/88
		Idaho (0)			
		Kansas (17)			
2890	First Fed	Coffeyville	75	−37.98	−17.22
2692	First of Kansas	Hays	54	−3.47	−1.29
2868	First Fed	Hutchinson	167	−26.72	−12.71
2844	Valley Fed	Hutchinson	201	−18.63	−6.43
2726	Anchor Savings	Kansas City	796	−4.61	−1.14
2848	Sun Savings	Kansas City	172	−19.03	−11.08
2887	Colonial Savings	Liberal	61	−33.76	−3.75
2816	Barber Co Savings	Medicine Lodge	49	−13.25	−3.62
2569	First Fed	Newton	135	−.07	−.23
2794	Mid-America Fed	Parsons	78	−10.19	−8.92
2797	Peoples Savings	Parsons	81	−10.36	−8.38
2763	Colonial Savings	Prairie Ville	146	−7.10	−4.65
2665	Peoples Heritage	Salina	2,015	−2.24	2.74
2735	Shawnee Fed	Topeka	212	−5.25	−4.71
2910	Topeka Savings	Topeka	82	−50.47	−24.78
2854	First Fed	Wellington	153	−21.12	−14.99
2639	Mid Kansas Fed	Wichita	866	−1.37	.27
		Montana (0)			

Nebraska (9)

2661	Custer Fed	Broken Bow	55	-2.19	-2.34
2574	Columbus Fed	Columbus	112	-.19	-.13
2621	Equitable Savings	Columbus	83	-1.10	-.67
2791	Equitable Fed	Fremont	216	-10.01	-7.49
2877	Platte Valley Fed	Gering	305	-30.13	-20.67
2847	Midwest Fed	Nebraska City	128	-18.95	-14.46
2803	Occidental Nebraska	Omaha	635	-11.05	-4.96
2915	Nile Valley Fed	Scotsbluff	52	-55.57	-43.31
2638	First Fed	York	67	-1.35	-.61

Nevada (0)

New Mexico (6)

2826	American Fed	Albuquerque	187	-13.81	-6.46
2742	New Mexico Fed	Albuquerque	244	-5.57	-4.53
2936	Sandia Fed	Albuquerque	693	-84.32	-58.07
2903	Sun Country	Albuquerque	70	-47.53	-43.03
2708	Security Savings	Carlsbad	37	-3.94	2.20
2924	Valley Fed Bank	Roswell	160	-70.57	-46.63

North Dakota (2)

2740	First Fed	Bismarck	124	-5.44	-6.24
2678	Midwest Fed	Minot	1,087	-2.70	1.40

Oklahoma (6)

1978	Cross Roads	Checotah	27	3.73	6.97
2653	Duncan Savings	Duncan	147	-1.69	.66

Table 4 Savings and Loans Taken over by Government or Insolvent in 1980s (*continued*)

National Rank	Institution	City	Assets ($ millions)	NW% 3/31/89	NW% 9/30/88
2717	Continental Fed	Oklahoma City	636	-4.32	-.30
2672	Family Fed	Sapulpa	55	-2.55	-.39
2802	First Fed	Seminole	32	-11.04	-6.89
2675	Great Plains Fed	Weatherfield	118	-2.64	1.08
		Oregon (1)			
2673	Family Fed	Dallas	165	-2.59	-1.31
		South Dakota (1)			
2617	Yankton Savings	Yankton	39	-.95	-1.59
		Utah (3)			
2849	Mountainwest	Ogden	228	-19.39	-11.72
2647	American Savings	Salt Lake City	2,132	-1.51	-.37
2912	Deseret Fed	Salt Lake City	157	-51.02	-49.16
		Washington (1)			
1622	Gibralter Savings	Bellevue	1,771	4.86	5.83
		Wyoming			
2592	Provident Fed	Casper	268	-.41	-.35

Source: "The S&Ls: Where They Stand," *USA Today*, August 14, 1989.

NOTES

1. No Money in Kansas

1. *Lincoln Farmer's Alliance*, quoted in Norman Pollack, *The Populist Response to Industrial America* (Cambridge: Harvard University Press, 1962), 16–17.

2. John Davis, "The National Monopoly or Financial Devil Fish of America," in John Davis Scrapbook E, Kansas State Historical Society (KHS), Topeka, Kans. See also George Anderson, *Essays on the History of Banking* (Lawrence, Kans.: Coronado Press, 1972).

3. James Newbill, W. R. Gedosh, and Roger Van Winkle, *The American Spectrum* (Belmont, Calif.: Wadsworth, 1972), 65.

4. James R. Emry, "Billions for the Bankers, Debts for the People," pamphlet published in Phoenix, Arizona, 1982. See also William Greider, *Secrets of the Temple: How the Federal Reserve Runs the Country* (New York: Simon and Schuster, 1987), 668–69.

5. Examples of views on banks and bankers in different eras appear in James R. Sharp, *The Jacksonians Versus the Banks: Politics in the States after the Panic of 1837* (New York: Columbia University Press, 1970), 7, 11; Robert P. Sharkey, *Money, Class, and Party: An Economic Study of the Civil War and Reconstruction* (Baltimore: Johns Hopkins University Press, 1959); Martin Mayer, *The Bankers* (New York: Weabright and Talley, 1974); S. C. Gwynne, *Selling Money* (New York: Penguin, 1987 [orig. pub. 1986]); and Irwin Unger, *The Greenback Era: A Social and Political History of American Finance, 1865–1879* (Princeton: Princeton University Press, 1964).

6. Greider, *Secrets of the Temple*, 709. Greider's calls for "democratic money" seemed dredged straight out of Jacksonian campaign literature. However, to justify such demands, he, while meticulously avoiding any mainstream economist (except Milton Friedman, whom he quotes but whose research he never challenges), has to somehow explain away the economic boom of the Reagan Revolution while simultaneously criticizing Paul Volcker, the chairman of the Federal Reserve Board during the period about which Greider wrote. Not only did Greider fail miserably, but he did us the unexpected favor of providing a timely example of rhetoric we frankly had thought was long gone. Greider's polemic lacks the anti-Semitism of earlier antibanker tracts, but in most other ways it maintains perfect continuity with the earlier materials.

7. On Arkansas and the southern banking experience, see Larry Schweikart, *Banking in*

the American South from the Age of Jackson to Reconstruction (Baton Rouge: Louisiana State University Press, 1987), and on Wisconsin and the Old Northwest, see William G. Shade, *Banks or No Banks: The Money Issue in Western Politics, 1832–1865* (Detroit: Wayne State University Press, 1972), and Sharp, *Jacksonians Versus the Banks,* 190–210.

8. *Elmwood Free Press,* December 24, 1859, quoted in George L. Anderson, "Some Phases of Currency and Banking in Territorial Kansas," in *Territorial Kansas: Studies Commemorating the Centennial* (Lawrence: University of Kansas Social Science Studies, 1954), 103–47 (quotation on p. 104); and John J. Ingalls to his father, April 3, 1860, "Some Ingalls Letters" *Collections,* KHS.

9. *Lawrence Republican,* June 25, 1857; *Elmwood Free Press,* November 12, 1859; *Emporia Kansas News,* September 12, 1857.

10. See, for example, Gerald D. Nash, *The American West in the Twentieth Century: A Short History of an Urban Oasis* (Albuquerque: University of New Mexico Press, 1977 [Orig. pub. 1973]), 4–5; idem, *American West Transformed: The Impact of World War II* (Bloomington: Indiana University Press, 1985); Ray Allen Billington, *The Far Western Frontier, 1830–1860* (New York: Harper, 1956), xvii–xviii; idem, *Westward Expansion,* 5th ed. (New York: Macmillan, 1982); and Roger L. Nichols, ed. *American Frontier and Western Issues: A Historiographical Review* (New York: Greenwood Press, 1986).

11. Nash, *American West in the Twentieth Century,* 4–5.

12. Note, for example, that the tenth Federal Reserve District has its reserve bank headquarters in Minneapolis, which is not included in this study.

13. John Haeger, "Economic Development of the American West," in Nichols, ed., *American Frontier and Western Issues,* 27–50, esp. 38–39, and notes 59–62. Among Haeger's citations are Bray Hammond's article "Banking in the Early West: Monopoly, Prohibition, and Laissez Faire," *Journal of Economic History* 8 (May 1948): 1–25; Fritz Redlich, *The Molding of American Banking: Men and Ideas,* 2 vols. (New York: Johnson Reprint Co., 1968 [orig. pub. 1947]); Richard Sylla "American Banking and Growth in the Nineteenth Century: A Partial View of the Terrain," *Explorations in Economic History* 9 (Winter, 1971–72): 197–227; and Guy S. Callender, "The Early Transportation and Banking Enterprises of the States in Relation to the Growth of Corporations," *Quarterly Journal of Economics* 17 (November 1902): 111–62. While these are important, indeed even landmark, pieces, they hardly represent the considerable body of new literature to appear from economists, historians, and private institutions.

14. Leonard J. Arrington, "Banking Enterprises in Utah, 1847–1880," *Business History Review* 24 (December 1955): 312–34, and his *Great Basin Kingdom* (Cambridge, Mass.: Harvard University Press, 1955); W. Turrentine Jackson, *The Enterprising Scot: Investors in the American West after 1873* (Edinburgh: Edinburgh University Press, 1968), and his numerous articles cited throughout this work; Kirkpatrick Sale, *Power Shift: The Rise of the Southern Rim and Its Challenge to the Eastern Establishment.* (New York: Vintage Books, 1975); Nash, *American West in the Twentieth Century,* 104–5, 167–68; and idem, *American West Transformed,* 24–25, 32, 34.

15. An overview of these works can be found in Larry Schweikart and Lynne Pierson Doti, "Banking in the West: A Bibliographical Overview," in *Banking in the West,* ed. Larry Schweikart (Manhattan, Kans.: Sunflower University Press, 1984), 88–94. Among the works on individual western-state banking cited therein are Roland Stucki, *Commercial Banking in Utah, 1847–1966* (Salt Lake City: University of Utah, Bureau of Economics and Business Research, 1967); Eugene Halaas, *The Banking Structure of Colorado: Historic Developments and Recent Changes,* Occasional Studies no. 1 (Denver: University of Denver, College of Business Administration, Division of Research, 1969); A. R. Gutowsky, *Arizona Banking* (Tempe: Arizona State University, College of Business, 1967); Ira Cross, *Financing an Empire: History of Banking in California* (Chicago: S. J. Clarke Publishing Co., 1927);

W. E. Kuhn, *History of Nebraska Banking: A Centennial Retrospect*, Business Research Bulletin no. 72 (Lincoln: University of Nebraska, College of Business Administration, 1968); George L. Anderson, "A Century of Banking in Kansas," in *Kansas: The First Century*, ed. John Bright, (New York: Lewis Historical Publishing Co., 1956), 2: 403–22; James Smallwood, *An Oklahoma Adventure: Of Banks and Bankers* (Norman: University of Oklahoma Press, 1979); L. Milton Woods, *Sometimes the Books Froze: Wyoming's Economy and Its Banks* (Boulder: Colorado Associated University Press, 1985); Thomas F. Cargill and Kerry S. Sullivan, "An Historical Perspective of Nevada Banking," *Journal of the West* 23 (April 1984): 21–28; and Orin Kay Burrell, *Gold in the Woodpile: An Informal History of Banking in Oregon* (Eugene: University of Oregon Books, 1967).

16. Some examples include, from Colorado, Thomas Jacob Noel, *Growing through History with Colorado, The Colorado National Banks: The First 125 Years, 1862–1987* (Denver: Colorado National Banks and University of Colorado, Colorado Studies Center, 1987); and from California, Marquis and Besse Rowland James, *Biography of a Bank: The Story of the Bank of America, N. T. and S. A.* (New York: Harper & Brothers, 1954). Numerous other examples will appear in the notes to subsequent chapters.

17. The ethical problems of writing business histories are discussed in Charles Dellheim, "Business in Time: The Historian and Corporate Culture," *The Public Historian* 8 (Spring 1986): 9–22; and Carl Rant, "The Public Historian and Business History," ibid., 31–38. Still, practitioners of corporate history often fail to realize that much of the value in writing histories of existing institutions is that they are success stories. Without them, we might well know from historical evidence why businesses fail, but not why they succeed. Moreover, without access to internal documents, we can only make reasonable guesses as to a company's strategy. See, for example, Allen Kaufman and Gordon Walker, "Strategy-History Connection: The Case of Exxon," ibid., 23–39.

18. Charles W. Calomiris, "Deposit Insurance: Lessons from the Record," *Economic Perspectives*, May/June 1989, 10–30; idem., "Is Deposit Insurance Necessary?" *Journal of Economic History* 50 (June 1990): 283–96; and idem., "Do 'Vulnerable' Economies Need Deposit Insurance? Lessons from the U.S. Agricultural Boom and Bust of the 1920s," unpublished paper, Federal Reserve Bank of Chicago, 1989, in authors' possession; Lance E. Davis, "The Investment Market, 1870–1914: The Evolution of a National Market," *Journal of Economic History* 25 (September 1969): 355–99; Milton Friedman and Anna J. Schwartz, *A Monetary History of the United States, 1867–1960* (Princeton: Princeton University Press, 1963); Richard Sylla, *American Capital Markets, 1846–1914: A Study of the Effect of Public Policy on Economic Development* (New York: Arno Press, 1975); Eugene White, *The Regulation and Reform of the American Banking System, 1900–1929* (Princeton: Princeton University Press, 1983). See also John A. James, *Money and Capital Markets in Postbellum America* (Princeton: Princeton University Press, 1978); and C. A. E. Goodhart, *The New York Money Market and the Finance of Trade* (Cambridge: Harvard University Press, 1969).

19. Ross Robertson, *The Comptroller and Bank Supervision: An Historical Approach* (Washington, D.C.: Office of the Comptroller of the Currency, 1968), 22–23 (quotation on p. 23).

20. For general banking histories, consult Redlich, *The Molding of American Banking;* Ray Westerfield, *Historical Survey of Branch Banking in the United States* (New York: American Bankers Association Policy Commission, 1939); Benjamin Klebaner, *Commercial Banking in the United States: A History* (Hinsdale, Illinois: Dryden Press, 1974); Philip Cagan, "The First Fifty Years of National Bank Act—Historical Appraisal," *Banking and Monetary Studies*, ed. Dean Carson (Homewood, Ill.: Richard D. Irwin Inc., 1963); Bray Hammond, *Banks and Politics in America from the Revolution to the Civil War* (Princeton: Princeton University Press, 1957); John Jay Knox, *A History of Financial Intermediaries* (New York: Random House, 1971); William Graham Sumner, *A History of Banking in the*

United States (New York: Augustus M. Kelley, 1971); Paul Trescott, *Financing American Enterprise: The Story of Commercial Banking* (New York: Harper and Row, 1963); James Livingston, *Origins of the Federal Reserve: Money, Class, and the Corporate Capital, 1890–1913* (Ithaca: Cornell University Press, 1986); George D. Green, *Finance and Economic Development in the Old South: Louisiana Banking, 1804–1861,* (Stanford: Stanford University Press, 1972).

21. Green makes this point in *Finance and Economic Development,* 48–52; as does Schweikart, *Banking in the American South,* 254–66.

22. Woods, *Sometimes the Books Froze,* 1.

23. Larry Schweikart, *A History of Banking in Arizona* (Tucson: University of Arizona Press, 1982), 9.

24. Cross, *Financing an Empire,* 1: 44, 47, 159; Neil Roy Knight, "History of Banking in Washington" (Ph.D. diss., University of Washington, 1935), 76.

25. Contrary to the claims of sociologist Andrew Beveridge, customers viewed the earliest western banks as currency and exchange stations, not as credit institutions. See Andrew A. Beveridge, "Credit to the Community: American Banking's Tribal Roots," (Master's Thesis, Graduate School and University Center, City University of New York, Spring 1988), 18–23.

26. Lewis Davids, " 'Fur' Money and Banking in the West," *Journal of the West,* April 1984, 7–10; Hiram Mark Chittenden, *The American Fur Trade of the Far West: A History of Pioneering Trading Posts and Early Fur Companies of the Missouri Valley and the Rocky Mountains and of the Overland Commerce with Santa Fe,* 3 vols. (New York: F. P. Harper, 1902). In frontier Arkansas, a resolution to make wolf pelts legal currency led to a brawl inside the chamber of the state House of Representatives in which the Speaker of the House used a bowie knife to slash to death his opponent on the floor of the chamber. See Ted Worley, "The Control of the Real Estate Bank of the State of Arkansas, 1836–1855," *Mississippi Valley Historical Review,* December 1950, 403–26. An excellent historiography of the fur trade appears in Gordon B. Dodds, "The Fur Trade and Exploration," in *Historians and the American West,* ed. Michael P. (Lincoln: University of Nebraska Press, 1983), 57–75.

27. See Richard Henry Dana, *Two Years Before the Mast* (New York: A. L. Burt Co., 1840).

28. Philip D. Thomas, "Thomas James, Hugh Glenn, and Jacob Fowler, 1821–1823," in *Frontier Adventures,* ed. Joseph Stout, Jr., (Oklahoma City: Oklahoma Historical Society, 1976), 61–79; Harry R. Stevens, "Hugh Glenn," in *The Mountain Man and the Fur Trade of the Far West,* ed. LeRoy R. Hafen, (Glendale: Arthur C. Clarke, 1965), 2: 165–74.

29. Smallwood, *An Oklahoma Adventure,* 4–5.

30. *Daily Oklahoman,* April 23, 1939; Edwin C. McReynolds, *Oklahoma: A History of the Sooner State* (Norman: University of Oklahoma Press, 1954), 170.

31. James Neal, Notes, 1942, Oklahoma Bankers Association Archives (OBA), Oklahoma City.

32. Earling A. Erickson, "Money and Banking in a 'Bankless' State: Iowa, 1846–1857," *Business History Review* 43 (Summer 1969): 171–91; F. Cyril James, *The Growth of Chicago Banks,* 2 vols. (New York: Harper & Row, 1938); Arthur Rolnick and Warren Weber, "Free Banking, Wildcat Banking, and Shinplasters," *Federal Reserve Bank of Minnesota Quarterly Review,* Fall 1982, 10–19; idem, "New Evidence on the Free Banking Era," *American Economic Review* 72 (December 1983): 1080–91; idem, "The Causes of Free Bank Failures," *Journal of Monetary Economics* 14 (November 1984): 267–91; idem, "Banking Instability and Regulation in the U.S. Free Banking Era," *Federal Reserve Bank of Minneapolis Quarterly Review,* Summer 1985, 2–9; idem, "Inherent Instability in Banking: The Free Banking Experience," *CATO Journal* 5 (Winter 1986): 877–90; Andrew Economopoulos, "Illinois Free Banking Experience," *Journal of Money Credit and Banking* 20 (May 1988): 249–64; Kenneth Ng, "Free Banking Laws and Barriers to Entry in Banking, 1838–1860,"

Journal of Economic History 48 (December 1988): 877–90; and Mortimer Speigelman, "The Failure of the Ohio Life Insurance and Trust Company, 1857," *Ohio Archeological and Historical Quarterly* 57 (1948): 247–65. The overwhelming evidence from the studies by Rockoff, Rolnick and Weber, Economopoulos, and others is that free banking's success depended on whether the laws permitted par valuation of the bonds backing the notes or instead demanded market valuation. The latter experienced virtually no difficulties, suggesting that there were really no inherent problems in free banking. See also Charles Calomiris and Larry Schweikart, "Was the South Backward: Differences in Antebellum Banking during Normalcy and Crisis," Federal Reserve Bank of Chicago Working Paper, 1989; idem, "Regulations and Markets as Determinants of the Performance and Vulnerability of Antebellum Banks," paper presented at the annual meeting of the American Economic Association, December 1987; and idem, "Southern Banks and the Panic of 1857: Evidence from Alabama, Georgia, and Virginia," unpublished paper, all in the authors' possession.

33. Schweikart, *Banking in the American South*, chap. 7; and idem, "Southern Banks and Economic Growth in the Antebellum Period: A Reassessment," *Journal of Southern History* 53 (February 1987): 19–36.

34. W. B. Worthen, *Early Banking in Arkansas* (Little Rock: Democrat Printing and Litho Co., 1906), 144–45; Larry Schweikart, "Entrepreneurial Aspects of Antebellum Banking," in *American Business History: Case Studies*, ed. C. Joseph Pusateri and Henry C. Dethloff (New York: Harlan Davidson, 1986), 122–39 (esp. p. 138); Larry Schweikart, "Arkansas Antebellum Banks," *Southern Studies* 26 (Fall 1987): 188–201. Despite the absence of "official" banking facilities, it is clear that far more private bankers plied their trade throughout the South, and, most likely, the Old Northwest, than has previously been thought. See Larry Schweikart, "Private Bankers in the Antebellum Period," *Southern Studies* 25 (Summer 1986): 125–34; and Richard Sylla, "Forgotten Men of Money: Private Bankers in Early U.S. History," *Journal of Economic History*, December 1969, 173–88.

35. Schweikart, *Banking in the American South*, 176–78.

36. Joseph M. Grant and Lawrence L. Crum, *The Development of State Chartered Banking in Texas* (Austin: University of Texas, Bureau of Business Research, 1978), 9, 15–16. Although in 1837 the legislature prohibited note issue by private banks, and in 1845 stated in the new constitution that "No corporate body shall . . . [have] banking or discounting privileges," it did not specifically prohibit note issue anew, nor did it close two banks then in existence (*Constitution of 1845*, Article 7, Section 30). Moreover, soon after the new constitution came into existence, "Mills money," issued by the firm of R. and D. G. Mills in Galveston, circulated widely with no apparent attempt by the state to prohibit the notes (Grant and Crum, *Development of State Chartered Banking in Texas*, 16–17). See also Avery Luverve Carlson, *A Monetary and Banking History of Texas* (Fort Worth: Fort Worth National Bank, 1930).

37. Carlson, *Monetary and Banking History of Texas*, 5.

38. William M. Gouge, *The Fiscal History of Texas* (Philadelphia: J. B. Lippincott, 1852).

39. John Kay Knox, *A History of Banking in the United States* (New York: Augustus M. Kelley, 1969 [orig. pub. 1903], 784, quoted in Anderson, "Some Phases of Currency and Banking," 115.

40. Kuhn, *History of Nebraska Banking*, 1–6.

41. *Kansas City [Missouri] Western Journal of Commerce*, November 14, 1857.

42. "Letters of John and Sarah Everett, 1854–1864," *Kansas Historical Quarterly* 8 (February 1939): 3–34, (May 1939): 143–74, (August 1939): 279–310, and (November 1939): 350–83. See also Thomas C. Wells, "Letters of a Kansas Pioneer, 1855–1860," *Kansas Historical Quarterly* 5 (May and August 1936): 143–318, and (November 1936): 381–418.

43. Alfred Theodore Andreas, *History of the State of Kansas*. . . . (Chicago: A. T. Andreas, 1883), 1: 137–78; *Topeka Daily Capital*, August 25, 1929.

44. For evidence related to gunrunning, see David M. Potter, *The Impending Crisis, 1848–1861*, ed. Don E. Fehrenbacher (New York: Harper, 1976), 199–224; Samuel A. Johnson, *The Battle Cry of Freedom: The New England Emigrant Aid Company in the Kansas Crusade* (Lawrence: University of Kansas Press, 1954), 16–50; W. H. Isely, "The Sharps Rifle Episode in Kansas History," *American Historical Review* 12 (1907): 546–66; and Walter L. Flemming, "The Buford Expedition to Kansas," *American Historical Review* 6 (1900): 38–48. On federal expenditures, see Anderson, "Some Phases of Currency and Banking," 110–12.

45. Quoted in George L. Anderson, "A Century of Banking in Kansas," 403, 404.

46. Anderson, "Some Phases of Currency and Banking," 103. One early Nebraska historian estimated the circulation per capita in 1857 at $100, although this number is questionable given the complaints of frontier settlers. Even so, the volume of money often related only slightly to its value, which fluctuated (wildly at times) depending on the ease of redemption, available specie, etc. See Henry W. Yates, "Early Nebraska Currency and Per Capita Circulation," *Proceedings of the Nebraska State Historical Society* 1, no. 2, (1894): 67–76.

47. Eugene H. Adams, Lyle W. Dorsett, and Robert S. Pulcipher, *The Pioneer Western Bank—First of Denver, 1860–1980*, ed. Robert S. Pulcipher (Denver: First Interstate Bank of Denver, NA, 1984), 4–20; Noel, *Growing through History with Colorado*, xvi. Aspects of mining in Colorado and other parts of the West are discussed extensively by historians. A review of the literature appears in Clark C. Spence, "Western Mining," *Historians and the American West*, 96–122.

48. Noel, *Growing through History*, xvi.

49. Bill Skidmore, *Treasure State Treasury: Montana Banks, Bankers, and Banking, 1864–1984* (Helena: Thurber Printing Co., 1985), 3.

50. Ibid. See also, Thomas Jacob Noel, *Denver's Larimer Street: Main Street, Skid Row and Urban Renaissance* (Denver: Historic Denver, Inc., 1981).

51. Jerome C. Smiley, *History of Denver with Outlines of the Earlier History of the Rocky Mountain Country* (Denver: The Denver Times/Sun Times Publishing Co., 1901), 302; Neil King, "History of Banking in Denver, Colorado, 1858–1950" (Master's thesis, Graduate School of Banking, Rutgers University, 1952).

52. J. H. M., Barrows, Millard & Co. to David Moffat, Jr., May 18, 1861, Collection 598, Agnes Wright Spring Papers, Colorado Historical Society (CHS), Denver. See also Ezra Millard to David Moffat, Jr., March 2, 1861; and Barrows, Millard & Co. to David Moffat, Jr., May 23, 1861; both in ibid.

53. Adams et al., *Pioneer Western Bank*, 6–9; Fred R. Niehaus, *Development of Banking in Colorado* (Denver: Mountain States Publishing Company, 1942), 11, 16–17; *Leavenworth Kansas Weekly Herald*, February 11, 1860. Although the first coins issued by Clark, Gruber & Co. were pure gold, they proved to be too soft and susceptible to abrasion, so in 1861 the mint added alloys.

54. *Leavenworth Kansas Weekly Herald*, February 11, 1860.

55. Woods, *Sometimes the Books Froze*, 10.

56. King, "History of Banking in Denver," 17–21.

57. *Rocky Mountain News*, August 1, 1860, quoted in Spring Papers, "Notes," MSS 598, CHS.

58. Noel, *Growing through History with Colorado*, 1–2; Skidmore, *Treasure State Treasury*, 4.

59. R. G. Dun & Co. quoted in ibid, xxiv.

60. Augustus to Luther Kountze, April 7, 1863, in Kountze Collection, Denver Public Library (uncatalogued as of this writing).

61. Skidmore, *Treasure State Treasury*, 15.

62. Clark C. Spence, *Montana: A History* (New York: W. W. Norton Co., 1978), 27.

63. Ibid., 28.

64. Skidmore, *Treasure State Treasury*, 4.

65. E. G. Leipheimer, *The First National Bank of Butte: Seventy-Five Years of Continuous Banking Operation, 1877 to 1952, Under the Successive Ownership and Management of Three Men Each Named Andrew Jackson Davis* (St. Paul: Brown and Bigelow, 1952), 1–8.

66. Robert E. Driscoll, *The Black Hills of South Dakota: Its Pioneer Banking History* (New York: Newcomen Society, 1951), 2–9.

67. Ibid., 9; Doane Robinson, *History of South Dakota*, (n.p., 1904), 1: 473–74; Judith Barjenbruch, "The First National Bank of Vermillion, 1875–1937" (Master's thesis, University of South Dakota, 1975), iii.

68. Charles Dahler to Warren Hussey, August 10, 1867, Letterbook 1, Hussey, Dahler and Company Letterbooks, 5 vols. Auerback Collection, Bancroft Library, University of California.

69. See C. James Wall, "Gold Dust and Greenbacks," *Montana: The Magazine of Western History* 7 (Spring 1957): 24–31, 63; Carl J. White, "Financial Frustrations in Territorial Montana," *Montana: The Magazine of Western History* 17 (Spring 1967): 34–45.

70. Charles Dahler to James Hughes, August 16, 1867, Letterbook 1, Hussey, Dahler and Company Letterbooks, Auerbach Collection, University of California Berkeley.

71. Frank Soule, John H. Gihon, and James Nisbet, *The Annals of San Francisco* (Palo Alto: Louis Osborn, 1966), 173; Cross, *Financing an Empire*, 1:159.

72. Dana, *Two Years Before the Mast*, 257.

73. Soule et. al., *Annals of San Francisco*, 173; Cross, *Financing and Empire*, 1: 43.

74. Dwight L. Clarke, *William Tecumseh Sherman: Gold Rush Banker* (San Francisco: California Historical Society, 1969).

75. Thomas Senior Berry, *Early California: Gold, Prices, and Trade* (Richmond, Va.: the Bostwick Press, 1984), 14. Barry notes that gold shipments influenced prices more than gold production.

76. Cross, *Financing an Empire*, 1: 41.

77. Neill Compton Wilson, *400 California Street: The Story of the Bank of California, National Association, and Its First 100 Years in the Financial Development of the Pacific Coast*, (San Francisco: Bank of California, 1969).

78. Lynne Pierson Doti, "Banking in California: Some Evidence on Structure, 1878–1905" (Ph.D. diss., University of California, Riverside, 1978), 1–55.

79. Russell R. Elliott, *History of Nevada* (Lincoln: University of Nebraska Press, 1973), 61–62.

80. Ibid., 63.

81. Privately minted coins from early California constitute a major exhibit at the Smithsonian Institutions, Museum of Science and Industry. Oregon has its famous beaver dollar: five-dollar and ten-dollar pieces were coined by eight Oregon businessmen who constituted the Oregon Exchange Company. Some $58,000 was minted in 1849. See Arthur Throckmorton, *Oregon Argonauts: Merchant Adventures on the Western Frontier* (Cortland: Oregon Historical Society, 1961), 99–100. Sherman also referred to privately minted coins (Clarke, *William Tecumseh Sherman*, 77), and Dwight Clark, Sherman's biographer, stated that the Philadelphia Mint in 1851 reported coinage activities by at least fifteen private California mints (ibid.).

82. See Elliot, *History of Nevada*, 125–26, for the first view; and W. H. Blauvelt, "Banking," in *The History of Nevada*, ed. Sam P. Davis, (Reno: The Elms Publishing Co., 1913), 1: 629–30, for the second. Blauvelt was the cashier of the Bank of California for several years.

83. On Sharon, see Cecil G. Tilton, *William Chapman Ralston: Courageous Builder* (Boston: The Christopher Publishing House, 1935), 137–59.

268 otes to Pages 15–17

84. Wilson, *400 California Street*, 16, 27; Thomas F. Cargill and Kerry S. Sullivan, "An Historical Perspective of Nevada Banking," 21–28.

85. George Lyman, *Ralston's Ring: California Plunders the Comstock Lode* (New York: Charles Scribner's Sons, 1937), 54.

86. Arrington, *Great Basin Kingdom*, 171–92; and idem, "Banking Enterprises in Utah," 312–15.

87. Stucki, *Commercial Banking in Utah*, 3.

88. Ibid.

89. *New York Herald*, June 22, 1849; Arrington, *Great Basin Kingdom*, 171–92; Stucki, *Commercial Banking in Utah*, 5.

90. Stucki, *Commercial Banking in Utah*, 4.

91. Dale W. Adams, "Chartering the Kirtland Bank," *Brigham Young University Studies* 23 (1983): 467–82; Marvin S. Hill, C. Keith Rooker, and Larry T. Wimmer, "The Kirtland Economy Revisited: A Market Critique of Sectarian Economics," *Brigham Young University Studies* 17 (Summer 1977): 391–472.

92. *Journal of the History of the Church of Jesus Christ of the Latter Day Saints*, Feb. 3, 1849, quoted in Stucki, *Commercial Banking in Utah*, 4.

93. Arrington, *Great Basin Kingdom*, 191; Dale R. Hawkins, "Banking in Utah," (Master's thesis, University of Utah, 1951), 4.

94. Frederick Kesler Diary, January 19, 1858, Frederick Kesler Papers, Box 1, "Diary 1858," University of Utah Library (UU).

95. Ibid., February 1, 1858. See also the entry for January 22, 1858. Other material on Brigham Young's economics appears in J. R. T. Hughes, *The Vital Few* (London: Oxford University Press, 1979 [orig. pub. 1965]), 67–116. On the affairs of the Kirtland bank, see Harry W. Beardsley, *Joseph Smith and His Mormon Empire* (Boston: Houghton Mifflin, 1931), 166, 319; Fawn M. Brodie, *No Man Knows My History* (New York: Knopf, 1946), 194–207; C. C. Huntington, "A History of Banking and Currency in Ohio Before the Civil War," *Ohio Archeological and Historical Publications* 14 (1915): 412–65; and Larry Schweikart, "Making Money the Old Fashioned Way," *Timeline* (December 1989/January 1990): 32–43.

96. Woods, *Sometimes the Books Froze*, 10.

97. Ibid., 1; Stanley P. Hirshson, *Grenville M. Dodge* (Bloomington: University of Indiana Press, 1967), 153. On the Union Pacific, see Maury Klein, *The Union Pacific: The Birth of a Railroad, 1863–1893* (New York: Doubleday, 1987).

98. *Cheyenne Leader*, September 24, 1867.

99. Ibid., October 1, 1867.

100. Woods, *Sometimes the Books Froze*, 14–15.

101. Arthur Throckmorton, "The Role of the Merchant on the Oregon Frontier: The Early Business Career of Henry W. Corbett, 1851–1869," *Journal of Economic History* 16 (December 1956): 539–50.

102. Throckmorton, *Oregon Argonauts*, 23–24.

103. In the spring of 1844, Hudson's Bay Company had accounts totalling $29,330 for between three hundred and four hundred Americans (ibid., 36).

104. Ibid., 50.

105. Knight, "History of Banking in Washington."

106. Barry Provorse, *The PeoplesBank Story* (Bellevue, Wash.: Documentary Book Publishers, 1987), 3.

107. Martin Fitzgerald, ed. *Sixty Milestones of Progress: 1859–1919* (Portland: James, Kerns, and Abbott, 1919); Harold L. Edmunds, "Pioneer Banking Houses of the Dalles, Ore.: 1867–1933: The Story of French and Company and Its Competitors," unpublished

typescript, Oregon Historical Society (ORHS), 2–6; James H. Gilbert, "The Development of Banking in Oregon," 13–15, 27.

108. Throckmorton, "Role of the Merchant on the Oregon Frontier," 549. See also E. Kimbark MacColl and Harry H. Stein, "The Economic Power of Portland's Early Merchants, 1857–1861," *Oregon Historical Quarterly*, Summer 1988, 117–156. MacColl and Stein accept Throckmorton's mercantilist assertion that "gold that might have been used for greater development of the territory was exported in sizeable quantities" by the early merchants (quoted in ibid., 118). Exactly how a raw territory could benefit from the abundant gold without exchanging it for a convenient circulating medium and items such as tools, saddles, plows, steam engines must have escaped the early merchants.

109. Elwyn B. Robinson, *History of North Dakota* (Lincoln: University of Nebraska Press, 1966), 31.

110. Harry N. Scheiber, *Ohio Canal Era, 1820–1861* (Athens, Ohio: Ohio University, 1969); Albert Fishlow, *American Railroads and the Transformation of the Antebellum Economy* (Cambridge, Mass.: Harvard University Press, 1965); Carter Goodrich, ed., *Canals and American Economic Development* (New York: Columbia University Press, 1961); idem., *Government Promotion of American Canals and Railroads, 1800–1890* (New York: Columbia University Press, 1960); Robert W. Fogel, *Railroads and American Economics Growth: Essays in Econometric History* (Baltimore: Johns Hopkins University Press, 1964).

111. Harry N. Scheiber, Harold G. Vatter, Harold Underwood Faulkner, *American Economic History*, 9th ed. (New York: Harper & Row, 1976), 154.

112. Charles Schultz, "Hayne's Magnificent Dream: Factors Which Influenced the Efforts to Join Cincinnati and Charleston by Railroad, 1835–1860" (Ph.D. diss., Ohio State University, 1966); Schweikart, *Banking in the American South*, 225–26.

113. See for example, Vincent C. Carosso, *The Morgans: Private International Bankers, 1854–1913* (Cambridge, Mass.: Harvard University Press, 1987), 95, 98–99, 101–2; Jeffrey Williamson, "Watersheds and Turning Points: Conjectures on the Long Term Impact of Civil War Financing," *Journal of Economic History* 34 (September 1974): 636–61; Stephen Salsbury, "The Effects of the Civil War on American Industrial Development," in *The Economic Impact of the American Civil War*, ed. Ralph Andreano (Cambridge, Mass.: Schenkman Publishing Co., 1962), 161–68; Harry N. Scheiber, "Economic Change in the Civil War Era," *Civil War History* 21 (1965): 396–411; and Allan Nevins, *The Ordeal of the Union: The War for the Union*, 2 vols. (New York: Scribner, 1960 [orig. pub. 1959]).

2. SYMBOLS OF SAFETY

1. Lewis Atherton, "The Pioneer Merchant in Mid-America," in *The Changing Economic Order: Readings in American Business and Economic History*, ed. Alfred D. Chandler, Jr., Stuart Bruchey, and Louis Galambos (New York: Harcourt Brace & World, 1968), 113–24. See also David Dary, *Entrepreneurs of the Old West* (New York: Knopf, 1986).

2. *Franklin Missouri Intelligencer*, July 16, 1821.

3. Erickson, "Money and Banking in a 'Bankless' State," 171–91 (quotation on p. 173); Hoyt Sherman, "Early Banking in Iowa," *Annals of Iowa* 5 (1901): 1–13; "List of the Private Bankers in the Principal Cities and Towns of the United States," *Banker's Magazine*, n.s. 5 (1855): 471–72.

4. The most important article on the effects of these laws remains Paul Wallace Gates, "The Role of the Land Spectator in Western Development," *The Pennsylvania Magazine of History and Biography* (July 1942): 314–33; idem, "The Homestead Law in an Incongruous Land System," *American Historical Review* 41 (July 1936): 652–81; and Allan Bogue and Margaret Bogue, "Profits and the Frontier Land Speculator," *Journal of Economic History* 17 (March

1957): 1–24. In contrast to Gates, Ray A. Billington's "The Origin of the Land Speculator as a Frontier Type," (*Agricultural History* 19 [October 1945]: 204–11) saw the speculator as important to frontier development, and not always coming out ahead. See also Shaw Livermore, *Early American Land Companies* (Princeton: Princeton University Press, 1939).

5. *Summer [Kansas] Gazette*, April 8 and May 15, 1858.

6. Cyrus K. Holliday to wife, March 18, 1855, "Letters of Cyrus Kurtz Holliday, 1854–1859," *Kansas Historical Quarterly* 6 (August 1937): 241–94 (quotation on p. 256).

7. *Freedom's Champion*, April 23, 1859; *Emporia News*, May 26, July 7, 1860.

8. This is Gates's position in the "Role of the Land Speculator in Western Development." See also Theodore Salutos, "Land Policy and Its Relation to Agricultural Production and Distribution, 1862–1933," *Journal of Economic History* 22 (December 1962): 445–60 for similar sentiments.

9. See Bogue and Bogue, "Profits and the Land Speculator."

10. Edward H. Rastatter, "Nineteenth Century Public Land Policy: The Case for the Speculator," in *Essays in Nineteenth Century Economic History: The Old Northwest*, ed. David C. Klingaman and Richard K. Vedder (Athens: Ohio University Press, 1975), 118–37 (quotation on p. 135). See also Peter D. McClelland, "New Perspectives on the Disposal of Western Lands in Nineteenth Century America," *Business History Review* 42 (Spring 1969): 77–83.

11. Similar charges of exorbitant rates charged to sharecroppers in the postbellum South were, according to one small sample, totally justified by risk. See, for the argument on exorbitant rates, Roger L. Ransom and Richard Sutch, *One Kind of Freedom: The Economic Consequences of Emancipation* (Cambridge: Cambridge University Press, 1977), 130–31; and for the refutation, see Schweikart, *Banking in the American South*, 199–201.

12. *Elmwood Free Press*, June 9, 1860.

13. W. Turrentine Jackson, "Wells Fargo: Symbol of the Wild West?" *Western Historical Quarterly* 3 (April 1972): 179–96 (quotation on p. 180).

14. Erickson, "Money and Banking in a 'Bankless' State," 175.

15. Edward H. Stiles, *Recollections and Sketches of Notable Lawyers and Public Men of Early Iowa. . . .* (Des Moines: The Homestead Publishing Co., 1916), 128–29; idem, *Portrait and Biographical Album of Jefferson and Van Buren Counties, Iowa. . . .* (Chicago: Lake City Publishing Co., 1890), 282–83; idem, *History of Lucas County* (Des Moines: State Historical Company, 1881), 673–74.

16. Erickson, "Money and Banking in a 'Bankless' State," 181.

17. Stiles, *Recollections and Sketches*, 124–29.

18. Erickson, "Money and Banking in a 'Bankless' State," 181. Bray Hammond's explanation—that the Democrats succumbed to the "pressure and temptations of enterprise"—hardly explained the confusion within the Democratic party over money from the 1830s through the 1890s (*Banks and Politics*, 625). Another approach is offered in Larry Schweikart, "Jacksonian Ideology, Currency Control, and 'Central' Banking: A Reappraisal" (*The Historian*, November 1988, 78–102), in which the inherent centralizing dynamic within the Democratic party is discussed.

19. Julius Sterling Morton, *Illustrated History of Nebraska: A History of Nebraska from the Earliest Explorations of the Trans-Mississippi Region* (Lincoln: Jacob North Company, 1905–13) 2: passim.

20. Ruth Gallaher, "Money in Pioneer Iowa, 1838–1855," *Iowa Journal of History and Politics*, 33 (1934): 27–28; H. W. Lathrop, "Some Iowa Bank History," *Iowa Historical Record* 8 (1897): 59–60.

21. Morton, *Illustrated History of Nebraska*, 2: 3–4; J. F. McClain, "Beginnings," pamphlet in Nebraska State Historical Society (NHS), 1952, 3–4. The legislature contemplated "not less than fifteen new banks" during this period (ibid., 3).

22. R. Mickel to Cook, Sargent and Downey, February 6, 1857, Cook, Sargent, and Downey Papers, Iowa Historical Society (IHS).

23. Luther A. Brewer and Barthinius A. Wick, *History of Linn County, Iowa* (Cedar Rapids: Torch Press, 1911), 439; Robert P. Swierenga, *Pioneers and Profits: Land Speculation on the Iowa Frontier* (Ames: Iowa State University Press, 1968), 109–10. Swierenga found that speculators made much higher rates of profit on frontier lands than the Bogues found, but these profits reflected an attempt by "nonbank" lenders to avoid Iowa's 10-percent usury law. Even so, the rates he reports can be explained by risk (see note 11 above).

24. Erickson, "Money and Banking in a 'Bankless' State," 183.

25. Ibid.; Howard H. Preston, *History of Banking in Iowa* (Iowa City: State Historical Society, 1922), 63; Addison E. Sheldon, *Nebraska, the Land and the People* (Chicago: Lewis Publishing Co., 1931), 1: 274.

26. Morton, *Illustrated History of Nebraska*, 2: 26; Erickson, "Money and Banking in a 'Bankless' State," 183–84.

27. Preston, *History of Banking in Iowa*, 63–64; Sheldon, *Nebraska*, 1: 274.

28. Lathrop, "Some Iowa Bank History," 60; Morton, *Illustrated History of Nebraska*, 11, 26.

29. For comparative behavior of banks, see Hugh Rockoff, *The Free Banking Era: A Reexamination* (New York: Arno Press, 1975) and Charles W. Calomiris and Larry Schweikart, "Regulations and Markets as Determinants of the Performance and Vulnerability of Antebellum Banks" (paper presented at the annual meeting of the American Economic Association, Chicago, December 1987, in authors' possession).

30. Erickson, "Money and Banking in a 'Bankless' State," 189–91.

31. Ralph Emerson Twitchell, *Leading Facts of New Mexican History* (Cedar Rapids, Iowa: The Torch Press, 1917), 5: 29; Ralph V. Edgel, *A Brief History of Banking in New Mexico, 1870–1959*, Bureau of Business Research Series, no. 39 (Albuquerque: University of New Mexico, 1962), 4–5. See also Paul A. F. Walter, "New Mexico's Pioneer Bank and Bankers," *New Mexico Historical Review* 21 (July 1946): 209–25; and idem, *Banking in New Mexico Before the Railroad Came!* (New York: Newcomen Society, 1955).

32. Larry Schweikart, "Early Banking in New Mexico from the Civil War to the Roaring Twenties," *New Mexico Historical Review* 63 (January 1988): 1–24.

33. As Hugh Rockoff notes, several states had adopted free banking, including many that fared well in the panic of 1857. See his *Free Banking Era*, and compare with Charles W. Calomiris and Larry Schweikart, "Was the South Backward?: North/South Differences in Antebellum Banking During Normalcy and Crisis" (Federal Reserve Bank of Chicago, Working Paper, 1989).

34. Arthur Rolnick and Warren Weber, "Explaining the Demand for Free Bank Notes," *Journal of Monetary Economics* 21 (January 1988): 47–71.

35. Sidney Ratner, James H. Soltow, and Richard Sylla, *The Evolution of the American Economy: Growth, Welfare and Decision Making* (New York: Basic Books, 1979), 344–51. See also Phillip Cagan, "The First Fifty Years of the National Banking System—an Historical Appraisal," 15–42.

36. Ratner et al., *Evolution of the American Economy; Veazie Bank* vs. *Fenno*, 8 Wall. 533 (1869), upheld the tax on bank notes. See also *The Seventy-Third Annual Report of the Comptroller of the Currency for the Year Ended October 31, 1935* (Washington: Government Printing Office, 1936), 817–43, which reviews in detail the government acts and summarizes the history of national banks and their notes, and *National Banks of the United States: Their Organization Management and Supervision, 1812–1910* (New York: The National City Bank of New York, 1910).

37. Helen Hill Updike, *The National Banks and American Economic Development, 1870–1900* (New York: Garland Publishing, Inc., 1985), 11, 13.

38. Ibid., 13; Sylla, "American Banking and Economic Growth in the Nineteenth Century," 657–86; Lynne Pierson Doti, "Banking in California: Some Evidence on Structure, 1878–1905" (Ph.D. diss., University of California, Riverside, 1978), 139. Doti notes that the percentage had shrunk throughout California's nineteenth-century banking history. In 1879, 1889, and 1899, banks with more than $50,000 in capital comprised 85 percent, 64 percent, and 55.7 percent, respectively, and the number of private banks with that level of capital was 33 percent (ibid.).

39. These sentiments had become clearer by the time the Populists appeared. See Norman Pollack, *The Populist Response to Industrial America* (Cambridge: Harvard University Press, 1962), 110, for example. Compare these views with those of the Jacksonians in Schweikart, *Banking in the American South*, 11–47, 145–89.

40. Those who see the National Bank Act as restrictive include Richard Sylla, "Federal Policy, Bank Market Structure, and Capital Mobilization in the United States, 1863–1913," *Journal of Economic History* 29 (December 1969): 659–65; Davis, "The Investment Market, 1870–1914: The Evolution of a National Market," 355–99; and John A. James, *Money and Capital Markets in Postbellum America*.

41. Richard H. Keehn and Gene Smiley, "Mortgage Lending by National Banks," *Business History Review* 51 (Winter 1977): 474–91 (quotation on p. 475).

42. *National Banks of the United States*, 47–57, 75–89; *Seventy-Third Report of the Comptroller*, 817–22.

43. Ransom and Sutch, *One Kind of Freedom*, 107–13; Schweikart, *Banking in the American South*, 311–13. See also Sylla, "Federal Policy."

44. Gerald Stanley, "Merchandising in the Southwest: The Mark I. Jacobs Company of Tucson, 1867–1875," *American Jewish Archives* 23 (April 1971): 86–102; William J. Parrish, *The Charles Ilfeld Company: A Study of the Rise and Decline of Merchant Capitalism in New Mexico* (Cambridge, Mass.: Harvard University Press, 1961), chap. 4 and 5.

45. *Tucson Daily Citizen*, October 27, 1929; *Tucson Weekly Arizonian*, January 22, 1870; Stanley, "Merchandising in the Southwest," 90.

46. Richard L. Gordon and Arlene A. Gordon, "The Mark I. Jacobs Family: A Discursive View," *Western States Jewish Quarterly* 13 (January 1981): 99–106; Stanley, "Merchandising in the Southwest," 86–88.

47. Larry Schweikart, "You Count It: The Birth of Banking in Arizona," *Journal of Arizona History*, Autumn 1981, 349–68.

48. Stanley, "Merchandising in the Southwest," 96; Invoice Record, Vols. 8–9, Jacobs Collection, University of Arizona Library (UA), Tucson.

49. Mark Jacobs to Lionel and Barron Jacobs, January 30, 1871, box 1, file 1870–71, Jacobs Collection, UA.

50. Mark Jacobs to Lionel and Barron Jacobs, January 16, 1871, box 1, file 1870–71, Jacobs Collection, UA.

51. Paul Hughes (*Bank Notes* [Phoenix: Phoenician Books, 1971]) and Charles F. Parker ("The Beginnings of Banking in Arizona," *Arizona Highways* 29 [August 1952]: 4–7, 38–39) both accept the position that the Bank of Arizona was the first bank in the territory. Clearly, however, both the Jacobs Company and Lord and Williams could claim that title in all but the most technical sense. See *Fifty Years of Growth in Tucson* (Tucson: Southern Arizona Bank and Trust Co., 1953), 6.

52. *Oklahoma City Daily Oklahoman*, October 23, 1939.

53. Smallwood, *An Oklahoma Adventure*, 7.

54. E. H. Kelley Scrapbook, 1955, Kelley Collection, Oklahoma Historical Society (OHS), Oklahoma City.

55. Smallwood, *An Oklahoma Adventure*, 7.

56. Lyman, *Ralston's Ring;* Tilton, *William Chapman Ralston; Fifty Years of Growth in Tucson,* 6; Schweikart, *History of Banking in Arizona,* 9.

57. Throckmorton, "The Role of the Merchant on the Oregon Frontier," 539–50; James H. Gilbert, "The Development of Banking in Oregon," 5–30; *Portland Oregonian,* December 6, 1851, March 6 and April 13, 1852. See also MacColl and Stein, "The Economic Power of Portland's Early Merchants," 117–56.

58. Wells Fargo History Department, "Wells Fargo Historical Highlights," (pamphlet published by Wells Fargo Bank, 1982), 1–3, provides a very brief overview of that company. More extensive studies include W. Turrentine Jackson, *Wells Fargo Stagecoaching in Montana Territory* (Helena: Montana Historical Society Press, 1979); idem, "A New Look at Wells Fargo, Stagecoaches, and the Pony Express," *California Historical Society Quarterly* 45 (1966): 291–324; idem, "Stages, Mails and Express in Southern California: The Role of Wells, Fargo & Co., in the Pre-Railroad Era," *California Historical Society Quarterly* 56 (1974): 233–72; idem, "Wells Fargo Staging Over the Sierras," *California Historical Society Quarterly* 44 (1970): 99–133; and Edward Hungerford, *Wells Fargo: Advancing the American Frontier* (New York: Random House, 1949).

59. Roscoe P. Conkling and Margaret B. Conkling, *The Butterfield Overland Mail, 1857–1869,* (Glendale, A. H. Clark Co., 1947), 1: 27–41; "John Butterfield," *Dictionary of American Biography,* 3: 374–75.

60. See also the discussion of Butterfield in Rodman W. Paul, *The Far West and the Great Plains in Transition, 1859–1900* (New York: Harper & Row, 1988), 55–56.

61. *Dictionary of American Biography,* 4: 271–72.

62. Ibid., 19: 639–40. See also W. Turrentine Jackson's sketches of Butterfield, Wells, and Fargo in *The Reader's Encyclopedia of the American West,* ed. Howard R. Lamar (New York: Crowell, 1977), 144, 1250, 360–61, respectively.

63. Wells Fargo History Dept., "Wells Fargo Historical Highlights," 3; Paul, *Far West,* 56–57.

64. Jackson, "Stages, Mails and Express," 233.

65. Wells Fargo History Dept., "Wells Fargo Historical Highlights," 4–6.

66. Jackson, "Stages, Mails and Express," 234.

67. Jackson, "New Look at Wells Fargo," 297.

68. Ibid., 296–301.

69. This discussion is taken from Paul, *Far West,* 57–58.

70. Wells Fargo History Dept., "Wells Fargo Historical Highlights," 5.

71. Ibid.

72. Jackson, "Wells Fargo: Symbol of the Wild West?" 181.

73. "D.O. Mills," unpublished typescript, Bancroft Library, University of California, Berkeley.

74. Robert Cleland and Frank Putnam, *Isais Hellman and the Farmers and Merchant Bank* (San Marino, Calif.: Huntington Library, 1965), 15.

75. Earl Pomeroy, *The Pacific Slope: A History of California, Oregon, Washington, Idaho, Utah and Nevada* (New York: Knopf, 1965), 88; Lamar, ed., *Reader's Encyclopedia,* 359.

76. Paul B. Trescott, *Financing American Enterprise,* 80–83.

77. "Merchants National Bank Records," User's Guide, Montana Historical Society Archives (MHS), Helena, Montana.

78. Ibid. To cite just a few other merchant bankers: E. S. Tyler and Company of Fargo and E. J. Lander and Company of Grand Forks, Dakota Territory (Samuel Torgerson, "Early Banking in North Dakota," *The Quarterly Journal of the University of North Dakota* 13 [1922–23]: 283–88); W. C. 'Woodman' Stone of Wichita ("Wichita Banking and How it Grew," *The Wichitan,* October 1978, 22–24); and Thatcher Brothers of Pueblo, Colorado

("The Story of the First National Bank is the Story of Pueblo, Colorado," pamphlet [Pueblo: First National Bank, 1922?]).

79. Background material on the Speigelbergs is found in Floyd S. Fierman, *The Speigelbergs of New Mexico: Merchants and Bankers, 1844–1893* (El Paso: Texas Western College Press, 1964), and William Parish Notebook 2, William Parish Papers, Zimmerman Library, University of New Mexico (UNM), Albuquerque. Parish's compilation of extensive unpublished research on New Mexico banks is contained in notebooks in this collection.

80. Schweikart, "Early Banking in New Mexico," 6.

81. Walter, "New Mexico's Pioneer Bank," 216–17, 219–22; Wayne L. Mauzy, *A Century in Santa Fe: The Story of the First National Bank of Santa Fe* (Santa Fe: Vergara Printing Co., 1970), 10.

82. Walter, "New Mexico's Pioneer Bank," 221–22.

83. Stephen Elkins to Northrup and Chick, April 29, 1872, letterbook 3, First National Bank of Santa Fe Collection, UNM.

84. Stockholder List, January 1, 1880, Chavez Collection, UNM.

85. Willi Speigelberg to Felipe Chavez, January 20, 1879, Chavez Collection, UNM.

86. Stephen Elkins to Northrup and Chick, September 14, 1872, letterbook 3, First National Bank of Santa Fe Collection, UNM.

87. Lehman Speigelberg to Levi Speigelberg, August 31, 1872, and September 14, 1872, Speigelberg letterbook, Second National Bank Collection, Museum of New Mexico (MNM), Santa Fe.

88. Willi Speigelberg to Levi Speigelberg, October 17, 1872, Second National Bank Collection, MNM.

89. Lehman Speigelberg to the comptroller of the currency, August 23, 1872, Second National Bank Collection, MNM.

90. Willi Speigelberg to Levi Speigelberg, October 17, 1872, Speigelberg letterbook, Second National Bank Collection, MNM; Mauzy, *Century in Santa Fe,* 13–14.

91. Cashier's letterbook, November 17, 1874, letterbook 9, First National Bank of Santa Fe Collection, UNM; Schweikart, "Early Banking in New Mexico," 5–7.

92. Felipe Chavez to the comptroller of the currency, May 24, 1894, September 3, 1895, all in Records of the Comptroller of the Currency, National Archives, Washington, D.C. See also A. J. Preston to comptroller, May 23, 1898, and Eugene Fiske to comptroller, January 17, 1905, ibid.

93. Biographical material on the Kountzes comes from Noel, *Growing through History with Colorado.*

94. Lyle W. Dorsett, "Equality of Opportunity on the Urban Frontier: Access to Credit in Denver, Colorado Territory, 1858–1876," in *The Urban West,* ed. Gerald Nash (Manhattan, Kans.: Sunflower University Press, 1979), 9. A good description of R. G. Dun's credit-rating practices in Denver can be found on pp. 75–81.

95. Adams, Dorsett, and Pulcipher, *The Pioneer Western Bank,* 17–19.

96. Skidmore, *Treasure State Treasury,* 9–10. See also Clarence Groth, "Montana Banking History" (Master's thesis, Graduate School of Banking, Ruthers University, 1955).

97. *Arizona Gazette,* May 16 and December 18, 1882; February 20 and November 17, 1882; January 12, 1883.

98. Geoffrey P. Mawn, "Phoenix, Arizona: Central City of the Southwest" (Ph.D. diss., Arizona State University, 1979), 85–89; William J. Murphy to Laura F. Murphy, April 23, 27, 1883, box 2, file 1883, William J. Murphy Collection, Arizona State University Library (ASU); Merwin Murphy, "William John Murphy and the Building of the Arizona Canal," manuscript 1974, William J. Murphy Collection, ASU.

99. William J. Murphy to Laura Murphy, March 29 and 30, 1884, William J. Murphy Collection, ASU.

100. Mawn, "Phoenix, Arizona," 89–90; *Weekly Phoenix Herald*, April 17, 1884; Merwin Murphy, "Murphy and the Building of the Arizona Canal," manuscript 1974, William J. Murphy Collection, ASU, 14; stock certificates of First National Bank of Phoenix, 11, 14, 15, ASU (which show the haste with which the Valley Bank was created—the name "First National Bank" is crossed off and "Valley Bank" written in). See also William Hendricks, *M. H. Sherman: A Pioneer Developer of the Pacific Southwest* (Pasadena: Castle Press for Sherman Foundation, 1973).

101. Kelley Scrapbook, 1948, Kelley Collection, OHS; *Oklahoma Daily Journal*, November 21, 1890; Smallwood, *An Oklahoma Adventure*, 16–17.

102. White, "Financial Frustrations in Territorial Montana," 34–45.

103. *Denver Tribune* quoted in Duane Smith, "The Bank that Built Durango," 1981, pamphlet, CHS, n.p.

104. Throckmorton, "Role of the Merchant," 539–45.

105. H. W. Corbett to Nourse Mason Company, December 11, 1857, Corbett and Failing Papers, University of Oregon (UO); and H. W. Corbett to Croton Manufacturing Co., February 8, 1858, Corbett and Failing Papers, College of the Pacific (CP).

106. Throckmorton, "Role of the Merchant," 549; H. W. Corbett to Charles Pope and C. Holman, June 9, 1862; Failing and Hatt to John A. Hatt, February 25, April 1, June 1 and 12, 1863, all in Corbett and Failing Papers, Oregon Historical Society (ORHS).

107. Failing and Hatt to John A. Hatt, June 1, 1863, Corbett and Failing Papers, ORHS.

108. Gilbert, "Development of Banking in Oregon," 7.

109. Provorse, *The PeoplesBank Story*, 1–5.

110. William B. Moore, "John Henry Dill, 1868–1942," *Chronicles of Oklahoma* 10 (September 1942): 289–91.

111. Woods, *Sometimes the Books Froze*, 20–21.

112. *Wyoming Bankers Association Proceedings of the Fourteenth Annual Convention Held at Laramie, Wyoming, September 19, 1922* (Cheyenne: Wyoming Bankers Association, 1923), n.p.

113. J. H. Triggs, *History of Cheyenne and Northern Wyoming, Embracing the Gold Fields of the Black Hills, Powder River and Big Horn Countries* (Omaha: Herald Printing House, 1876), 15; *Snake River [Wyoming] Press*, November 18, 1982.

114. Woods, *Sometimes the Books Froze*, 18–20.

115. Stucki, *Commercial Banking in Utah*, 10.

116. Arrington, "Banking Enterprises in Utah," 312–34 (esp. p. 322).

117. Ibid., 221–22.

118. Ibid., 322.

119. *Deseret News*, September 27 and 30, 1873; *Salt Lake City Herald*, September 27 and 28, 1873.

120. *Spokane Northwest Mining Truth*, February 16, 1920, 41–42; Arrington, "Banking Enterprises in Utah," 322–23.

121. Thomas McFadden, "Banking in the Boise Region: The Origins of the First National Bank of Idaho," *Idaho Yesterdays* 11 (Spring 1967): 3–17; Arrington, "Banking Enterprises in Utah," 323.

122. McFadden, "Banking in the Boise Region"; Arrington, "Banking Enterprises in Utah," 323.

123. Silas D. Aulls to Ambrose Hewlett, April 21 and 24, 1888, "Misc. Aulls, Silas," KHS.

124. Leipheimer, *The First National Bank of Butte*, 1–18.

125. Skidmore, *Treasure State Treasury*, 16; John Hakula, "Samuel T. Hauser and the Economic Development of Montana" (Ph.D. diss., Indiana University, 1961), 23, 90–95, 108–17.

126. Harry R. Stevens, "Bank Enterprisers in a Western Town, 1815–1822," *Business*

History Review, 29 (1955): 139–56 (quotation on p. 145). Innumerable other examples of this pattern exist for the West. For examples in South Dakota, see Judith Barjenbruch, "The First National Bank of Vermillion, 1875–1937" (Master's thesis, University of South Dakota, 1975), 1–2.

127. Ira Cross, *Financing an Empire*, 1: 38; Smallwood, *An Oklahoma Adventure*, 18.

128. First National Bank of Helena Records, User's Guide, MHS.

129. *Oklahoma City Daily Oklahoman*, April 23, 1939.

130. Woods, *Sometimes the Books Froze*, 19; Floyd Fierman, "Jewish Pioneering in the Southwest," *Arizona and the West* 2 (Spring 1960): 54–72; Ernest J. Hopkins, *Financing the Frontier* (Phoenix: Arizona Printers, 1950), 10, 13.

131. Jesse N. Smith, "Diary" and "The Story of the . . . Bank of Northern Arizona," both in AHS; Noel, *Growing through History*, 1.

132. Woods, *Sometimes the Books Froze*, 36.

133. Exchange Bank Memobook, Ledgerbook, February 20, 1896, Archives, OHS; E. W. Jones, *Early Day History of Perry, Oklahoma* (Perry, Oklahoma: n.p., 1931), 13.

134. Driscoll, *The Black Hills of South Dakota*, 9; A. B. Cahalan, *Territorial Banking in Hand County, South Dakota* (Omaha: Cockle Printing Co., n.d. [1956]), 6.

135. *Albuquerque Morning Democrat*, June 26, 1890, box 1, folder 72, "Business Misc.," Chavez Collection, UNM. The choice of words is illuminating: how often did newspapers mention the floor or fixtures of a new general store?

136. *Denver Republican* quoted in Noel, *Growing through History*, 28.

137. *Prescott [Arizona] Weekly Miner*, September 3, 1877.

138. Adams, Dorsett, and Pulcipher, *Pioneer Western Bank*, 4, 13.

139. Nancy Avery, "Wichita Banking and How it Grew," *The Wichitan*, October 1978, 22–24 (photo on p. 22).

140. See photo in Skidmore, *Treasure State Treasury*, 27.

141. Anne Bloomfield, "David Farquharson, Pioneer California Architect," *California History* 59 (1980): 16–33; *Articles of Incorporation and Conditions of Agreement with Depositors [of the California Savings and Loan Society]* (San Francisco, 1873).

142. Clarke, *William Tecumseh Sherman*, 26.

143. *Pueblo Chieftan* quoted in "The Story of the First National Bank," pamphlet, 7–8. Compare with the descriptions of hundreds of other banks in the West, for example, Bohm and Aub in Helena: "elegant furniture . . . [rooms] fitted in a luxurious manner. . . ." *Helena Weekly Herald*, June 18, 1868.

144. See the photo of the Bank of Arizona in Schweikart, *Banking in Arizona*, 16.

145. Information on James King of William appears in Cross, *Financing an Empire*, 58–61. Again, reports emphasizing fireproofing are universal.

146. Soule, Gihon, and Nisbet, *Annals*, 329.

147. Noel, *Growing through History*, 28. It should be noted, though, that by the time the bank purchased its building, its assets totaled $2 million.

148. "The Story of the First National Bank," pamphlet, 11.

149. Willson, *400 California Street*, 26, 29.

150. Cara McFarland, *The United States National Bank of Portland, Oregon* (Portland: Binfords & Mort, Publishers, 1942), 14.

151. Clarke, *William Tecumseh Sherman*, 18.

152. "The Story of the National Bank," 5–6.

153. Theo Ackerman, "Reminiscences of Banking in the Early Days of Russell County," manuscript, KHS.

154. White, "Financial Frustrations in Territorial Montana," 34–45.

155. Christopher Nelson, "Bank Architecture in the West," *Journal of the West* 23 (April 1984): 77–87 (quotation on p. 82). Although its location only a few miles on the other side of the Kansas border technically puts Asa Beebe Cross's Bank of Commerce in Kansas City

out of our definition of the West, this 1883 bank clearly was illustrative of "western" banks. Built at a cost of $40,000, the bank "quickly became and remained for many years a city landmark." See George Ehrlich, "The Bank of Commerce by Asa Beebe Cross: 'A Building of the Latest Architecture,'" *Journal of the Society of Architectural Historians* 43 (1984): 168–72 (quotation on p. 170). For another bank exterior in Billings (1891), see Skidmore, *Treasure State Treasury*, 45.

156. "Bank Architecture in New York," *Bankers Magazine*, February 1855, 582.

157. A. C. David, "Private Residence for Banking Firms," *Architectural Record*, July 1903, 13–28.

158. *Vermillion [South Dakota] Dakota Residence*, February 17, 1876.

159. See the comments of A. B. Robbs, Jr., (in Larry Schweikart, *That Quality Image: The History of Continental Bank* [Tappan, N.Y.: Custombook, 1988], 59), responding to criticism in the *Arizona Republic*, April 30, 1980, and January 28, 1981; and in *Scottsdale Magazine*, Fall 1981. The value of the bank's furnishings appear in Sotheby's Appraisal, May 31, 1985, Financial Center File, boxes 16, 19–20, Continental Bank Archives, Chase Bank, Scottsdale, Arizona.

160. Nelson, "Bank Architecture in the West," 77–87. Although the period is somewhat later than that under discussion, the same attitudes applied in Montana bank design between 1910 and 1922. See "Solid, Safe, and Secure: Country Banks in Montana," *Montana: The Magazine of Western History* 36 (Spring 1986): 77–79.

161. Philip Sawyer, "The Planning of Bank Buildings," *The Architectural Review* 12 (1905): 24–31.

162. Willson, *400 California Street*, photo on p. 24; photo in "Fifty Years of Progress: The Golden Anniversary of the Establishment of Credit in Seattle, 1870–1920," pamphlet (Seattle: Dexter Horton N. B., n.d.) Seattle Public Library.

163. See photo in Schweikart, *A History of Banking in Arizona*, 16; Neil M. Loomis, sketch in *Wells Fargo* (New York: Bramhall House, 1968), 95; and Theodore Davie, "San Diego Trust & Savings Bank: A Well-Known Member of the Community for Ninety-Five Years," *Journal of San Diego History* 30 (1984): n.p. Cross's Bank of Commerce in Kansas City, Missouri, also featured this design. See Ehrlich, "Bank of Commerce," 171. Note that while the photo in Schweikart is dated circa 1898, the interior of the banking house that it depicts had been standing for roughly twenty years. The photo of the San Diego Trust and Savings is dated 1889. The Parrott Building, designed by John Parrott, was possibly the first stone building in San Francisco. Reportedly, the stone was cut in China and sent to San Francisco with instructions for assembly. The Chinese unfortunately had cut the stone according to their own strong traditions, and when San Francisco Chinese found the site did not suit the design, they would not help build it. Parrott completed the building, but had to have it "exorcised" before Chinese would enter it. (Hungerford, Edward, *Wells Fargo: Advancing the American Frontier* [New York: Random House, 1949], 13.)

164. Wim de Wit, "The Banks and the Image of Progressive Banking," in *Louis Sullivan: The Function of Ornament*, ed. Wim de Wit (New York: Chicago Historical Society, the Saint Louis Art Museum, and W. W. Norton & Company, 1986); Robert Twombly, *Louis Sullivan: His Life and Work* (New York: Elisabeth Sifton Books, 1986), 410–17, 421, 426–27. For pictures of vaults, see the First Bank of California and the Dexter Horton bank mentioned in note 162. See also William T. Morgan, "Strongboxes on Main Street: Prarie Style Banks," *Landscape* 24 (1980): 35–40; and Cross, *Financing an Empire*, 1: 39, which lists the companies that had safes used for deposit purposes at the time of liquidation. Pictures of the vault, and banks' interiors in general, appear in Skidmore, *Treasure State Treasury*, 27, 59, 71. See especially pp. 59 and 71, with the vaults in view.

165. de Wit, "Banks and the Image of Progressive Banking"; Twombly, *Louis Sullivan*, 410–17, 421, 426–27.

166. *Ruby City [Idaho] Owyhee Avalanche*, June 9, 1866. Other ads or photographs of

typical ads can be found in box 6, "Advertisement" folder, First National Bank of Santa Fe Collection, UNM; *Albuquerque Morning Democrat*, June 26, 1890. Note that virtually all photographs of banks focus on either the vault area or the outside facade of the building.

167. Marshall Sprague, *First Century at the First* (n.p., 1973), 3.

168. Ibid., 7.

169. The *Pueblo [Colorado] Chieftan*, quoted in "Story of the First National Bank," pamphlet, 4. A closeup 1886 photo of the vault in First National Bank of Great Falls appears in Skidmore, *Treasure State Treasury*, 41; as does a 1907 photo of the new vault for the State Savings Bank of Butte being pulled by a team of fourteen horses (p. 54).

170. Cahalan, *Territorial Banking in Hand County*, 4.

171. Newspaper clipping in Cook, Sargent, and Parker papers, box 1, series 4, folder 3, NSHS. See also the *Arkansas Gazette*, June 19, 1839, and October 30, 1839, for similar reports by frontier Arkansas banks.

172. Harold R. Edmonds, "Pioneer Banking Houses of the Dalles, Ore. 1867–1933: The Story of French and Company and its Competitors," typescript (n.d.), p. 2, OHS.

173. Burt Brown Barker, "Early History: The First National Bank of Portland, Ore.," typescript (1941), p. 23, OHS.

174. Clarke, *William Tecumseh Sherman*, 26.

175. Silas D. Aulls to Ambrose Hewlett, December 23, 1888, "Misc. Aulls, Silas," KHS.

176. Clarke, *William Tecumseh Sherman*, 26.

177. R. L. Clarke to Cook and Sargent, September 6, 1854, Cook, Sargent & Parker Papers, box 1, series 1, folder 1, NSHS.

178. Photo (circa 1984) in author's possession.

179. James and James, *Biography of a Bank*, 44; Twombly, *Louis Sullivan*, 410–11.

180. H. L. Sherman, *A History of Newport Beach* (Newport Beach: City of Newport Beach, 1931), 112.

181. Schweikart, *A History of Banking in Arizona*, 19; John and Lillian Theobald, *Wells Fargo in Arizona Territory*, ed. Bert Fireman, (Tempe: Arizona Historical Foundation, 1978); material on Nevada robberies was furnished by Nevada national bank historian Douglas McDonald in correspondence to the authors. The advent of the automobile increased the vulnerability of country banks to robbers, especially in the Midwest. See L. Edge, *Run the Cat Roads: A True Story of Bank Robberies in the 1930's* (New York: Dembrer Books, 1981).

182. This discussion is taken from the "Dalton Gang," in Lamar, ed., *Reader's Encyclopedia*, 285–286.

183. Adams, Dorsett, and Pulcipher, *Pioneer Western Bank*, 76–79.

184. Moses B. Hazeltine to A. C. Cook Commercial Mining Co., Lewis Collection, First National [now First Interstate] Bank Collection. Since this writing, the collection has been transferred to Northern Arizona University, Flagstaff, and recatalogued.

185. Hughes, *Bank Notes*, 16; *Helena Weekly Herald*, July 15, 1869, cited in Skidmore, *Treasure State Treasury*, 20.

186. On the Baum and Aub scandal, see Wall, "Gold Dust and Greenbacks," 24–31, 63.

187. General patterns of banking procedure are discussed in A. B. Johnson, *A Treatise on Banking: The Duties of A Banker and His Personal Requests Therefore* (New York: Greenwood Press, 1968 [orig. pub. 1850]; and are also seen in discussions in Schweikart, *Banking in the American South*, 83–84, 88–90, 190–212.

188. Barrows, Millard and Company to David Moffat, September 20, 1861, collection 598, Agnes Wright Spring Papers, CHS.

189. Eugene Kelly to Donohoe, Kelly and Company, telegram, October 1, 1864, MSS JL2/1/2 and JL2/1/3, Stanford University Library.

190. See the letterbooks of the Second National Bank, Second National Bank Collection, MNM; Noel, *Growing through History*, 1–38; and Murphy, "William John Murphy," passim.

191. Silas D. Aulls to Ambrose Hewlett, April 24, 1888, June 3, 1889, May 15, 1888, and May 23, 1888, "Misc. Aulls, Silas," KHS.

192. J. Rogers to H. C. Harrison, December 30, 1881, and February 3, 1882; Harrison Papers, KHS.

193. Joseph Leet to J. K. Caulkins, June 17, 1887, Warwick Downing Papers, CHS.

194. Joseph Leet to M. T. Kendall, June 18, 1887; to T. V. Munson, June 24, 1887; and to aunt, June 17, 1887, all in ibid.

195. Joseph Leet to C. F. Maurer, January 23, 1888, ibid.

196. Dorsett, "Equality of Opportunity"; Skidmore, *Treasure State Treasury*, 20.

197. Lee M. Ford, "Bob Ford, Sun River Cowman," *Montana: The Magazine of Western History* 18 (Spring 1967): 30–43.

198. B. F. White quoted in Skidmore, *Treasure State Treasury*, 20; *Montana Banker*, August 1932, 15.

199. Isaac Moore to his brother, September 3, 1866, Montana Historical Society, quoted in Skidmore, *Treasure State Treasury*, 11.

200. J. A. Graves, *My Seventy Years in California* (Los Angeles: Times Mirror Press, 1927), 317–19.

201. Claude Singer, *U.S. National Bank of Oregon and U.S. Bancorp, 1891–1904* (Portland: U.S. Bancorp, 1984), 7. For a recollection of life as a small-town bank teller, see Thomas Ryan Riley, *Things to Remember: Recollections of a Long Life* (Fond du Lac, Wisc.: Badger Freund, Inc., n.d.), in NSHS.

202. Records of Donohue Kelly Banking Company, "Records 1863–1919," box JL2 448, Stanford University Library.

203. S. B. Wheelock to Felipe Chavez, May 28, 1872, quoted in Parish Notebook 3, 1872, William Parish Papers, UNM; William Sherman to Lucas-Turner Bank of St. Louis, quoted in Clarke, *William Tecumsch Sherman*, 239.

204. Lionel Jacobs to Selim M. Franklin, November 1, November 5, and December 12, 1887, box 2, file 1887–1891, Franklin Collection, UA.

205. Larry Schweikart, "Frontier Banking in Colorado: A New Perspective on Public Confidence and Regulation, 1862–1907," *Essays and Monographs in Colorado History* 8 (Fall 1988): 15–33; Herbert O. Brayer, "Boom Town Banker", *Bulletin of the Business History Society*, 19 (1945): 27–30 (another version of this article appeared in the *Westerners Brand Book*, vol. 3 [Denver: Denver Posse of Westerners, 1947], which includes crucial entries that the history society version omitted]; Neil King, "History of Banking in Denver, Colorado, 1858–1950," (Master's thesis, Graduate School of Banking, Rutgers University, 1952), 17–60.

206. Hughes, *Bank Notes*, 17; Speech by Will Hazeltine, July 13, 1873, in First Interstate Bank Collection, Lewis Collection, Northern Arizona University; and Larry Schweikart interview with Sherman Hazeltine, May 20, 1980.

207. Cashier, November 6 and December 7, 1872, letterbook 6, First National Bank of Santa Fe Collection, UNM.

208. Willi to J. W. Seligman, November 4, 1872, and to Levi Speigelberg, November 2 and 6, and December 7, 1872, all in Second National Bank Collection, MNM.

209. Lionel Jacobs to Mark I. Jacobs, April 5, June 28, February 22, 1879, Bound Letters, vol. 78, Jacobs Collection, UA; and Pima County Bank to Martin Kales, April 23, 1880, vol. 79, Jacobs Collection, UA.

210. Material on Palen is found in the R. J. Palen letterbook, cited and copied in the William Parish notebook 2, Parish Papers, First National Bank of Santa Fe Collection, UNM. See cashier's letters of April 17, 1879, April 26, 1882, October 11 and 17, 1883 therein; and Stephen Elkins to R. J. Palen, August 8, 1878, letterbook 19, cashier's letters of November 20, December 4, 1878, letterbook 20, First National Bank of Santa Fe Collection, UNM.

211. Cashier's letters, November 11, 1879, October 11, 17, 1883, November 24, 1884, Palen letterbook cited in Parish notebook 2, Parish Papers, UNM.

212. Cashier's letters of April 4, 1884, February 22, 1887, December 31, 1888, June 12, 1884, ibid. See also Mauzy, *A Century in Santa Fe,* 17.

213. Tilton, *William Chapman Ralston,* 384–85.

214. Resolution, n.d., Minutes of the Board of Directors, Minutebook, City Bank of Leadville, CHS.

215. Minutes of meetings, June 9, 1882, January 8, 9, March 24, 28, April 18, 19, 26, June 9, September 17, 1883, January 16, 1884, (quotation from January 9, 1883 meeting), all in ibid. Howell, according to the minutes of the January 8, 1883, meeting, was entrusted with funds totaling $18,000 from an Ohio bank for use in purchasing securities at Gilman Sims in New York, but did not do so.

216. C. C. Davis, the new president, and D. A. Crowell, the vice president, became the executors of assignment (Minutes of the Board of Directors, January 16, 1884, ibid.)

217. Minutes of the Board of Directors of the Denver National Bank, July 6, 1882–January 12, 1892, various dates, Denver National Bank Minutebook, CHS.

218. *The Laramie Boomarang,* October 17, 1891.

219. Appendix tables 1 and 2 capture some of those statistics collected by government agencies.

220. Alfred D. Chandler, *Visible Hand: The Managerial Revolution in American Business* (Harvard: Belknap, 1977).

3. CONTROLLING THE "INJUDICIOUS BANKER"

1. Gabriel Kolko, *Railroads and Regulation, 1872–1916* (Princeton: Princeton University Press, 1965).

2. Morton Albaugh, "The Injudicious Banker and How to Control Him," *Kansas Bankers Association Proceedings of the Sixteenth Annual Meeting* (1903), 64–65.

3. Naomi Lamoreaux, in a manuscript, "From Entrepreneurs to Bankers: The Professionalization of Banking in Late Nineteenth Century New England," generously made available to the authors, has noted that in the early to mid-nineteenth century similar changes swept through New England Banks. Those institutions, frequently founded for the specific purpose of lending to the businesses of the directors or officers, curtailed such activity as they came to rely less on the capital of the founders and more on the funds of depositors for lending. Also see her papers "Institutional Form and Economic Performance: New England Banking in the Late Nineteenth Century" and "Banks and Insider Lending in Jacksonian New England: A Window on Social Structure and Values," in the authors' files, as well as her article "Banks, Kinship, and Economic Development: The New England Case," *Journal of Economic History* 46 (September 1986): 647–67.

4. Albaugh, "Injudicious Banker," 68.

5. *Banker's Almanac,* December 1855, 468–75; John Jay Knox, *A History of Banking in the United States* (New York: Augustus M. Kelley, 1969 [orig. pub. 1903]), 843; Cross, *Financing an Empire,* 1: 39–41.

6. J. Rogers to H. C. Harrison, Harrison Papers, KHS.

7. Albaugh, "Injudicious Banker," 68.

8. Johnson, *A Treatise on Banking,* 26, 31, 33, 43–44.

9. Herbert O. Brayer, "Boom Town Banker—Central City, Colorado, 1880," *Bulletin of the Business Historical Society* 19 (June 1945): 67–95. Another version of this article, but edited differently by retaining critical passages (as will be seen below) appears in the *Western Brand Book,* vol. 3 (Denver: Denver Posse of Westerners, 1947). This version will be cited as "Boom Town Banker [2]", and the *BBHS* version will be cited as "Brom Town Banker [1]."

10. Ibid. [1], 72.

11. Ibid. [2], 32.

12. Ibid. [1], 72–74.

13. Ibid., 74–75.

14. Ibid. [2], p. 37, 40–41. Kimber and Fullerton was a partnership formed to exploit mining claims and leases. Fullerton was also a director of the bank.

15. Judith Millar Barjenbruch, "The First National Bank of Vermillion, 1875–1937" (Master's thesis, University of South Dakota, 1975), 17.

16. Estimates of the number of banks in each state are provided in Appendix table 1. Kuhn, *History of Nebraska Banking*, 9–11; Mabel Frances Neal, "The History of Banking in Nebraska, 1854–1889" (Master's thesis, University of Nebraska, 1933), 45, 77, 80–81; Emmett John Vaughn, "Capital Accumulation in Nebraska Since 1854" (Ph.D. diss., University of Nebraska, 1964), 86.

17. Kuhn, *History of Nebraska Banking*, 11.

18. Robertson, *The Comptroller and State Supervision*, 71, 77.

19. William B. Thorpe, Diary and Examiner's Books, box 1, folder 1, MS. 3638. NSHS, Lincoln. All references that follow are taken from the examination book, which, although not paginated, is alphabetized by bank name.

20. Walter Fulkerson to Charles Sumner Jobes, October 29, 1901 [? date obscured], Jobes Correspondence and Miscellaneous Papers, KHS.

21. Chester Long to Charles Sumner Jobes, March 21, 1901, ibid. Jobes's remarkable brother, Andrew, had been cashier at the Mississippi bank, then purchased it from Charles. A telegrapher who had worked with railroads, Andrew organized and managed the Attica State Bank from 1885 to 1887; was vice president and then controlling partner in the Kansas National Bank of Wichita; founded the Bank of Commerce in Wichita (changed in 1889 to National Bank of Commerce); moved to Kansas City, Missouri, in 1908 as president of First National Bank; was a director of Citizens National Bank in Fort Scott; and organized Santana [Kansas] National Bank in 1913 and Elkhart [Kansas] State Bank in 1915. See the biographical sketch, ibid., taken from W. E. Connelley, *Kansas and Kansans*, 1918 ed., KHS.

22. Grant S. Youmans, *Legalized Bank Robbery* (Minot, N. Dak.: Grant S. Youmans, 1914), 40.

23. Charles Dawes to Charles Sumner Jobes, May 22, 1899, ibid.

24. Cahalan, *Territorial Banking in Hand County*, 4; Barjenbruch, "First National Bank of Vermillion" (Master's thesis), 3.

25. Youmans, *Legalized Bank Robbery*. Eventually, Youmans who claimed his bank was closed in retaliation for his support of a local union, concluded that the only way to have banks that would serve the public would be if the U.S. government owned all banks (p. 112). Yet when the federal agencies got more deeply involved in bank regulation during the Great Depression, bankers complained even more bitterly than ever that the regulators played politics with banks.

26. *Vermillion [South Dakota] Dakota Republican*, March 22, 1877.

27. Barjenbruch, "First National Bank of Vermillion" (Master's thesis), 4, 12.

28. Mortgage Records of Clay County, South Dakota, books E and F.

29. Barjenbruch, "First National Bank of Vermillion" (Master's thesis), 6.

30. Glenn H. Miller, Jr., "The Hawkes Papers: A Case Study of a Kansas Mortgage Brokerage Business, 1871–1888," *Business History Review* 32 (Summer 1958): 293–310.

31. C. M. Hawkes to Rebecca Clarke, June 8, 1875, Hawkes Papers, KHS.

32. Miller, "Hawkes Papers," 300–302, 307.

33. H. Peers Brewer, "Eastern Money and Western Mortgages in the 1870s," *Business History Review* 50 (Autumn 1976): 356–80.

34. James H. Thomas, *The Fourth: A History of the Fourth National Bank and Trust*

Company (Wichhita: Fourth National Bank and Trust Company and the Center for Entrepreneurship and Small Business Management, Wichita State University, 1980), 10. See also Keehn and Smiley, "Mortgage Lending by National Banks," 474–91.

35. Lynne Pierson Doti, "Banking in California: Some Evidence on Structure, 1878–1905" (Ph.D. diss., University of California, Riverside, 1978), 114–35, 375–80.

36. E. Kimbark MacColl, *The Growth of a City: Power and Politics in Portland, Oregon, 1915–1950* (Portland: Georgian Books, 1979), p. 67–69; E. Kimbark MacColl, *The Shaping of a City: Business and Politics in Portland, Oregon, 1885–1915* (Portland: Georgian Press, 1976), 82.

37. Farmers and Merchants Bank, Record Book, MS. 10272, North Dakota Historical Society (NDHS), Bismarck.

38. Floyd S. Fierman, *The Speigelbergs of New Mexico, Merchant Bankers of Early Santa Fe, 1844–1893* (El Paso: Texas Western College, 1964), 33–34.

39. Jno. H. Charles to T. C. Powers, April 20, 1897, "Powers, T. C.," box 5, Isaac Post Baker Papers, NDHS. These papers were being catalogued and indexed at the time of this writing, and the archivists who permitted research in the collection advised that some box numbers may change.

40. Letterbook 12, First National Bank of Santa Fe Collection, UNM. See entries for May 26 and June 29, 1876.

41. Ibid., September 25 and November 6, 1876.

42. Adams, Dorsett, Pulcipher, *The Pioneer Western Bank*, 38.

43. See, for example, William G. Robbins, "The 'Plundered Province' Thesis and the Recent Historiography of the American West," *Pacific Historical Review* 55 (November 1986): 577–97; and Richard D. Lamm and Michael McCarthy, *The Angry West: A Vulnerable Land and Its Future* (Boston: Houghton-Mifflin, 1982). Lamm's vision of the future while he served as governor of Colorado became so dismal that even the highly biased television news show "60 Minutes" referred to him as "Governor Gloom."

44. These were important services, as judged by citizens' complaints in the *Vermillion [South Dakota] Dakota Republican*, April 20, 1882; May 14, 1885; January 14, April 19, and July 15, 1886; and January 2, 1890.

45. *Minutes of the Common Council of the City of Phoenix*, December 12, 1884.

46. Clarke, *William Tecumseh Sherman*, 60; MacColl, *Shaping of a City*, 275. The Portland Railway Company had a bonded debt of $812,000.

47. Fitzgerald, ed., *Sixty Milestones of Progress*, 60; MacColl, *Shaping of a City*, 181.

48. Burt Brown Barker, "Early History of the First National Bank of Oregon," typescript, 1941, p. 62 OHS; MacColl, *Shaping of a City*, 166–68.

49. Material on Hunter appears in Adams, Dorsett, and Pulcipher, *Pioneer Western Bank*; and the Absalom Hunter Papers, CHS.

50. Absalom V. Hunter to Charles Cavender, March 17, 1910, Absalom Hunter Papers, CHS. Cavender was the secretary to Ibex Mining Company and was involved in Hunter's Free Coinage Mining Company, so undoubtedly Hunter's reference to the office was to one of these mining businesses.

51. Ibid., May 11, 17, 18, 24, 1910.

52. Adams, Dorsett, and Pulcipher, *Pioneer Western Bank*, 124.

53. Absalom V. Hunter to George Trimble, June 25, 1911, ibid. Trimble was the receiver for the Bank of Leadville. Hunter's papers imply that First National had considered a merger with that bank's assets. See also the June 5, 1911, letter to Trimble.

54. Adams, Dorsett, and Pulcipher, *Pioneer Western Bank*, 111.

55. Ibid., 117, 126, 131, 132–33.

56. Articles of Incorporation, March 10, 1890; Organizational Meeting Records, February

15, 1890; Directors Minutebook, April 5, 1893; all in Provo Commercial and Savings Bank Records, Lee Library, Brigham Young University (BYU).

57. Directors Minutebook, July 5, 1893, April 17, 1900, ibid.

58. Gilbert, "The Development of Banking in Oregon," 6–30.

59. James J. Hunter, *Partners in Progress, 1864–1950: A Brief History of the Bank of California, N.A., and the Region it has Served for 85 Years* (Princeton: Newcomen Society, 1950), 21; Wilson, *400 California Street*, 19, 21.

60. Wilson, *400 California Street*, 15; telegraph from Edward Kelly to Donohoe, Kelly and Co., October 1, 1864, MS. JL2/1/2, Stanford University Library, Stanford, California.

61. Lloyd W. Mints, *A History of Banking Theory in Great Britain and The United States* (Chicago: University of Chicago Press, 1945), 207.

62. E. Brown to William C. Ralston, November 10, 1864, September 30, 1869, file 77/88, Ralston Papers, Bancroft Library, University of California, Berkeley, California; George Bradbury to William C. Ralston, September 30, 1869, file 77/88, #2125, ibid.

63. James Lees to D. O. Mills and William C. Ralston, September 11, 1869, 77/88c, #7820, ibid.

64. Lyman, *Ralston's Ring*, 328.

65. Ibid., 222.

66. Tilton, *William Chapman Ralston*, 342.

67. Trescott, *Financing American Enterprise* 80–81.

68. Tilton, *William Chapman Ralston*, 357.

69. Trescott, *Financing American Enterprise*, 81. It is interesting that the Bank of the State of Missouri survived the panic of 1873, only to crumble under a host of poor loans to bridge and jetty projects (ibid., 77).

70. Thomas, *The Fourth*, 14–16.

71. Skidmore, *Treasure State Treasury*, 50.

72. Stucki, *Commercial Banking in Utah*, 135–38.

73. Woods, *Sometimes the Books Froze*, 146–71.

74. Trescott, *Financing American Enterprise*, 153–54.

75. George L. Anderson, "From Cattle to Wheat: The Impact of Agricultural Developments on Banking in Early Wichita," in *Essays on the History of Banking*, ed. George Anderson (Lawrence: Coronado Press, 1972), 53–65 (quotation on p. 55).

76. O. H. Harker to David Moffat, February 5, 1884, Collection 598, "Loose Papers," CHS.

77. Minutebook of the Board of Directors, Denver National Bank, August 1, 19, 1893, Denver National Bank, Collection 195, CHS.

78. Ibid., June 20, 1894; and R. W. Woodbury to John McNeil, June 23, 1894, contained in ibid.

79. Ibid., June 23, 1894; and R. W. Woodbury to John McNeil, July 20, 1894, contained in ibid.

80. Ibid., July 28, 1894.

81. See meetings of August 4, 1894, March 16, 1895, September 15, 1900, and April 20, 1902, and letter of the comptroller of the currency to John McNeil, January 5, 1895, contained in ibid.

82. Schweikart, "Early Banking in New Mexico," 16.

83. Mauzy, *A Century in Santa Fe*, 12.

84. Frank Bond, "Memoirs of Forty Years in New Mexico," paper read before the Ten Dons club, Albuquerque, New Mexico, quoted in Frank Grubbs, "Frank Bond, Gentleman Sheepherder of Northern New Mexico, 1893–1915" (Master's thesis, University of New Mexico, 1958), 18.

85. Schweikart, "Early Banking in New Mexico," 17.

86. Alexander J. Noyes, "The Banks and the Panic of 1893," *Political Science Quarterly* 9 (March 1894): 12–30 (quotation on p. 12).

87. Ibid., 16; Cross, *Financing an Empire*, vol. 2: 617.

88. Neil Roy Knight, "History of Banking in Washington" (Ph.D. diss., University of Washington, 1935), 176, 193.

89. Provorse, *The PeoplesBank Story*, 16–18.

90. Knight, "History of Banking in Washington" (Ph.D. diss.), 199.

91. Gilbert, "Development of Banking in Oregon," 21–22.

92. Skidmore, *Treasure State Treasury*, 50–51.

93. Cleland and Putnam, *Isaias Hellman and the Farmers and Merchants Bank*, 59.

94. Ibid., 61–62.

95. Martin Kales to P. J. McCormack, November 21, 1893, Lewis Collection, First National [now, First Interstate] Bank Collection, NAU.

96. Will Hazeltine to Phillip Hull [n.d., but established as 1893], ibid.

97. Will Hazeltine to J. W. Johnston, March 28, 1893, ibid.

98. *Tucson Daily Citizen*, May 28, 1909; *Globe [Arizona] Silver Belt*, December 8, 1908.

99. Grubbs, "Frank Bond" (Master's thesis), 36.

100. William M. Pease, "Tales of Pioneering," manuscript, n.d. [circa 1910], South Dakota Historical Society (SDHS). Because many pages of the manuscript have indistinguishable page numbers, no pages will be included in citations.

101. Ibid.

102. Issac Post Baker to J. B. Forgan, November 25, 1907, box 28, "Corresp. 1907–08," Isaac Post Baker Papers, NDHS.

103. Blauvelt, "Banking," 1: 634.

104. Noel, *Growing through History*, 30.

105. Youmans, *Legalized Bank Robbery*, 13.

106. Schweikart, *History of Banking in Arizona*, 44–45; Cornelius Bremer, *American Bank Failures* (New York: A.M.S. Press, 1968), 26–28; Noyes, "Banks and the Panic of 1893," 12–30. Noyes's figures, taken from Dun's Mercantile Agency, are probably as unreliable as the comptroller's figures.

107. Cross, *Financing an Empire*, 895. Mansel Blackford, in "Banking and Bank Legislation in California, 1890–1915," *Business History Review* 47 (Winter 1973): 482–507, seemed puzzled that "Californians lagged behind other bankers in establishing clearing houses" (p. 486). But the late creation of clearinghouses was predictable in a branch-banking state, and was a sign of systemic strength not weakness. Compare the two systems in Charles W. Calomiris and Larry Schweikart, "Was the South Backward? North/South Differences in Antebellum Banking During Normalcy and Crisis," Federal Reserve Bank of Chicago Working Paper, 1989.

108. Robert J. Chandler, *San Francisco Clearinghouse Certificates: Last of California's Private Money* (Reno: McDonald Publishing House, 1986), 7; quotation in Blackford, "Banking and Bank Legislation in California," 490.

109. Examination of Donohoe and Kelly Bank, January 17, 1909, MS. JL2/7/89, Stanford University Library.

110. Cross, *Financing an Empire*, 889.

111. Carl Copping Plehn, "The San Francisco Clearinghouse Certificates of 1907–1908," reprinted in Chandler, *San Francisco Clearinghouse Certificates*, 20; Richard H. Timberlake, Jr., "The Central Banking Role of Clearinghouse Associations," *Journal of Money, Credit and Banking* 16 (February 1984): 1–15. Plehn reported scrip returning from Hawaii, Berlin, and China (Chandler, *San Francisco Clearinghouse Certificates*, 30), and a Los

Angeles Savings Bank is still holding open a redemption fund for outstanding clearinghouse scrip (Cross, *Financing an Empire*, 889).

112. Cleland and Putnam, *Isaias Hellman*, 22, 78.

113. See Calomiris and Schweikart, "Was the South Backward?" (unpublished paper).

114. George L. Anderson, "Banks, Mails, and Rails, 1880–1915," in *The Frontier Challenge: Responses to the Trans-Mississippi West*, ed. John G. Clarke (Lawrence: University of Kansas, 1971), 275–307.

115. Cornelius Bremer, *American Bank Failures* (New York: AMS Press, 1968), 26–28; Noyes, "Banks and the Panic of 1893," 12–30. see note 106 concerning Noyes's figures.

116. Arizona State Banking Department Records; Walter C. Madsen, "History of Banking in Arizona" (Master's thesis, University of Washington Pacific Coast Banking School, 1974), 20–24.

117. Guy LeRoy Stevick, "The Denver Savings Bank: Why It Failed," 1908, pamphlet in CHS, 1–37 (quotations on pp. 1, 2).

118. Idib.; Carol Martel and Larry Schweikart, "Arizona Banking and the Collapse of Lincoln Thrift," *Arizona and the West*, 28 (Fall 1986): 246–63.

119. See Stevick, "Denver Savings Bank" (pamphlet, CHS).

120. See the comment in Kuhn, *History of Nebraska Banking*, 11 and Roger Kirkwood, *The Story of Banking in Kansas, 1887–1980* (Topeka: Kansas Bankers Association, 1981), 15–18, and compare with Eric Monkkonen's similar sentiments in *"The Bank of Augusta* v. *Earle:* Corporate Growth v. States' Rights," *Alabama Historical Quarterly*, Summer 1972, 113–130.

121. See, for example, "The Rise and Fall of Alec Swan," *The American West* 4 (August 1967): 21–68. Alexander Swan, vice president and director of First National Bank of Cheyenne, found himself late on a $25,000 payment, which triggered a run on his other interests. The collapse of his business and his subsequent resignation from the bank shocked his associates. Another important cattle rancher, John Hunton, who had taken in $38,000 the year before, in 1887 wrote "Am busted beyond all doubt" (quoted in Woods, *Sometimes the Books Froze*, 43).

122. Woods, *Sometimes the Books Froze*, 44, 48.

123. Ibid., 50; Gerald C. Fischer, *American Banking Structure* (New York: Columbia University Press, 1968), 26.

124. Doti, "Banking in California" (Ph.D. diss.), 87–88.

125. See Board of Bank Commissioners of the State of California, *Annual Reports to the Governor and the Legislature* (Sacramento: State Printing Office, various years), Introduction.

126. Doti, "Banking in California" (Ph.D. diss.), 89–91.

127. LeRoy Armstrong and J. O. Denny, *Financial California: An Historical Review of the Beginnings and Progress of Banking in the State* (New York: Arno, 1980 [orig. pub. 1916]), 23.

128. Board of Bank Commissioners of the State of California, *Annual Reports to the Governor and Legislature* (Sacramento: State Printing Office, 1879), 12.

129. Benjamin C. Wright, *Banking in California, 1849–1910* (San Francisco: H. S. Crocker Company, 1910. Reprinted by New York: Arno Press, 1980), 108–9.

130. MacColl, *Shaping of a City*, 354.

131. *[Portland] Oregon Journal*, August 21, 1907; "1907 Scrapbook," Abbot L. Mills Papers, UO.

132. Ross quoted in MacColl, *Shaping of a City*, 355.

133. *[Portland] Oregon Journal*, November 10, 1907; MacColl, *Shaping of a City*, 355.

134. Kuhn, *History of Nebraska Banking*, 10; J. F. McLain, "Beginnings" (pamphlet), 1952, pp. 5–6, NSHS.

135. James C. Olson, *History of Nebraska*, 2d ed. (Lincoln: University of Nebraska Press, 1966), 254; Kuhn, *History of Nebraska Banking*, 11–12.

136. Kirkwood, *Story of Banking in Kansas*, 16–17.

137. Stucki, *Commercial Banking in Utah*, 77–78.

138. Ibid., 78–79.

139. Halaas, *Banking Structure in Colorado*, 28–30; George Anderson, "Banking and Monetary Problems," in *Essays on the History of Banking*, ed. George Anderson (Lawrence: Coronado Press, 1972), 76–98.

140. Halaas, *Banking Structure in Colorado*, 28–30. Halaas only implies this process, but questions remain. Why, for example, didn't ambitious *national* bankers seek branching privileges before statehood?

141. White, *Regulation and Reform*, 15; Fischer, *American Banking Structure*, 26.

142. White, *Regulation and Reform*, 18, 20.

143. Cargill and Sullivan, "An Historical Perspective of Nevada Banking," 21–28.

144. Ibid., 24; Lyman, *Ralston's Ring*, 54–55; Elliott, *History of Nevada*, 128; Joseph L. King, *History of the San Francisco Stock and Exchange Board* (San Francisco: Stanley-Taylor Co., 1910), 209.

145. See Schweikart, *History of Banking in Arizona*.

146. Doti, "Banking in California" (Ph.D. diss.) 44–46; Armstrong and Denny, *Financial California*, 18. Although California took the banking sections of its constitution from New York, the constitution as a whole was modeled on that of Iowa.

147. Schweikart, *Banking in the American South*, chap. 4.

148. See the results in Calomiris and Schweikart, "Regulations and Markets," (unpublished paper); and idem, "Was the South Backward?" (unpublished paper); as well as Calomiris's "Do 'Vulnerable' Economies Need Deposit Insurance? Lessons from the U.S. Agricultural Boom and Bust of the 1920s" (unpublished paper, Federal Reserve Bank of Chicago, 1989, in authors' possession; and his "Is Deposit Insurance Necessary?," *Journal of Economic History* 50 (June 1990) 283–95.

149. Schweikart, *History of Banking in the American South*, chap. 4; John Ray Cable, *The Bank of the State of Missouri* (New York: Columbia University Press, 1923).

150. Robertson, *The Comptroller and Bank Supervision*, 197.

151. George Barnett, *State Banks and Trust Companies since the Passage of the National Bank Act* (Washington, D.C.: U.S. Government Printing Office, 1910), 135.

152. J. Crumb, "Banking and Regulation in California" (Ph.D. diss., University of California, Berkeley, 1935).

153. See, for example, Gary Gilbert and William Longbrake, "The Effects of Branching by Financial Institutions on Competition, Productive Efficiency, and Stability: An Examination of the Evidence, (Part II, *Journal of Bank Research* 4 (Winter 1974): 298–307; Ernest Baltensperger, "Economics of Scale, Firm Size, and Concentration in Banking," *Journal of Money, Credit and Banking* 4 (August 1972): 467–88; Donald Jacobs, "The Interaction Effects of Restrictions on Branching and Other Bank Regulations," *Journal of Finance* 20 (May 1965): 332–49; R. F. Lanzellotti and T. R. Savings, "State Branching Restrictions and Availability of Branching Services: A Comment," *Journal of Money, Credit and Banking*, 1 (November 1969): 778–88; Louis H. Launch and Neil B. Murphy, "A Test of the Impact of Branching on Deposit Variability," *Journal of Financial and Quantitative Analysis* 5 (September 1970): 323–27; George J. Benston, "Economics of Scale and Financial Institutions," *Journal of Money, Credit and Banking* 4 (May 1972): 312–41; idem, "The Optimum Banking Structure: Theory and Evidence," *Journal of Bank Research* 3 (Winter 1973): 220–37; Donald R. Fraser and Peter S. Ross, "Bank Entry and Bank Performance," *Journal of Finance* 27 (March 1972): 65–78; Lyle E. Gramley, *A Study of Scale Economies in Banking* (Kansas City, Mo.: Federal Reserve Bank of Kansas City, 1962); Paul M. Horwitz and Bernard Schull, "The Impact of

Branch Banking on Bank Performance," *The National Banking Review* 11 (December 1974): 143–89; Jack R. Vernon, "Regulatory Barriers to Branching and Merger and Concentration on Banking Markets," *Southern Economic Journal* 37 (January 1971): 349–55; Richard F. Wacht, "Branch Banking and Risk," *Journal of Financial and Quantitative Analysis* 3 (March 1968): 97–107.

154. White, *Regulation and Reform*, 14–15, 61, 82–83. This point is also made by James Livingston *(Origins of the Federal Reserve System)* although he views the conflict as being one between a small group of perceptive bankers trying to restore "capital's" position vis-à-vis labor. Those short-sighted country bankers (in his view) simply failed to appreciate the threat to their "class" posed by labor.

155. White, *Regulation and Reform*, 15; Fischer, *American Banking Structure*, 26.

156. George L. Anderson, "Western Attitude toward National Banks, 1873–74," in *Essays on the History of Banking*, ed. George L. Anderson (Lawrence, Kansas: Coronado Press, 1972), 9–20 (quotations on pp. 9, 10.

157. See George Anderson, "The National Banking System, 1865–1875: A Sectional Institution" (Master's thesis, University of Illinois, 1933). Two views of the causes of the note shortages and the related price changes during the greenback suspension of 1862–78 currently dominate the scholarly debate. Friedman and Schwartz *(A Monetary History of the United States)* have cited the supply of greenbacks and the demand for money as an explanation for the changes in prices in the "greenback era." Paul Studenski and Herman E. Krooss *(Financial History of the United States*, 2d edition [New York: McGraw Hill, 1963]), and Charles W. Calomiris ("Price and Exchange Rate Determination During the Greenback Suspension," *Oxford Economic Papers* 90 [1988]: 719–50) argue that expectations about resumption accounted for the changes in rates and prices. We subscribe here to the latter view.

158. *Iola [Kansas] Register*, October 4, 1873; *Topeka Blade*, September 22, 1873; and Anderson, "National Banking System" (Master's thesis), 12–13.

159. John Davis, scrapbook E. KHS, quoted in Anderson, "National Banking System," 13–14.

160. Tom Messelt, "Montana's Bank Failures of the Twenties," pamphlet, n.d., pp. 2, 3, MHS.

161. Cashier to comptroller of the currency, June 5, 1878, letterbook 18, First National Bank of Santa Fe Collection, UNM. See also cashier to comptroller of the currency, June 4, 1877, ibid.

162. Minutes of the meetings of the Board of Directors, August 8, 1877, August 1, 1878, February 15, 1879, all in Parish notebook 2, William Parish Papers, UNM.

163. Cashier's letter, December 4, 1878, letterbook 20, First National Bank Collection, MNM.

164. Moldon J. Proussor, "Hugo Seaberg, New Mexican Capitalist, 1869–1945" (Master's thesis, University of Denver, 1968), 19–38.

165. *Congressional Record*, 53 Cong., 2d Sess., 26: 840–41, quoted in Anderson, "Banking and Monetary Problems," 89.

166. *Congressional Record*, 53 Cong., 3d Sess., 27: 43–44; 54 Cong., 2d Sess., 29: 2284; and 56 Cong., 1st Sess., 33: 589, all quoted in Anderson, "Banking and Monetary Problems," 89.

167. Lincoln *Farmers' Alliance*, quoted in Pollack, ed., *The Populist Mind*, 21; and the *Platte County [Nebraska] Argus*, quoted in ibid., 42.

168. George W. Holmes, *"Since 1871": A Short History of the First National Bank of Lincoln, Nebraska* (New York: Newcomen Society, 1951), 12.

169. Quoted in Woods, *Sometimes the Books Froze*, 104.

170. Peter Huntoon, "The Wyoming National Bank Massacre," *Journal of the West* 23 (April 1984): 29–48.

171. Blauvelt, "Banking," 1: 624–39 (quotation on p. 635). On the creation of the California Bankers Association, see Mansel Blackford, *The Politics of Business in California, 1890–1920* (Columbus: Ohio State University Press, 1977), 103.

172. Thomas O'Brien to member bankers, South Dakota Bankers Association, March 7, 1930, "South Dakota Bankers Association, 1929–1931," MS. 2, I. M. Beebe Papers, SDHS.

173. Livingston, *Origins of the Federal Reserve*, 90.

174. William H. Harvey, *Coin's Financial School*, ed. Richard Hofstadter (Cambridge, Mass.: Belknap Press, 1963 [orig. pub. 1894]). Despite claims that Harvey's book circulated widely in the South and West, it appears that, except for some silver regions, the tract mainly hit audiences in the Old Northwest and South. See Richard Hofstadter, *"Coin's Financial School* and the Mind of 'Coin' Harvey," in ibid., 1–80.

175. Livingston, *Origins of the Federal Reserve*, 103–6.

176. Ibid., 106–7.

177. See A. P. Hepburn, *A History of Coinage and Currency in the United States* (New York: MacMillan, 1903), xv–xx; *Report of the Monetary Commission . . . Recommending a Complete Currency System* (Indianapolis: H. H. Hanna, 1897), 3–11.

178. M. N. Dolley, "Reform of the Currency, and Its Relation to the State Banking Institutions of the United States," November 21, 1911, pamphlet, KHS.

179. Livingston, *Origins of the Federal Reserve*, 150.

180. Ibid., 165–66. See also Robert P. Sharkey, "Commercial Banking," in *Economic Change in the Civil War Era*, ed. David T. Gilchrist (Greenville, Del.: Elutherian Mills-Hagley Foundation, 1965), 23–40; Davis, "The Investment Market," 395–99; Sylla, "Federal Policy," 657–86.

181. Livingston, *Origins of the Federal Reserve*, 173–74.

182. Woodlock, quoted in ibid., 178.

183. White, *Regulation and Reform*, 23.

184. Eugene White, "The Membership Problem of the Federal Reserve System Before the Great Depression," unpublished paper in authors' possession.

185. White, *Regulation and Reform*, 24–27, quotation on p. 29.

186. Kuhn, *History of Nebraska Banking*, 13. See also B. Frank Watson, "A History of the Nebraska Bank Guaranty Law," 1933, pamphlet, NSHS; William Frank, "Results of Seventeen Years Banking in Nebraska under the Depositors' Guaranty Fund Law," Grand Island, Nebraska, 1930, pamphlet, NSHS; and Dan R. Stephens, "The Guarranty Law Situation," Fremont, Nebraska, 1929, pamphlet, NSHS; and Calomiris, "Do 'Vulnerable' Economies Need Deposit Insurance?" (unpublished paper).

187. *Noble State Bank* v. *Haskell*, 219 U.S. (1910), 104.

188. See "Nebraska Is Remarkable State and Tells a Story No Other State Can Tell" 1926, pamphlet, NSHS.

189. Holmes, ". . .Since 1871," 17.

190. George H. Shibley, "History of Guaranty of Bank Deposits in the States of Oklahoma, Texas, Nebraska, and South Dakota, 1908–1914" pamphlet, 8–9 (quotation on p. 9), reproduced in *Senate Document* no. 522, 63d Cong. 2d Sess. (Washington: Government Printing Office, 1914).

191. White, *Regulation and Reform*, 196–97 (quotation on p. 196).

192. Kuhn, *History of Nebraska Banking*, n, 20, 59; Holmes, *"Since 1871"*, 18.

193. Thornton Cooke, "The Guaranty of Bank Deposits," quoted in Shibley, "History of Guaranty of Bank Deposits," 11. See also Roland I. Roblinson, "Unit Banking Evaluated," in *Banking and Monetary Studies*, ed. Deane Carson (Homewood, Ill.: Richard D. Irwin, 1963), 291–305; Paul D. Horvitz, "Branch Banking, Mergers, and Competition," ibid., 306–18. Robinson, in 1963, aptly described the process as a "glacially slow drift toward branch banking" (p. 293).

194. C. A. Glazier to William F. Armstrong, May 9, July 29, 1905, box 3, folder 10, William F. Armstrong papers, Utah State Historical Society (USHS).

195. Charles Tingley to President and Board of Directors, August 22, 1905, ibid.

196. Thomas Holt to Clarence Collins, June 19, 1914, box 3, folder 6, William F. Armstrong papers, USHS.

197. Noel, *Growing through History*, 46.

198. Pease, "Tales of Pioneering," n.p.; Leipheimer, *First National Bank of Butte*, 22.

199. Woods, *Sometimes the Books Froze*, 87.

200. Skidmore, *Treasure State Treasury*, 82.

201. C. D. Brinton to Moyle and Van Cott, August 31, [1914?], William F. Armstrong Papers, USHS.

202. Minutes of a Meeting of the Executive Committee, McCornick and Company, Bankers, April 5, 1910, "McCornick & Co.," MS. A864, USHS.

203. Minutes of the Board of Directors, May 3, June 7, 1910, August 1, 6, 1911, ibid.

204. Skidmore, *Treasure State Treasury*, 73.

205. Pease, "Tales of Pioneering," n.p.

206. Ibid.

207. Clarence W. Groth, "Sowing and Reaping: Montana Banking, 1910–1925," *Montana: The Magazine of Western History* 20 (Autumn 1970): 28–35.

208. Pease, "Tales of Pioneering," n.p.

209. Ibid.

4. MAKING THE LOCAL BANKERS THE GOATS

1. San Francisco banks obviously were forced, by the earthquake and fire of 1906, to construct new buildings ahead of schedule. For this burst of new construction in the West, see Noel, *Growing through History*, 52–73; Jackson A. Graves, *My Seventy Years in California* (Los Angeles: Times/Mirror Press, 1927), 125; John Russell McCarthy, *Joseph Francis Sartori, 1858–1946* (Los Angeles: The Ward Ritchie Press, 1948), 65; Wilson, *400 California Street*, 65; James and James, *Biography of a Bank*, 43–45; Adams, Dorsett, and Pulcipher, *Pioneer Western Bank*, 128–29; and George W. Holmes, "*Since 1871*," 19. In addition, Portland experienced a burst of growth from 1907 to 1915, including several buildings erected by banks or the estates of bankers, such as the Wells Fargo (Porter) building, the Corbett & Failing Banks, Northwestern National Bank, and Wilcox buildings. See MacColl, *Shaping of a City*, 435.

2. Alfred Hopkins, *The Fundamentals of Good Bank Building* (New York: The Bankers Publishing Co., 1929), 36.

3. Noel, for example, dedicates several pages to color photos of murals in the bank by artist Allen True (*Growing through History*, 67–73).

4. Ibid., 7.

5. J. R. Walters to cashier, April 7, 1917, box 27, "Correspondence: State Bank Examiner, 1909–1922," Issac Post Baker Papers, NDHS.

6. Smallwood, *An Oklahoma Adventure*, 76–79; Skidmore, *Treasure State Treasury*, 69.

7. Noel, *Growing through History*, 60–61.

8. Provorse, *PeoplesBank Story*, 34.

9. *Report of the [Arizona] State Bank Comptroller*, (Phoenix: Arizona State Printing Office, 1916), 4.

10. Schweikart, *History of Banking in Arizona*, 59–60.

11. Skidmore, *Treasure State Treasury*, 69.

12. Schweikart, *History of Banking in Arizona*, 60.

13. Smallwood, *An Oklahoma Adventure*, 91.

14. Eugene P. Gum, memoranda, 1924–1930, "Report on Bank Robberies and Burglaries in Oklahoma, 1920–1930," OBA; Smallwood, *An Oklahoma Adventure*, 93.

15. Marcus P. Beebe to J. B. Allen, December 22, 1928, box 1, folder 1, I. M. Beebe Papers, SDHS; Smallwood, *An Oklahoma Adventure*, 93.

16. Eugene P. Gum, memoranda, 1924–1930, "Report on Bank Robberies," OBA.

17. Smallwood, *An Oklahoma Adventure*, 91–94; *Oklahoma Banker*, April 1925, 9–11; and November 1925, 19–20.

18. Smallwood, *An Oklahoma Adventure*, 93–94.

19. "Report of the Secretary, Treasurer, Committees," South Dakota Bankers Association, box 1, no folder, I. M. Beebe Papers, SDHS.

20. W. S. Gordon to Marcus P. Beebe, March 17, 1927, box 1, folder 1, I. M. Beebe Papers, SDHS.

21. Secretary for George Wingfield to [cashier], Virginia City Bank, July 27, 1925, box 115, folder "1925," George Wingfield Papers, Nevada Historical Society (NHS), Reno, Nevada.

22. See box 1, folder 6, I. M. Beebe Papers, SDHS.

23. W. C. McFadden to members of the North Dakota Bankers Association, July 16, 1930, in "South Dakota Bankers Association, 1929–1931," MSS, I. M. Beebe Papers, SDHS.

24. Glen Barrett, *Small Town Banking in the Good Ol' Days*, (Boise: Boise State University Press, 1975), 70.

25. W. S. Gordon to Marcus P. Beebe, November 5, 1930, box 1, folder 2, I. M. Beebe Papers, SDHS.

26. W. C. McFadden to Marcus P. Beebe, December 11, 1931, ibid.

27. William Ridgeway, "He Had No Gun," *Arizona Days and Ways*, May 15, 1955, 9.

28. Roscoe Willson, "Old Lawman Outshoots Robbers," *Arizona Days and Ways*, July 4, 1965, 26–27.

29. Schweikart, *History of Banking in Arizona*, 67.

30. Provorse, *PeoplesBank Story*, 67.

31. Jerome E. Edwards, *Pat McCarran: Political Boss of Nevada* (Reno: University of Nevada Press, 1982), 36.

32. Ibid., 33.

33. George Wingfield to H. C. Clapp, March 6, 1926, series 7, box 108, "Carson Valley Bank, 1926," George Wingfield Papers, NHS.

34. *Reno Evening Gazette* quoted in Edwards, *Pat McCarran*, 36.

35. Edwards, *Pat McCarran*, 36.

36. Frederick W. Kiesel to George Wingfield, May 9, 1927, series 7, box 108, "Carson Valley Bank, 1927," George Wingfield Papers, NHS.

37. North Dakota Banking Board memo, October 25, 1917, box 27, "Banking and Home Building," Issac Post Baker Papers, NDHS.

38. Skidmore, *Treasure State Treasury*, 82.

39. See Richard Hofstader, *The Age of Reform: From Bryan to FDR* (New York: Vintage, 1955).

40. Singer, *U.S. National Bank of Oregon and U.S. Bancorp*, 29, 38–48.

41. Knight, "History of Banking in Washington" (Ph.D. diss.), 360–80.

42. Biographies and sketches of Giannini appear in Julian Dana, *A. P. Giannini: Giant in the West, a Biography* (New York: Prentice Hall, 1947); and "A. P. Giannini," in Lamar, *Readers' Encyclopedia of the American West*, 438–39. The best work on the Bank of Italy remains James and James, *Biography of a Bank*.

43. Julian Dana, *A. P. Giannini*, 49–195. For an interesting look at the political side of Giannini's activities on behalf of the bank and branching, see William Hively, "The Italian

Connection and the Bank of America's First Billion," *Journal of the West* 23 (April 1984): 56–64.

44. Julian Dana, *A. P. Giannini*, 87, 90–91; James and James, *Biography of a Bank*, 60–63, 78–80.

45. Ibid., 78–80, 96–99.

46. F. A. Little to Issac Post Baker, January 22, 1918, box 36, "Little, F. A. 1917–1922," Isaac Post Baker Papers, NDHS. The notion that the Federal Reserve Board had contributed to the farm problems—and, to some, was the root cause of the farmers' plight—is found in C. B. Billinghurst, "The Farmer's Dollar and the Wall Street Banks Flurry of April 1920: The Farmer's Dollar Was Taken from the West to Brace up Weak Banks in the East; A Feature in the Problem of Farm Relief" (n.d.), pamphlet, SDHS.

47. F. A. Little to Issac Post Baker, August 10, November 27, 1918; F. A. Little to G. H. Russ, Jr., March 19, 1921, box 36, "Little, F. A. 1917–1922," Isaac Post Baker Papers, NDHS.

48. A. C. Johnson to E. M. Thompson, June 21, 1918, box 35, "American National Bank, Helena, 1916–1922," ibid.

49. G. H. Russ, Jr., to American National Bank, November 2, 1921, ibid.

50. Barjenbruch, "The First National Bank of Vermillion," (Master's thesis), 49.

51. These data are reported in Calomiris, "Do 'Vulnerable' Economies Need Deposit Insurance?" (unpublished paper), 11.

52. On the causes of the Great Depression, see Elmus Wicker, "A Reconsideration of the Banking Panic of 1930," *Journal of Economic History* 40 (September 1980): 571–83; Friedman and Schwartz, *A Monetary History of the United States;* Peter Temin, *Did Monetary Forces Cause the Great Depression?* (New York: W. W. Norton, 1976).

53. Peter Huntoon, "The National Bank Failures in Wyoming, 1924," *Annals of Wyoming*, Fall 1982, 34–44.

54. Skidmore, *Treasure State Treasury*, 79; Groth, "Montana Banking History" (Master's thesis); Groth, "Saving and Reaping," 28–35.

55. Curtis L. Mosher, *The Causes of Banking Failure in the Northwestern States* (Minneapolis: Federal Reserve Bank of Minneapolis, September 1930), 18. See also F. M. Bailey, *The Small Bank Problem* (Minneapolis: Federal Reserve Bank of Minneapolis, September 1930).

56. Tom Messelt, Sr., "Montana's Bank Failures of the Twenties," n.d., pamphlet, pp. 1, 8–9, 13–14, MHS.

57. Mosher, *Causes of Banking Failure*, 19.

58. This story is related in MacColl, *Growth of a City*, 189–90, 371–79.

59. Memo, February 3, 1925, J. C. Ainsworth Papers, University of Oregon (UO).

60. MacColl, *Growth of a City*, 377.

61. *[Portland] Oregon Journal*, March 30, 1927. See also the Northwestern Bank file in the J. C. Ainsworth papers, UO.

62. MacColl, *Growth of a City*, 377.

63. MacColl discusses Meier in ibid., 385–90.

64. Ibid., 401–3.

65. Mary Scott Rowland, "Kansas Farming and Banking in the 1920s," *Kansas Historical Quarterly*, August 1985, 186–99 (see table 3 on p. 192); Huntoon, "National Bank Failures in Wyoming," 35. Huntoon notes that some men—such as Benjamin F. Yoder, Thomas A. Cosgriff, John L. Baird, George E. Abbott, and A. H. Marble—who owned a bank that failed also either owned or were directors of other banks. Yet several of these individuals' chains survived the depression, and the Cosgriffs emerged "unscathed" (ibid., 44). Although the Wyoming chains ran into trouble over the falling livestock prices that plagued Wingfield's banks, they often survived, suggesting that the chain structure itself was not the causal factor in the Wingfield collapse.

66. Woods, *Sometimes the Books Froze,* 100–132.

67. Marriner Eccles, *Beckoning Frontiers: Public and Personal Recollections,* ed. Sidney Hyman (New York: Knopf, 1951), 57–68. See also Frederick Lundquist, "An Analysis of Banking in Utah's Economy, 1875–1953" (Master's thesis, University of Utah, 1963), 70–71.

68. MacColl, *Growth of a City,* 201; MacColl, *Shaping of a City,* 364–66.

69. Ibid., 202. See also Burrell, *Gold in the Woodpile,* 90–91.

70. MacColl, *Growth of a City,* 209.

71. Ibid., 209–11.

72. Ibid., 368.

73. Provorse, *PeoplesBank Story,* 77–78. See also Shelby Scates, *FIRSTBANK: The Story of Seattle First National Bank* (Seattle: First National Bank, 1970); Elliot Marple and Bruce H. Olson, *The National Bank of Commerce of Seattle, 1889–1969* (Palo Alto, Calif.: Pacific Books, 1970); and Howard H. Preston, *Trust Banking in Washington* (Seattle: University of Washington Press, 1953).

74. Barjenbruch, "First National Bank of Vermillion" (Master's thesis), 63; Holmes, "*Since 1871,*" 20.

75. Schweikart, *History of Banking in Arizona,* 86–95; Robert Browder and Thomas Smith, *Independent: A Biography of Lewis W. Douglas* (New York: Alfred A. Knopf, 1986).

76. Frank C. Brophy to Melzar M. Whittlesey, April 16, 1934, box 37, file 1214, Arizona Historical Society (AHS). This collection was unprocessed as of this writing. Note that there are two letters from Brophy to Whittlesey with this date in file 1214.

77. J. Patrick McGahan, "The Development and Effect of Banking in Utah, 1933–1945," (Master's thesis, University of Utah, 1963), 11; Utah Bankers Association, Minutes, Salt Lake City Clearinghouse, Salt Lake City, Utah; Edgel, *Brief History,* 16.

78. Edgel, *Brief History,* 14–15.

79. Rowland, "Kansas Farming and Banking," 192, 194, 195–97.

80. See Calomiris, "Do 'Vulnerable' Economies Need Deposit Insurance?" The specific developments in each of the deposit-insurance states appear in Calomiris, "Deposit Insurance," 10–30.

81. Calomiris, "Do 'Vulnerable' Economies Need Deposit Insurance?" 44, 53, and table 23.

82. Ibid., 8, 9, 21, 22, and table 13.

83. Ibid., 28–31.

84. Edgel, *Brief History,* 14–15.

85. Barrett, *Small Town Banking,* 86.

86. Provorse, *PeoplesBank Story,* 104.

87. James S. Olsen, "The Boise Bank Panic of 1932," *Idaho Yesterdays,* Winter 1974, 18–29 (quotation on p. 26); *[Boise] Idaho Daily Statesman,* Sept. 18, Oct. 18, 25, Nov. 1, 1932.

88. Sidney Hyman, *Challenge and Response: First Security Corporation, First Fifty Years, 1928–1978* (Salt Lake City: University of Utah, Graduate School of Business, 1978), 152–58.

89. Harold Chucker, *Banco at Fifty: A History of Northwest Bancorporation, 1929–1979* (Minneapolis: Northwest Bancorporation, 1979), 10–13; Larry Schweikart interview with Bob Hedrickson, president of First National Bank and Trust Company of Bismarck, North Dakota, April 27, 1988.

90. Schweikart interview with Bob Hedrickson, April 27, 1988.

91. James S. Olson, "Rehearsal for Disaster: Hoover, the R.F.C., and the Banking Crisis in Nevada, 1932–1933," *Western Historical Quarterly,* April 1975, 149–61.

92. "George Wingfield" in Lamar, ed., *Reader's Encyclopedia,* 1275; Russell Elliott, *History of Nevada* (Lincoln: University of Nebraska Press, 1973), 286–87; Cargill and Sullivan, "An Historical Perspective on Nevada Banking," 21–28.

93. Clel Georgetta, *Golden Fleece in Nevada* (Reno: Venture Publishing Co., 1972), 383–425.

94. See, for example, George Wingfield to H. C. Clapp, January 20, 1926, "Carson Valley Bank, 1926"; idem to H. C. Clapp, June 17, 1921, "Carson Valley Bank, 1921"; idem to F. P. Strasberg, September 20, 1916, "Churchill County Bank, 1916"; idem to L. W. Horton, January 9, 1930, "Carson Valley Bank, 1930"; all in series 7, box 108, George Wingfield Papers, NHS; idem to E. W. Blair, January 22, 1927, "Churchill County Bank, 1927," series 7, box 109, ibid; and idem to E. W. Blair, February 28, 1929, "Churchill County Bank, Jan.–Ap. 1929," series 7, box 109, ibid.

95. George Wingfield to H. C. Clapp, June 23, 1921, "Carson Valley Bank, 1921," series 7, box 108, ibid.

96. George Wingfield to H. C. Clapp, August 16, 1923, "Carson Valley Bank, 1923," Series 7, box 108, ibid.

97. George Wingfield to L. W. Horton, July 23, 1928, "Carson Valley Bank, 1928," series 7, box 108, ibid.

98. George Wingfield to H. C. Clapp, October 7, 1925, "Carson Valley Bank, 1925," series 7, box 108, ibid.

99. Treasury Department Report, February 19, 1923, "Carson Valley Bank, Taxes, 1923," series 7, box 108, ibid.

100. George Wingfield to C. W. Foote, January 17, 1918, "Churchill County Bank, 1918," series 7, box 108, ibid.

101. George Wingfield to E. W. Blair, August 10, 1927, "Churchill County Bank, 1927," series 7, box 108, ibid.

102. See, for example, Cargill and Sullivan, "An Historical Perspective on Nevada Banking," 26; and Elliott, *History of Nevada,* 286–87.

103. "Carson Valley Bank," Net Earnings, 1919–1931, series 7, box 8, "Carson Valley Bank, Jan.–July, 1932," George Wingfield Papers, NHS.

104. See the minutes of the RFC, July 30, 1932, record group 234, National Archives, Secretarial Division, Washington, D.C.; Olson, "Rehearsal for Disaster," 150.

105. Income tax forms, "Carson Valley Bank, Taxes," series 7, box 108, George Wingfield Papers, NHS.

106. H. C. Clapp to George Wingfield, December 11, 1922, "Carson Valley Bank, 1922," series 7, box 108, ibid.

107. Audit, March 31, 1928, "Carson Valley Bank, 1928, Special Audit," series 7, box 108, ibid.

108. E. W. Blair to George Wingfield, February 28, 1929, "Churchill County Bank, Jan.–Ap. 1929," series 7, box 109, ibid; George Wingfield to E. W. Blair, September 6, 1927, "Churchill County Bank, 1927," series 7, box 108, ibid.

109. See George Wingfield to E. W. Blair, February 26, 1929, "Churchill County Bank, Jan.–Ap. 1929," series 7, box 109, ibid.; and "Churchill County Bank, Audit, 1929," ibid.

110. Olson, "Rehearsal for Disaster," 151.

111. See Georgetta, *Golden Fleece,* 403–4.

112. Larry Schweikart interview with Harold Gorman, August 30, 1989.

113. E. W. Blair to George Wingfield, July 28, 1932, "Churchill County Bank, July–Dec. 1929," series 7, box 109, George Wingfield Papers, NHS.

114. Olson, "Rehearsal for Disaster," 153–55.

115. Georgetta, *Golden Fleece,* 405; memo to Reconstruction Finance Corporation, n.d. [1932], "Reno National Bank, Feb.–July 1932," series 7, box 113, George Wingfield Papers, NHS.

116. T. E. Harris to J. G. Moore, n.d., "First National Bank of Winnemucca, Aug.–Dec. 1932," series 7, box 111, ibid.

117. F. G. Willis to George Wingfield, August 11, 1932, series 7, box 113, "Reno National Bank, Aug. 1932," ibid.

118. J. G. Moore to George Wingfield, November 6, 1932, "First National Bank of Winnemucca, Aug.–Dec. 1952," series 7, box 111, ibid.; William J. Henley to George Wingfield, November 5, 1932, "Virginia City Bank, 1932," series 7, box 115, ibid.

119. J. G. Moore to George Wingfield, November 6, 1932, series 7, box 111, "First National Bank of Winnemucca, Aug.–Dec. 1952," ibid.

120. W. J. Henley to J. Sheehan, November 15, 1932, series 7, box 115, "Virginia City Bank, 1932," ibid.

121. J. G. Moore to George Wingfield, December 16, 1932, series 7, "First National Bank of Winnemucca, Aug.–Dec. 1932," ibid.

122. F. G. Awalt, "Assessment Upon the Shareholders," January 6, 1933, series 7, box 113, "Reno National Bank, 1933," ibid.

123. "To the Depositors of the Riverside Bank," January 25, 1933, series 7, box 113, Riverside Bank, 1933, ibid.

124. "Bank Depositors . . . ," reprint in "George Wingfield Correspondence, re: Banking Reorganization, 1933," series 1, box 40, ibid.

125. "Wingfield's Future," *Santa Barbara Daily News*, February 14, 1933, clipping in series 1, box 40, ibid.

126. Ibid.

127. W. J. Henley to George Wingfield, February 21, 1933, series 7, box 715, "Virginia City Bank, 1933," ibid.

128. Georgetta, *Golden Fleece*, 406–7.

129. Ibid., 407.

130. Ibid., 410–11.

131. "Proposed Balance Sheet, Wingfield Banks," *Reno Evening Gazette*, February 22, 1933; "The Plan for Reorganization and Reopening of Nevada's Closed Banks," in George Wingfield Correspondence re: Banking Reorganization, Printed Matter," series 1, box 40, George Wingfield Papers, NHS.

132. "Proposed Balance Sheet, Wingfield Banks," *Reno Evening Gazette*, Feb. 22, 1933.

133. "Plan for Reorganization" (George Wingfield Papers, NHS), Georgetta, *Golden Fleece*, 420.

134. Georgetta, *Golden Fleece*, 420–22.

135. Ibid., 421.

136. George Wingfield to James G. Wakefield, July 5, 1929, series 7, box 113, "Reno National Bank, June–Dec. 1929," George Wingfield Papers, NHS.

137. Georgetta, *Golden Fleece*, 422.

138. M. D. Cravath to C. T. Smith, February 8, 1932, series 1, box 1, folder 3, MS. 3987, Stockmen's National Bank–Rushville, Nebr., NSHS. See also Cravath to Jereme Wadd, February 8, 1932, ibid.

139. Woods, *Sometimes the Books Froze*, 106, 110.

140. Arthur Seligman to the comptroller of the currency, February 11, 1930, box 107, First National Bank of Santa Fe Collection, UNM.

141. Ibid.; "Notes of a Meeting of the Board of Directors," n.d. [1911], box 107, ibid.

142. "Notes," box 107, ibid.

143. Paul Walter to Arthur Seligman, December 12, 1930, box 114, "Paul Walter File," ibid. Many other bankers have expressed similar objections. For example, see A. E. Dahl, *Banker Dahl of South Dakota: An Autobiography* (Rapid City: Fenske Book Co., 1965), 151–52. Dahl's criticism, although made in the 1950s, is relevant because at other times he was extremely supportive of the examiners.

144. Skidmore, *Treasure State Treasury*, 83.

145. Ibid., 79.

146. George Becker to the president and the board of directors, February 11, 1930, January 15, 1931, Ogden State Bank, Minutebook of the Board of Directors, BYU.

147. Ibid.

148. Ibid. Interviews with North Dakota bank presidents who recalled the Depression support the view that federal examiners lacked a sense of the territory. Federal officials insisted, for example, that First National Bank of McClusky change management, despite the fact that the officers had "done a good job" (Larry Schweikart interviews with John Davis, April 26, 1988 and Bob Hedrickson, April 27, 1988).

149. Larry Schweikart interview with John Davis, April 26, 1988.

150. George P. Comer to M. D. Cravath, March 8, 1930, series 1, box 1, folder 1, MS. 3987, Stockmen's National Bank–Rushville, Nebr., NSHS. Nevertheless, Comer a year later referred to another national bank examiner as a "fair man," indicating he did not distrust the judgement of all regulators. (George P. Comer to M. D. Cravath, January 30, 1931, series 1, box 1, folder 2, ibid.).

151. M. D. Cravath to George P. Comer, February 19, 1931, series 1, box 1, folder 2, MS. 3987, ibid.

152. Noel, *Growing through History*, 82.

153. Ibid., 84.

154. Provorse, *PeoplesBank Story*, 105.

155. William Jervey, "When the Banks Closed: Arizona's Bank Holiday of 1933," *Arizona and the West*, Summer 1968, 127–53; *[Phoenix] Arizona Republic*, March 3, 1933.

156. *Bisbee Daily Review*, March 4, 1933; *Tucson Daily Citizen*, March 4, 5, 8, 1933; Schweikart, *History of Banking in Arizona*, 91. See also the telegram from the Alabama Bankers Association to the Nebraska state superintendent of banks, March 11, 1933, confirming that many of the banks in that district did not have to close and for Nebraska bankers to wire their senators and representatives if that was the situation in Nebraska. MS. 8769, series 1, box 1, folder 1, J. Floyd McLain, MSS, NSHS.

157. *Bisbee Daily Review*, March 4, 1933.

158. Herold quoted in Schweikart, *History of Banking in Arizona*, 91. W. G. Bowman, a member of the Democratic National Committee and chairman of the First National Bank of Nogales, congratulated the bank officials for their defiance (*Tucson Daily Citizen*, March 6, 1933).

159. Barret, *Small Town Banking*, 88.

160. Noel, *Growing through History*, 84.

161. Ibid., 79.

162. Ibid., 85.

163. Ibid., 86.

164. For the impact of the RFC's habit of publishing information on troubled banks, see Richard Keehn and Gene Smiley, "U.S. Bank Failures, 1932–1933: A Provisional Analysis," *Essays in Business and Economic History*, 6: 136–56.

165. See Larry Schweikart, "*Brophy* vs. *Douglas:* A Case Study in Corporate Control," *Journal of the West* 23 (April 1984): 49–55.

166. *[Phoenix] Arizona Republic*, April 4, 1934.

167. Bimson quoted in Schweikart, *History of Banking in Arizona*, 103.

168. Material on Walter Bimson is found in Hopkins, 217–18; Interview with W. R. Montgomery, July 22, 1980, ASU; Don Dedera, "Walter Reed Bimson, Arizona's Indispensable Man, Compleat Banker," *Saturday Evening Post*, April 10, 1954, 23; Carl Bimson, speech "Transformation in the Desert—The Story of Arizona's Valley Bank," Newcomen Society reprint, March 20, 1962, ASU; and Larry Schweikart interviews with Carl Bimson, March and April 1980.

169. Hopkins, *Financing the Frontier*, 217–18; Dedera, "Walter Reed Bimson," 26.

170. Draft of an article on Bimson by Ernest J. Hopkins in authors' possession.

171. Schweikart, *History of Banking in Arizona*, 89.

172. Dedera, "Walter Reed Bimson," 1, 26.

173. Untitled list of banking principles, series 7, box 113, "Reno National Bank, Jan.–May 1930," George Wingfield Papers, NHS.

174. Smallwood, *An Oklahoma Adventure*, 111–12.

175. Leonard H. Arrington, *Tracy-Collins Bank and Trust Co.* (Midvale, Utah: Eden Hill Publishing Co., 1984), 122–23.

176. A. L. Hoppaugh to Preston Nutter, September 3, 13, 1932, box 96, folder 2, Preston Nutter Collection, UU.

177. George P. Comer to M. D. Cravath, January 15, 1930, series 1, box 1, folder 1, MS. 3987, Stockmen's National Bank–Rushville, Nebr., NSHS. By the end of the year, however, Comer was less optimistic: "The banking situation . . . is certainly 'bum' and the newspapers are full of accounts of *failure* after failure." (George P. Comer to M. D. Cravath, December 20, 1930, series 1, box 1, folder 1, ibid.).

178. Undated memo, circa January 1930, from unidentified employee or director, possibly George P. Comer, series 1, box 1, folder 4, MS. 3987, ibid.

179. See above memo and George P. Comer to M. D. Cravath, January 15, 1930, series 1, box 1, folder 1, MS. 3987, ibid. For other correspondence on Duncan's attempted takeover of the bank, see George P. Comer to M. D. Cravath, December 13, 1930, and January 16, 1931, both in series 1, box 1, folder 4, ibid.; and M. D. Cravath to George P. Comer, January 1931, series 1, box 1, folder 4, ibid.

180. George P. Comer to M. D. Cravath, January 15, 1930, series 1, box 1, folder 1, MS. 3987, ibid. See also C. L. Smith to M. D. Cravath, January 25, 1931, and M. D. Cravath to C. L. Smith, January 28, 1931, both in series 1, box 1, folder 2, MS. 3987, ibid.

181. Undated memo, series 1, box 1, folder 4, MS. 3987, ibid.

182. M. D. Cravath to George P. Comer, February 19, 1931, series 1, box 1, folder 2, MS. 3987, ibid.

183. George P. Comer to M. D. Cravath, March 7, 1931, series 1, box 1, folder 2, MS. 3987, ibid.

184. M. D. Cravath to George P. Comer, August 20, 1931, series 1, box 1, folder 3, MS. 3987, ibid.

185. George P. Comer to M. D. Cravath, January 30, 1932, series 1, box 1, folder 3, MS. 3987, ibid.

186. George P. Comer to M. D. Cravath, March 25, 1931, series 1, box 1, folder 2, MS. 3987, ibid.

187. A. N. Gehrt to M. D. Cravath, March 11, 1932, series 1, box 1, folder 3, MS. 3987, ibid.

188. Ibid. See also M. D. Cravath to A. N. Gehrt, March 17, 1932, series 1, box 1, folder 3, MS. 3987, ibid.

189. Sidney Hyman, *Marriner S. Eccles, Private Entrepreneur and Public Servant* (Stanford: Stanford University, Graduate School of Business, 1976), 78–80.

190. Ibid., 80–81.

191. Ibid., 81.

192. Ibid.

193. Material on Eccles also appears in Eccles's own book *Beckoning Frontiers*.

194. Hyman, *Marriner S. Eccles*, 36, 39.

195. Ibid., 70–73.

196. Ibid., 94–100.

197. Ibid., 135.

198. Ibid., 129, 139.

199. Browder and Smith, *Independent*, 81; Frank Friedel, *Franklin D. Roosevelt: Launching the New Deal* (Boston: Little, Brown, 1973), 241–42.

200. Browder and Smith, *Independent*, 92–93, 107.

201. James and James, *Biography of a Bank*, 185–201.

202. Ibid., 269–70.

203. Ibid., 168.

204. Ibid., 194.

205. Ibid., 195.

206. Ibid., 199.

207. Ibid., 225.

208. Ibid., 234.

209. Ibid., 292.

210. Ibid., 310.

211. Singer, *U.S. National Bank of Oregon*, 49, 50, 61–64.

212. Ibid., 323–45.

213. Ibid., 358.

214. MacColl, *Growth of a City*, 395–401.

215. Irwin Wright to Paul Walter, August 24, 1934, box 151, folder "National—1934," First National Bank of Santa Fe Collection, UNM.

216. Paul Walter to Irwin Wright, August 27, 1934, box 151, folder "National—1934," ibid.

217. George P. Comer to M. D. Cravath, January 30, 1932, series 1, box 1, folder 3, MS. 3987, Stockmen's National Bank–Rushville, Nebr., NSHS.

218. Noel, *Growing through History*, 86.

219. Paul Walter to Irwin Wright, August 27, 1934, box 151, folder "National—1934," First National Bank of Santa Fe Collection, UNM.

220. Ibid.

221. Minutes of the thirtieth annual convention of the Utah Bankers Association, quoted McGahan, "The Development and Effect of Banking in Utah" (Master's thesis), 27–28.

222. Paul Walter to Irwin Wright, August 27, 1934, box 151, folder "National—1934," First National Bank of Santa Fe Collection, UNM.

223. W. D. Hover to ?, July 18, 1934, box 15, file 1, Hilliard and Hilliard, Receivers, MS. 311, CHS.

224. W. D. Hover to the comptroller of the currency, October 29, 1934, box 15, file 1, Hilliard and Hilliard, Receivers, MS. 311, ibid.

225. Noel, *Growing through History*, 75.

226. Kuhn, *History of Nebraska Banking*, 20–24. See also "Farmers and Merchants Bank, Edison, Nebraska, 25th Anniversary, 1929–1954," 1954, pamphlet, NSHS.

227. Smallwood, *An Oklahoma Adventure*, 106–11.

228. Schweikart, *History of Banking in Arizona*, 102; *[Phoenix] Arizona Republic*, April 13 and 19, 1937; *Coast Banker*, December 1937, 333.

229. AZ State Banking Department, condensed statements Gutowsky, *Arizona Banking*, 24.

230. See Lynne Pierson Doti and Larry Schweikart, "Financing the Post-War Housing Boom in Phoenix and Los Angeles, 1945–1960," *Pacific Historical Review* 58 (May 1989): 173–94.

231. Schweikart, *History of Banking in Arizona*, 104.

232. Speech, October 1952, "Speeches of Carl Bimson," Valley National Bank (VNB), Phoenix, 127–36; "The Brash Banker of Arizona," *Saturday Evening Post* 226 (April 10, 1954), 23.

233. Hopkins, *Financing the Frontier*, 247; Carl Bimson, "Formula for Frontier Financ-

ing," 1956, "Speeches of Carl Bimson, p. 232, VNB; Schweikart, *History of Banking in Arizona*, 104.

234. Hopkins, *Financing the Frontier*, 248.

235. Schweikart, *History of Banking in Arizona*, 105.

236. Hyman, *Challenge and Response*, 143–67, 176.

237. See Schweikart, *That Quality Image*.

238. Nash, *American West Transformed*, 3–14.

5. BRASH BANKERS AND BIG BOOSTERS

1. Skidmore, *Treasure State Treasury*, 112.

2. Adams, Dorsett, and Pulcipher, *Pioneer Western Bank*, 161.

3. Smallwood, *An Oklahoma Adventure*, 130.

4. Skidmore, *Treasure State Treasury*, 112.

5. Hyman, *Challenge and Response*, 196.

6. Schweikart, *History of Banking in Arizona*, 109.

7. Skidmore, *Treasure State Treasury*, 112.

8. Singer, *U.S. National Bank of Oregon and U.S. Bankcorp, 1891–1984*, 78.

9. Provorse, *The PeoplesBank Story*, 133.

10. Vance Coleman Moore, "The Effects of World War II on Banking in the State of Washington" (Master's thesis, University of Washington, 1950), 121.

11. James R. Modrall, "The History of the Albuquerque National Bank from the Beginning to 1965" (New York: Newcomen Society, 1965), n.p.

12. Edgel, *Brief History*, 21.

13. Hyman, *Challenge and Response*, 194–95.

14. Ibid., 168, 187–88. On Marriner Eccles's inflationary warnings, see Marriner S. Eccles, "Price Fixing Is Not Enough," *Fortune*, August 1941, 56–57, 150, 152, 154, 157.

15. Hyman, *Challenge and Response*, 197.

16. James and James, *Biography of a Bank*, 460–62.

17. Speech of George Eccles, June 22, 1951, quoted in Hyman, *Challenge and Response*, 199–200.

18. Adams, Dorsett, and Pulcipher, *Pioneer Western Bank*, 161.

19. Hyman, *Challenge and Response*, 184–85.

20. James and James, *Biography of a Bank*, 463–64. On Consolidated Vultee, see William Wagner, *Reuben Fleet and the Story of Consolidated Aircraft* (Fallbrook, California: Aero Publishers, 1976).

21. James and James, *Biography of a Bank*, 464.

22. Ibid., 466–67. See also W. A. Beck and S. T. Gaskins, "Henry J. Kaiser: Entrepreneur of the American West," *Journal of the West* 25 (1986): 64–72; Mark S. Foster, "Giant of the West: Henry J. Kaiser and Regional Industrialization, 1930–1950," *Business History Review* 59 (1985): 1–23; and David R. Dorn, "Ships for Victory," U.S. Naval Institute *Proceedings*, February 1989, 69–75.

23. An excellent description of the U.S. war-production effort appears in Paul Johnson, *Modern Times: A History of the World from the Twenties to the Eighties* (New York: Harper Colophon Books, 1983), 401–2.

24. James and James, *Biography of a Bank*, 468.

25. Johnson, *Modern Times*, 402.

26. Roger Lotchin, "The Metropolitan-Military Complex in Comparative Perspective: San Francisco, Los Angeles, and San Diego, 1919–1941," *Journal of the West*, 1979, 19–30 (quotation on p. 26).

27. Skidmore, *Treasure State Treasury*, 113.

28. Edgel, *Brief History*, p. 18.

29. James and James, *Biography of a Bank*, p. 471.

30. Edgel, *Brief History*, 18.

31. Gerald Nash, in *The American West Transformed*, while appreciating the importance of government spending in the West during the war, underestimates the contributions of individuals and booster groups in perceiving the opportunities for growth associated with those expenditures. One indicator of the fact that government spending itself cannot generate long-lasting growth is the disparity among sunbelt cities themselves. El Paso, for example, suffered no dearth of government money or military contracts. But, lacking determined boosters, it soon fell behind similar cities, such as San Diego, Phoenix, and Oklahoma City. For a comparison of Phoenix, Tucson, Albuquerque, and El Paso, see Bradford Luckingham, *The Urban Southwest: A Profile History of El Paso, Albuquerque, Tucson, and Phoenix* (El Paso: Texas Western Press, University of Texas at El Paso, 1982). Compare with Roger Sale, *Seattle: Past to Present* (Seattle: University of Washington Press, 1976). For boosterism in general see the entire issue of *The Journal of the West* 18 (July 1979); Bradford Luckingham, "The American West: An Urban Perspective," *Journal of Urban History* 7 (November 1981), 99–105; and idem, "The Urban Dimension of Western History," in *Historians and the American West*, ed. Michael Malone (Lincoln: University of Nebraska Press, 1983), 323–43. The original work on boosterism remains Carl Abbott, *Boosters and Businessmen: Popular Economic Thought and Urban Growth in the Antebellum Middle West* (Westport, Conn.: Greenwood Press, 1981).

32. MacColl, *Growth of a City*, 583.

33. Provorse, *PeoplesBank Story*, 132.

34. Hyman, *Challenge and Response*, 180. On these and other bases, see Leonard J. Arrington, Thomas G. Alexander, and Eugene A. Erb, Jr., "Utah's Biggest Business: Ogden Air Material Area at Hill Air Force Base, 1938–1965," *Utah Historical Quarterly* 23 (Winter 1965): 9–33; Thomas G. Alexander, "Ogden's 'Arsenal of Democracy,' 1920–1955," *Utah Historical Quarterly* 23 (Summer 1965): 237–47; Leonard J. Arrington and Thomas G. Alexander, "They Kept 'Em Rolling: Toole Army Depot, 1942–1962," *Utah Historical Quarterly* 23 (Winter 1963): 3–25; Leonard J. Arrington and Archer L. Durham, "Anchors Aweigh in Utah: The U.S. Naval Supply Depot at Clearfield, 1942–1962," *Utah Historical Quarterly* 31 (Spring 1963): 109–26.

35. Hyman, *Challenge and Response*, 180–81.

36. Woods, *Sometimes the Books Froze*, 134.

37. William E. Koenker, *Post-War Banking Trends in North Dakota*, North Dakota Economic Studies, no. 3 (Fargo: University of North Dakota, Bureau of Business and Economic Research, n.d.), 5.

38. A. E. Dahl, *Banker Dahl of South Dakota: An Autobiography* (Rapid City: Festive Book Co., 1965), 102–16, 127.

39. Woods, *Sometimes the Books Froze*, 133–34; Edgel, *Brief History*, 18.

40. Adams, Dorsett, and Pulcipher, *Pioneer Western Bank*, 174.

41. Noel, *Growing through History*, 94.

42. Skidmore, *Treasure State Treasury*, 113.

43. Moore, "Effects of World War II" (Master's thesis), 30.

44. Robert L. Johnson, *Commercial Banking in South Dakota* (Vermillion, S. Dak.: South Dakota University Press, Business Research Bureau, School of Business of South Dakota University, 1964), no. 83, pp. 6, 20. See also U. E. Montgomery, *Manufacturing in South Dakota, 1939–1958* (Vermillion, S. Dak.: South Dakota University Press, Business Research Bureau, School of Business of South Dakota University, 1962), no. 78; Ralph Brown, "The South Dakota Economy: The Historical Perspective," *South Dakota Business Review* 45 (June 1988)

45. Robinson, *History of North Dakota*, 424–31, 443.

46. Larry Schweikart interview with Carl Bimson, March 1980; Keith Monroe, "Bank Knight in Arizona," *American Magazine* 140 (November 1945): 24–25, 116–22; Dedera, "Walter Reed Bimson," 1, 21–29.

47. Singer, *U.S. National Bank*, 84; Wilfred A. Clarke, *History of the Bank of New Mexico: The Past Is Prologue* (New York: Newcomen Society, 1972), 12.

48. Smallwood, *An Oklahoma Adventure*, 151.

49. *Oklahoma Banker*, January 1944, 6. See also James Smallwood, "Financing Urban Growth on the Great Plains, 1945–1970," paper presented at the annual meeting of the Western Economic Association, Lake Tahoe, June 22, 1989, in authors' possession.

50. Smallwood, "Financing Urban Growth" (unpublished paper), 6. See also James H. Thomas, *The Financial Center of Kansas: A History of the Fourth National Bank and Trust Company [of Wichita]* (Oklahoma City: Western Heritage Books, Center for Entrepreneurship and Small Business Administration, Wichita State University, 1980).

51. Larry Schweikart interview with Carl Bimson, March 1980; Monroe, "Bank Knight in Arizona." On the role of FHA lending in general, see Marc Weiss, "Own Your Own Home: American Real Estate Industry and Housing Policy," unpublished paper in authors' possession.

52. Schweikart, *History of Banking in Arizona*, 104.

53. Smallwood, *An Oklahoma Adventure*, 139, 147.

54. Noel, *Growing through History*, 91.

55. Clarke, *History of the Bank of New Mexico*, 19–20.

56. Dahl, *Banker Dahl*, 134.

57. Adams, Dorsett, and Pulcipher, *Pioneer Western Bank*, 161–62, 165, 168, 184.

58. Schweikart, *History of Banking in Arizona*, chap. 6.

59. For material on A. B. Robbs, Jr., see Schweikart, *That Quality Image*.

60. A. B. Robbs Trust Company Ledger, Continental Bank Archives, Chase Bank of Arizona, Scottsdale.

61. Schweikart, *That Quality Image*, 9.

62. Harold Martin, "The New Millionaires of Phoenix," *Saturday Evening Post*, September 30, 1961.

63. Schweikart, *That Quality Image*, 13–15.

64. Ibid. Material on David Murdock appears in a memo to Larry Schweikart from Lilymae Penton, vice president of Murdock Development Company.

65. See Doti and Schweikart, "Financing the Post-War Housing Boom," 173–94.

66. James and James, *Biography of a Bank*, 470, 490.

67. Federal Reserve Board of Governors, *Federal Reserve All Bank Statistics, 1896–1955* (Washington, D.C.: Federal Reserve Board, 1959), 150; James Gillies and Clayton Curtis, *Institutional Residential Mortgage Lending in Los Angeles County, 1946–51: Six Significant Years of Mortgage Lending* (Los Angeles: University of California, Bureau of Business and Economic Research, 1956), p. 65. See also Hyman Minsky, "Commercial Banking and Rapid Economic Growth in California," in *California Banking in a Growing Economy: 1946–1975*, ed. Hyman Minsky (Berkeley: University of California Press, 1965), 79–134.

68. United States Savings and Loan League, *Savings and Loan Annuals, 1949* (Chicago: United States Savings and Loan League, 1949), n.p.

69. See Doti and Schweikart, "Financing the Post-War Housing Boom," table 4, reprinted from Albert Schaaf, "The Savings Function and Mortgage Investment by California Banks and Financial Institutions," in *California Banking*, Hyman Minsky, ed., 249–86 (table on p. 256). The $512 million figure comes from the *Savings and Loan Annuals, 1954*, n.p.

70. James Cox, "Institutional Mortgage Lending in the Los Angeles Metropolitan Area, 1953–54 and 1957–58" (Ph.D. diss., University of California, 1962), 115–17.

71. Minsky, "Commercial Banking," 121.

72. Gillies and Curtis, *Institutional Mortgage Lending*, Appendix, table 7.

73. Schaaf, "Savings Function," *California Banking*, 260–61.

74. Wells Fargo Annual Reports, 1959 and 1975.

75. See Doti and Schweikart, "Financing the Post-War Housing Boom," table 3.

76. Howard Jones, "The History of Banking in the Utah Economy, 1933–1963" (Master's thesis, University of Utah, 1964), 56–57.

77. Hyman, *Challenge and Response*, 175.

78. Ibid., 173, 261, 265.

79. Murray Moler, "A Centennial History of Commercial Security Bank, 1875–1975," manuscript, n.d., n.p. (second page in chapter 5), USHS.

80. Dahl, *Banker Dahl*, 141, 154–65.

81. Adams, Dorsett, and Pulcipher, *Pioneer Western Bank*, 162, 174.

82. Allen Dupont Breck, *John Evans of Denver: Portrait of a Twentieth Century Banker*, University of Denver, The West in American History Series, no. 5 (Boulder: Pruett Publishing Company, 1972), 146.

83. Halaas, *Banking Structure in Colorado*, 2.

84. Smallwood, *Oklahoma Adventure*, 152.

85. Hyman, *Challenge and Response*, 181.

86. Ibid., 183–84.

87. Michael Konig, "Postwar Phoenix, Arizona: Banking and Boosterism," *Journal of the West* 23 (April 1984): 72–76.

88. See Michael Konig, "Toward Metropolis Status: Charter Government and the Rise of Phoenix, Arizona, 1945–1960" (Ph.D. diss., Arizona State University, 1983); idem, transcript of interview with Frank Snell, December 7, 1978, on file in Phoenix History Project, Western Savings Building, Phoenix, idem, transcript of interview with Patrick Downey, July 8, 1978, ibid.

89. "Many Magazines Tell Phoenix Story," *Phoenix Action*, November 1949; "Disinterested Outsiders Say Phoenix Best Publicized City in the U.S.—Here's Why," *Phoenix Action*, February 1950; Martin, "New Millionaires"; "The Brash Banker of Arizona," 23.

90. Patterson quoted in George Anderson, "Banking and Monetary Problems," 93.

91. Peter Wiley and Robert Gottleib, *Empires in the Sun: The Rise of the New American West* (Tucson: University of Arizona Press, 1985), 122.

92. MacColl, *Growth of a City*, 593–601.

93. Downey quoted in Pomeroy, *The Pacific Slope*, 94. See also Remi Nadeau, *City Makers: The Men Who Transformed Los Angeles. . . .* (New York: Doubleday, 1948), 44–48.

94. Noel, *Growing through History*, 94. For a discussion of other Colorado suburbs' booster efforts and the importance of the sunbelt suburbs as a whole, see Carl Abbott, "The Suburban Sunbelt," *Journal of Urban History* 13 (May 1987): 275–301.

95. Adams, Dorsett, and Pulcipher, *Pioneer Western Bank*, 174.

96. Breck, *John Evans*, 152–54, 160–61.

97. "Great Family: Evans of Denver," *Life*, June 15, 1959, 103–11.

98. Noel, *Growing through History*, 96, 124.

99. Skidmore, *Treasure State Treasury*, 113–15.

100. MacColl, *Growth of a City*, 607, 624–34.

101. *Oregon Journal*, February 4, 1917.

102. MacColl, *Growth of a City*, 65.

103. *[Portland] Oregon Journal*, February 4, 1917.

104. MacColl, *Growth of a City*, 66.

105. Ibid., 625–39.

106. See Abbott's comments on the relationship between the suburban boosters and the growth of sunbelt cities in "Suburban Sunbelt," 294–95 (quotation on p. 295). See also Abbott's *The New Urban America: Growth and Politics in Sunbelt Cities* (Chapel Hill: University of North Carolina Press, 1981) and Richard Bernard and Bradley Rice, eds. *Sunbelt Cities: Politics and Growth Since World War II* (Austin: University of Texas Press, 1983).

107. Wiley and Gottleib, *Empires in the Sun,* 123–24.

108. Adams, Dorsett, and Pulcipher, *Pioneer Western Bank,* 175.

109. Ibid., 174–75.

110. On Transamerica, see James and James, *Biography of a Bank,* and George H. Koster, with Elizabeth Summers, *The Transamerica Story: 50 Years of Service and Looking Forward* (San Francisco: Transamerica Corporation, 1978).

111. Hyman, *Marriner S. Eccles,* 325.

112. Ibid., 339.

113. Ibid., 324–25.

114. Edward S. Herman, "The Board of Governors v. Transamerica: Victory from Defeat," *The Antitrust Bulletin* 4 (March 1964): 521–39.

115. Koster, *Transamerica Story,* 29–32.

116. See, for example, Walter A. Buenger and Joseph Pratt, *But Also Good Business: Texas Commerce Banks and the Financing of Houston and Texas, 1886–1986* (College Station: Texas A & M University Press, 1986).

117. William E. Koenker, *Post-War Banking Trends in North Dakota,* Economic Studies, no. 3 (Fargo: University of North Dakota, Bureau of Business and Economic Research, n.d.), 7–8.

118. Provorse, *PeoplesBank Story,* 170. See also Marple and Olson, *National Bank of Commerce;* and Scates, *FIRSTBANK.*

119. See Albert R. Gutowsky, "History of Commercial Banking in Oregon," *Oregon Business Review* 24 (August 1965): 1–6.

120. Edward S. Herman quoted in Edward S. Herman, "The Transamerica Case: A Study of the Federal Reserve Board Anti-Trust Proceedings" (Ph.D. diss., University of California, Berkeley, 1953), 80.

121. Gutowsky, "History of Commercial Banking," 4.

122. Edgel, *Brief History,* 22–23.

123. Skidmore, *Treasure State Treasury,* 120.

124. *Helena People's Voice,* March 29, 1957.

125. Skidmore, *Treasure State Treasury,* 117. See also Patricia P. Douglas, *Montana Banking Study* (Helena: Helena Branch of the Federal Reserve Bank of Minneapolis, 1971); and Lothar I. Iverson, *Montana and U.S. Banks—A Comparison of Assets and Liabilities, 1934–1950* (Missoula: Montana State University [AOW University of Montana] at Missoula, Bureau of Economic Research, School of Business Administration, 1952).

126. Ibid., 14, table 2.

127. Koenker, *Post-War Banking Trends in North Dakota,* 14.

128. Smallwood, *Oklahoma Adventure,* 141–43.

129. George Gilder, *The Spirit of Enterprise* (New York: Simon and Schuster, 1984), 23–41.

130. Schweikart, *History of Banking in Arizona,* 128–31; Wiley and Gottleib, *Empires in the Sun,* 145, 168.

131. James and James, *Biography of a Bank,* 399, 403–11.

132. Skidmore, *Treasure State Treasury,* 118.

133. Smallwood, *Oklahoma Adventure,* 154–55.

134. Ibid., p. 155.

135. Horwitz and Schull, "The Impact of Branch Banking on Bank Performance," 143–89. Bernard Schull and Paul Horwitz, "Branch Banking and the Structure of Competition," in *Studies in Banking Competition and the Banking Structure*, ed. Comptroller of the Currency, reprinted in *The National Banking Review* 1 (March 1964): 106; Fischer, *American Banking Structure*.

136. Gerry Findley, *Mergers and Acquisitions among California Banks, 1955–1965* (Temple City, Calif.: G. Findley, 1965), 1–42.

137. Fischer, *American Banking Structure*, 132. Hellman quoted in Lynne Pierson Doti, "Banking in California: The Second Branching Era," paper presented at the annual meeting of the Western Economic Association, San Francisco, July 1981, 12.

138. Ibid.

139. Ibid.

140. Fischer, *American Banking Structure*, 285.

141. Ibid.

142. James and James, *Biography of a Bank*, 494. A good description of Kaiser's automotive ventures is found in David Halberstam, *The Reckoning* (New York: Avon, 1986), 323–25.

143. Ibid.

144. Quotations appear in Halberstam, *The Reckoning*, 332, 334.

145. Provorse, *PeoplesBank Story*, 153–54.

146. Carl Bimson, "Report Before the American Bankers Association," April 20–24, 1956, 120–27, Speeches of Carl Bimson, VNB; Speech of Carl Bimson, "Vital Vitamin in the Body Economic," March 19, 1956, ibid.

147. Roger E. Bolton, *Defense Purchases and Regional Growth* (Washington, D.C.: The Brookings Institution, 1966) 91–93, 99.

148. Provorse, *PeoplesBank Story*, 139.

149. Wiley and Gottleib, *Empires in the Sun*, 198–200.

150. For the Greens' story, see Provorse, *PeoplesBank Story* as well as Gordon Newell, *The Green Years* (Seattle: Superior Publishing Company, 1969).

151. Provorse, *PeoplesBank Story*, 51–75.

152. Ibid., 148.

6. THE ASIAN INVASION

1. Sale, *Power Shift*, 17–53.

2. See Schweikart, *That Quality Image*, 10–11; A. B. Robbs Trust Company "Dispatch," January–November 1961, box 1, folder 4, Continental Bank [now Chase Bank] Archives (CB), Scottsdale, Arizona.

3. Larry Schweikart interviews with A. B. Robbs, Jr., June 27, 1985, tape 3, CB.

4. Schweikart, *That Quality Image*, 13–15.

5. Larry Schweikart interviews with Lilymae Penton, July 19, 1985, tape 12, CB. Penton, now a senior vice president in Murdock Development Company, at the time of the actions was a senior vice president for the Robbs Trust Company.

6. A. B. Robbs Trust Company Minutes, August 15, 1963, box 6; "Application to Organize a National Bank," August 26, 1963, box 13, folder 1; Larry Schweikart interviews with A. B. Robbs, Jr., June 27, 1985, tape 3, all in CB.

7. A. B. Robbs Trust Company Minutes, August 15, 1963, CB.

8. Larry Schweikart interviews with George Steinhilber, July 2, 1985, tape 6, CB. See also Doti and Schweikart, "Financing the Post-War Housing Boom," 173–94; and Larry Schweikart, "Financing Urban Growth: Entrepreneurial Creativity and Western Cities, 1945–1975," *Urban History* 26 (February 1989): 177–86.

9. Schweikart, *That Quality Image*, 72, taken from Sheshunoff, *Banks of the West*.

10. See Larry Schweikart, "Dynamic Legacy: Thunderbird Bank, the First Twenty Years, 1964–1984," privately printed by Thunderbird Bank, 1985.

11. Edgel, *Brief History*, 25–26.

12. Luckingham, *The Urban Southwest*.

13. Lynne Pierson Doti, "Nationwide Branching: Some Lessons from California," in *Essays in Economic and Business History*, vol. 9, ed. Ed Perkins (Los Angeles: University of Southern California for the Economic and Business Historical Society, forthcoming, 1991).

14. Fischer, *American Banking Structure*, 210–11, 221.

15. Findley, *Mergers and Acquisitions*, I-20–I-22.

16. Based on information from Findley "Mergers and Acquisitions," I-2–I-5.

17. Smallwood, *Oklahoma Adventure*, 170–72.

18. Irvine H. Sprague, *Bailout: An Insider's Account of Bank Failures and Rescues* (New York: Basic Books, 1987), 109–213.

19. Woods, *Sometimes the Books Froze*, 141–43.

20. Glen Barrett, *Idaho Banking, 1863–1976* (Boise: Boise University Press, 1976), 94.

21. Schweikart, *A History of Banking in Arizona*, 144–47; idem, *That Quality Image*; "Dynamic Legacy."

22. Schweikart, *History of Banking in Arizona*, 144–47; Schweikart, interviews with anonymous bank sources.

23. Gutowsky, "History of Commercial Banking in Oregon," 1–6.

24. Singer, *U.S. National Bank*, 111.

25. Adams, Dorsett, and Pulcipher, *Pioneer Western Bank*, 205–6.

26. Jay Fell, Jr., *Twenty-Five Years of Banking in the Rockies: The Story of United Banks of Colorado* (Denver: United Banks of Colorado, 1989).

27. Noel, *Growing through History*, 123–24. See also Adams, Dorsett, and Pulcipher, *Pioneer Western Bank*, 196, 205, for First of Denver's response to the problem.

28. Noel, *Growing through History*, 123–29.

29. On construction in Phoenix, see Schweikart, *History of Banking in Arizona*, 158–61; and in Denver, see Noel, *Growing through History*, 94, and Adams, Dorsett, and Pulcipher, *Pioneer Western Bank*, 184–85, 188–89.

30. James Smallwood, notes on Oklahoma banks, in authors' possession.

31. Singer, *U.S. National Bank*, 112.

32. The role of foreign investment in the U.S. is discussed in Reginald McGrane, *Foreign Bondholders and American State Debts* (New York: McMillan, 1935).

33. Green, *Finance and Economic Development in the Old South*, discusses the problems that the English went through trying to collect on Louisiana bonds, for example. The antebellum experiences of Mississippi and Florida are found in Schweikart, *Banking in the American South*, 48–90, 170–82.

34. "Buying into a Good Thing," *National Review*, October 14, 1988, 17. See also Jack Anderson, "Who Owns America?" *Parade Magazine*, April 16, 1989, 4–6; Martin Tolchin and Susan Tolchin, *Buying into America: How Foreign Money Is Changing the Face of Our Nation* (New York: Times Books, 1988); and Clyde V. Prestowitz, Jr., *Trading Places: How We Allowed Japan to Take the Lead* (New York: Basic Books, 1988), for updated versions of the "Yellow Peril" alarms. Anderson's piece is especially misleading, for it deals only with current purchases (i.e., "who's buying America") and not the percentage of the total that those purchases represent, or how they are offset by Americans' purchases overseas. A vastly different view of the trade deficit appears in George Gilder, *Microcosm: The Quantum Revolution in Economics and Technology* (New York: Simon and Schuster, 1989).

35. "Buying into a Good Thing," 17.

36. See Don Russ, "The Asian Invasion," *Bankers Magazine* 166 (January/February 1981): 48–52.

37. Benjamin C. Wright, *Banking in California, 1849–1910* (New York: Arno Press, 1980 [orig. pub. 1910]), 48–49, 52–53, 55, 61, 66.

38. Lyman, *Ralston's Ring*, 210.

39. Wright, *Banking in California*, 61.

40. Cross, *Financing an Empire*, 884; Clarke, *William Tecumseh Sherman*, 73.

41. "Banks of All Flags," *Forbes*, September 5, 1980, 15, 18.

42. Robert A. Johnson, "California's Competitive Banking," *The Banker* 127 (October 1977): 77.

43. David Fairlamb, "Japanese Banks Invade the West," *Dun's Business Month*, June 1986, 52–53.

44. James Houpt, "Foreign Ownership of U.S. Banks: Trends and Effects," *Journal of Bank Research* 14 (Summer 1983): 144–56. See also Ellen Goldberg, "Competitive Cost Analysis of Foreign Owned U.S. Banks," *Journal of Bank Research* 13 (Autumn 1982): 144–59.

45. Chaucer F. Yang, "The Impact of Foreign Bank Invasion in the United States," *Los Angeles Business and Economics* 4 (Summer/Fall 1979): 38–41.

46. Paul E. Homrighausen, "One Large Step toward Less-Check: The California Automated Clearing House System," *Business Lawyer* 28 (July 1973): 1143–60.

47. Ibid., 1159.

48. "Here Come the Cards," *Forbes*, February 15, 1969, 39–40.

49. Garrison A. Southard, Jr., "California Master Charge," *Bankers Monthly Magazine* 7 (February 1968): 40–42.

50. Gary Hector, *Breaking the Bank: The Decline of BankAmerica* (Boston: Little Brown and Company, 1988), 69. See also Moira Johnston, *The Roller Coaster: The Bank of America in the World Economy* (N.Y.: Ticknor & Fields, 1990).

51. Material on ATMs was provided from the clipping file of the American Bankers Association. For a comparative look at ATM installment strategy, see John Donald Wilson, *The Chase: The Chase Manhattan Bank, N.A., 1945–1985* (Boston: Harvard Business School Press, 1986), 161, 288, 315, 321, and 405 n. 26; and Harold van B. Cleveland and Thomas F. Huertas, *Citibank, 1812–1970* (Cambridge, Mass.: Harvard University Press, 1985).

52. Bill Orr, "California, a Foot-Dragger in ATMs, Comes to Life," *ABA Banking Journal* 71 (September 1979): 139–44 (quotation on p. 139).

53. Hector, *Breaking the Bank*, 69.

54. Hyman, *Challenge and Response*, 378–79.

55. Adams, Dorsett, and Pulcipher, *Pioneer Western Bank*, 186.

56. Dahl, *Banker Dahl*, 244–57.

57. Hyman, *Challenge and Response*, 381–82.

58. These descriptions appear in Hector, *Breaking the Bank*, 72–124 (quotation on p. 75).

59. Ibid., 78, 82.

60. Ibid., 86, 90.

61. Kirkpatrick Sale, *Power Shift*, 32.

62. Kirkpatrick Sale, *Power Shift*, 32.

63. Ibid., 33.

64. Schweikart, *History of Banking in Arizona*, 161, n. 17.

65. Ibid., 16. *Financial World*, March 15, 1979, 24–25.

66. Schweikart, *History of Banking in Arizona*, 164 n. 21.

67. Ibid.

68. Hyman, *Challenge and Response*, 402.

69. Tom Barry, *New Mexico's Financial Institutions: An Investigation* (Albuquerque: New Mexico People and Energy, 1980), 2. Compare New Mexico with Arizona at the time that critics contended that too much concentration of assets existed there. See Larry Schweikart,

"Collusion or Competition? Another Look at Banking in the Postwar Period, 1950–1964," *Journal of Arizona History* 28 (Summer 1987): 189–200.

70. Barry, *New Mexico's Financial Institutions*, 2, 6, 13–14, 23.

71. Ibid., 13–14, 23.

72. Larry Schweikart, "Financial Concentration and the Growth of Phoenix," in *Phoenix: The First Century*, G. Wesley Johnson (Norman: University of Oklahoma Press, forthcoming).

73. Charles Lockwood and Christopher B. Leincberger, "Los Angeles Comes of Age," *Atlantic Monthly*, January 1988, 31–62 (quotation on p. 35); Hector, *Breaking the Bank*, 267.

74. Hector, *Breaking the Bank*, 267.

75. Connie Bruck, *The Predator's Ball* (New York: Penguin, 1989 [orig. pub. 1988]), 78–88.

76. Samuel C. Webb and Leland F. Cox, "Correspondent Banking in Wichita," *Business Journal* (College of Business Administration, Wichita State University), no. 30 (September 1968); 12–16 (quotation on p. 12).

77. Thomas, *The Fourth*, 80, 93.

78. "Building for the Future," *IV Front*, June/July 1987, 4.

79. Barry, *New Mexico's Financial Institution*, 1, 12.

80. Wiley and Gottleib, *Empires in the Sun*, 137.

81. See Fell, *Twenty-Five Years of Banking*, 2–4.

82. Fell, *Twenty-Five Years of Banking*, 7.

83. Ibid., 12.

84. Quoted in Alice Kessler-Harris, *Out to Work: A History of Wage-Earning Women in the United States* (Oxford: Oxford University Press, 1982), 230.

85. Barrett, *Idaho Banking*, 155, 183.

86. Kessler-Harris, *Out to Work*, 236.

87. "The Last Word in Service for our Women Customers," *IV Front*, June/July 1987, 5.

88. Provorse, *PeoplesBank Story*, 131.

89. Singer, *U.S. National Bank*, 80.

90. Provorse, *PeoplesBank*, 180.

91. Schweikart, *History of Banking in Arizona*, 142; Kent Richards, "The Lady Is a Banker," *Phoenix* 4 (June 1969): 70–76; Larry Schweikart interviews with Anna Foster, various dates, 1980; Memo, Carl Bimson to Larry Schweikart, September, 1980; Larry Schweikart interview with Anna Foster, August 29, 1980; Singer, *U.S. National Bank*, 71.

92. Barry, *New Mexico's Financial Institutions*, 19.

93. Hector, *Breaking the Bank*, 22.

94. Adams, Dorsett, and Pulcipher, *Pioneer Western Bank*, 206–7.

95. Larry Schweikart interview with Sherman Hazeltine, May 20, 1980, and various informal discussions with Sherman and Cynthia Hazeltine, 1980.

96. "How's your Bank, Honey," *MS.*, January–February, 1989, 142.

97. Larry Schweikart interview with Ruby Nelson, June 24, 1985, tape 1, CB.

98. Larry Schweikart interview with Lilymae Penton, July 19, 1985, tape 12, CB.

99. Hector, *Breaking the Bank*.

100. Interviews with various anonymous bankers.

101. Adams, *Pioneer Western Bank*, 180–81.

7. FROM DEREGULATION TO NEW FRONTIERS

1. See "Arizona's Deepening Real-Estate Slump Is Hammering Hard at Banking Firms," *The Wall Street Journal*, October 23, 1989.

2. Material on the destabilizing effects of deposit insurance is seen in Robert D. Auerbach, *Money, Banking, and Financial Markets*, 3d ed. (New York: Macmillan Publishing Co., 1988), 140–44; Rolnick and Weber, "Inherent Instability in Banking: The Free Banking Experience," *Cato Journal*, Winter 1986, 877–90; and Lawrence J. White, "Regulatory Sources of Instability in Banking," *Cato Journal*, Winter 1986, 890–97; John Kareken and Neil Wallace, "Deposit Insurance and Bank Regulation: A Partial-Equilibrium Exposition," *Journal of Business*, July 1978, 413–38.

3. Carol Martel and Larry Schweikart, "Arizona Banking and the Collapse of Lincoln Thrift," *Arizona and the West*, 28 (Autumn 1986): 246–63.

4. James Ring Adams, *The Big Fix: Inside the S&L Scandal, How an Unholy Alliance of Politics and Money Destroyed America's Banking System* (New York: John Wiley & Sons, 1990); and Paul Zane Pilzer with Robert Deitz, *Other People's Money: The Inside Story on the S&L Mess* (New York: Simon and Schuster, 1989). On the S&L troubles, see "The S&L Mess," *USA Today*, August 14, 1989; Ned Eichler, *The Thrift Debacle* (Berkeley: University of California Press, 1989); and "S&L Crisis Focuses on Chairman," *Dayton Daily News*, July 9, 1989.

5. James Ring Adams, "The Big Fix," *American Spectator* 22 (March 1989): 21–22; R. Cort Kirkwood and Terrence P. Jeffrey, "Quis Custodiet?" *National Review*, April 21, 1989, 35–36. Among other questionable activities, Wright protected Don Dixon, the head of Vernon Savings and Loan, who provided a corporate jet for the ex-Speaker.

6. "S&L Crisis Focuses on Chairman."

7. "Lincoln Savings Posts $847 Million 1st Half Loss," *Orange County [Calif.] Register*, July 28, 1989.

8. David Greenwald and Ricardo Sandoval, "Keating Jailed on Fraud Charges," *Orange County [Calif.] Register*, September 19, 1990, 1.

9. "Shaky Comeback: Knapp's New Firm Seems Short on Money, Long on Failed Deals," *Wall Street Journal*, May 30, 1989. The renaming of S&Ls, allowed by the 1982 Garn–St Germain Amendment, became common as the industry's troubles deepened, creating more danger of contagion to the banks.

10. For a list of all S&Ls in the country and their status, see "The S&Ls: Where They Stand," *USA Today*, August 14, 1989. See also Lawrence J. White, "Problems of the FSLIC: A Former Policy Maker's View," *Contemporary Policy Issues* 8 (April 1990): 62–81; and Angelo R. Mascaro, "Aftermath of the Thrift Crisis: Balancing the Economy's Books," *Contemporary Policy Issues* 8 (April 1990): 95–106.

11. For material on the real-estate problems, see "Arizona's Deepening Real-Estate Slump"; "Big Banks Form 'Bad Banks' to Discard Problem Loans," *Arizona Republic*, November 20, 1988; "Commercial Real-Estate Bog Muddying Valley Banks Boots," ibid., June 26, 1989; and Terry Greene, "And the Money Kept Flowing," *New Times*, June 21–27, 1989, 22, 26–28, 30–32.

12. The FDIC report is summarized in "Accounting for Bank Problems," *USA today*, May 29, 1990.

13. "Rough Times Ahead for USA Banks," ibid. The large eastern banks suffered almost as badly as those in the West: due to real-estate problems, Chase Manhattan reported $1.3 billion in nonperforming real-estate assets, Citicorp $1.9 billion on a $13.7 billion portfolio of real-estate loans, and Chemical Bank $1.2 billion on $10 billion worth of loans. See Beth Belton, "Big Banks Teeter in Real-Estate Crisis" *USA Today*, July 10, 1990.

14. "Arizona Bank Performance 48th in Nation," *[Phoenix] Arizona Republic*, July 25, 1989.

15. "Arizona's Deepening Real-Estate Slump"; "Commercial Real-Estate Bog Muddying Valley Bank's Boots."

16. "Arizona's Deepening Real-Estate Slump."

17. Louis E. Jeffries, "Nebraska Bank Failures and the State of Nebraska Banking," *Business in Nebraska* 39 (June 1988): 1–5 (Bureau of Business Research, University of Nebraska-Lincoln).

18. "Big Banks form 'Bad Banks' to Discard Problem Loans."

19. Irvine H. Sprague, *Bailout*, 109–34. See also Gerald P. O'Driscoll, "Bank Failures: The Deposit Insurance Connection," *Contemporary Policy Issues* 6 (April 1988): 1–12. In September 1990, Henry Gonzales, chairman of the House Banking Committee, revealed a plan to reduce the coverage of FDIC insurance to $30,000 per account.

20. Irving H. Sprague, *Bailout*, 113, 134.

21. "Security Pacific Plans Stake in Unit of Mitsui Bank Ltd.," *Wall Street Journal*, July 28, 1989.

22. Jack Anderson, "Who Owns America?"

23. Joel Kotkin and Yoriko Kishimoto, *The Third Century: America's Resurgence in the Asian Era* (New York: Crown Publishers, 1988).

24. Henry R. Nau, *The Myth of America's Decline: Leading the World Economy into the 1990s* (New York: Oxford University Press, 1990).

25. *[Phoenix] Arizona Republic*, June 25, 1989.

26. "Small Business Surge in U.S. West Region Outpouring Big Firms," ibid., June 28, 1989.

27. Gilder, *Microcosm*. See also idem, "The Message of the Microcosm," *American Spectator*, December 1987, 16–19; and idem, "The Revitalization of Everything: the Law of the Microcosm," *Harvard Business Review*, March–April 1988, 49–61. Walter Wriston's similar ideas appear in "Technology and Sovereignty," *Foreign Affairs*, Winter 1988, 63–75.

28. "Building a Factory? Try N. H.," *USA Today*, July 14, 1988.

29. Richard Timberlake, "Banking Legislation in the 1980s," in *Encyclopedia of American Business History and Biography: Banking and Finance in the 20th Century*, ed. Larry Schweikart (Columbia: Bruccoli Clark Layman, 1990).

30. Gary Binger, "South Dakota Banking: The Low Down on High Finance in Middle America, a History of the Citibanking Revolution" (manuscript), 10, 13 (Preamble to House Bill 1046), 18, South Dakota State Archives.

31. *Sioux Falls Argus Leader*, March 8, 1980, quoted in ibid., 21.

32. Binger, "South Dakota Banking," 31–33, 89–90, South Dakota State Archives.

33. Ibid., 68.

34. Walter Wriston, "Looking Backward at the Nineteen Eighties," speech before the Reserve City Bankers, Boca Raton, Florida, March 21, 1980, quoted in ibid., 84.

35. Calomiris, "Deposit Insurance: Lessons from the Record," 10–30; idem, "Is Deposit Insurance Necessary? A Historical Perspective" *Journal of Economic History* 50 (June 1990): 283–95.

36. Richard L. Nelson, "Optimal Banking Structure: Implications for Interstate Banking," *Contemporary Policy Issues* 6 (April 1988): 13–23.

37. Dean F. Amel and Michael J. Jacowski, "Trends in Banking Structure Since the Mid-1970s." *Federal Reserve Bulletin*, March 1989, 120–33.

38. Woods, *Sometimes the Books Froze*, 140.

39. Amel and Jacowski, "Trends in Banking," 131, table 9.

40. Woods, *Sometimes the Books Froze*, 140.

41. Lockwood and Leinberger, "Los Angeles Comes of Age," 31–62.

42. Hanson quoted in Kotkin and Kishimoto, *The Third Century*, 201.

43. "BankAmerica Pulls Itself from the Brink," *USA Today*, May 24, 1989.

44. See Hector, *Breaking the Bank*.

45. Ibid., 163. Although no longer in banking, Transamerica, the one-time holding company of Bank of America, also had blundered into a major disaster when it purchased the United Artists motion picture company in 1967. The movie company never helped TransAmerica because, with one exception, the public did not identify United Artists with Transamerica. The exception proved fatal, however, for despite several major hits, the company failed utterly to control the budget of Michael Cimino's *Heaven's Gate*, a picture budgeted at $7 million that finally appeared in 1983 after UA spent close to $40 million on it. The disaster prompted Transamerica to see UA to MGM. See Steven Bach, *Final Cut: Dreams and Disaster in the Making of Heaven's Gate* (New York: William Morrow and Company, 1985).

46. Hector, *Breaking the Bank*, 165–69.

47. Irvine H. Sprague, *Bailout*, 135–48.

48. Hector, *Breaking the Bank*, 207–14.

49. Ibid., 251–53, 277–88 (quotation on p. 277).

50. Christopher Conte, "Small Town Bankers Fight to Keep Curbs on Big Rival's Growth," *Wall Street Journal*, June 3, 1983.

51. "A Solid Year, with Regionals Leading the Way," *Business Week*, April 7, 1986.

52. Daniel M. Clark, "Diversification: The Watchword at Security Pacific," *ABA Banking Journal* 78, no. 5 (May 1986).

53. Steven Davis, *Excellence in Banking: A Profile of Superior Management Based on Insight into Citibank, Deutschbank, Morgan and Thirteen Other Selected Banks* (New York: St. Martin's Press, 1987).

54. Laura Seagall and John Allen, "Security Pacific: Richard J. Flamson III Runs the Most Diversified Institution in California," *The Executive*, Nov. 1985, 18–24 (quotation on p. 18).

55. Koster, *TransAmerica Story*, 33–34; Daniel C. Kibble, *Their Bank—Our Bank, the Quality Bank: A History of the First Interstate Bank of California* (Costa Mesa, Calif.: Professional Publications, 1981), 196–98.

56. Kibble, *Their Bank—Our Bank*, 218–19, 227–28.

57. Ibid., 257–59.

58. Ibid., 276.

59. *Time* article quoted in "Pinola's Introduction," manuscript supplied by First Interstate Bank.

60. Schweikart, *History of Banking in Arizona*, 164.

61. Kibble, *Their Bank—Our Bank*, 304.

62. Robert Bryan, "First Interstate: California's Restless Giant," *Bankers Monthly* 103, no. 10 (October 1986): 25.

63. These prices come from the Shearson-Lehman offering in the appendix of Schweikart, *That Quality Image*. Similar occurrences were noted across the Sunbelt, where the real-estate boom of the 1970s had inflated the market value, but not the book value, of the banks' physical assets. For other examples, see John G. Sproat and Larry Schweikart, *Making Change: South Carolina Banking in the Twentieth Century* (Columbia, S.C.: Bruccoli Clark Layman, 1990), 161–89.

64. See U.S. National Bank, "News Releases," May 19, 1987, and February 8, June 30, November 17, December 15, 1988, and January 3, 1989, U.S. National Bank, Portland, Ore.

65. The same pattern appeared in South Carolina. See Sproat and Schweikart, *Making Change*, 161–89.

66. See also Edward Loomis, *Bank Burning: A Documentary Novel from Isla Vista* (Santa Barbara: Capricorn Press, 1970).

67. Kirk Scharfenberg, "The Community as Bank Examiner," *Working Papers for a New Society* 7 (1980): 30–35.

68. Ibid., 31–32.

69. Schweikart, *That Quality Image*, 67–68.

70. Scharfenberg, "Community as Bank Examiner," 33–34.

71. Ibid., 35.

72. Richard Bernard, ed. *Snowbelt Cities: Metropolitan Politics in the Northeast and Midwest since World War II* (Bloomington, Ind.: Indiana University Press, 1990), 1.

BIBLIOGRAPHY

ABBREVIATIONS

AHS	Aryona Historical Society, Tucson
ASU	Arizona State University Library, Tempe
BYU	Brigham Young University, Provo
CB	Chase Bank of Arizona, Scottsdale
CHS	Colorado Historical Society, Denver
KHS	Kansas Historical Society, Topeka
MHS	Montana Historical Society Archives, Helena
MNM	Museum of New Mexico, Santa Fe
NAU	Northern Arizona University, Flagstaff
NDHS	North Dakota Historical Society, Bismarck
NHS	Nevada Historical Society, Reno
NSHS	Nebraska State Historical Society, Lincoln
OBA	Oklahoma Bankers Association Archives, Oklahoma City
OHS	Oklahoma Historical Society, Oklahoma City
ORHS	Oregon Historical Society, Portland
SDHS	South Dakota Historical Society, Pierre
UA	University of Arizona, Tucson
UNM	University of New Mexico, Albuquerque
UO	University of Oregon, Eugene
USHS	Utah State Historical Society, Salt Lake City
UU	University of Utah Library
VNB	Valley National Bank, Phoenix

ARCHIVAL MATERIALS

Arizona Historical Society, Tucson (AHS)
Arizona State University Library (ASU)
   William J. Murphy Collection
   Jesse N. Smith, Diary

Jesse N. Smith, "The Story of the . . . Bank of Northern Arizona"
Brigham Young University (BYU)
  Ogden State Bank, Minutebook of the Board of Directors
  Provo Commercial and Savings Bank Records, Lee Library
Chase Bank of Arizona (CB), Scottsdale
  Continental Bank Archives
Colorado Historical Society (CHS), Denver
  Absalom Hunter Papers
  Agnes Wright Spring Papers
  Collection 598, "Loose Papers"
  Denver National Bank, Collection 195
  Hilliard & Hilliard, Receivers, MS. 311
  Minutebook, City Bank of Leadville
  Warwick Downing Papers
Denver Public Library, Denver
  Kountze Collection
Huntington Library, San Marino
  Bacon Papers
Iowa Historical Society (IHS)
  Cook, Sargent, and Downey Papers
Kansas Historical Society (KHS), Topeka
  Collections, Ingalls Papers
  W. E. Connelley, *Kansas and Kansas*, 1918 ed.
  Harrison Papers
  Hawkes Papers
  Jobes Correspondence and Miscellaneous Papers
  John Davis Scrapbook E
  "Misc. Aulls, Silas"
Montana Historical Society Archives (MHS), Helena
  First National Bank of Helena Records, User's Guide
  Merchants National Bank Records, User's Guide
Museum of New Mexico (MNM), Santa Fe
  Second National Bank Collection
National Archives, Washington, D.C.
  1932 National Archives, Secretarial Division
  Records of the Comptroller of the Currency
Nebraska State Historical Society (NSHS), Lincoln
  Cook, Sargent, and Parker Papers
  "Farmers and Merchants Bank, Edison, Nebraska, 25th Anniversary, 1929–1954" (1954 pamphlet)
  J. Floyd McClain MSS
  Stockmen's National Bank–Rushville, Nebraska
  William B. Thorpe, Diary and Examiner's Books
Nevada Historical Society (NHS), Reno
  George Wingfield Papers
North Dakota Historical Society (NDHS), Bismarck
  Farmers and Merchants Bank, Record Book, MS. 10272
  Issac Post Baker Papers
Northern Arizona University (NAU), Flagstaff
  Lewis Collection, First National [now, First Interstate] Bank Collection
Oklahoma Bankers Association Archives (OBA), Oklahoma City

James Neal, Notes, 1942
"Report on Bank Robberies and Burglaries in Oklahoma, 1920–1930"
Oklahoma Historical Society (OHS), Oklahoma City
  Exchange Bank Memobook, Ledgerbook, Archives
  Kelley Collection
Oregon Historical Society (ORHS)
  Corbett and Failing Papers
South Dakota Historical Society (SDHS)
  I. M. Beebe Papers
  William M. Pease, "Tales of Pioneering" (manuscript), n.d. [circa 1910]
South Dakota State Archives
  Gary Binger, "South Dakota Banking: The Low Down on High Finance in Middle America, a History of the Citibanking Revolution"
Stanford University Library
  MSS JL2/1/2, JL2/1/3, JL2/7/89
  Records of Donohue Kelly Banking Company
University of Arizona Library (UAL), Tucson
  Franklin Collection
  Jacobs Collection
University of California, Berkeley, Bancroft Library
  Auerback Collection
  Ralston Papers
University of New Mexico (UNM), Albuquerque
  Chavez Collection
  First National Bank of Santa Fe Collection
  William Parish Papers, Zimmerman Library
University of Oregon (UO), Eugene
  Abbot L. Mills Papers
  Corbett and Failing Papers
  J. C. Ainsworth Papers
University of Utah Library (UU)
  Frederick Kesler Papers
  Preston Nutter Collection
Utah State Historical Society (USHS)
  "McCornick & Co.," MS. A864
  William F. Armstrong papers
Valley National Bank (VNB), Phoenix
  "Speeches of Carl Bimson"

GOVERNMENT DOCUMENTS

Arizona State Banking Department Records
Articles of Incorporation and Conditions of Agreement with Depositors [of the California Savings and Loan Society], San Francisco, 1873.
Board of Bank Commissioners of the State of California, *Annual Reports to the Governor and the Legislature* (Sacramento: State Printing Office, various years).
Clay County, South Dakota, mortgage records, books E and F
Common Council of the City of Phoenix, Minutes, December 12, 1884.
Comptroller of the Currency. *The Seventy-Third Annual Report of the Comptroller of the Currency for the Year Ended October 31, 1935*. Washington: Government Printing Office, 1936.

Congressional Record, 53d Cong., 2d Sess., 1894 vol. 26.
————. 53d Cong., 3d Sess., 1895, vol. 27.
————. 54th Cong., 2d Sess., 1896, vol. 29.
————. 56th Cong., 1st Sess., 1899, vol. 33.
Federal Reserve Board of Governors. *Federal Reserve All Bank Statistics, 1896–1955.* Washington, D.C.: Federal Reserve Board, 1959.
New York State Banking Department, *Postwar Banking Developments in New York State.* Albany: New York State Banking Dept., 1958.
Noble State Bank v. *Haskell,* 219 U.S. 104.
Report of the [Arizona] State Bank Comptroller. Phoenix: Arizona State Printing Office, 1916.
Shibley, George H. "History of Guaranty of Bank Deposits in the States of Oklahoma, Texas, Nebraska, and South Dakota, 1908–1914." Pamphlet reproduced in *Senate Document* no. 522, 63d Cong., 2d Sess. Washington: Government Printing Office, 1914.
Utah Bankers Association Salt Lake City Clearinghouse, minutes, Salt Lake City
Veazie Bank v. *Fenno,* 8 Wall. 533 (1869).
Wyoming Bankers Association Proceedings of the Fourteenth Annual Convention Held at Laramie, Wyoming, September 19, 1922. Cheyenne: Wyoming Bankers Association, 1923.

BOOKS

Abbott, Carl. *Boosters and Businessmen: Popular Economic Thought and Urban Growth in the Antebellum Middle West.* Westport, Conn.: Greenwood Press, 1981.
————. *The New Urban America: Growth and Politics in Sunbelt Cities.* Chapel Hill: University of North Carolina Press, 1981.
Adams, Eugene H., Lyle W. Dorsett, and Robert S. Pulcipher. *The Pioneer Western Bank— First of Denver, 1860–1980.* Edited by Robert S. Pulcipher. Denver: First Interstate Bank of Denver, NA, 1984.
Adams, James Ring. *The Big Fix: Inside the S&L Scandal, How an Unholy Alliance of Politics and Money Destroyed America's Banking System.* New York: John Wiley & Sons, 1990.
Anderson, George, *Essays on the History of Banking.* Lawrence: Coronado Press, 1972.
Andreas, Alfred Theodore. *History of the State of Kansas Containing a Full Account of Its Growth from an Uninhabited Territory to a Wealthy and Important State; Of Its Early Settlement; Its Rapid Increase in Population and the Marvelous Development of Its Great Natural Resources. Also, a Supplementary History and Description of Its Counties, Cities, Towns, and Villages, Their Advantages, Industries, Manufacturers and Commerce; To Which Are Added Biographical Sketches and Portraits of Prominent Men and Early Settlers.* 2 vols. Chicago: A. T. Andreas, 1883.
Armstrong, Leroy, and J. O. Denny. *Financial California: An Historical Review of the Beginnings and Progress of Banking in the State.* New York: Arno Press, 1980 [orig. pub. 1916].
Arrington, Leonard H. *Great Basin Kingdom.* Cambridge, Mass.: Harvard University Press, 1955.
————. *Tracey-Collins Bank and Trust Co.* Midvale, Utah: Eden Hill Publishing Co., 1984.
Auerbach, Robert D. *Money, Banking, and Financial Markets.* 3d ed. New York: Macmillian Publishing Co., 1988.
Bach, Steven. *Final Cut: Dreams and Disaster in the Making of Heaven's Gate.* New York: William Morrow and Co., 1985.
Bailey, F. M. *The Small Bank Problem.* Minneapolis: Federal Reserve Bank of Minneapolis, 1930.
Barnett, George. *State Banks and Trust Companies since the Passage of the National Bank Act.* Washington, D.C.: U.S. Government Printing Office, 1910.

Barrett, Glen. *Idaho Banking, 1863–1976.* Boise: Boise University Press, 1976.
––––––. *Small Town Banking in the Good Ol' Days.* Boise: Boise State University Press, 1975.
Barry, Tom. *New Mexico's Financial Institutions: An Investigation.* Albuquerque: New Mexico People and Energy, 1980.
Beardsley, Harry M. *Joseph Smith and His Mormon Empire.* Boston: Hougthton Mifflin, 1931.
Bemer, Cornelius. *American Bank Failures.* New York: A.M.S. Press, 1968.
Bernard, Richard, ed. *Snowbelt Cities: Metropolitan Politics in the Northeast and Midwest since World War II.* Bloomington: Indiana University Press, 1990.
Bernard, Richard, and Bradley Rice, eds. *Sunbelt Cities: Politics and Growth since World War II.* Austin: University of Texas Press, 1983.
Berry, Thomas Senior. *Early California: Gold, Prices, and Trade.* Richmond, Va.: Bostwick Press, 1984.
Billington, Ray Allen. *The Far Western Frontier, 1830–1860.* New York: Harper, 1956.
––––––. *Westward Expansion.* 5th ed. New York: Macmillan Publishing Co., 1982.
Blackford, Mansel. *The Politics of Business in California, 1890–1920.* Columbus: Ohio State University Press, 1977.
Bolton, Roger E. *Defense Purchases and Regional Growth.* Washington, D.C.: Brookings Institution, 1966.
Brayer, Herbert O. *Westerners Brand Book.* Vol. 3. Denver: Denver Posse of Westerners, 1947.
Breck, Allen Dupont. *John Evans of Denver: Portrait of a Twentieth-Century Banker.* University of Denver, "The West in American History Series," no. 5. Boulder: Pruett Publishing Co., 1972.
Bremer, Cornelius. *American Bank Failures.* New York: AMS Press, 1968.
Brewer, Luther A., and Barthinius A. Wick. *History of Linn County, Iowa.* Cedar Rapids: Torch Press, 1911.
Brodie, Fawn M. *No Man Knows My History.* New York: Alfred A. Knopf, 1946.
Browder, Robert, and Thomas Smith. *Independent: A Biography of Lewis W. Douglas.* New York: Alfred A. Knopf, 1986.
Bruck, Connie. *The Predator's Ball.* New York: Penguin, 1989.
Buenger, Walter A., and Joseph Pratt. *But Also Good Business: Texas Commerce Banks and the Financing of Houston and Texas, 1886–1986.* College Station: Texas A & M University Press, 1986.
Burrell, Orin Kay. *Gold in the Woodpile: An Informal History of Banking in Oregon.* Eugene: University of Oregon Books, 1967.
Cable, John Ray. *The Bank of the State of Missouri.* New York: Columbia University Press, 1923.
Cahalan, A. B. *Territorial Banking in Hand County South Dakota.* Omaha: Cockle Printing Co., n.d. [1956].
Carlson, Avery Luverve. *A Monetary and Banking History of Texas.* Fort Worth: Fort Worth National Bank, 1930.
Carosso, Vincent C. *The Morgans: Private International Bankers, 1854–1913.* Cambridge, Mass.: Harvard University Press, 1987.
Chandler, Alfred D. *Visible Hand: The Managerial Revolution in American Business.* Harvard: Belknap, 1977.
Chandler, Robert J. *San Francisco Clearinghouse Certificates: Last of California's Private Money.* Reno: McDonald Publishing House, 1986.
Chittenden, Hiram Mark. *The American Fur Trade of the Far West: A History of Pioneering Trading Posts and Early Fur Companies of the Missouri Valley and the Rocky Mountains and of the Overland Commerce with Santa Fe.* 3 vols. New York: F. P. Harper, 1902.

Chucker, Harold. *Banco at Fifty: A History of Northwest Bancorporation, 1929–1979*. Minneapolis: Northwest Bancorporation, 1979.

Clarke, Dwight L. *William Tecumseh Sherman: Gold Rush Banker*. San Francisco: California Historical Society, 1969.

Clarke, Wilfred A. *History of the Bank of New Mexico: The Past Is Prologue*. New York: Newcomen Society, 1972.

Cleland, Robert, and Frank Putnam. *Isaias Hellman and the Farmers and Merchants Bank*. San Marino, Calif.: Huntington Library, 1965.

Cleveland, Harold van B., and Thomas F. Huertas. *Citibank, 1812–1970*. Cambridge, Mass.: Harvard University Press, 1985.

Conkling, Roscoe P., and Margaret B. Conkling. *The Butterfield Overland Mail, 1857–1869*, 3 vol. Glendale: A. H. Clark Co., 1947.

Cross, Ira. *Financing an Empire: History of Banking in California*. 4 vols. Chicago: S. J. Clarke, 1927.

Dahl, A. E. *Banker Dahl of South Dakota: An Autobiography*. Rapid City: Fenske Book Co., 1965.

Dana, Julian. *A. P. Giannini: Giant in the West, a Biography*. New York: Prentice Hall, 1947.

Dana, Richard Henry. *Two Years Before the Mast*. New York: A. L. Burt Co., 1840.

Dary, David. *Entrpreneurs of the Old West*. New York: Alfred A. Knopf, 1986.

Davis, Steven. *Excellence in Banking: A Profile of Superior Management Based on Insight into Citibank, Deutschbank, Morgan and Thirteen Other Selected Banks*. New York: St. Martin's Press, 1987.

Douglas, Patricia P. *Montana Banking Study*. Helena: Helena Branch of the Federal Reserve Bank of Minneapolis, 1971.

Driscoll, Robert E. *The Black Hills of South Dakota: Its Pioneer Banking History*. New York: Newcomen Society, 1951.

Eccles, Marriner. *Beckoning Frontiers: Public and Personal Recollections*. Edited by Sidney Hyman. Stanford: Stanford University Graduate School of Business, 1976 [orig. publ. 1951].

Edge, L. *Run the Cat Roads: A True Story of Bank Robberies in the 1930's*. New York: Dembrer Books, 1981.

Edgel, Ralph V. *A Brief History of Banking in New Mexico, 1870–1959*. Bureau of Business Research Series, no. 39. Albuquerque: University of New Mexico, 1962.

Edwards, Jerome E. *Pat McCarren: Political Boss of Nevada*. Reno: University of Nevada Press, 1982.

Eichler, Ned. *The Thrift Debacle*. Berkeley: University of California Press, 1989.

Elliott, Russell R. *History of Nevada*. Lincoln: University of Nebraska Press, 1973.

Fell, Jay, Jr. *Twenty-Five Years of Banking in the Rockies: The Story of United Banks of Colorado*. Denver: United Banks of Colorado, 1989.

Fierman, Floyd S. *The Speigelbergs of New Mexico: Merchants and Bankers of Early Santa Fe, 1844–1893*. El Paso: Texas Western College Press, 1964.

Fifty Years of Growth in Tucson. Tucson: Southern Arizona Bank and Trust Co., 1953.

Findley, Gerry. *Mergers and Acquisitions among California Banks, 1955–1965*. Temple City, Calif.: G. Findley, 1965.

Fischer, Gerald C. *American Banking Structure*. New York: Columbia University Press, 1968.

Fishlow, Albert. *American Railroads and the Transformation of the Antebellum Economy*. Cambridge, Mass.: Harvard University Press, 1965.

Fitzgerald, Martin, ed. *Sixty Milestones of Progress: 1859–1919*. Portland: James, Kerns, and Abbott, 1919.

Fogel, Robert W. *Railroads and American Economics Growth: Essays in Econometric History.* Baltimore: Johns Hopkins University Press, 1964.

Friedman, Milton, and Anna J. Schwartz. *A Monetary History of the United States, 1867–1960.* Princeton: Princeton University Press, 1963.

Georgetta, Clel. *Golden Fleece in Nevada.* Reno: Venture Publishing Co., 1972.

Gilder, George. *Microcosm: The Quantum Revolution in Economics and Technology.* New York: Simon and Schuster, 1989.

———. *The Spirit of Enterprise.* NEw York: Simon and Schuster, 1984

Gillies, James, and Clayton Curtis. *Institutional Residential Mortgage Lending in Los Angeles County, 1946–51: Six Significant Years of Mortgage Lending.* Los Angeles: University of California, Bureau of Business and Economic Research, 1956.

Goodhart, C. A. E. *The New York Money Market and the Finance of Trade.* Cambridge, Mass.: Harvard University Press, 1969.

Goodrich, Carter, ed. *Canals and American Economic Development.* New York: Columbia University Press, 1961.

———. *Government Promotion of American Canals and Railroads, 1800–1890.* New York: Columbia University Press, 1960.

Gouge, William M. *The Fiscal History of Texas.* Philadelphia: J. B. Lippincott, 1852.

Gramley, Lyle E. *A Study of Scale Economies in Banking.* Kansas City, Mo.: Federal Reserve Bank of Kansas City, 1962.

Grant, Joseph M., and Lawrence L. Crum. *The Development of State Chartered Banking in Texas.* Austin: University of Texas, Bureau of Business Research, 1978.

Graves, Jackson A. *My Seventy Years in California.* Los Angeles: Times Mirror Press, 1927.

Green, George D. *Finance and Economic Development in the Old South: Louisiana Banking, 1804–1861.* Stanford: Stanford University Press, 1972.

Greider, William. *Secrets of the Temple: How the Federal Reserve Runs the Country.* New York: Simon and Schuster, 1987.

Gressley, Gene M. *Bankers and Cattlemen.* New York: Alfred A. Knopf, 1966.

Gutowsky, A. R. *Arizona Banking.* Tempe: Arizona State University, College of Business, 1967.

Gwynne, S. C. *Selling Money.* New York: Penguin, 1987 [orig. pub. 1986].

Halaas, Eugene T. *The Banking Structure in Colorado: Historic Developments and Recent Changes.* Occasional Studies, no. 1. Denver: The University of Denver, College of Business Administration, Division of Business Research, 1969.

Halberstam, David. *The Reckoning.* New York: Avon, 1986.

Hammond, Bray. *Banks and Politics in America from the Revolution to the Civil War.* Princeton: Princeton University Press, 1957.

Harvey, William H. *Coin's Financial School.* Edited by Richard Hofstadter. Cambridge, Mass.: Belknap Press, 1963 [orig. pub. 1894].

Hector, Gray. *Breaking the Bank: The Decline of BankAmerica.* Boston: Little, Brown and Co., 1988.

Hendricks, William. *M. H. Sherman: A Pioneer Developer of the Pacific Southwest.* Pasadena, Calif.: Castle Press for Sherman Foundation, 1973.

Hepburn, Alonzo Barton. *A History of Coinage and Currency in the United States.* New York: Macmillan, 1903.

Hirshson, Stanley P. *Grenville M. Dodge.* Bloomington: Indiana University Press, 1967.

Hofstader, Richard. *The Age of Reform: From Byan to FDR.* New York: Vintage, 1955.

Holmes, George W. *"Since 1871": A Short History of the First National Bank of Lincoln, Nebraska.* New York: Newcomen Society, 1951.

Hopkins, Alfred. *The Fundamentals of Good Bank Building.* New York: Bankers Publishing Co., 1929.

Hopkins, Ernest J. *Financing the Frontier*. Phoenix: Arizona Printers, 1950.

Hughes, J. R. T. *The Vital Few*. London: Oxford University Press, Expanded Ed. 1979 [orig. pub. 1965].

Hughes, Paul. *Bank Notes*. Phoenix: Phoenician Books, 1971.

Hungerford, Edward. *Wells Fargo: Advancing the American Frontier*. New York: Random House, 1949.

Hunter, James J. *Partners in Progress, 1864–1950: A Brief History of the Bank of California, N.A., and the Region It Has Served for 85 Years*. Princeton: Newcomen Society, 1950.

Hyman, Sidney. *Challenge and Response: First Security Corporation, First Fifty Years, 1928–1978*. Salt Lake City: University of Utah, Graduate School of Business, 1978.

———. *Marriner S. Eccles, Private Entrepreneur and Public Servant*. Stanford: Stanford University, Graduate School of Business, 1976.

Iverson, Lothar I. *Montana and U.S. Banks—A Comparison of Assets and Liabilities, 1934–1950*. Missoula: Montana State University [AOW University of Montana] at Missoula, Bureau of Economic Research, School of Business Administration, 1952.

Jackson, W. Turrentine. *The Enterprising Scot: Investors in the American West after 1873*. Edinburgh: Edinburgh University Press, 1968.

———. *Wells Fargo Stagecoaching in Montana Territory*. Helena: Montana Historical Society Press, 1979.

James, F. Cyril. *The Growth of Chicago Banks*. 2 vols. New York: Harper & Row, 1938.

James, John A. *Money and Capital Markets in Postbellum America*. Princeton: Princeton University Press, 1978.

James, Marquis, and Besse Rowland James. *Biography of a Bank: The Story of the Bank of America, N.T. & S.A.* New York: Harper & Brothers, 1954.

Johnson, A. B. *A Treatise on Banking: The Duties of a Banker and His Personal Requests Therefore*. New York: Greenwood Press, 1968 [orig. pub. 1850].

Johnson, Paul. *Modern Times: A History of the World from the Twenties to the Eighties*. New York: Harper Colophon Books, 1983.

Johnson, Robert L. *Commercial Banking in South Dakota* Vermillion, S. Dak.: South Dakota University Press, Business Research Bureau, School of Business of South Dakota University, 1964.

Johnson, Samuel A. *The Battle Cry of Freedom: The New England Emigrant Aid Company in the Kansas Crusade*. Lawrence: University of Kansas Press, 1954.

Johnston, Moira. *Roller Coaster: Bank of America in the World Economy*. New York: Ticknor & Fields, 1990.

Jones, E. W. *Early Day History of Perry, Oklahoma*. Perry, Okla.: n.p., 1931.

Junker, Rozanne Enerson. *The Bank of North Dakota: An Experiment in State Ownership*. Santa Barbara, California: Fithian Press, 1989.

Kessler-Harris, Alice. *Out to Work: A History of Wage-Earning Women in the United States*. Oxford: Oxford University Press, 1982.

Kibble, Daniel C. *Their Bank—Our Bank, the Quality Bank: A History of First Interstate Bank of California*. Costa Mesa: Calif.: Professional Publications, 1981.

King, Joseph L. *History of the San Francisco Stock and Exchange Board*. San Francisco: Stanley-Taylor Co., 1910.

Kirkwood, Roger. *The Story of Banking in Kansas, 1887–1980*. Topeka: Kansas Bankers Association, 1981.

Klebaner, Benjamin. *Commercial Banking in the United States: A History*. Hinsdale, Ill.: Dryden Press, 1974.

Klein, Maury. *The Union Pacific: The Birth of a Railroad, 1863–1893*. New York: Doubleday, 1987.

Knox, John Jay. *A History of Banking in the United States.* New York: Augustus M. Kelley, 1969 [orig. pub. 1903].

Koenker, William E. *Post-War Banking Trends in North Dakota.* North Dakota Economic Studies, no. 3. Fargo: University of North Dakota, Bureau of Business and Economic Research, n.d.

Kolko, Gabriel. *Railroads and Regulation, 1872–1916.* Princeton: Princeton University Press, 1965.

Koster, George H., with Elizabeth Summers. *The Transamerica Story: 50 Years of Service and Looking Forward.* San Francisco: Transamerica Corporation, 1978.

Kotkin, Joel, and Yoriko Kishimoto. *The Third Century: America's Resurgence in the Asian Era.* New York: Crown Publishers, 1988.

Kross, Herman, and Martin Blyn. *A History of Financial Intermediaries.* New York: Random House, 1971.

Kuhn, W. E. *History of Nebraska Banking: A Centennial Retrospect.* Business Research Bulletin no. 72. Lincoln: University of Nebraska, College of Business Administration, Bureau of Business Research, 1968.

Lamar, Howard R., ed. *The Reader's Encyclopedia of the American West.* New York: Crowell, 1977.

Lamm, Richard D., and Michael McCarthy. *The Angry West: A Vulnerable Land and Its Future.* Boston: Houghton-Mifflin, 1982.

Leipheimer, E. G. *The First National Bank of Butte: Seventy-Five Years of Continuous Banking Operation, 1877 to 1952, Under the Successive Ownership and Management of Three Men Each Named Andrew Jackson Davis.* St. Paul: Brown and Bigelow, 1952.

Livermore, Shaw. *Early American Land Companies.* Princeton: Princeton University Press, 1939.

Livingston, James. *Origins of the Federal Reserve: Money, Class, and the Corporate Capital, 1890–1913.* Ithaca: Cornell University Press, 1986.

Loomis, Edward. *Bank Burning: A Documentary Novel from Isla Vista.* Santa Barbara: Capricorn Press, 1970.

Loomis, Niel M. *Wells Fargo.* New York: Bramhall House, 1968.

Luckingham, Bradford. *The Urban Southwest: A Profile History of El Paso, Albequerque, Tuscon, and Phoenix.* El Paso: Texas Western Press, University of Texas at El Paso, 1982.

Lyman, George D. *Ralston's Ring: California Plunders the Comstock Lode.* New York: Charles Scribner's Sons, 1937.

McCarthy, John Russell. *Joseph Francis Sartori, 1858–1946.* Los Angeles: Ward Ritchie Press, 1948.

MacColl, E. Kimbark. *The Growth of a City: Power and Politics in Portland, Oregon, 1915–1950.* Portland: Georgian Books, 1979.

———. *The Shaping of a City: Business and Politics in Portland, Oregon, 1885–1915.* Portland: Georgian Press, 1976.

McFarland, Cara. *The United States National Bank of Portland, Oregon.* Portland: Binfords & Mort, Publishers, 1942.

McGrane, Reginald. *Foreign Bondholders and American State Debts.* New York: Macmillan Publishing Co., 1935.

McReynolds, Edwin C. *Oklahoma: A History of the Sooner State.* Norman: University of Oklahoma Press, 1954.

Marple, Elliot, and Bruce H. Olson. *The National Bank of Commerce of Seattle, 1889–1969.* Palo Alto, Calif.: Pacific Books, 1970.

Mauzy, Wayne L. *A Century in Santa Fe: The Story of the First National Bank of Santa Fe.* Santa Fe: Vergara Printing Co., 1970.

Mayer, Martin. *The Bankers.* New York: Weabright and Talley, 1974.

Mints. Lloyd W. *A History of Banking Theory in Great Britain and the United States.* Chicago: University of Chicago Press, 1945.

Montgomery, U. E. *Manufacturing in South Dakota, 1939–1958.* Vermillion, S. Dak.: South Dakota University Press and Business Research Bureau, School of Business of South Dakota University, 1962.

Morton, Julius Sterling. *Illustrated History of Nebraska: A History of Nebraska from the Earliest Explorations of the Trans-Mississippi Region.* 3 vols. Lincoln: Jacob North Company, 1905–13.

Mosher, Curtis L. *The Causes of Banking Failure in the Northwestern States.* Minneapolis: Federal Reserve Bank of Minneapolis, 1930.

Nadeau, Remi. *City Makers: The Men Who Transformed Los Angeles.* New York: Doubleday, 1948.

Nash, Gerald D. *The American West in the Twentieth Century: A Short History of an Urban Oasis.* Albuquerque: University of New Mexico Press, 1977 [orig. pub. 1973].

———. *American West Transformed: The Impact of World War II.* Bloomington: Indiana University Press, 1985.

National Banks of the United States: Their Organization, Management and Supervision, 1812–1910. New York: National City Bank of New York, 1910.

Nau, Henry R. *The Myth of America's Decline: Leading the World Economy into the 1990s.* New York: Oxford University Press, 1990.

Newbill, James, W. R. Gedosh, and Roger Van Winkle. *The American Spectrum.* Belmont, Calif.: Wadsworth, 1972.

Newell, Gordon. *The Green Years.* Seattle: Superior Publishing Co., 1969.

Nichols, Roger L., ed. *American Frontier and Western Issues: A Historiographical Review.* New York: Greenwood Press, 1986.

Niehaus, Fred R. *Development of Banking in Colorado.* Denver: Mountain States Publishing Co., 1942.

Noel, Thomas Jacob. *Denver's Larimer Street: Main Street, Skid Row and Urban Renaissance.* Denver: Historic Denver, 1981.

———. *Growing through History with Colorado, the Colorado National Banks: The First 125 Years, 1862–1987.* Denver: Colorado National Banks and University of Colorado, Colorado Studies Center, 1987.

Olson, James C. *History of Nebraska.* 2d ed. Lincoln: University of Nebraska Press, 1966.

Olson, James S. *Saving Capitalism: The Reconstruction Finance Corporation and the New Deal, 1933–1940* (Princeton: Princeton University Press, 1988).

Parrish, William J. *The Charles Ilfeld Company: A Study of the Rise and Decline of Merchant Capitalism in New Mexico.* Cambridge: Mass.: Harvard University Press, 1961.

Paul, Rodman W. *The Far West and the Great Plains in Transition, 1859–1900.* New York: Harper & Row, 1988.

Pilzer, Paul Zane, with Robert Dietz. *Other People's Money: The Inside Story on the S&L Mess.* New York: Simon and Schuster, 1989.

Plehn, Carl Copping. *San Francisco Clearinghouse Certificates: Last of California's Private Money.* Reno: McDonald Publishing House, 1986.

Pollack, Norman. *The Populist Response to Industrial America.* Cambridge: Harvard University Press, 1962.

Pomeroy, Earl. *The Pacific Slope: A History of California, Oregon, Washington, Idaho, Utah and Nevada.* New York: Alfred A. Knopf, 1965.

Potter, David M. *The Impending Crisis, 1848–1861.* Edited by Don E. Fehrenbacher. New York: Harper, 1976.

Preston, Howard H. *History of Banking in Iowa.* Iowa City: State Historical Society, 1922.

————. *Trust Banking in Washington.* Seattle: University of Washington Press, 1953.

Prestowitz, Clyde V., Jr. *Trading Places: How We Allowed Japan to Take the Lead.* New York: Basic Books, 1988.

Provorse, Barry. *The PeoplesBank Story.* Bellevue, Wash.: Documentory Book Publishers, 1987.

Ransom, Roger L., and Richard Sutch. *One Kind of Freedom: The Economic Consequences of Emancipation.* Cambridge: Cambridge University Press, 1977.

Ratner, Sidney, James H. Soltow, and Richard Sylla. *The Evolution of the American Economy: Growth, Welfare and Decision Making.* New York: Basic Books, 1979.

Redlich, Fritz. *The Molding of American Banking, Men and Ideas.* 2 vols. New York: Johnson Reprint Co., 1968 [orig. pub. 1947].

Riley, Thomas Ryan. *Things to Remember: Recollections of a Long Life.* Fond du Lac, Wisc.: Badger, Freund, Inc., n.d.

Robertson, Ross. *The Comptroller and Bank Supervision: An Historical Appraisal.* Washington, D.C.: Office of the Comptroller of the Currency, 1968.

Robinson, Doane. *History of South Dakota.* 2 vols. n.p., 1904.

Robinson, Elwyn B. *History of North Dakota.* Lincoln: University of Nebraska Press, 1966.

Rockoff, Hugh. *The Free Banking Era: A Reexamination.* New York: Arno Press, 1975.

Sale, Kirkpatrick, *Power Shift: The Rise of the Southern Rim and Its Challenge to the Eastern Establishment.* New York: Vintage Books, 1975.

Sale, Roger. *Seattle: Past to Present.* Seattle: University of Washington Press, 1976.

Scates, Shelby. *FIRSTBANK: The Story of Seattle-First National Bank.* Seattle: First National Bank, 1970.

Scheiber, Harry N. *Ohio Canal Era, 1820–1861.* Athens, Ohio: Ohio University, 1969.

Scheiber, Harry N., Harold G. Vatter, and Harold Underwood Faulkner. *American Economic History.* 9th ed. New York: Harper & Row, 1976.

Schweikart, Larry, ed. *Banking in the West.* Manhattan Kansas: Sunflower University Press, 1984.

Schweikart, Larry. *A History of Banking in Arizona.* Tucson: University of Arizona Press, 1982.

————. *Banking in the American South from the Age of Jackson to Reconstruction.* Baton Rouge: Louisiana State University Press, 1987.

————. *That Quality Image: The History of Continental Bank.* Tappan, N.Y.: Custombook, 1988.

Shade, William G. *Banks or No Banks: The Money Issue in Western Politics, 1832–1865.* Detroit: Wayne State University Press, 1972.

Sharkey, Robert P. *Money, Class, and Party: An Economic Study of the Civil War and Reconstruction.* Baltimore: Johns Hopkins University Press, 1959.

Sharp, James R. *The Jacksonians Versus the Banks: Politics in the States after the Panic of 1837.* New York: Columbia University Press, 1970.

Sheldon, Addison E. *Nebraska, the Land and the People.* 3 vols. Chicago: Lewis Publishing Co., 1931.

Sherman, H. L. *A History of Newport Beach.* Newport Beach: City of Newport Beach, 1931.

Singer, Claude. *U.S. National Bank of Oregon and U.S. Bancorp, 1891–1904.* Portland: U.S. Bancorp, 1984.

Skidmore, Bill. *Treasure State Treasury: Montana Banks, Bankers, and Banking, 1864–1984.* Helena: Thurber Printing Co., 1985.

Smallwood, James. *An Oklahoma Adventure: Of Banks and Bankers.* Norman: University of Oklahoma Press, 1979.

Smiley, Jerome C. *History of Denver with Outlines of the Earlier History of the Rocky Mountain Country.* Denver: Denver Times/Sun Times Publishing Co., 1901.

Soule, Frank, John H. Gihon, and James Nisbet. *The Annals of San Francisco.* Palo Alto: Louis Osborn, 1966.

Spence, Clark C. *Montana: A History.* New York: W. W. Norton Co., 1978.

Sprague, Irvine H. *Bailout: An Insider's Account of Bank Failures and Rescues.* New York: Basic Books, 1987.

Sprague, Marshall. *First Century at the First.* n.p., 1973.

Sproat, John G., and Larry Schweikart. *Making Change: South Carolina Banking in the Twentieth Century.* Columbia: Bruccoli Clark Layman, 1990.

Stiles, Edward H. *History of Lucas County.* Des Moines: State Historical Co., 1881.

———. *Portrait and Biographical Album of Jefferson and Van Buren Counties, Iowa.* Chicago: Lake City Publishing Co., 1890.

———. *Recollections and Sketches of Notable Lawyers and Public Men of Early Iowa.* Des Moines: Homestead Publishing Co., 1916.

Stucki, Roland. *Commercial Banking in Utah, 1847–1966.* Salt Lake City: University of Utah, Bureau of Economics and Business Research, 1967.

Studenski, Paul, and Herman E. Krooss. *Financial History of the United States.* 2d ed. New York: McGraw Hill, 1963.

Sumner, William Graham. *A History of Banking in the United States.* New York: Augustus M. Kelley, 1971.

Swierenga, Robert P. *Pioneers and Profits: Land Speculation on the Iowa Frontier.* Ames: Iowa State University Press, 1968.

Sylla, Richard. *American Capital Markets, 1846–1914: A Study of the Effect of Public Policy on Economic Development.* New York: Arno Press, 1975.

Temin, Peter. *Did Monetary Forces Cause the Great Depression?* New York: W. W. Norton & Company, Inc., 1976.

Theobald, John, and Lillian Theobald. *Wells Fargo in Arizona Territory.* Edited by Bert Fireman. Tempe: Arizona Historical Foundation, 1978.

Thomas, James H. *The Fourth: A History of the Fourth National Bank and Trust Company.* Wichita: Fourth National Bank and Trust Company and the Center for Entrepreneurship and Small Business Management, Wichita State University, 1980.

Throckmorton, Arthur. *Oregon Argonauts: Merchant Adventures on the Western Frontier.* Portland: Oregon Historical Society, 1961.

Tilton, Cecil G. *William Chapman Ralston: Courageous Builder.* Boston: Christopher Publishing House, 1935.

Tolchin, Martin, and Susan Tolchin. *Buying into America: How Foreign Money Is Changing the Face of Our Nation.* New York: Times Books, 1988.

Trescott, Paul D. *Financing American Enterprise: The Story of Commercial Banking.* New York: Harper and Row, 1963.

Triggs, J. H. *History of Cheyenne and Northern Wyoming, Embracing the Gold Fields of the Black Hills, Powder River and Big Horn Countries.* Omaha: Herald Printing House, 1876.

Twenty-Five Years of Banking in the Rockies: The Story of United Banks of Colorado. Denver: United Banks of Colorado, 1989.

Twitchell, Ralph Emerson. *Leading Facts of New Mexican History.* 5 vols. Cedar Rapids: Torch Press, 1917.

Twombly, Robert. *Louis Sullivan: His Life and Work.* New York: Elisabeth Sifton Books, 1986.

Unger, Irwin. *The Greenback Era: A Social and Political History of American Finance, 1865–1879.* Princeton: Princeton University Press, 1964.

United States Savings and Loan League. *Savings and Loan Annuals,* various years.

Updike, Helen Hill. *The National Banks and American Economic Development, 1870–1900*. New York: Garland Publishing, Inc., 1985.

Wagner, William. *Reuben Fleet and the Story of Consolidated Aircraft*. Fallbrook, Calif.: Aero Publishers, 1976.

Walter, Paul A. F. *Banking in New Mexico before the Railroad Came!* New York: Newcomen Society, 1955.

Weingarden, Lauren S. *Louis Sullivan: The Banks*. Cambridge, Mass.: The MIT Press, 1987.

Westerfield, Ray. *Historical Survey of Branch Banking in the United States*. New York: American Bankers Association Policy Commission, 1939.

White, Eugene. *The Regulation and Reform of the American Banking System, 1900–1929*. Princeton: Princeton University Press, 1983.

Wiley, Peter, and Robert Gottleib. *Empires in the Sun: The Rise of the New American West*. Tucson: University of Arizona Press, 1985.

Wilson, John Donald. *The Chase: The Chase Manhattan Bank, N.A., 1945–1985*. Boston: Harvard Business School Press, 1986.

Wilson, Neill Compton. *400 California Street: The Story of the Bank of California, National Association, and Its First 100 Years in the Financial Development of the Pacific Coast*. San Francisco: Bank of California, 1964.

Woods, L. Milton. *Sometimes the Books Froze: Wyoming's Economy and Its Banks*. Boulder: Colorado Associated University Press, 1985.

Worthen, W. B. *Early Banking in Arkansas*. Little Rock: Democrat Printing and Litho Co., 1906.

Wright, Benjamin C. *Banking in California, 1849–1910*. New York: Arno Press, 1980 [orig. pub. 1910].

Youmans, Grant S. *Legalized Bank Robbery*. Minot, N. Dak.: Grant S. Youmans, 1914.

ARTICLES

Abbott, Carl. "The Suburban Sunbelt." *Journal of Urban History* 13 (May 1987): 275–301.

"Accounting for Bank Problems." *USA Today*, May 29, 1990.

Adams, Dale W. "Chartering the Kirtland Bank." *Brigham Young University Studies* 23 (1983): 467–82.

Adams, James Ring. "The Big Fix." *American Spectator* 22 (March 1989): 21–24.

Albaugh, Morton. "The Injudicious Banker and How to Control Him." *Kansas Bankers Association Proceedings of the Sixteenth Annual Meeting*, 1903.

Alexander, Thomas G. "Ogden's 'Arsenal of Democracy,' 1920–1955." *Utah Historical Quarterly* 23 (Summer 1965): 237–47.

Amel, Dean F., and Michael J. Jacowski. "Trends in Banking Structure since the Mid-1970s." *Federal Reserve Bulletin*, March 1989, 120–33.

Anderson, George L. "Banking and Monetary Problems." In *Essays on the History of Banking*, edited by George Anderson, 93. Lawrence: Coronado Press, 1972.

———. "Banks, Mails, and Rails, 1880–1915." In *The Frontier Challenge: Responses to the Trans-Mississippi West*, edited by John G. Clarke, 275–307. Lawrence: University of Kansas, 1971.

———. "A Century of Banking in Kansas." In *Kansas: the First Century*, edited by John Bright, 2: 403–22. New York: Lewis Historical Publishing Co., 1956.

———. "From Cattle to Wheat: The Impact of Agricultural Developments on Banking in Early Wichita." In *Essays on the History of Banking*, edited by George L. Anderson, 53–65. Lawrence: Coronado Press, 1972.

———. "Some Phases of Currency and Banking in Territorial Kansas." In *Territorial Kansas:*

Studies Commemorating the Centennial. 103–47. Lawrence: University of Kansas Social Science Studies, 1954.

————. "Western Attitude toward National Banks, 1873–74." In *Essays on the History of Banking*, edited by George L. Anderson, 9–20. Lawrence: Coronado Press, 1972.

Anderson, Jack. "Who Owns America?" *Parade Magazine*, April 16, 1989, 4–6.

"Arizona Bank Performance 48th in Nation." [*Phoenix*] *Arizona Republic*, July 25, 1989.

"Arizona's Deepening Real-Estate Slump Is Hammering Hard at Banking Firms." *Wall Street Journal*, October 23, 1989.

Arrington, Leonard J. "Banking Enterprises in Utah, 1847–1880." *Business History Review* 24 (December 1955): 312–34.

Arrington, Leonard J., and Thomas G. Alexander. "They Kept 'Em Rolling: Toole Army Depot, 1942–1962." *Utah Historical Quarterly* 23 (Winter 1963): 3–25.

Arrington, Leonard J., Thomas G. Alexander, and Eugene A. Erb, Jr. "Utah's Biggest Business: Ogden Air Material Area at Hill Air Force Base, 1938–1965." *Utah Historical Quarterly* 23 (Winter 1965): 9–33.

Arrington, Leonard J., and Archer L. Durham. "Anchors Aweigh in Utah: The U.S. Naval Supply Depot at Clearfield, 1942–1962." *Utah Historical Quarterly* 31 (Spring 1963): 109–26.

Atherton, Lewis. "The Pioneer Merchant in Mid-America." In *The Changing Economic Order: Readings in American Business and Economic History*, edited by Alfred D. Chandler, Jr., Stuart Bruchey, and Louis Galambos, 113–24. New York: Harcourt Brace & World, 1968.

Avery, Nancy. "Wichita Banking and How it Grew." *The Wichitan*, October 1978, 22–24.

Baltensperger, Ernest. "Economics of Scale, Firm Size, and Concentration in Banking." *Journal of Money, Credit and Banking* 4 (August 1972): 467–488.

"BankAmerica Pulls Itself from the Brink." *USA Today*, May 24, 1989.

"Bank Architecture in New York." *Bankers Magazine*, February 1855, 582.

"Banks of All Flags." *Forbes*, September 5, 1980, 15, 18.

Beck, W. A., and S. T. Gaskins, "Henry J. Kaiser: Entrepreneur of the American West." *Journal of the West* 25 (1986): 64–72.

Belton, Beth. "Big Banks Teeter in Real-Estate Crisis." *USA Today*, July 10, 1990.

Benston, George J. "Economics of Scale and Financial Institutions." *Journal of Money, Credit and Banking* 4 (May 1972): 312–41.

————. "The Optimum Banking Structure: Theory and Evidence." *Journal of Bank Research* 3 (Winter 1973): 220–37.

"Big Banks Form 'Bad Banks' to Discard Problem Loans." [*Phoenix*] *Arizona Republic*, November 20, 1988.

Billington, Ray A. "The Origin of the Land Speculator as a Frontier Type." *Agricultural History* 19 (October 1945): 204–11.

Blackford, Mansel. "Banking and Bank Legislation in California, 1890–1915," *Business History Review* 47 (Winter 1973): 482–507.

Blauvelt, W. H. "Banking." In *The History of Nevada*, 2 vols., edited by Sam P. Davis, 1: 629–30. Reno: The Elms Publishing Co., 1913.

Bloomfield, Anne. "David Farquharson, Pioneer California Architect." *California History* 59 (1980): 16–33.

Bogue, Allan, and Margaret Bogue. "Profits and the Frontier Land Speculator." *Journal of Economic History* 17 (March 1957): 1–24.

"The Brash Banker of Arizona," *Saturday Evening Post* 226 (April 10, 1954): 23.

Brayer, Herbert O. "Boom Town Banker—Central City, Colorado, 1880." *Bulletin of the Business Historical Society* 19 (June 1945): 67–95.

Brewer, H. Peers. "Eastern Money and Western Mortgages in the 1870s." *Business History Review* 50 (Autumn 1976): 356–80.

Brown, Ralph. "The South Dakota Economy: The Historical Perspective." *South Dakota Business Review* 35 (June 1988).

Bryan, Robert. "First Interstate: California's Restless Giant." *Bankers Monthly* 103, no. 10 (October 1986): 25.

"Building a Factory? Try N.H." *USA Today*, July 14, 1988.

"Building for the Future." *IV Front*, June/July 1987, 4.

"Buying into a Good Thing." *National Review*, October 14, 1988, 17.

Cagan, Philip. "The First Fifty Years of the National Bank Act—Historical Appraisal." In *Banking and Monetary Studies*, edited by Deane Carson, 15–42. Homewood, Ill.: Richard D. Irwin, Inc., 1963.

Callender, Guy S. "The Early Transportation and Banking Enterprises of the States in Relation to the Growth of Corporations." *Quarterly Journal of Economics* 17 (November 1902): 111–62.

Calomiris, Charles W. "Deposit Insurance: Lessons from the Record." *Economic Perspectives*, May/June 1989, 10–30.

———. "Is Deposit Insurance Necessary? A Historical Perspective." *Journal of Economic History* 50 (June 1990: 283–95.

———. "Price and Exchange Rate Determination During the Greenback Suspension." *Oxford Economic Papers* 90 (1988): 719–50.

Cargill, Thomas F., and Kerry S. Sullivan. "An Historical Perspective on Nevada Banking." *Journal of the West* 23 (April 1984): 21–28.

Clark, Daniel M. *ABA Banking Journal* 78, no. 5 (May 1986).

"Commercial Real-Estate Bog Muddying Valley Bank Boots." [Phoenix] *Arizona Republic*, June 26, 1989.

Conkling, Roscoe P. "John Butterfield." In *Dictionary of American Biography* 3: 374–75. N.Y.: C. Schribner's Sons, 1943.

Conte, Christopher. "Small Town Bankers Fight to Keep Curbs on Big Rival's Growth." *Wall Street Journal*, June 3, 1983.

David, A. C. "Private Residence for Banking Firms." *Architectural Record*, July 1903, 13–28.

Davids, Lewis. " 'Fur' Money and Banking in the West." *Journal of the West*, April 1984, 7–10.

Davie, Theodore. "San Diego Trust & Savings Bank: A Well Known Member of the Community for Ninety-Five Years." *Journal of San Diego History* 30 (1984): n.p.

Davis, Lance E. "The Investment Market, 1870–1914: The Evolution of a National Market." *Journal of Economic History* 25 (September 1965): 355–99.

Dedera, Don. "Walter Reed Bimson: Arizona's Indispensible Man, Compleat Banker." *Arizona Highways* 69 (April 1973): 1, 21–29.

Dellheim, Charles. "Business in Time: The Historian and Corporate Culture." *Public Historian* 8 (Spring 1986): 9–22.

de Wit, Wim. "The Banks and the Image of Progressive Banking." In *Louis Sullivan: The Function of Ornament*, edited by Wim de Wit, 159–97. New York: Chicago Historical Society, the Saint Louis Art Museum, and W. W. Norton & Company, 1986.

"Disinterested Outsiders Say Phoenix Best Publicized City in the U.S.—Here's Why." *Phoenix Action*, February 1950.

Dodds, Gordon B. "The Fur Trade and Exploration." In *Historians and the American West*, edited by Michael P. Malone. Lincoln: University of Nebraska Press, 1983.

Dorn, David R. "Ships for Victory." U.S. Naval Institute *Proceedings*, February 1989, 69–75.

Dorsett, Lyle W. "Equality of Opportunity on the Urban Frontier: Access to Credit in

Denver, Colorado Territory, 1858–1876." In *The Urban West*, edited by Gerald Nash, 75–81. Manhattan, Kans.: Sunflower University Press, 1979.

Doti, Lynne Pierson. "Nationwide Branching: Some Lessons from California." In *Essays in Economic and Business History*, edited by Edwin J. Perkins, 9. Los Angeles: University of Southern California for the Economic and Business Historical Society, forthcoming.

Doti, Lynne Pierson, and Larry Schweikart. "Financing the Post-War Housing Boom in Phoenix and Los Angeles, 1945–1960." *Pacific Historical Review* 58 (May 1989): 173–94.

Eccles, Marriner S. "Price Fixing Is Not Enough." *Fortune*, August 1941, 56–57, 150, 152, 154, 157.

Economopoulos, Andrew. "Illinois Free Banking Experience." *Journal of Money Credit and Banking* 20 (May 1988): 249–64.

Ehrlich, George. "The Bank of Commerce by Asa Beebe Cross: 'A Building of the Latest Architecture.'" *Journal of the Society of Architectural Historians* 43 (1984): 168–72.

Erickson, Earling A. "Money and Banking in a 'Bankless' State: Iowa, 1846–1857." *Business History Review* 43 (Summer 1969): 171–91.

Fairlamb, David. "Japanese Banks Invade the West." *Dun's Business Month*, June 1986, 52–53.

Fierman, Floyd. "Jewish Pioneering in the Southwest." *Arizona and the West* 2 (Spring 1960): 54–72.

Flemming, Walter L. "The Buford Expedition to Kansas." *American Historical Review* 6 (1900): 38–48.

Ford, Lee M. "Bob Ford, Sun River Cowman." *Montana: The Magazine of Western History* 18 (Spring 1967): 30–43.

Foster, Mark S. "Giant of the West: Henry J. Kaiser and Regional Industrialization, 1930–1950." *Business History Review* 59 (1985): 1–23.

Fraser, Donald R., and Peter S. Ross. "Bank Entry and Bank Performance." *Journal of Finance* 27 (March 1972): 65–78.

Gallaher, Ruth. "Money in Pioneer Iowa, 1838–1855." *Iowa Journal of History and Politics* 33 (1934): 27–28.

Gates, Paul Wallace. "The Homestead Law in an Incongruous Land System." *American Historical Review* 41 (July 1936): 652–81.

———. "The Role of the Land Speculator in Western Development." *The Pennsylvania Magazine of History and Biography* 64 (July 1942): 314–33.

Gilbert, Gary, and William Longbrake. "The Effects of Branching by Financial Institutions on Competition, Productive Efficiency, and Stability: An Examination of the Evidence, Part II," *Journal of Bank Research* 4 (Winter 1974): 298–307.

Gilbert, James H. "The Development of Banking in Oregon." *University of Oregon Bulletin* 9 (September 1911): 5–30.

Gilder, George. "The Message of the Microcosm." *American Spectator* (December 1987): 16–19.

———. "The Revitalization of Everything: The Law of Microcosm." *Harvard Business Review* (March–April 1988): 49–61.

Goldberg, Ellen. "Competitive Cost Analysis of Foreign Owned U.S. Banks," *Journal of Bank Research* 13 (Autumn 1982): 144–59.

Golden, Richard L., and Arlene A. "The Mark I. Jacobs Family: A Discursive View." *Western States Jewish Quarterly* 13 (January 1981): 99–106.

"Great Family: Evans of Denver." *Life*, June 15, 1959, 103–11.

Greene, Terry. "And the Money Kept Flowing." *New Times*, June 21–27, 1989, 22, 26–28, 30–32.

Greenwald, David, and Ricardo Sandoval. "Keating Jailed on Fraud Charges." *Orange County [Calif.] Register*, September 19, 1990, 1.

Groth, Clarence W. "Savings and Reaping: Montana Banking, 1910–1925." *Montana: The Magazine of Western History* 20 (Autumn 1970); 28–35.

Gutowsky, Albert R. "History of Commercial Banking in Oregon." *Oregon Business Review* 24 (August 1965): 1–6.

Haeger, John. "Economic Development of the American West." In *American Frontier and Western Issues: A Historiographical Review*, edited by Roger L. Nichols, 27–50. New York: Greenwood Press, 1986.

Hammond, Bray. "Banking in the Early West: Monopoly, Prohibition, and Laissez Faire." *Journal of Economic History* 8 (May 1948): 1–25.

"Here Come the Cards." *Forbes*, February 15, 1969, 39–40.

Herman, Edward S. "Board of Governors v. Transamerica: Victory from Defeat." *The Antitrust Bulletin* 4 (March 1964): 521–39.

Hill, Marvin S., C. Keith Rooker, and Larry T. Wimmer. "The Kirtland Economy Revisited: A Market Critique of Sectarian Economics." *Brigham Young University Studies* 17 (Summer 1977): 391–72.

Hively, William. "The Italian Connection and the Bank of America's First Billion." *Journal of the West* 23 (April 1984): 56–64.

Homrighausen, Paul E. "One Large Step toward Less-Check: The California Automated Clearing House System." *Business Lawyer* 28 (July 1973): 1143–60.

Horvitz, Paul D. "Branch Banking, Mergers, and Competition." In *Banking and Monetary Studies*, edited by Deane Carson, 306–18. Homewood, Ill.: Richard D. Irwin, 1963.

Horwitz, Paul M., and Bernard Schull. "The Impact of Branch Banking on Bank Performance." *The National Banking Review* 11 (December 1974): 143–89.

Houpt, James. "Foreign Ownership of U.S. Banks: Trends and Effects." *Journal of Bank Research* 14 (Summer 1983): 144–56.

"How's Your Bank, Honey." *Ms.*, January–February 1989, 142.

Huntington, C. C. "A History of Banking and Currency in Ohio Before the Civil War." *Ohio Archeological and Historical Publications* 14 (1915): 412–65.

Huntoon, Peter. "National Bank Failures in Wyoming, 1924." *Kansas Historical Quarterly*, August 1985, 35.

———. "The National Bank Failures in Wyoming, 1924." *Annals of Wyoming*, Fall 1982, 34–44.

———. "The Wyoming National Bank Massacre." *Journal of the West* 23 (April 1984): 29–48.

Isely, W. H. "The Sharps Rifle Episode in Kansas History." *American Historical Review* 12 (1907): 546–66.

Jackson, W. Turrentine, "A New Look at Wells Fargo, Stagecoaches, and the Pony Express." *California Historical Society Quarterly* 45 (1966): 291–324.

———. "Stages, Mails and Express in Southern California: The Role of Wells, Fargo & Co. in the Pre-Railroad Era." *California Historical Society Quarterly* 56 (1974): 233–72.

———. "Wells Fargo: Symbol of the Wild West?" *Western Historical Quarterly* 3 (April 1972): 179–96.

———. "Wells Fargo's Pony Expresses." *Journal of the West* 11 (1972): 412–17.

———. "Wells Fargo Staging over the Sierras." *California Historical Society Quarterly* 44 (1970): 99–133.

Jacobs, Donald. "The Interaction Effects of Restrictions on Branching and Other Bank Regulations." *Journal of Finance* 20 (May 1965): 332–49.

Jeffries, Louis E. "Nebraska Bank Failures and the State of Nebraska Banking." *Business in Nebraska* (Bureau of Business Research, Univ. of Nebraska-Lincoln) 41 (June 1988): 1–5.

Jervey, William. "When the Banks Closed: Arizona's Bank Holiday of 1933." *Arizona and the West*, Summer 1968, 127–53.

Johnson, Robert A. "California's Competitive Banking." *The Banker* 127 (October 1977): 77.

Kareken, John, and Neil Wallace. "Deposit Insurance and Bank Regulation: A Partial-Equilibrium Exposition." *Journal of Business,* July 1978, 413–38.

Kaufman, Allen, and Gordon Walker. "Strategy-History Connection: The Case of Exxon." *The Public Historian* 8 (Spring 1986): 23–39.

Keehn, Richard N., and Gene Smiley. "Mortgage Lending by National Banks." *Business History Review* 51 (Winter 1977): 474–91.

———. "U.S. Bank Failures, 1932–1933: A Provisional Analysis." In *Essays in Business and Economic History* 6 (1988): 136–56.

Kirkwood, R. Cort, and Terrence P. Jeffrey. "Quis Custodiet?" *National Review,* April 21, 1989, 35–36.

Konig, Michael. "Postwar Phoenix, Arizona: Banking and Boosterism," *Journal of the West* 23 (April 1984): 72–76.

Lamoreaux, Naomi. "Banks, Kinship, and Economic Development: The New England Case." *Journal of Economic History* 46 (September 1986): 647–67.

Lanzellotti, R. F., and T. R. Savings. "State Branching Restrictions and the Availability of Branching Services: A Comment." *Journal of Money, Credit and Banking* 1 (November 1969): 778–88.

"The Last Word in Service for Our Women Customers." *IV Front,* June/July 1987, 5.

"List of Private Bankers in the Principal Cities and Towns of the United States." *Bankers Magazine,* N.S. 5 (1855): 471–72.

Lathrop, H. W. "Some Iowa Bank History." *Iowa Historical Record* 8 (1897): 59–60.

Lauch, Louis H., and Neil B. Murphy. "A Test of the Impact of Branching on Deposit Variability." *Journal of Financial and Quantitative Analysis* 5 (September 1970): 323–27.

"Letters of Cyrus Kurtz Holliday, 1854–1859." *Kansas Historical Quarterly* 6 (August 1937): 241–94.

"Letters of John and Sarah Everett, 1854–1864." *Kansas Historical Quarterly* 8 (February 1939): 3–34; (May 1939): 143–74; (August 1939): 279–310; and (November 1939): 350–83.

"Lincoln Savings Posts $847 Million 1st Half Loss." *Orange County [Calif.] Register,* July 28, 1989.

Lockwood, Charles, and Christopher B. Leincberger. "Los Angeles Comes of Age." *Atlantic Monthly,* January 1988, 31–62.

Lotchin, Roger. "The Metropolitan-Military Complex in Comparative Perspective: San Francisco, Los Angeles, and San Diego, 1919–1941." *Journal of the West* 18 July 1978: 19–30.

Luckingham, Bradford. "The American West: An Urban Perspective." *Journal of Urban History* 7 (November 1981): 99–105.

———. "The Urban Dimension of Western History." In *Historians and the American West,* edited by Michael Malone, 323–43. Lincoln: University of Nebraska Press, 1983.

McClelland, Peter D. "New Perspectives on the Disposal of Western Lands in Nineteenth Century America." *Business History Review* 42 (Spring 1969): 77–83.

MacColl, E. Kimbark, and Harry H. Stein. "The Economic Power of Portland's Early Merchants, 1851–1861." *Oregon Historical Quarterly,* Summer 1988, 117–56.

McFadden, Thomas. "Banking in the Boise Region: The Origins of the First National Bank of Idaho." *Idaho Yesterdays* 11 (Spring 1967): 3–17.

"Many Magazines Tell Phoenix Story." *Phoenix Action,* November 1949: 2.

Martel, Carol, and Larry Schweikart. "Arizona Banking and the Collapse of Lincoln Thrift." *Arizona and the West* 28 (Fall 1986): 246–63.

Martin, Harold. "The New Millionaires of Phoenix." *Saturday Evening Post,* September 30, 1961.

Mascaro, Angelo R. "Aftermath of the Thrift Crisis: Balancing the Economy's Books." *Contemporary Policy Issues* 8 (April 1990): 95–106.

Miller, Glenn H., Jr. "The Hawkes Papers: A Case Study of a Kansas Mortgage Brokerage Business, 1871–1888." *Business History Review* 32 (Summer 1958): 293–310.

Minsky, Hyman. "Commercial Banking and Rapid Economic Growth in California." In *California Banking in a Growing Economy*, edited by Hyman Minsky, 79–134. Berkeley: University of California Press, 1965.

Monkkonen, Eric. "*The Bank of Augusta* v. *Earle*: Corporate Growth v. States' Rights." *Alabama Historical Quarterly*, Summer 1972, 113–30.

Monroe, Keith. "Bank Knight in Arizona." *American Magazine* 140 (November 1945): 24–25, 116–22.

Moore, William B. "John Henry Dill, 1868–1942." *Chronicles of Oklahoma* 10 (September 1942): 289–91.

Morgan, William T. "Strongboxes on Main Street: Prairie Style Banks." *Landscape* 24 (1980): 35–40.

Nelson, Christopher. "Bank Architecture in the West." *Journal of the West* 23 (April 1984): 77–87.

Nelson, Richard L. "Optimal Banking Structure: Implications for Interstate Banking." *Contemporary Policy Issues* 6 (April 1988): 13–23.

Ng, Kenneth. "Free Banking Laws and Barriers to Entry in Banking, 1838–1860." *Journal of Economic History* 48 (December 1988): 877–90.

Noyes, Alexander J. "The Banks and the Panic of 1893." *Political Science Quarterly* 9 (March 1894): 12–30.

O'Driscoll, Gerald P. "Bank Failures: The Deposit Insurance Connection." *Contemporary Policy Issues* 6 (April 1988): 1–12.

Olson, James S. "The Boise Bank Panic of 1932." *Idaho Yesterdays*, Winter 1974, 18–29.

———. "Rehearsal for Disaster: Hoover, the R.F.C., and the Banking Crisis in Nevada, 1932–1933." *Western Historical Quarterly*, April 1975, 149–61.

Orr, Bill. "California, a Foot-Dragger in ATMs, Comes to Life." *ABA Banking Journal* 71 (September 1979): 139–44.

Parker, Charles F. "The Beginnings of Banking in Arizona." *Arizona Highways* 29 (August 1952): 4–7, 38–39.

Rant, Carl. "The Public Historian and Business History." *Public Historian* 8 (Spring 1986): 31–38.

Rastatter, Edward H. "Nineteenth Century Public Land Policy: The Case for the Speculator." In *Essays in Nineteenth Century Economic History: The Old Northwest*, edited by David C. Klingaman and Richard K. Vedder, 118–37. Athens: Ohio University Press, 1975.

Richards, Kent. "The Lady Is a Banker." *Phoenix* 4 (June 1969): 70–76.

Ridgway, William. "He Had No Gun." *Arizona Days and Ways*, May 15, 1955, 9.

"The Rise and Fall of Alec Swan." *American West* 4 (August 1967): 21–68.

Robbins, William G. "The 'Plundered Province' Thesis and the Recent Historiography of the American West." *Pacific Historical Review* 55 (November 1986): 577–97.

Robinson, Roland I. "Unit Banking Evaluated." In *Banking and Monetary Studies*, edited by Deane Carson, 291–305. Homewood, Ill.: Richard D. Irwin, 1963.

Rolnick, Arthur, and Warren Weber. "Banking Instability and Regulation in the U.S. Free Banking Era." *Federal Reserve Bank of Minneapolis Quarterly Review*, Summer 1985, 2–9.

———. "The Causes of Free Bank Failures." *Journal of Monetary Economics* 14 (November 1984): 267–91.

———. "Explaining the Demand for Free Bank Notes." *Journal of Monetary Economics* 21 (January 1988): 47–71.

———. "Free Banking, Wildcat Banking, and Shinplasters." *Federal Reserve Bank of Minnesota Quarterly Review*, Fall 1982, 10–19.

————. "Inherent Instability in Banking: The Free Banking Experience." *CATO Journal* 5 (Winter 1986): 877–90.

————."New Evidence on the Free Banking Era." *American Economic Review* 72 (December 1983): 1080–91.

"Rough Times Ahead for USA Banks." *USA Today*, May 29, 1990.

Rowland, Mary Scott. "Kansas Farming and Banking in the 1920s." *Kansas Historical Quarterly*, August 1985, 186–99.

Russ, Don. "The Asian Invasion." *Bankers Magazine* 166 (January/February 1981): 48–52.

Salsbury, Stephen. "The Effects of the Civil War on American Industrial Development." In *The Economic Impact of the American Civil War*, edited by Ralph Andreano, 161–68. Cambridge, Mass.: Schenkman Publishing Co., 1962.

Salutos, Theodore. "Land Policy and Its Relation to Agricultural Production and Distribution, 1862–1933." *Journal of Economic History* 22 (December 1962): 445–60.

"S&L Crisis Focuses on Chairman." *Dayton Daily News*, July 9, 1989.

"The S&L Mess." *USA Today*, August 14, 1989.

Sawyer, Philip. "The Planning of Bank Buildings." *Architectural Review* 12 (1905): 24–31.

Scharfenberg, Kirk. "The Community as Bank Examiner." *Working Papers for a New Society* 7 (1980): 30–35.

Scheiber, Harry N. "Economic Change in the Civil War Era." *Civil War History* 21 (1965): 396–411.

Schull, Bernard, and Paul Horwitz. "Branch Banking and the Structure of Competition." In *Studies in Banking Competition and the Banking Structure*, edited by Comptroller of the Currency. Reprinted in *National Banking Review* 1 (March 1964): 106.

Schweikart, Larry. "Arkansas Antebellum Banks." *Southern Studies* 26 (Fall 1987): 188–201.

————. "*Brophy* v. *Douglas*: A Case Study in Corporate Control." *Journal of the West* 23 (April 1984): 49–55.

————. "Collusion or Competition? Another Look at the Banking in the Postwar Period, 1950–1964." *Journal of Arizona History* 28 (Summer 1987): 189–200.

————. "Early Banking in New Mexico from the Civil War to the Roaring Twenties." *New Mexico Historical Review* 63 (January 1988): 1–24.

————. "Entrepreneurial Aspects of Antebellum Banking." In *American Business History: Case Studies*, edited by C. Joseph Pusateri and Henry C. Dethloff, 122–39. New York: Harlan Davidson, 1986.

————. "Financial Concentration and the Growth of Phoenix." In *Phoenix: The First Century*, edited by G. Wesley Johnson. Norman: University of Oklahoma Press, forthcoming.

————. "Financing Urban Growth: Entrepreneurial Creativity and Western Cities, 1945–1975." *Urban History* 26 (February 1989): 177–86.

————. "Frontier Banking in Colorado: A New Perspective on Public Confidence and Regulation, 1862–1907." *Essays and Monographs in Colorado History* 8 (Fall 1988): 15–33.

————. "Jacksonian Ideology, Currency Control, and 'Central' Banking: A Reappraisal." *The Historian* (November 1988): 78–102.

————. "Making Money the Old Fashioned Way." *Timeline* (Dec. 1989/Jan. 1990): 32–43.

————. "Private Bankers in the Antebellum Period." *Southern Studies* 25 (Summer 1986): 125–34.

————. "Southern Banks and Economic Growth in the Antebellum Period: A Reassessment." *Journal of Southern History* 53 (February 1987): 19–36.

————. "You Count It: The Birth of Banking in Arizona." *Journal of Arizona History*, Autumn 1981, 349–68.

Schweikart, Larry, and Lynne Pierson Doti. "Banking in the West: A Bibliographical Overview." In *Banking in the West*, edited by Larry Schweikart, 88–94. Manhattan, Kans.: Sunflower University Press, 1984.

Seagall, Laura, and John Allen. "Security Pacific: Richard J. Flamson III Runs the Most Diversified Institution in California." *Executive*, November 1985, 18–24.

"Security Pacific Plans Stake in Unit of Mitsui Bank Ltd." *Wall Street Journal*, July 28, 1989.

"Shaky Comeback: Knapp's New Firm Seems Short on Money, Long on Failed Deals." *Wall Street Journal*, May 30, 1989.

Sharkey, Robert P. "Commercial Banking." In *Economic Change in the Civil War Era*, edited by David T. Gilchrist, 23–31. Greenville, Del.: Elutherian Mills-Hagley Foundation, 1965.

Sherman, Hoyt. "Early Banking in Iowa." *Annals of Iowa* 5 (1901): 1–13.

———. "List of the Private Bankers in the Principal Cities and Towns of the United States." *Banker's Magazine*, n.s., 5 (1855): 471–472.

"Small Business Surge in U.S. West Region Outpouring Big Firms." *[Phoenix] Arizona Republic*, June 28, 1989.

"Solid, Safe, and Secure: Country Banks in Montana." *Montana* 36 (Spring 1986): 77–79.

"A Solid Year, With Regionals Leading the Way." *Business Week*, April 7, 1986.

Southard, Garrison A., Jr. "California Master Charge." *Bankers Monthly Magazine* 7 (February 1968): 40–42.

Speigelman, Mortimer. "The Failure of the Ohio Life Insurance and Trust Company, 1857." *Ohio Archeological and Historical Quarterly* 57 (1948): 247–65.

Spence, Clark C. "Western Mining." In *Historians and the American West*, edited by Michael Malone, 96–122. Lincoln: University of Nebraska Press, 1983.

Stanley, Gerald. "Merchandising in the Southwest: The Mark I. Jacobs Company of Tucson, 1867–1875." *American Jewish Archives* 23 (April 1971): 86–102.

Stevens, Harry R. "Bank Enterprises in a Western Town, 1815–1822." *Business History Review* 29 (1955): 139–56.

———. "Hugh Glenn." In *The Mountain Men and the Fur Trade of the Far West*, edited by LeRoy R. Hafen, 2: 165–74. Glendale: Arthur C. Clarke, 1965.

Sylla, Richard. "American Banking and Growth in the Nineteenth Century: A Partial View of the Terrain." *Explorations in Economic History* 9 (Winter 1971–72): 197–227.

———. "Federal Policy, Bank Market Structure, and Capital Mobilization in the United States, 1863–1913." *Journal of Economic History* 29 (December 1969): 659–65.

———. "Forgotten Men of Money: Private Bankers in Early U.S. History." *Journal of Economic History*, December 1969, 173–88.

"The S&Ls: Where They Stand." *USA Today* (Aug. 14, 1989).

Thomas, Phillip D. "Thomas James, Hugh Glenn, and Jacob Fowler, 1821–1823." In *Frontier Adventures*, edited by Joseph Stout, Jr., 61–79. Oklahoma City: Oklahoma Historical Society, 1976.

Throckmorton, Arthur. "The Role of the Merchant on the Oregon Frontier: The Early Business Career of Henry W. Corbett, 1851–1869." *Journal of Economic History* 16 (December 1956): 539–50.

———. "The Central Banking Role of Clearinghouse Associations." *Journal of Money, Credit, and Banking* 16 (February 1984): 1–15.

Torgerson, Samuel. "Early Banking in North Dakota." *Quarterly Journal of the University of North Dakota* 13 (1922–1923): 283–88.

———. "Wichita Banking and How it Grew." *Wichitan*, October 1978, 22–24.

Vernon, Jack R. "Regulatory Barriers to Branching and Merger and Concentration on Banking Markets." *Southern Economic Journal* 37 (January 1971): 349–55.

Wacht, Richard F. "Branch Banking and Risk." *Journal of Financial and Quantitative Analysis* 3 (March 1968): 97–107.

Wall, C. James. "Gold Dust and Greenbacks." *Montana: The Magazine of Western History* 7 (Spring 1957): 24–31, 63.

Walter, Paul A. F. "New Mexico's Pioneer Bank and Bankers." *New Mexico Historical Review* 21 (July 1946): 209–25.

Webb, Samuel C., and Leland F. Cox. "Correspondent Banking in Wichita." *Business Journal* (College of Business Administration, Wichita State University), September 1958, 12–16.

Wells, Thomas C. "Letters of a Kansas Pioneer, 1855–1860." *Kansas Historical Quarterly* 5 (May and August 1936): 143–318; and (November 1936): 381–418.

Wendt, Paul F. "Earnings and Capital Problems of California Banks, 1946 to 1975." In *California Banking in a Growing Economy, 1946–1975*, edited by Hyman Minsky, 306. Berkeley: University of California Press, 1965.

White, Carl J. "Financial Frustrations in Territorial Montana." *Montana: The Magazine of Western History* 17 (Spring 1967): 34–45.

White, Lawrence J. "Problems of the FSLIC: A Former Policy Maker's View." *Contemporary Policy Issues* 8 (April 1990): 62–81.

––––––. "Regulatory Sources of Instability in Banking." *Cato Journal* (Winter 1986): 890–97.

Williamson, Jeffrey. "Watersheds and Turning Points: Conjectures on the Long Term Impact of Civil War Financing." *Journal of Economic History* 34 (September 1974): 636–61.

Willson, Roscoe. "Old Lawman Outshoots Robbers." *Arizona Days and Ways*, July 4, 1965, 26–27.

Worley, Ted. "The Control of the Real Estate Bank of the State of Arkansas, 1836–1855." *Mississippi Valley Historical Review*, December 1950, 403–26.

Wriston, Walter. "Technology and Sovereignty." *Foreign Affairs*, Winter 1988, 63–75.

Yang, Chaucer F. "The Impact of Foreign Bank Invasion in the United States." *Los Angeles Business and Economics* 4 (Summer/Fall 1979): 38–41.

Yates, Henry W. "Early Nebraska Currency and Per Capita Circulation." *Proceedings of the Nebraska State Historical Society* 1, no. 2 (1894): 67–76.

Dissertations and Theses

Anderson, George. "The National Banking System, 1865–1875: A Sectional Institution." Master's thesis, University of Illinois, 1933.

Beveridge, Andrew A. "Credit to the Community: American Banking's Tribal Roots." Master's thesis, Graduate School and University Center, City University of New York, 1988.

Barjenbruch, Judith. "The First National Bank of Vermillion, 1875–1937." Master's thesis, University of South Dakota, 1975.

Cox, James. "Institutional Mortgage Lending in the Los Angeles Metropolitan Area, 1953–54 and 1957–58." Ph.D. diss., University of California, 1962.

Crumb, J. "Banking and Regulation in California." Ph.D. diss., University of California, Berkeley, 1935.

Doti, Lynne Pierson. "Banking in California: Some Evidence on Structure, 1878–1905." Ph.D. diss., University of California, Riverside, 1978.

Groth, Clarence. "Montana Banking History." Master's thesis, American Bankers Association Graduate School of Banking, Rutgers University, 1955.

Grubbs, Frank. "Frank Bond, Gentleman Sheepherder of Northern New Mexico, 1893–1915." Master's thesis, University of New Mexico, 1958.

Hakula, John. "Samuel T. Hauser and the Economic Development of Montana." Ph.D. diss., Indiana University, 1961.

Hawkins, Dale R. "Banking in Utah." Master's thesis, University of Utah, 1951.

Herman, Edward S. "The Transamerica Case: A Study of the Federal Reserve Board Anti-Trust Proceedings." Ph.D. diss., University of California, Berkeley, 1953.

Jones, Howard. "The History of Banking in the Utah Economy, 1933–1963." Master's thesis, University of Utah, 1964.

King, Neil. "History of Banking in Denver, Colorado, 1858–1950." Master's thesis, American Bankers Association Graduate School of Banking, Rutgers University, 1952.

Knight, Neil Roy. "History of Banking in Washington." Ph.D. diss., University of Washington, 1935.

Konig, Michael. "Toward Metropolis Status: Charter Government and the Rise of Phoenix, Arizona, 1945–1960." Ph.D. diss., Arizona State University, 1983.

Lundquist, Frederick. "An Analysis of Banking in Utah's Economy, 1875–1953." Master's thesis, University of Utah, 1963.

McGahan, J. Patrick. "The Development and Effect of Banking in Utah, 1933–1945." Master's thesis, University of Utah, 1963.

Madsen, Walter C. "History of Banking in Arizona." Master's thesis, University of Washington Pacific Coast Banking School, 1974.

Martin, George Preston. "A Comparison of the Economic Roles of Multiple Outlet Banking and Unit Banking in California, 1920–1950." Ph.D. diss., Indiana University, 1952.

Mawn, Geoffrey P. "Phoenix, Arizona: Central City of the Southwest." Ph.D. diss., Arizona State University, 1979.

Moore, Vance Coleman. "The Effects of World War II on Banking in the State of Washington." Master's thesis, University of Washington, 1950.

Neal, Mabel Frances. "The History of Banking in Nebraska, 1854–1889." Master's thesis, University of Nebraska, 1933.

Prousser, Moldon J. "Hugo Seaberg, New Mexican Capitalist, 1869–1945." Master's thesis, University of Denver, 1968.

Schultz, Charles. "Hayne's Magnificent Dream: Factors Which Influenced the Efforts to Join Cincinnati and Charleston by Railroad, 1835–1860." Ph.D. diss., Ohio State University, 1966.

Vaughn, Emmett John. "Capital Accumulation in Nebraska Since 1854." Ph.D. diss., University of Nebraska, 1964.

PAMPHLETS AND UNPUBLISHED MANUSCRIPTS

Ackerman, Theo. "Reminiscences of Banking in the Early Days of Russell County." Manuscript, n.d., KHS.

Barker, Burt Brown. "Early History: The First National Bank of Portland, Ore." Manuscript, n.d., OHS.

———. "Early History: The First National Bank of Portland, Ore." Typescript, 1941, OHS.

Billinghurst, C. B. "The Farmer's Dollar; the Wall Street Banks Flurry of April 1920: The Farmer's Dollar Was Taken from the West to Brace up Weak Banks in the East; A Feature in the Problem of Farm Relief." Pamphlet, n.p., n.d., SDHS.

Calomiris, Charles W. "Do 'Vulnerable' Economies Need Deposit Insurance? Lessons from the U.S. Agricultural Boom and Bust of the 1920s." Unpublished paper, Federal Reserve Bank of Chicago, 1989.

Calomiris, Charles, and Larry Schweikart. "Regulations and Markets as Determinants of the Performance and Vulnerability of Antebellum Banks." Paper presented at the annual meeting of the American Economic Association, Chicago, December 1987.

———. "Southern Banks and the Panic of 1857: Evidence from Alabama, Georgia, and Virginia." Unpublished paper, n.d.

———. "Was the South Backward?: Differences in Antebellum Banking during Normalcy and Crisis." Federal Reserve Bank of Chicago Working Paper, 1989.

Dolley, M. N. "Reform of the Currency, and Its Relation to the State Banking Institutions of the United States." Pamphlet, n.p., November 21, 1911, KHS.

Doti, Lynne Pierson. "Banking in California: The Second Branching Era." Paper presented at the annual meeting of the Western Economic Association, San Francisco, July 1981.

Edmunds, Harold R. "Pioneer Banking Houses of The Dalles, Ore., 1867–1933: The Story of French and Company and Its Competitors." Typescript, n.d., OHS.

Emry, James R. "Billions for the Bankers, Debts for the People." Pamphlet published in Phoenix, Arizona, 1982.

"Fifty Years of Progress: The Golden Anniversary of the Establishment of Credit in Seattle, 1870–1920." Pamphlet published by Dexter Horton N.B., n.d., Seattle Public Library.

Frank, William. "Results of Seventeen Years Banking in Nebraska under the Depositors' Guaranty Fund Law." Pamphlet, Grand Island, Nebraska, 1930, NSHS.

Lamoreaux, Naomi. "Banks and Insider Lending in Jacksonian New England: A Window on Social Structure and Values." Typescript.

———. "From Entrepreneurs to Bankers: The Professionalization of Banking in Late Nineteenth Century New England." Typescript.

———. "Institutional Form and Economic Performance: New England Banking in the Late Nineteenth Century." Typescript.

Messelt, Thomas, Sr. "Montana's Bank Failures of the Twenties." Pamphlet, n.d.

Moler, Murray. "A Centennial History of Commerical Security Bank, 1875–1975." Manuscript, n.d., n.p., USHS.

Murphy, Merwin. "William John Murphy and the Building of the Arizona Canal." Manuscript, 1974, ASU.

"Nebraska is a Remarkable State and Tells a Story No Other State Can Tell." Pamphlet, 1926, NSHS.

Schweikart, Larry. "Dynamic Legacy: Thunderbird Bank, the First Twenty Years, 1964–1984." Pamphlet, privately printed by Thunderbird Bank, 1985.

Smallwood, James. "Financing Urban Growth on the Great Plains, 1945–1975." Paper presented at the annual meeting of the Western Economic Association, Lake Tahoe, June 1989.

Smith, Duane. "The Bank That Built Durango." Pamphlet, n.p., 1981, CHS.

Stephens, Dan R. "The Guaranty Law Situation." Pamphlet, Fremont, Nebraska, 1929, NSHS.

Stevick, Guy LeRoy. "The Denver Savings Bank: Why It Failed." Pamphlet, n.p., 1908, CHS.

"The Story of the First National Bank Is the Story of Pueblo, Colorado." Pamphlet, First National Bank, Pueblo, 1922?

U.S. National Bank. "News Releases." U.S. National Bank, Portland, 1987 and 1988, various dates.

Watson, B. Frank. "A History of the Nebraska Bank Guaranty Law." Pamphlet, 1933, NSHS.

Weiss, Mark. "Own Your Own Home: American Real Estate Industry and Housing Policy." Paper presented at the annual meeting of the American Historical Association, Chicago, December 1988, in authors' possession.

Wells Fargo History Department. "Wells Fargo Historical Highlights." Pamphlet, Wells Fargo Bank, 1982.

White, Eugene. "The Membership Problem of the Federal Reserve System before the Great Depression." Unpublished paper, n.d., in authors' possession.

INTERVIEWS

Konig, Michael. Transcript of interview with Patrick Downey, July 8, 1978, on file in Phoenix History Project, Western Savings Building, Phoenix.

————. Transcript of interview with Frank Snell, December 7, 1978, on file in Phoenix History Project, Western Savings Building, Phoenix.

Schweikart, Larry. Interviews with anonymous bank sources, various dates.

————. Interviews with Carl Bimson, March and April 1980.

————. Interview with John Davis, April 26, 1988.

————. Interviews with Anna Foster, various dates, 1980.

————. Interview with Harold Gorman, August 30, 1989.

————. Interview with Sherman Hazeltine, May 20, 1980.

————. Interview with Bob Hedrickson, president of First National Bank and Trust Company of Bismarck, North Dakota, April 27, 1988.

————. Interview with W. R. Montgomery, July 22, 1980, ASU.

INDEX